T0130728

Get the eBook FREE!

(PDF, ePub, Kindle, and liveBook all included)

We believe that once you buy a book from us, you should be able to read it in any format we have available. To get electronic versions of this book at no additional cost to you, purchase and then register this book at the Manning website.

Go to https://www.manning.com/freebook and follow the instructions to complete your pBook registration.

That's it!
Thanks from Manning!

Functional Programming in C#
SECOND EDITION

ENRICO BUONANNO

MANNING
SHELTER ISLAND

Manning Publications Co.
20 Baldwin Road
PO Box 761
Shelter Island, NY 11964

Development editor:	Marina Michaels
Technical development editor:	René van den Berg
Review editor:	Adriana Sabo
Production editor:	Deirdre S. Hiam
Copy editor:	Frances Buran
Proofreader:	Melody Dolab
Technical proofreader:	Paul Louth
Typesetter and cover designer:	Marija Tudor

ISBN 9781617299827
Printed in the United States of America

A Mirtillo

contents

Functional programming (FP) has become an important and exciting part of mainstream programming. The majority of new languages and frameworks created in the 2010s are functional, leading some to predict that the future of programming is functional. Meanwhile, popular object-oriented (OO) languages like C# and Java have seen the introduction of more functional features with every new release, enabling a multiparadigm programming style. And yet, adoption in the C# community has been slow. Why is this so? One reason, I believe, is the lack of good literature:

- Most FP literature is written in and for functional languages, especially Haskell. For developers with a background in OOP, this poses a programming-language barrier to learning FP concepts. Even though many of the concepts apply to a multiparadigm language like C#, learning a new paradigm *and* a new language at once is a tall order.
- Even more importantly, most of the books in the literature tend to illustrate functional techniques and concepts with examples from the domains of mathematics or computer science. For the majority of programmers who work on Line of Business (LOB) applications day in and day out, this creates a domain gap and leaves them wondering how relevant these techniques may be for real-world applications.

These shortcomings posed major stumbling blocks in my own path to learning FP. After tossing aside the *n*-th book that explained something known as currying by showing how the add function can be curried with the number 3, creating a function that can add 3 to any number (can you think of any application where this would be even remotely useful?), I decided to pursue my own research path. This involved learning half a dozen functional languages and experimenting to find out which concepts from FP could be effectively applied in C# and in the kind of applications most developers are paid to write. My research culminated in the writing of this book.

This book bridges the language gap for C# developers by showing how you can leverage functional techniques in this language. It also bridges the domain gap by showing how functional techniques can be applied to typical business scenarios. I take a pragmatic approach and cover functional techniques to the extent that they're useful in a typical LOB application scenario and dispense with most of the theory behind FP. Ultimately, you should care about FP because it gives you the following:

- *Power*—This simply means that you can get more done with less code. FP raises the level of abstraction, allowing you to write high-level code while freeing you from low-level technicalities that add complexity but no value.
- *Safety*—FP is adverse to state mutation. This means that a program written in the functional style is unlikely to go into an invalid state. Furthermore, a conservative approach to state mutation is extremely beneficial when dealing with concurrency. A program written in the imperative style may work well in a single-threaded implementation but cause all sorts of bugs when concurrency comes in. Functional code offers much better guarantees in concurrent scenarios, so it's only natural that we're seeing a surge of interest in FP in the era of multicore processors.
- *Clarity*—We spend more time maintaining and consuming existing code than writing new code, so it's important that our code be clear and intention-revealing. As you learn to think functionally, achieving this clarity becomes more natural.

If you've programmed in an OO style for some time, it may take a bit of effort and willingness to experiment before the concepts in this book come to fruition. To make sure learning FP is an enjoyable and rewarding process, I have two recommendations:

- *Be patient.* You may have to read some sections more than once. You may put the book down for a few weeks and find that when you pick it up again, something that seemed obscure suddenly starts to make sense.
- *Experiment in code.* You won't learn unless you get your hands dirty. The book provides many examples and exercises, and many of the code snippets can be tested in the REPL.

Your colleagues may be less eager to explore than you. Expect them to protest at your adoption of this new style and to look perplexedly at your code and say things like, "Why not just do *x*?" (where *x* is boring, obsolete, and usually harmful). Don't discuss. Just sit back and watch them eventually turn around and use your techniques to solve issues they run into again and again.

acknowledgments

I'd like to thank Paul Louth, who not only provided inspiration through his language-ext library (from which I borrowed many good ideas) but also graciously reviewed the book at various stages.

Manning's thorough editorial process ensured that the quality of this book is infinitely better than if I had been left to my own means. For this, I'd like to thank the team that collaborated on the book, including Mike Stephens, development editor Marina Michaels, technical editor René van den Berg, project manager Deirdre Hiam, and proofer Melody Dolab.

Special thanks to Daniel Marbach and Tamir Dresher for their technical insights, as well as to all those who took part in the peer reviews, including David Paccoud, Foster Haines, George Onofrei, Goetz Heller, Oliver Forral, Jeremy Caney, Kent Spillner, Matt Van Winkle, Jedidja Bourgeois, Mark Elston, Najeeb Arif, Oliver Korten, and Robert Wilk.

Thanks to Scott Wlaschin for sharing his articles at http://fsharpforfunand profit.com and to the many other members of the FP community, who share their knowledge and enthusiasm through articles, blogs, and open source.

about this book

This book aims to show how you can leverage functional techniques in C# to write code that is concise, elegant, robust, and maintainable.

Who should read this book?

This book is for an ambitious breed of developer. You know .NET and C# or a similar language like Java, Swift, or Kotlin. You have experience developing real-world applications and are familiar with OOP concepts, patterns, and best practices. But, you're looking to expand your arsenal by learning functional techniques so that you can make the most out of C# as a multiparadigm language.

If you're trying or planning to learn a functional language, this book will also be hugely valuable because you'll learn how to think functionally in a language you're familiar with. Changing the way you think is the hard part; once that's achieved, learning the syntax of any particular language is relatively easy.

How this book is organized: A road map

The book consists of 19 chapters divided into 4 parts:

- Part 1 covers the basic principles of functional programming. We'll start by looking at what functional programming is and how C# supports programming in a functional style. We'll then look at the power of higher-order functions and the importance of pure functions. By the end of part 1, you'll have both the conceptual and practical tools to start learning more specific functional techniques.
- Part 2 shows some practical applications of functional techniques: how to design types and function signatures and how simple functions can be composed into complex programs. By the end of part 2, you'll have a good feel for

what a program written in a functional style looks like and for the benefits that this style has to offer.

- With these basic concepts covered, we'll pick up some speed in part 3 and move on to wider-reaching concerns such as functional error handling, modularizing and composing an application, and the functional approach to understanding state and representing change. By the end of part 3, you'll have acquired a set of tools enabling you to effectively tackle many programming tasks using a functional approach.

- Part 4 tackles more advanced topics including lazy evaluation, stateful computations, asynchrony, data streams, and concurrency. Each chapter in part 4 introduces important techniques that have the potential to completely change the way you write and think about software.

You'll find a more detailed breakdown of the topics in each chapter and a representation of what chapters are required before reading any particular chapter inside the front cover.

Coding for real-world applications

The book aims to stay true to real-world scenarios. To do this, many examples deal with practical tasks such as reading configuration, connecting to a database, validating HTTP requests, and so on—things you may already know how to do, but that you'll see with the fresh perspective of functional thinking.

Throughout the book, I use a long-running example to illustrate how FP can help when writing LOB applications. For this, I've chosen an online banking application for the fictitious Bank of Codeland (BOC)—naff, I know, but at least it has the obligatory three-letter acronym. Because most people have access to an online banking facility, it should be easy to imagine the required functionality and see how the problems discussed are relevant to real-world applications.

I use several other scenarios to illustrate how to solve typical programming problems in a functional style. The constant back and forth between practical examples and FP concepts will, hopefully, help bridge the gap between theory and practice, something I found wanting in the existing literature.

Leveraging functional libraries

A language like C# may have functional features, but to fully leverage these, you'll often use libraries that facilitate common tasks. In this book, you'll learn about

- `System.Linq`—Yes, in case you didn't know, it's a functional library! I assume you're familiar with it, given that it's such an important part of .NET.

- `System.Collections.Immutable`—This is a library of immutable collections, which we'll start using in chapter 11.

- `System.Interactive` and `System.Reactive`—These libraries (you may know them as the *interactive extensions* and *reactive extensions* for .NET) allow you to work with data streams, which we'll discuss in chapters 16 and 18.

This leaves out plenty of other important types and functions that are staples of FP. As a result, several independent developers have written libraries to fill those gaps. To date, the most complete of these is language-ext, a library written by Paul Louth to improve the C# developer's experience when coding functionally.[1]

In the book, I don't use language-ext directly; instead, I'll show you how I developed my own library of functional utilities, called `LaYumba.Functional`, even though it largely overlaps with language-ext. This is pedagogically more useful for several reasons:

- The code will remain stable after the book is published.
- You get to look under the hood and see that powerful functional constructs are deceptively simple to define.
- You can concentrate on the essentials. I'll show you the constructs in their purest form so that you won't be distracted by the details and edge cases that a full-fledged library addresses.

About the code

This second edition of *Functional Programming in C#* uses C# 10 and .NET 6.[2] Many, if not all, of the techniques can be applied in previous versions of the language, although doing so usually involves some extra typing. The appendix shows specifically how to work with immutable data and pattern matching if you're working with earlier versions of C# that don't include these as language features.

You can get executable snippets of code from the liveBook (online) version of this book at https://livebook.manning.com/book/functional-programming-in-c-sharp -second-edition. You can execute many of the shorter snippets in a REPL, thereby gaining hands-on practice with immediate feedback. The more extended examples are available for download at https://github.com/la-yumba/functional-csharp-code-2, along with the exercises' setup and solutions. You can also download the book's source code from www.manning.com/books/functional-programming-in-c-sharp -second-edition.

Code listings in the book focus on the topic being discussed and therefore may omit `using` statements, namespace declarations, trivial constructors, or sections of code that appeared in a previous listing and remain unchanged. If you'd like to see the full, compiling version of a listing, you'll find it in the code repository.

---

[1] language-ext is open source and available on GitHub and NuGet: https://github.com/louthy/language-ext.
[2] C# 10 and .NET 6 are still in preview at the time of writing, so some discrepancies are possible. These will be pointed out where relevant in the book.

liveBook discussion forum

Purchase of *Functional Programming in C#, Second Edition* includes free access to live-Book, Manning's online reading platform. Using liveBook's exclusive discussion features, you can attach comments to the book globally or to specific sections or paragraphs. It's a snap to make notes for yourself, ask and answer technical questions, and receive help from the author and other users. To access the forum, go to https://livebook.manning.com/book/functional-programming-in-c-sharp-second-edition/welcome/v-7/. You can also learn more about Manning's forums and the rules of conduct at https://livebook.manning.com/#!/discussion.

Manning's commitment to our readers is to provide a venue where a meaningful dialogue between individual readers and between readers and the author can take place. It is not a commitment to any specific amount of participation on the part of the author, whose contribution to the forum remains voluntary (and unpaid). We suggest you try asking the author some challenging questions lest his interest stray! The forum and the archives of previous discussions will be accessible from the publisher's website as long as the book is in print.

about the author

ENRICO BUONANNO obtained an MS in Computer Science from Columbia University in 2001 and has been working as a software developer and architect ever since. He's worked on mission-critical projects for prestigious companies in FinTech (including the Bank for International Settlements, Barclays, and UBS) and other technology-driven businesses.

Part 1

Getting started

In this part, I'll introduce you to the basic techniques and principles of functional programming.

Chapter 1 starts by looking at what functional programming is and how C# supports programming in a functional style.

Chapter 2 shows how functions are represented in C# and then delves into higher-order functions, a fundamental technique of FP.

Chapter 3 explains what pure functions are, why purity has important implications for a function's testability, and why pure functions lend themselves well to parallelization and other optimizations.

In these introductory chapters, I try to leverage existing knowledge you might have (particularly about LINQ and about unit testing) to illustrate practical applications of the principles of FP.

By the end of part 1, you'll have a clear idea of what FP is and what features of C# enable you to code in a functional style, and you'll begin to see the benefits that FP has to offer.

Introducing functional programming

This chapter covers

- Benefits and tenets of functional programming
- Functional features of the C# language
- Using records and pattern matching for type-driven programs

Functional programming (FP) is a programming *paradigm*: a different way of thinking about programs than the mainstream imperative paradigm you're probably used to. For this reason, learning to think functionally is challenging but also very enriching. My ambition is that, after reading this book, you'll never look at code with the same eyes as before!

The learning process can be a bumpy ride. You're likely to go from frustration at concepts that seem obscure or useless to exhilaration when something clicks in your mind, and you're able to replace a mess of imperative code with just a couple of lines of elegant, functional code. This chapter will address some questions you may have as you start on this journey. What exactly is functional programming? Why should I care? Can I code functionally in C#? Is it worth the effort?

1.1   *What is this thing called functional programming?*

What exactly is functional programming (FP)? At a high level, it's a programming style that emphasizes functions while avoiding state mutation. This definition is already two-fold as it includes two fundamental concepts:

- Functions as first-class values
- Avoiding state mutation

Let's see what these mean.

Running snippets in the REPL

As you go through the snippets in this chapter and in the book, I encourage you to type them in a REPL. A *REPL* (Read-Eval-Print-Loop) is a command-line interface that lets you experiment with the language by typing in statements and getting immediate feedback. You may want to try out a few variations on the examples I show you; getting your hands dirty by messing with real code will get you learning fastest.

If you use Visual Studio, you can start the REPL by going to View > Other Windows > C# Interactive. Alternatively, you can use LINQPad. Unfortunately, at the time of writing, these options are only available on Windows. On other OSs, you can use the `csi` command, even though it's not as feature-rich.

1.1.1   *Functions as first-class values*

In a language where functions are first-class values, you can use them as inputs or outputs of other functions, you can assign them to variables, and you can store them in collections. In other words, you can do with functions all the operations that you can do with values of any other type.

For example, type the contents of the following listing into the REPL.

Listing 1.1   A simple example of using a function as a first-class value

```
var triple = (int x) => x * 3;          ◁─┐ Defines a function that returns
                                             the triple of a given integer
var range = Enumerable.Range(1, 3);                  ◁─┐ Creates a list with
                                                          the values [1, 2, 3]
var triples = range.Select(triple);     ◁─┐ Applies triple to all
                                             the values in range
triples // => [3, 6, 9]
```

In this example, you invoke `Select` (an extension method on `IEnumerable`), giving it the range and the `triple` function as arguments. This creates a new `IEnumerable` containing the elements obtained by applying the `triple` function to each element in the input range.

Notice that prior to C# 10 you needed to explicitly declare the delegate type for `triple` like so:

```
[source,csharp]

Func<int, int> triple = x => x * 3;
```

The code in listing 1.1 demonstrates that functions are indeed first-class values in C# because you can assign the multiply-by-3 function to the variable `triple` and give it as an argument to `Select`. Throughout the book, you'll see that treating functions as values allows you to write powerful and concise code.

1.1.2 Avoiding state mutation

If we follow the functional paradigm, we should refrain from state mutation altogether: once created, an object *never* changes, and variables should never be reassigned (so that, in fact, they're *variable* in name only). The term *mutation* indicates that a value is changed in place, updating a value stored somewhere in memory. For example, the following code creates and populates an array, and then it updates one of the array's values in place:

```
int[] nums = { 1, 2, 3 };
nums[0] = 7;

nums // => [7, 2, 3]
```

Such updates are also called *destructive updates* because the value stored prior to the update is destroyed. These should always be avoided when coding functionally. (Purely functional languages don't allow in-place updates at all.)

Following this principle, sorting or filtering a list should not modify the list in place but should create a new, suitably filtered or sorted list without affecting the original. Type the code in the following listing into the REPL to see what happens when sorting or filtering a list using LINQ's `Where` and `OrderBy` functions.

Listing 1.2 Functional approach: `Where` and `OrderBy` create new lists

```
var isOdd = (int x) => x % 2 == 1;
int[] original = { 7, 6, 1 };

var sorted = original.OrderBy(x => x);
var filtered = original.Where(isOdd);

original // => [7, 6, 1]          The original list
sorted   // => [1, 6, 7]          isn't affected.
filtered // => [7, 1]
```

Sorting and filtering yielded new lists.

As you can see, the original list is unaffected by the sorting or filtering operations, which yield new `IEnumerable`s. Let's look at a counterexample in the following listing. If you have an array, you can sort it in place by calling its `Sort` method.

Listing 1.3 Nonfunctional approach: `List<T>.Sort` sorts the list in place

```
int[] original = { 5, 7, 1 };
Array.Sort(original);

original // => [1, 5, 7]
```

In this case, after sorting, the original ordering is destroyed. We'll see why this is problematic next.

> **NOTE**   The reason you see both the functional and nonfunctional approaches in .NET libraries is historical: `Array.Sort` predates LINQ, which marked a decisive turn in a functional direction.

1.1.3   Writing programs with strong guarantees

Of the two concepts we just discussed, functions as first-class values initially seems more exciting, and we'll concentrate on it in chapter 2. But before we move on, I'd like to briefly demonstrate why avoiding state mutation is also hugely beneficial—it eliminates many complexities caused by mutable state.

Let's look at an example. (We'll revisit these topics in more detail, so don't worry if not everything is clear at this point.) Type the code in the following listing into the REPL.

Listing 1.4   Mutating state from concurrent processes

```
using static System.Linq.Enumerable;        Lets you call Range and WriteLine
using static System.Console;                 without full qualification

var nums = Range(-10000, 20001).Reverse().ToArray();
// => [10000, 9999, ... , -9999, -10000]

var task1 = () => WriteLine(nums.Sum());
var task2 = () => { Array.Sort(nums); WriteLine(nums.Sum()); };

Parallel.Invoke(task1, task2);               Executes both
// prints: 5004 (or another unpredictable value)   tasks in parallel
//         0
```

Here you define `nums` to be an array of all integers between 10,000 and -10,000; their sum should obviously be 0. You then create two tasks:

- `task1` computes and prints the sum.
- `task2` first sorts the array and then computes and prints the sum.

Each of these tasks correctly computes the sum if run independently. When you run both tasks in parallel, however, `task1` comes up with an incorrect and unpredictable result. It's easy to see why. As `task1` reads the numbers in the array to compute the sum, `task2` is reordering the elements in the array. That's somewhat like trying to read a book while somebody else flips the pages: you'd be reading some well-mangled sentences! This is shown graphically in figure 1.1.

What if we use LINQ's `OrderBy` method, instead of sorting the list in place? Let's look at an example.

```
var task3 = () => WriteLine(nums.OrderBy(x => x).Sum());
Parallel.Invoke(task1, task3);

// prints: 0
//         0
```

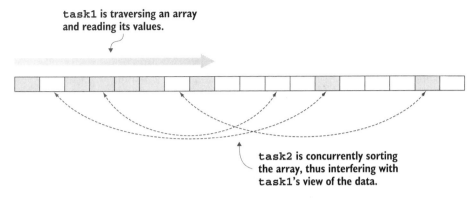

Figure 1.1   Modifying data in place can give concurrent threads an incorrect view of the data.

As you can see, using LINQ's functional implementation gives you a predictable result, even when you execute the tasks in parallel. This is because task3 isn't modifying the original array but rather creating a completely new view of the data, which is sorted: task1 and task3 read from the original array concurrently, but concurrent reads don't cause any inconsistencies, as figure 1.2 shows.

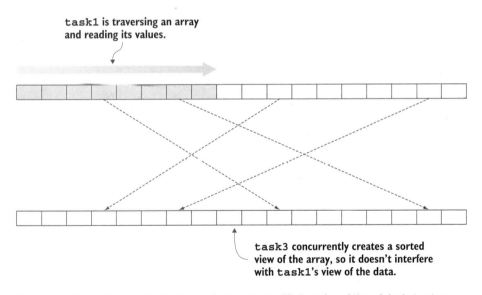

Figure 1.2   The functional approach: creating a new, modified version of the original structure

This simple example illustrates a wider truth: when developers write an application in the imperative style (explicitly mutating the program state) and later introduce concurrency (due to new requirements or a need to improve performance), they inevitably face a lot of work and potentially some difficult bugs. When a program is written in a functional style from the outset, concurrency can often be added for free or with substantially less effort. We'll discuss state mutation and concurrency more in chapters 3 and 11. For now, let's go back to our overview of FP.

Although most people will agree that treating functions as first-class values and avoiding state mutation are fundamental tenets of FP, their application gives rise to a series of practices and techniques, so it's debatable which techniques should be considered essential and included in a book like this. I encourage you to take a pragmatic approach to the subject and try to understand FP as *a set of tools* that you can use to address your programming tasks. As you learn these techniques, you'll start to look at problems from a different perspective: you'll start to think functionally.

Now that we have a working definition of FP, let's look at the C# language itself and at its support for FP techniques.

Functional vs. object-oriented?

I'm often asked to compare and contrast FP with object-oriented programming (OOP). This isn't simple, mainly because there are conflicting assumptions about what OOP should look like.

In theory, the fundamental principles of OOP (encapsulation, data abstraction, and so on) are orthogonal to the principles of FP, so there's no reason why the two paradigms can't be combined.

In practice, however, most object-oriented (OO) developers heavily rely on the imperative style in their method implementations, mutating state in place and using explicit control flow; they use OO design in the large and imperative programming in the small. The real question is that of *imperative versus functional* programming.

Another interesting question is how FP differs from OOP in terms of structuring a large, complex application. The difficult art of structuring a complex application relies on the following principles. They're generally valid, regardless of whether the component in question is a function, a class, or an application:

- *Modularity*—Software should be composed of discrete, reusable components.
- *Separation of concerns*—Each component should only do one thing.
- *Layering*—High-level components can depend on low-level components but not vice versa.
- *Loose coupling*—A component shouldn't know about the internal details of the components it depends on; therefore, changes to a component shouldn't affect components that depend on it.

These principles are also in no way specific to OOP, so the same principles can be used to structure an application written in the functional style. The difference will be in what the components are and which APIs they expose. In practice, the functional emphasis on pure functions (which we'll discuss in chapter 3) and composability (chapter 7) make it significantly easier to achieve some of these design goals.[a]

---

[a] For a more thorough discussion on why imperatively flavored OOP is a *cause* of (rather than a solution to) program complexity, see the article "Out of the Tar Pit," by Ben Moseley and Peter Marks (November, 2006) at http://mng.bz/xXK7.

1.2　How functional a language is C#?

Functions are indeed first-class values in C#, as demonstrated in the previous listings. In fact, C# had support for functions as first-class values from the earliest version of the language through the `Delegate` type, and the subsequent introduction of lambda expressions made the syntactic support even better. We'll review these language features in chapter 2.

There are some quirks and limitations when it comes to type inference, which we'll discuss in chapter 10, but overall the support for functions as first-class values is pretty good.

As for supporting a programming model that avoids in-place updates, the fundamental requirement in this area is that a language have garbage collection. Because you create modified versions of existing data structures, rather than updating their values in place, you want old versions to be garbage-collected as needed. Again, C# satisfies this requirement.

Ideally, the language should also *discourage* in-place updates. For a long time, this was C#'s greatest shortcoming: having everything mutable by default and no easy way to define immutable types was a hurdle when programming in a functional style. This all changed with the introduction of records in C# 9. As you'll see in section 1.2.3, records allow you to define custom immutable types without any boilerplate; in fact, it's easier to define a record than a "normal" class.

As a result of the features added over time, C# 9 offers good language support for many functional techniques. In this book, you'll learn to harness these features and to work around any shortcomings. Next, we'll review some language features of C# that are particularly relevant to FP.

1.2.1　The functional nature of LINQ

When C# 3 was released, along with version 3.5 of the .NET Framework, it included a host of features inspired by functional languages, including the LINQ library (`System.Linq`) and some new language features enabling or enhancing what you could do with LINQ. These features included extension methods, lambda expression, and expression trees.

LINQ is indeed a functional library (as you probably noticed, I used LINQ earlier to illustrate both tenets of FP). The functional nature of LINQ will become even more apparent as you progress through this book.

LINQ offers implementations for many common operations on lists (or, more generally, on "sequences," as instances of `IEnumerable` should technically be called), the most common of which are mapping, sorting, and filtering, see the "Common operations on sequences" sidebar. Here's an example combining all three operations:

```
Enumerable.Range(1, 100).
   Where(i => i % 20 == 0).
   OrderBy(i => -i).
   Select(i => $"{i}%")
// => ["100%", "80%", "60%", "40%", "20%"]
```

Notice how `Where`, `OrderBy`, and `Select` all take functions as arguments and don't mutate the given `IEnumerable` but return a new `IEnumerable` instead. This illustrates both tenets of FP you saw earlier.

LINQ facilitates querying not only objects in memory (LINQ to objects), but various other data sources as well, like SQL tables and XML data. C# programmers have embraced LINQ as the standard toolset for working with lists and relational data (accounting for a substantial amount of a typical codebase). On the upside, this means that you'll already have some sense of what a functional library's API feels like.

On the other hand, when working with other types, C# programmers generally stick to the imperative style of using flow-control statements to express the program's intended behavior. As a result, most C# codebases I've seen are a patchwork of functional style (when working with `IEnumerables` and `IQueryables`) and imperative style (when working with everything else).

What this means is that, although C# programmers are aware of the benefits of using a functional library such as LINQ, they haven't had enough exposure to the design principles behind LINQ to leverage those techniques in their own designs. That's something this book aims to address.

Common operations on sequences

The LINQ library contains many methods for performing common operations on sequences such as the following:

- *Mapping*—Given a sequence and a function, mapping yields a new sequence whose elements are obtained by applying the given function to each element in the original sequence (in LINQ, this is done with the `Select` method):

  ```
  Enumerable.Range(1, 3).Select(i => i * 3) // => [3, 6, 9]
  ```

- *Filtering*—Given a sequence and a predicate, filtering yields a new sequence including all the elements from the original sequence that satisfy the predicate (in LINQ, this is done with `Where`):

  ```
  Enumerable.Range(1, 10).Where(i => i % 3 == 0) // => [3, 6, 9]
  ```

- *Sorting*—Given a sequence and a key-selector function, sorting yields a sequence where the elements of the original sequence are ordered by the key (in LINQ, this is done with `OrderBy` and `OrderByDescending`):

  ```
  Enumerable.Range(1, 5).OrderBy(i => -i) // => [5, 4, 3, 2, 1]
  ```

1.2.2   Shorthand syntax for coding functionally

C# 6, C# 7, and C# 10 were not revolutionary releases, but they included many smaller language features that, taken together, provide more idiomatic syntax and hence a better experience for coding functionally. The following listing illustrates some of these features.

Listing 1.5   C# idioms relevant for FP

```
using static System.Math;                        ◁──┐  using static enables unqualified
                                                     │  access to the static members of
public record Circle(double Radius)              ◁──┘  System.Math, like PI and Pow.
{
    public double Circumference                      An expression-bodied property
        => PI * 2 * Radius;
```

```
public double Area
{
   get
   {
      double Square(double d) => Pow(d, 2);      ◁──┐  A local function is a method
      return PI * Square(Radius);                    │  declared within another method.
   }
}
}
```

IMPORTING STATIC MEMBERS WITH THE USING STATIC DIRECTIVE

The using static directive introduced in C# 6 allows you to import the static members of a class (in listing 1.5, the System.Math class). As a result, in this example you can invoke the PI and Pow members of Math without further qualification:

```
using static System.Math;

public double Circumference
   => PI * 2 * Radius;
```

Why is this important? In FP, we prefer functions whose behavior relies only on their input arguments because we can reason about and test these functions in isolation (contrast this with instance methods, whose implementation typically interacts with instance variables). These functions are implemented as static methods in C#, so a functional library in C# consists mainly of static methods.

using static allows you to more easily consume such libraries. This is even truer in C# 10, where global using static allows you to make functions available throughout your project. Although overuse of these directives can lead to namespace pollution, reasonable use can make for clean, readable code.

MORE CONCISE FUNCTIONS WITH EXPRESSION-BODIED MEMBERS

We declare the Circumference property with an *expression body*, introduced with =>, rather than with the usual *statement body* enclosed by curly braces:

```
public double Circumference
   => PI * 2 * Radius;
```

Notice how much more concise this is compared to the Area property in listing 1.5!

In FP, we tend to write lots of simple functions, many of them one-liners, and then compose these into more complex workflows. Expression-bodied methods allow you to do this with minimal syntactic noise. This is particularly evident when you want to write a function that returns a function—something you'll see a lot of in this book.

The expression-bodied syntax was introduced in C# 6 for methods and property getters. It was generalized in C# 7 to also apply to constructors, destructors, getters, and setters.

DECLARING FUNCTIONS WITHIN FUNCTIONS

Writing lots of simple functions means that many functions are called from one location only. C# allows you to make this explicit by declaring a function within the scope of another function. There are actually two ways to do this; the one I favor uses a delegate:

```
[source,csharp]

get
{
   var square = (double d) => Pow(d, 2);
   return PI * square(Radius);
}
```

This code uses a lambda expression to represent the function and assigns it to the square variable. (In C# 10, the compiler infers the type of square to be Func<double, double> so that you can declare it with the var keyword.) We'll look at lambda expressions and delegates more in depth in chapter 2.

Another possibility is to use *local functions*, effectively methods declared within a method—a feature introduced in C# 7.

```
get
{
   double Square(double d) => Pow(d, 2);
   return PI * Square(Radius);
}
```

Both lambda expressions and local functions can refer to variables within the enclosing scope for this reason, the compiler actually generates a class for each local function. To mitigate the possible performance impact, if a local function does not need to access variables from the enclosing scope, as is the case in this example, C# 8 allows you to declare the local function static like so:

```
static double Square(double d) => Pow(d, 2);
```

If you refer to a variable in the enclosing scope from within a local function that is marked as static, you'll get a compiler error.

1.2.3 *Language support for tuples*

C# 7 introduced new lightweight syntax for creating and consuming tuples, similar to the syntax found in many other languages. This was the most important feature introduced in C# 7.[1]

How are tuples useful in practice, and why are they relevant to FP? In FP, we tend to break tasks down into small functions. You may end up with a data type whose only purpose is to capture the information returned by one function, and that's expected as input by another function. It's impractical to define dedicated types for such

---

[1] C# 7 tuples supersede their clunky C# 4 predecessors, which were suboptimal in performance and unattractive in syntax, their elements being accessed via properties called Item1, Item2, and so on. Apart from the new syntax, the underlying implementation of tuples also changed. The old tuples are backed by the System.Tuple classes, which are immutable reference types. The new tuples are backed by the System .ValueTuple structs. Being structs, they're copied when passed between functions, yet they're mutable, so you can update their members within methods, which is a compromise between the expected immutability of tuples and performance considerations.

structures, which don't correspond to meaningful domain abstractions. That's where tuples come in.

Let's look at an example. Imagine you have a currency-pair identifier such as EURUSD, which identifies the exchange rate for Euros/US Dollars, and you'd like to break it up into its two parts:

- The *base currency* (EUR)
- The *quote currency* (USD)

For this, you can define a general function that splits a string at the given index. The following example shows this operation:

```
public static (string, string)      ◁── Declares a tuple as the
    SplitAt(this string s, int at)        method's return type
    => (s.Substring(0, at), s.Substring(at));   ◁── Constructs a tuple

var (baseCcy, quoteCcy) = "EURUSD".SplitAt(3);   ◁── Deconstructs
baseCcy  // => "EUR"                                   a tuple
quoteCcy // => "USD"
```

Furthermore, you can assign meaningful names to the elements of a tuple. This allows you to query them like properties:

```
public static (string Base, string Quote)   ◁── Assigns names to the elements
    AsPair(this string ccyPair)                   of the returned tuple
    => ccyPair.SplitAt(3);

var pair = "EURUSD".AsPair();
pair.Base  // => "EUR"     | Accesses the elements by name
pair.Quote // => "USD"
```

Let's see another example. You know you can use `Where` with a predicate to filter the values in a list:

```
var nums = Enumerable.Range(0, 10);
var even = nums.Where(i => i % 2 == 0);

even // => [0, 2, 4, 6, 8]
```

What if you want to know both the elements that satisfy the predicate and those that don't, in order to process them separately? For this, I've defined a method called `Partition`, which returns a tuple containing both lists:

```
var (even, odd) = nums.Partition(i => i % 2 == 0);

even // => [0, 2, 4, 6, 8]
odd  // => [1, 3, 5, 7, 9]
```

As these examples illustrate, tuple syntax allows you to elegantly write and consume methods that need to return more than one value. There's no good reason to define a dedicated type to hold together those values.

1.2.4 Pattern matching and record types

Versions 8 and 9 of C#, which appeared after the first edition of this book was published, bring us two important features that are directly inspired by functional languages:

- *Pattern matching*—Lets you use the `switch` keyword to match not only on specific values but also on the shape of the data, most importantly its type
- *Records*—Boilerplate-free immutable types with built-in support for creating modified versions

> **TIP** The appendix shows you how you can work with pattern matching and immutable types if you're working with legacy code and are stuck with an older version of C#.

I'll illustrate how you can use these through a practical example. If you've ever worked in e-commerce, you may have come across the need to evaluate the value-added tax (VAT) that your customers will pay with their purchases.[2]

Imagine you're tasked with writing a function that estimates the VAT a customer needs to pay on an order. The logic and amount of VAT depends on the country to which the item is sent and, of course, on the purchase amount. Therefore, we're looking to implement a function named `Vat` that will compute a `decimal` (the tax amount), given an `Order` and the buyer's `Address`. Assume that the requirements are as follows:

- For goods shipped to Italy and Japan, VAT will be charged at a fixed rate of 22% and 8%, respectively.
- Germany charges 8% on food products and 20% on all other products.
- The US charges a fixed rate on all products, but the rate varies for each state.

Before you read on, you might like to take a moment to think how you would go about tackling this task.

The following listing shows how you can use record types to model an `Order`. To keep things simple, I'm assuming that an `Order` cannot contain different types of `Products`.

Listing 1.6 Positional records

```
record Product(string Name, decimal Price, bool IsFood);        ⟵ A record without a body
                                                                    ends with a semicolon.

record Order(Product Product, int Quantity)        ⟵
{                                                       A record can have a
    public decimal NetPrice => Product.Price * Quantity;   body with additional
}                                                       members.
```

---

[2] VAT is also called *sales tax* or *consumption tax*, depending on the country you're in.

Notice how with a single line, you can define the Product type! The compiler generates a constructor, property getters, and several convenience methods such as Equals, GetHashCode, and ToString for you.

> **NOTE** Records in C# 9 are reference types, but C# 10 allows you to use record syntax to define value types by simply writing record struct rather than just record. Somewhat surprisingly, record structs are mutable, and you have to declare your struct as readonly record struct if you want it to be immutable.

The following listing shows how we can implement the first business rule, which applies to countries with a fixed VAT rate, like Italy and Japan.

Listing 1.7 Pattern matching on a value

```
static decimal Vat(Address address, Order order)
   => Vat(RateByCountry(address.Country), order);

static decimal RateByCountry(string country)
   => country switch
   {
      "it" => 0.22m,
      "jp" => 0.08m,
      _ => throw new ArgumentException($"Missing rate for {country}")
   };

static decimal Vat(decimal rate, Order order)
   => order.NetPrice * rate;
```

Here I've defined RateByCountry to map country codes to their respective VAT rates. Notice the clean syntax of a switch expression compared to the traditional switch statement with its clunky use of case, break, and return. Here we simply match on the *value* of country.

Also notice that the code in listing 1.7 assumes there is an Address type with a Country property. This can be defined as follows:

```
record Address(string Country);
```

What about the other fields that make up an address, like the street, postal code, and so on? No, I didn't forget or leave them out for simplicity. Because we only require the country for this calculation, it's legitimate to have an Address type that only encapsulates the information we need in this context. You could have a different, richer definition of Address in a different component, and define a conversion between the two, if required.

Let's move on and add the implementation for goods shipped to Germany. As a reminder, Germany charges 8% on food products and 20% on all other products. The code in the following listing shows how we can add this rule.

Listing 1.8   Deconstructing a record in a pattern-matching expression

```
static decimal Vat(Address address, Order order)
   => address switch
   {
      Address("de") => DeVat(order),
      Address(var country) => Vat(RateByCountry(country), order),
   };

static decimal DeVat(Order order)
   => order.NetPrice * (order.Product.IsFood ? 0.08m : 0.2m);
```

We've now added a `switch` expression within the `Vat` function. In each case, the given `Address` is deconstructed, allowing us to match on the value of its `Country`. In the first case, we match it against the literal value `"de"`; if this matches, we call the VAT computation for Germany, `DeVat`. In the second case, the value is assigned to the `country` variable and we retrieve the rate by country as previously. Note that it's possible to simplify the clauses of the `switch` expression as follows:

```
static decimal Vat(Address address, Order order)
   => address switch
   {
      ("de") _ => DeVat(order),
      (var country) _ => Vat(RateByCountry(country), order),
   };
```

Because the type of `address` is known to be `Address`, you can omit the type. In this example, you must include a variable name for the matching expression; here we use a *discard*, the underscore character. This is not required if the object being deconstructed has at least two fields.[3]

Property patterns

The previous listing shows how to match on the value of a field by deconstructing the `Address`; this is called a *positional pattern*. Now, imagine that your `Address` type were more complex, including half a dozen fields or so. In this case, a positional pattern would be noisy, as you'd need to include a variable name (at least a discard) for each field.

This is where *property patterns* are better suited. The following code shows how you can match on the value of a property:

```
static decimal Vat(Address address, Order order)
   => address switch
   {
      { Country: "de" } => DeVat(order),
      { Country: var c } => Vat(RateByCountry(c), order),
   };
```

---

[3] The problem is that in C# (`"de"`) is identical to `"de"`, so the compiler would think you're matching on a `string`, rather than an object with a single string field.

This syntax offers the advantage that you do not need to change anything if you later add an extra field to `Address`. In general, property patterns work best with your typical OO entities, whereas positional patterns work best with very simple objects whose definition is unlikely to change (like a 2D point), or with objects that were modeled around a specific pattern matching scenario, like the simplified `Address` type in the current example.

Now for the US. Here we also need to know the state to which the order is going because different states apply different rates. You can model this as follows:

```
record Address(string Country);
record UsAddress(string State) : Address("us");
```

That is, we create a dedicated type to represent a US address. This extends `Address` because it has additional data. (In my opinion, this is better than adding a `State` property to `Address` and having it be `null` for the majority of countries.) We can now complete our requirements as the following listing shows.

Listing 1.9   Pattern matching by type

```
static decimal Vat(Address address, Order order)
   => address switch
   {
      UsAddress(var state) => Vat(RateByState(state), order),
      ("de") _ => DeVat(order),
      (var country) _ => Vat(RateByCountry(country), order),
   };

static decimal RateByState(string state)
   => state switch
   {
      "ca" => 0.1m,
      "ma" => 0.0625m,
      "ny" => 0.085m,
      _ => throw new ArgumentException($"Missing rate for {state}")
   };
```

`RateByState` is implemented along the same lines as `RateByCountry`. What's more interesting is the pattern matching in `Vat`. We can now match on the `UsAddress` type, extracting the state, to find the rate applicable to that state.

TIP   This section illustrates the most common (and most useful) patterns that C# supports. In addition, you can use *relational patterns* to match, say, all values greater than 100, or *logical patterns* to combine several other patterns. Head to https://docs.microsoft.com/en-us/dotnet/csharp/language-reference/operators/patterns for the full specification.

And we're done! The whole thing is just over 40 lines, most functions are one-liners, and the three cases in our requirements are clearly expressed in the corresponding cases in the top-level `switch` expression. We didn't need to go crazy with functions (yet). We didn't need to create an interface with multiple implementations as an OO programmer (seeing this problem as a perfect candidate for the *strategy* pattern) probably would have. Instead, we just used a *type-driven* approach that is representative of how records and pattern matching can be used in statically-typed functional languages.

The resulting code is not only concise, but is also readable and extensible. You can see that it would be easy for any programmer to come in and add new rules for other countries or modify the existing rules if required.

1.3   *What you will learn in this book*

In this chapter, you've seen some of the basic ideas of FP and the C# features that allow you to program in a functional style. This book does not assume any prior knowledge of functional programming. It does assume you know .NET and C# well (or, alternatively, a similar language like Java, Swift, or Kotlin). This book is about functional programming, not C#. After reading this book, you will be able to

- Use higher-order functions to achieve more with less code and reduce duplication
- Use pure functions to write code that is easy to test and optimize
- Write APIs that are pleasant to consume and accurately describe your program's behavior
- Use dedicated types to handle nullability, system errors, and validation rules in a way that's elegant and predictable
- Write testable, modular code that can be composed without the overhead of an IoC container
- Write a Web API in a functional style
- Write complex programs with simple, declarative code, using high-level functions to process elements in a sequence or a stream of values
- Read and understand literature written for functional languages

Summary

- Functional programming (FP) is a powerful paradigm that can help you make your code more concise, maintainable, expressive, robust, testable, and concurrency-friendly.
- FP differs from object-oriented programming (OOP) by focusing on functions rather than objects, and on data transformations rather than state mutations.
- FP can be seen as a collection of techniques that are based on two fundamental tenets:
  - Functions are first-class values.
  - In-place updates should be avoided.
- C# is a multi-paradigm language that has steadily incorporated functional features, allowing you to reap the benefits of programming in a functional style.

Thinking in functions

This chapter covers

- Functions in math and in programming
- Representing functions in C#
- Leveraging higher-order functions

In chapter 1, you saw how treating functions as first-class values is one of the tenets of FP. This allows the programmer to up the ante and write functions that are parameterized by or create other functions. These are called *higher-order functions* (HOFs); they really raise the level of abstraction in our programs, allowing us to do more with less code.

But before we delve into HOFs, let's take a step back and see what we mean by functions: what they are both in the mathematical and programming jargon. We'll then look at the various constructs that C# offers to represent functions.

2.1   What's a function, anyway?

In this section, I'll clarify what I mean by *function*. I'll start with the mathematical use of the word and then move on to the various language constructs that C# offers to represent functions. This will give you some basic conceptual and practical tools so you can start to code functionally.

2.1.1   Functions as maps

In mathematics, a function is a map between two sets, respectively called the *domain* and *codomain*. That is, given an element from its domain, a function yields an element from its codomain. That's all there is to that. It doesn't matter whether the mapping is based on some formula or is completely arbitrary.

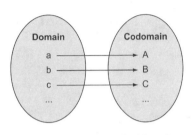

Figure 2.1   A mathematical function is simply a mapping. It maps elements from one set (the domain) to elements of another set (the codomain).

In this sense, a function is a completely abstract mathematical object, and the value that a function yields is determined *exclusively* by its input. You'll see that this isn't always the case with functions in programming.

For example, imagine a function mapping lowercase letters to their uppercase counterparts as in figure 2.1. In this case, the domain is the set *{a, b, c, ...}*, and the codomain is the set *{A, B, C, ...}*. (Naturally, there are functions for which the domain and codomain are the same set; can you think of an example?)

How does this relate to programming functions? In statically-typed languages like C#, *types* represent the sets (domain and codomain). For example, if you code the function in figure 2.1, you could use char to represent both the domain and the codomain. The type of your function could then be written as

```
char → char
```

The function maps chars to chars or, equivalently, given a char, it yields a char.

The types for the domain and codomain constitute a function's *interface*, also called its *type* or *signature*. You can think of this as a contract: a function signature declares that, given an element from the domain, it will yield an element from the codomain.[1] This may sound pretty obvious, but you'll see in chapter 4 that, in reality, violations of the signature contract abound.

Next, let's look at the C# language features that enable us to represent functions. By this I mean, not just mathematical functions, but what we refer to as functions in everyday programming talk.

2.1.2   Representing functions in C#

There are several language constructs in C# that you can use to represent functions:

- Methods (including local functions)
- Delegates
- Lambda expressions
- Dictionaries

---

[1] Interfaces in the OO sense are an extension of this idea: a set of functions with their respective input and output types or, more precisely, methods (which are essentially functions) that take this (the current instance) as an implicit argument.

If you're well versed in these, skip to section 2.2; otherwise, here's a quick refresher.

METHODS

Methods are the most common and idiomatic representation for functions in C#. For example, the `System.Math` class includes methods that represent many common mathematical functions. When programming functionally, we tend to overwhelmingly use static methods that only rely on their input arguments—they don't refer to any fields or properties in the enclosing static class, and therefore, you can think of them in isolation, like you would do with mathematical functions.

We discussed local functions in section 1.2.2. They're really methods declared inside a method. If you have a function that performs a specific task and you only need to call it in one place, it could be a candidate for a local function. The constructs that really enable you to program in a functional style are delegates and lambda expressions, so let's move on to those.

DELEGATES

Delegates are type-safe function pointers. *Type-safe* here means that a delegate is strongly typed. The types of the input and output values of the function are known at compile time, and consistency is enforced by the compiler.

Creating a delegate is a two-step process: you first declare the delegate type and then provide an implementation. (This is analogous to writing an `interface` and then instantiating a `class` implementing that interface.)

The first step is done by using the `delegate` keyword and providing the signature for the delegate. For example, the following listing shows the definition of the `Comparison<T>` delegate, which is included in the .NET Base Class Library.

Listing 2.1 Declaring a delegate

```
namespace System
{
    public delegate int Comparison<in T>(T x, T y);
}
```

As you can see, a `Comparison<T>` takes two `T`'s. It then yields an `int`, indicating which is greater.

Once you have a delegate type, you can instantiate it by providing an implementation. The following listing shows this approach.

Listing 2.2 Instantiating and using a delegate

```
var list = Enumerable.Range(1, 10).Select(i => i * 3).ToList();
list // => [3, 6, 9, 12, 15, 18, 21, 24, 27, 30]

Comparison<int> alphabetically = (l, r)          Provides an implementation
    => l.ToString().CompareTo(r.ToString());     of Comparison

list.Sort(alphabetically);                       ⟵ Uses the Comparison delegate
list // => [12, 15, 18, 21, 24, 27, 3, 30, 6, 9]   as an argument to Sort
```

As you can see, a delegate is just an *object* (in the technical sense) that represents an operation; in this case, a comparison. Like any other object, you can use a delegate as an argument for another method as in listing 2.2. Delegates are the language feature that makes functions first-class values in C#.

THE FUNC AND ACTION DELEGATES

.NET includes a couple of delegate families that can represent pretty much any function type:

- `Func<R>`—Represents a function that takes no arguments and returns a result of type `R`
- `Func<T1, R>`—Represents a function that takes an argument of type `T1` and returns a result of type `R`
- `Func<T1, T2, R>`—Represents a function that takes a `T1` and a `T2` and returns an `R`

And so on. These delegates represent functions of various *arities* (see the sidebar on "Function arity").

Since the introduction of `Func`, it has become rare to use custom delegates. For example, instead of declaring a custom delegate like this

```
delegate Greeting Greeter(Person p);
```

you can simply use

```
Func<Person, Greeting>
```

The type of `Greeter` as defined in this example is equivalent to or compatible with `Func<Person, Greeting>`. In both cases, it's a function that takes a `Person` and returns a `Greeting`. In practice, this means you can define a `Greeter` and pass it to a method that expects a `Func<Person, Greeting>` and vice versa, without any complaints from the compiler.

There's a similar delegate family to represent *actions*, functions that have no return value, such as `void` methods:

- `Action`—Represents an action with no input arguments
- `Action<T1>`—Represents an action with an input argument of type `T1`
- `Action<T1, T2>` and so on—Represent an action with several input arguments

The evolution of .NET has been away from custom delegates in favor of the more general `Func` and `Action` delegates. For instance, take the representation of a predicate:[2]

- In .NET 2, a `Predicate<T>` delegate was introduced. For example, the `FindAll` method used to filter a `List<T>` expects a `Predicate<T>`.
- In .NET 3, the `Where` method, also used for filtering but defined for the more general `IEnumerable<T>`, doesn't take a `Predicate<T>` but simply a `Func<T, bool>`.

---

[2] A *predicate* is a function that, given a value (say, an integer), tells you whether it satisfies some condition (say, whether it's even).

Both function types are equivalent. Using `Func` is recommended to avoid a proliferation of delegate types that represent the same function signature, but there's still something to be said in favor of the expressiveness of custom delegates. `Predicate<T>`, in my view, conveys intent more clearly than `Func<T, bool>` and is closer to the spoken language.

Function arity

Arity is a funny word that refers to the number of arguments that a function accepts. For instance

- A *nullary* function takes no arguments.
- A *unary* function takes one argument.
- A *binary* function takes two arguments.
- A *ternary* function takes three arguments.

And so on. In reality, all functions can be viewed as being unary because passing n arguments is equivalent to passing an n tuple as the only argument. For example, addition (like any other binary arithmetic operation) is a function whose domain is the set of all pairs of numbers.

LAMBDA EXPRESSIONS

Lambda expressions, called *lambdas* for short, are used to declare a function inline. The following listing demonstrates using a lambda to sort a list of numbers alphabetically.

Listing 2.3 Declaring a function inline with a lambda

```
var list = Enumerable.Range(1, 10).Select(i => i * 3).ToList();
list // => [3, 6, 9, 12, 15, 18, 21, 24, 27, 30]

list.Sort((l, r) => l.ToString().CompareTo(r.ToString()));
list // => [12, 15, 18, 21, 24, 27, 3, 30, 6, 9]
```

If your function is short, and you don't need to reuse it elsewhere, lambdas offer the most attractive notation. Also notice that in listing 2.3, the compiler not only infers l and r to be of type `int`, it also converts the lambda to the delegate type `Comparison<int>` expected by the `Sort` method, given that the provided lambda is compatible with this type.

Like methods, delegates and lambdas have access to the variables in the scope in which they're declared. This is particularly useful when leveraging *closures*, as in the following listing.[3]

---

[3] A *closure* is the combination of the lambda expression itself along with the context in which that lambda is declared (all the variables available in the scope where the lambda appears).

Listing 2.4   A lambda accessing a variable from the enclosing scope

```
var days = Enum.GetValues(typeof(DayOfWeek)).Cast<DayOfWeek>();
// => [Sunday, Monday, Tuesday, Wednesday, Thursday, Friday, Saturday]

IEnumerable<DayOfWeek> daysStartingWith(string s)
   => days.Where(d => d.ToString().StartsWith(s));        ◁─┐ References the s variable
                                                            │ from within the lambda, thus
                                                            │ capturing it in a closure

daysStartingWith("S") // => [Sunday, Saturday]
```

In this example, Where expects a function that takes a DayOfWeek and returns a bool.
In reality, the function expressed by the lambda expression also uses the value of
pattern, which is captured in a closure to calculate its result.

   This is interesting. If you were to look at the function expressed by the lambda
with a more mathematical eye, you might say that it's actually a binary function that
takes a DayOfWeek *and* a string (the pattern) as inputs and yields a bool. As programmers, however, we're usually mostly concerned about the function signature, so you
might be more likely to look at it as a unary function from DayOfWeek to bool. Both
perspectives are valid: the function must conform to its unary signature, but it
depends on two values to do its work.

Anonymous methods

For the sake of completeness, I should mention that C# 2 introduced a feature called
anonymous methods. These allow you to create a delegate like this:

```
Comparison<int> alphabetically = delegate (int l, int r)
{
    return l.ToString().CompareTo(r.ToString());
};
```

Anonymous methods were superseded in C# 3 when lambda expressions provided a
more concise syntax for doing the same, as you saw in listing 2.2. Anonymous methods survive as a vestigial feature of the language, but their use is discouraged. In the
context of C# features, the term *anonymous functions* refers both to anonymous
methods and to lambda expressions.

DICTIONARIES

Dictionaries are fittingly also called maps (or hash tables). They're data structures that
provide a direct representation of a function. They literally contain the association of
keys (elements from the domain) to *values* (the corresponding elements from the
codomain).

   We normally think of dictionaries as data, so it's enriching to change perspectives for
a moment and consider them as functions. Dictionaries are appropriate for representing functions that are completely arbitrary, where the mappings can't be computed but

must be stored exhaustively. For example, the following listing shows how you could map Boolean values to their names in French.

> **Listing 2.5 A dictionary exhaustively representing a function**

```
var frenchFor = new Dictionary<bool, string>
{
    [true] = "Vrai",
    [false] = "Faux",
};

frenchFor[true]                    Function application is
// => "Vrai"                       performed with a lookup.
```

The fact that functions can be represented with dictionaries also makes it possible to optimize computationally expensive functions by storing their computed results in a dictionary instead of recomputing them every time. This technique is called *memoization*.

For convenience, in the rest of the book, I'll use the term *function* to indicate one of the C# representations of a function. Keep in mind that this doesn't quite match the mathematical definition of the term. You'll learn more about the differences between mathematical and programming functions in chapter 3.

2.2 Higher-order functions (HOFs)

Now that you have an understanding of what FP is and we've reviewed the functional features of the language, it's time to start exploring some concrete functional techniques. We'll begin with the most important benefit of functions as first-class values— they give you the ability to define higher-order functions (HOFs).

HOFs are functions that take other functions as inputs or return a function as output or both. I'll assume that you've already used HOFs to some extent, as with LINQ, for example. We'll use HOFs *a lot* in this book, so this section should act as a refresher and will possibly introduce some use cases for HOFs that you may be less familiar with.

HOFs are fun, and most of the examples in this section can be run in the REPL. Make sure you try a few variations of your own along the way.

2.2.1 Functions that depend on other functions

Some HOFs take other functions as arguments and invoke them in order to do their work, somewhat like the way a company may subcontract some of its work to another company. You've seen some examples of such HOFs earlier in this chapter, including Sort (an instance method on List) and Where (an extension method on IEnumerable).

List.Sort when called with a Comparison delegate is a method that says, "OK, I'll sort myself, as long as you tell me how to compare any two elements that I contain." Sort does the job of sorting, but the caller can decide what logic to use for comparing.

Similarly, Where does the job of filtering, and the caller decides what logic determines whether an element should be included. You can represent the type of Where graphically as shown in figure 2.2.

Figure 2.2   `Where` **is a HOF that takes a predicate function as input. It uses the predicate to decide which elements to include in the returned list.**

The following listing shows an idealized implementation of `Where`.[4]

Listing 2.6   `Where`, a HOF that iteratively applies the given predicate

```
public static IEnumerable<T> Where<T>
    (this IEnumerable<T> ts, Func<T, bool> predicate)
{
    foreach (T t in ts)              Iterating over the list is an
        if (predicate(t))            implementation detail of Where.
            yield return t;          The criterion determining which items
}                                    are included is decided by the caller.
```

The `Where` method is responsible for the filtering logic. The caller provides the *predicate*, which is the criterion based on which the `IEnumerable` should be filtered.

As you can see, HOFs can help with the separation of concerns in cases where logic can't otherwise be easily separated. `Where` and `Sort` are examples of an *iterated application*—the HOF applies the given function repeatedly for every element in the collection.

One crude way of looking at this is that you're passing as the argument a function whose code will ultimately execute inside the body of a loop within the HOF. This is something you couldn't do by only passing static data. The general scheme is shown in figure 2.3.

Optional execution is another good candidate for HOFs. This is useful when you want to invoke a given function only in certain conditions, as figure 2.4 illustrates.

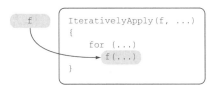

Figure 2.3   A HOF that iteratively applies the function given as an argument

Figure 2.4   A HOF that conditionally applies the function given as an argument

---

[4] This implementation is functionally correct, but it lacks the error checking and optimizations in the LINQ implementation.

For example, imagine a method that looks up an element from the cache. A delegate can be provided and can be invoked in case of a cache miss. The following listing shows how this is done.

Listing 2.7 A HOF that optionally invokes the given function

```
class Cache<T> where T : class
{
   public T Get(Guid id) => //...
   public T Get(Guid id, Func<T> onMiss)
      => Get(id) ?? onMiss();
}
```

The logic in onMiss could involve an expensive operation, such as a database call. You wouldn't want this to be executed unnecessarily.

The preceding examples illustrate HOFs that take a function as input and use it to perform a task or to compute a value. This is perhaps the most common pattern for HOFs, and it's sometimes referred to as *inversion of control*, where the caller of the HOF decides *what* to do by supplying a function, and the function decides *when* to do it by invoking the given function. Let's look at some other scenarios in which HOFs come in handy.

2.2.2 Adapter functions

Some HOFs don't *apply* the given function at all, but rather return a new function that's somehow related to the function given as an argument. For example, say you have a function that performs integer division:

```
var divide = (int x, int y) => x / y;
divide(10, 2) // => 5
```

You want to change the order of the arguments so that the divisor comes first. This could be seen as a particular case of a more general problem: changing the order of the arguments. You can write a generic HOF that modifies any binary function by swapping the order of its arguments:

```
static Func<T2, T1, R> SwapArgs<T1, T2, R>(this Func<T1, T2, R> f)
   => (t2, t1) => f(t1, t2);
```

Technically, it would be more correct to say that SwapArgs returns a new function, which invokes the given function with the arguments in the reverse order. But on an intuitive level, I find it easier to think that I'm getting back a modified version of the original function. You can now modify the original division function by applying SwapArgs:

```
var divideBy = divide.SwapArgs();
divideBy(2, 10) // => 5
```

Playing with this sort of HOF leads to the interesting idea that functions aren't set in stone: if you don't like the interface of a function, you can call it via another function that provides an interface that better suits your needs. That's why I call these *adapter functions.*[5]

2.2.3 Functions that create other functions

Sometimes you'll write functions whose primary purpose is to create other functions. You can think of them as *function factories.* The following example uses a lambda to filter a sequence of numbers, keeping only those divisible by 2:

```
var range = Enumerable.Range(1, 20);

range.Where(i => i % 2 == 0)
// => [2, 4, 6, 8, 10, 12, 14, 16, 18, 20]
```

What if you wanted something more general, like being able to filter for numbers divisible by any number *n*? You could define a function that takes *n* and yields a suitable predicate that evaluates whether any given number is divisible by *n*:

```
Func<int, bool> isMod(int n) => i => i % n == 0;
```

We haven't looked at a HOF like this before. It takes some static data and returns a function. Let's see how you can use it:

```
using static System.Linq.Enumerable;

Range(1, 20).Where(isMod(2)) // => [2, 4, 6, 8, 10, 12, 14, 16, 18, 20]
Range(1, 20).Where(isMod(3)) // => [3, 6, 9, 12, 15, 18]
```

Notice how you've gained not only in generality but also in readability! In this example, you're using the isMod HOF to produce a function, and then you're feeding it as input to another HOF, Where, as figure 2.5 shows.

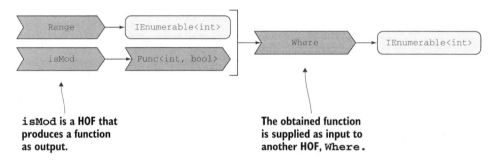

isMod is a **HOF** that produces a function as output.

The obtained function is supplied as input to another HOF, Where.

Figure 2.5   Here we define IsMod as a HOF that returns a function telling us whether a number is divisible by some given value. We then take the resulting predicate and use it as input to Where.

---

[5]   The well-known adapter pattern in OOP can be seen as applying the idea of adapter functions to an object's interface.

You'll see many more uses of HOFs in this book. Eventually, you'll look at them as regular functions, forgetting that they're higher order. Let's now look at how these can be used in a scenario closer to everyday development.

2.3 Using HOFs to avoid duplication

Another common use case for HOFs is to encapsulate setup and teardown operations. For example, interacting with a database requires some setup to acquire and open a connection and some cleaning up after the interaction to close the connection and return it to the underlying connection pool. The following listing shows what this looks like in code.

Listing 2.8 Connecting to a DB with some setup and teardown

```
string connString = "myDatabase";

var conn = new SqlConnection(connString));    │ Setup: acquire and
conn.Open();                                  │ open a connection

// interact with the database...

conn.Close();        │ Teardown: close and
conn.Dispose();      │ release the connection
```

The setup and teardown are always identical, regardless of whether you're reading or writing to the database, or performing one or many actions. The preceding code is usually written with a `using` block like this:

```
using (var conn = new SqlConnection(connString))
{
    conn.Open();
    // interact with the database...
}
```

This is both shorter and better, but it's still essentially the same.[6] Consider the following listing, showing a simple `DbLogger` class with a couple of methods that interact with the database. `Log` inserts a given log message, and `GetLogs` retrieves all logs since a given date.

Listing 2.9 Duplication of setup/teardown logic

```
using Dapper;        ◁─── Exposes Execute and Query as
                          extension methods on the connection
public class DbLogger
{
    string connString;          ◁─── Assume this is set
                                     in the constructor.
```

---

[6] It's shorter because `Dispose` is called as you exit the `using` block, which will, in turn, call `Close`. It's better because the interaction is then wrapped in a `try`/`finally` block, so the connection is disposed even if an exception is thrown in the body of the `using` block.

```
public void Log(LogMessage msg)
{
    using (var conn = new SqlConnection(connString))         ◁──┤ Setup
    {
        conn.Execute("sp_create_log", msg              Persists the LogMessage
            , commandType: CommandType.StoredProcedure);    to the database
    }
}                                        ◁──┐ Performs teardown
                                             │ as part of Dispose
public IEnumerable<LogMessage> GetLogs(DateTime since)
{
    var sql = "SELECT * FROM [Logs] WHERE [Timestamp] > @since";
    using (var conn = new SqlConnection(connString))         ◁──┤ Setup
    {
        return conn.Query<LogMessage>(sql              Queries the database and
            , new {since = since});                    deserializes the results
    }                             ◁──┤ Teardown
}
}
```

It's not essential that you understand the code in detail. The code uses Dapper (https://github.com/StackExchange/dapper-dot-net), a thin layer on top of ADO.NET, allowing you to interact with the database through a simple API:

- Query—Queries the database and returns the deserialized LogMessages
- Execute—Runs the stored procedure and returns the number of affected rows, which we're disregarding

The important thing to notice is that the two methods have some duplication; namely, the setup and teardown logic. Can we get rid of the duplication?

> **NOTE** In a real-world scenario, I'd recommend you always perform I/O operations asynchronously. In this example, GetLogs should really call QueryAsync and return a Task<IEnumerable<LogMessage>>). But asynchrony adds a level of complexity that's not helpful while you're trying to learn the already challenging ideas of FP. For pedagogical purposes, I'll wait until chapter 16 to discuss asynchrony.

As you can see, Dapper exposes a pleasant API, and it even opens the connection if necessary. But you're still required to create the connection, and you should dispose it as soon as possible once you're done with it. As a result, the "meat" of your database calls ends up sandwiched between identical pieces of code that perform setup and teardown. Let's look at how you can avoid this duplication by extracting the setup and teardown logic into a HOF.

You're looking to write a function that performs setup and teardown and that's parameterized on what to do in between. This is a perfect scenario for a HOF because you can represent the logic in between with a function.[7] Graphically, it looks like figure 2.6.

---

[7] For this reason, you may hear this pattern inelegantly called a "hole in the middle."

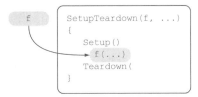

Figure 2.6 A HOF that wraps a given function between setup and teardown logic

Because connection setup and teardown are much more general than DbLogger, they can be extracted to a new ConnectionHelper class. The following listing provides an example of this.

Listing 2.10 Encapsulating setup and teardown of the DB connection into a HOF

```
using System.Data;
using System.Data.SqlClient;

public static class ConnectionHelper
{
   public static R Connect<R>
      (string connString, Func<IDbConnection, R> f)
   {
      using (var conn = new SqlConnection(connString))     ←┐
      {                                                       │  Setup
         conn.Open();                                        ←┘
         return f(conn);     ←── What happens in between
      }                           is now parameterized.
   }                 ←─┐
}                     │ Teardown
```

The Connect function performs the setup and teardown, and it's parameterized by what it should do in between. The signature of the body is interesting; it takes an IDbConnection (through which it will interact with the database) and returns a generic object R. In the use cases we've seen, R will be IEnumerable<LogMessage> in the case of the query and int in the case of the insert.

You can now use the Connect function in DbLogger as follows:

```
using Dapper;
using static ConnectionHelper;

public class DbLogger
{
   string connString;

   public void Log(LogMessage message)
      => Connect(connString, c => c.Execute("sp_create_log"
         , message, commandType: CommandType.StoredProcedure));

   string sql = @"SELECT * FROM [Logs] WHERE [Timestamp] > @since";

   public IEnumerable<LogMessage> GetLogs(DateTime since)
      => Connect(connString
         , c => c.Query<LogMessage>(sql, new {since = since}));
}
```

You got rid of the duplication in DbLogger, so DbLogger no longer needs to know the details about creating, opening, or disposing of the connection. By now, I hope you agree that HOFs are powerful tools, although overuse can make it difficult to understand what the code is doing. Use HOFs when appropriate but be mindful of readability: use short lambdas, clear naming, and meaningful indentation.

Exercises

I recommend you take the time to do the exercises and come up with a few of your own along the way. The code samples repository on GitHub (http://mng.bz/10Pj) includes placeholders so that you can write, compile, and run your code with minimal setup effort. It also includes solutions that you can check your results against:

1 Browse the methods of System.Linq.Enumerable (http://mng.bz/PX6n). Which are HOFs? Which do you think imply iterated application of the given function?

2 Write a function that negates a given predicate: when the given predicate evaluates to true, the resulting function evaluates to false and vice versa.

3 Write a method that uses quicksort to sort a List<int>, returning a new list rather than sorting it in place.

4 Generalize the previous implementation to take a List<T> and a Comparison<T> delegate.

Summary

- Mathematical functions simply define a mapping between two sets.
- You can represent functions in C# using methods, delegates, lambdas, and dictionaries.
- FP leverages higher-order functions (HOFs), which are functions that take other functions as input or output); hence, the necessity for the language to have functions as first-class values.

Why function
purity matters

3

This chapter covers

- What makes a function pure or impure
- Why purity matters in concurrent scenarios
- How purity relates to testability
- Reducing the impure footprint of your code

The initial name for this chapter was "The irresistible appeal of purity." But if it was so irresistible, we'd have more functional programmers, right? Functional programmers, you see, are suckers for *pure functions*: functions with no side effects. In this chapter, you'll see what that means exactly and why pure functions have some very desirable properties.

Unfortunately, this fascination with pure functions is partly why FP as a discipline has become disconnected from the industry. As you'll soon realize, there's little purity in most real-world applications. And yet, purity is still relevant in the real world, as I hope to show in this chapter.

We'll start by looking at what makes a function pure (or impure), and then you'll see how purity affects a program's testability and even correctness, especially in concurrent scenarios. I hope that by the end of the chapter, you'll find purity if not *irresistible* at least *definitely worth keeping in mind.*

3.1 *What is function purity?*

In chapter 2, you saw that mathematical functions are completely abstract entities. Although some programming functions are close representations of mathematical functions, this is often not the case. You often want a function to print something to the screen, to process a file, or to interact with another system. In short, you often want a function to *do* something, to have a *side effect.* Mathematical functions do nothing of the sort; they only return a value.

There's a second important difference: mathematical functions exist in a vacuum, so their results are determined strictly by their arguments. The programming constructs we use to represent functions, on the other hand, all have access to a *context*: an instance method has access to instance fields, a lambda has access to variables in the enclosing scope, and many functions have access to things that are completely outside the scope of the program, such as the system clock, a database, or a remote service, for instance.

That this context exists, that its limits aren't always clearly demarcated, and that it can consist of things that change outside of the program's control means that the behavior of functions in programming is substantially more complex to analyze than functions in mathematics. This leads to a distinction between *pure* and *impure* functions.

3.1.1 *Purity and side effects*

Pure functions closely resemble mathematical functions: they do nothing other than compute an output value based on their input values. Table 3.1 contrasts pure and impure functions.

Table 3.1   Requirements of pure functions

Pure functions	Impure functions
Output depends entirely on the input arguments.	Factors other than input arguments can affect the output.
Cause no side effects.	Can cause side effects.

To clarify this definition, we must define exactly what a side effect is. A function is said to have side effects if it does any of the following:

- *Mutates global state*—Global here means any state that's visible outside of the function's scope. For example, a private instance field is considered global because it's visible from all methods within the class.
- *Mutates its input arguments*—Arguments passed by the caller are effectively a state that a function shares with its caller. If a function mutates one of its arguments, that's a side effect that's visible to the caller.

- *Throws exceptions*—You can reason about pure functions in isolation; however, if a function throws exceptions, then the outcome of calling it is context-dependent. Namely, it differs depending on whether the function is called in a `try-catch`.
- *Performs any I/O operation*—This includes any interaction between the program and the external world, including reading from or writing to the console, the filesystem, or a database, and interacting with any process outside the application's boundary.

In summary, pure functions have no side effects, and their output is solely determined by their inputs. Note that both conditions must hold:

- *A function that has no side effects can still be impure.* Namely, a function that reads from global mutable state is likely to have an output that depends on factors other than its inputs.
- *A function whose output depends entirely on its inputs can also be impure.* It could still have side effects such as updating global mutable state.

The deterministic nature of pure functions (they always return the same output for the same input) has some interesting consequences. Pure functions are easy to test and to reason about.[1]

Furthermore, the fact that outputs only depend on inputs means that the order of evaluation isn't important. Whether you evaluate the result of a function now or later, the result does not change. This means that the parts of your program that consist entirely of pure functions can be optimized in a number of ways:

- *Parallelization*—Different threads carry out tasks in parallel.
- *Lazy evaluation*—Only evaluates values as needed.
- *Memoization*—Caches the result of a function so that it's only computed once.

On the other hand, using these techniques with impure functions can lead to rather nasty bugs. For these reasons, FP advocates that pure functions be preferred as far as possible.

3.1.2 Strategies for managing side effects

OK, let's aim to use pure functions whenever possible. But is it always possible? Is it ever possible? Well, if you look at the list of things considered as side effects, it's a pretty mixed bag, so the strategies for managing side effects depend on the types of side effects in question.

Mutating input arguments is the easiest of the lot. This side effect can always be avoided, and I'll demonstrate this next. It's also possible to always avoid throwing exceptions. We'll look at error handling without throwing exceptions in chapters 8 and 14.

---

[1] More theoretically inclined authors show how you can reason about pure functions algebraically to prove the correctness of your program; see, for example, Graham Hutton's *Programming in Haskell*, 2nd ed. Cambridge, UK: Cambridge University Press, 2016.

Writing programs (even stateful programs) without state mutation is also possible. You can write any program without ever mutating state.[2] This may be a surprising realization for an OO programmer and requires a real shift in thinking. In section 3.2, I'll show you a simple example of how avoiding state mutation enables you to easily parallelize a function. In later chapters, you'll learn various techniques to tackle more complex tasks without relying on state mutation.

Finally, I'll discuss how to manage I/O in section 3.3. By learning these techniques, you'll be able to isolate or avoid side effects and, thus, harness the benefits of pure functions.

3.1.3   *Avoid mutating arguments*

You can view a function signature as a contract: the function receives some inputs and returns some output. When a function mutates its arguments, this muddies the waters because the caller relies on this side effect to happen, even though this is not declared in the function signature. For this reason, I'd argue that mutating arguments is a bad idea in *any* programming paradigm. Nonetheless, I've repeatedly stumbled on implementations that do something along these lines:

```
decimal RecomputeTotal(Order order, List<OrderLine> linesToDelete)
{
   var result = 0m;
   foreach (var line in order.OrderLines)
      if (line.Quantity == 0) linesToDelete.Add(line);
      else result += line.Product.Price * line.Quantity;
   return result;
}
```

RecomputeTotal is meant to be called when the quantity of items in an order is modified. It recomputes the total value of the order and, *as a side effect*, adds the order lines whose quantities have changed to zero to the given linesToDelete list. This is represented in figure 3.1.

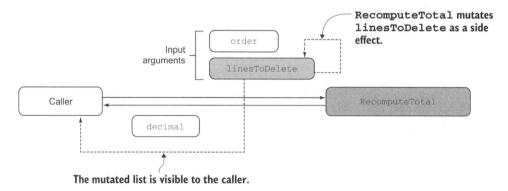

Figure 3.1   RecomputeTotal **mutates its input, and the caller depends on this side effect.**

---

[2] I should point out that *completely* avoiding state mutation is not always easy and not always practical. But avoiding state mutation most of the time is, and this is something you should be aiming toward.

The reason why this is such a terrible idea is that the behavior of the method is now tightly coupled with that of the caller: the caller relies on the method to perform its side effect, and the callee relies on the caller to initialize the list. As such, each method must be aware of the implementation details of the other, making it impossible to reason about the code in isolation.

> **WARNING**   Another problem with methods that mutate their argument is that, if you were to change the type of the argument from a `class` to a `struct`, you'd get a radically different behavior because structs are copied when passed between functions.

You can easily avoid this kind of side effect by returning all the computed information to the caller instead. It's important to recognize that the method is effectively computing two pieces of data: the new total for the order and the list of lines that can be deleted. You can make this explicit by returning a tuple. The refactored code would be as follows:

```
(decimal NewTotal, IEnumerable<OrderLine> LinesToDelete)
    RecomputeTotal(Order order)
    => (order.OrderLines.Sum(l => l.Product.Price * l.Quantity)
      , order.OrderLines.Where(l => l.Quantity == 0));
```

Figure 3.2 represents this refactored version and appears simplified. After all, now it's just a normal function that takes some input and returns an output.

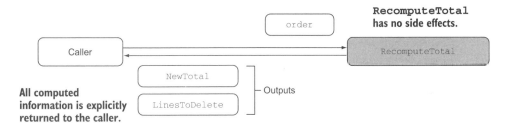

Figure 3.2   `RecomputeTotal` **refactored to explicitly return all the information it computes**

Following this principle, you can always structure your code in such a way that functions never mutate their input arguments. In fact, it would be ideal to enforce this by always using immutable objects—objects that once created cannot be changed. We'll discuss this in detail in chapter 11.

3.2   *Enabling parallelization by avoiding state mutation*

In this section, I'll show you a simple scenario that illustrates why pure functions can always be parallelized while impure functions can't. Imagine you want to format a list of strings as a numbered list:

- The casing should be standardized.
- Each item should be preceded with a counter.

To do this, you could define a `ListFormatter` class, with the following usage:

```
var shoppingList = new List<string>
{
    "coffee beans",
    "BANANAS",
    "Dates"
};

new ListFormatter()
   .Format(shoppingList)
   .ForEach(WriteLine);

// prints: 1. Coffee beans
//         2. Bananas
//         3. Dates
```

The following listing shows one possible implementation of `ListFormatter`.

Listing 3.1   A list formatter combining pure and impure functions

```
static class StringExt
{
    public static string ToSentenceCase(this string s)      ◁──┐ A pure
        => s == string.Empty                                   │ function
            ? string.Empty
            : char.ToUpperInvariant(s[0]) + s.ToLower()[1..];
}

class ListFormatter
{
    int counter;                                                   ┐ An impure function
                                                                   │ (it mutates
    string PrependCounter(string s) => $"{++counter}. {s}";   ◁──┘ global state).

    public List<string> Format(List<string> list)
        => list
            .Select(StringExt.ToSentenceCase)       │ Pure and impure functions
            .Select(PrependCounter)                  │ can be applied similarly.
            .ToList();
}
```

There are a few things to point out with respect to purity:

- `ToSentenceCase` *is pure (its output is strictly determined by the input).* Because its computation only depends on the input parameter, it can be made static without any problems.[3]
- `PrependCounter` *increments the counter, so it's impure.* Because it depends on an instance member (the counter), you can't make it static.
- *In the* `Format` *method, you apply both functions to items in the list with* `Select`, *irrespective of purity.* This isn't ideal, as you'll soon learn. In fact, there should ideally be a rule that `Select` should only be used with pure functions.

---

[3] In many languages, you'd have functions like this as freestanding functions, but methods in C# need to be inside a class. It's mostly a matter of taste where you put your static functions.

If the list you're formatting is big enough, would it make sense to perform the string manipulations in parallel? Could the runtime decide to do this as an optimization? We'll tackle these questions next.

3.2.1 Pure functions parallelize well

Given a big enough set of data to process, it's usually advantageous to process it in parallel, especially when the processing is CPU-intensive and the pieces of data can be processed independently. Pure functions parallelize well and are generally immune to the issues that make concurrency difficult. (For a refresher on concurrency and parallelism, see the sidebar on the "Meaning and types of concurrency").

I'll illustrate this by trying to parallelize our list-formatting functions with `ListFormatter`. Compare these two expressions:

```
list.Select(ToSentenceCase).ToList()
list.AsParallel().Select(ToSentenceCase).ToList()
```

The first expression uses the `Select` method defined in `System.Linq.Enumerable` to apply the pure function `ToSentenceCase` to each element in the list. The second expression is similar, but it uses methods provided by Parallel LINQ (PLINQ).[4] `AsParallel` turns the list into a `ParallelQuery`. As a result, `Select` resolves to the implementation defined in `ParallelEnumerable`, which applies `ToSentenceCase` to each item in the list, but now in parallel.

The list is split into chunks, and several threads are fired to process each chunk. The results are then harvested into a single list when `ToList` is called. Figure 3.3 shows this process.

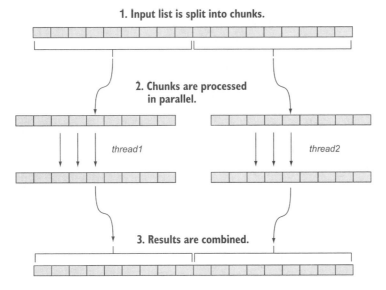

1. Input list is split into chunks.

2. Chunks are processed in parallel.

thread1   *thread2*

3. Results are combined.

Figure 3.3
Parallel processing
of data in a list

---

[4] PLINQ is an implementation of LINQ that works in parallel.

As you would expect, the two expressions yield the same results, but one does so sequentially and the other in parallel. This is nice. With just one call to `AsParallel`, you get parallelization *almost* for free.

Why *almost* for free? Why do you have to explicitly instruct the program to parallelize the operation? Why can't the runtime figure out that it's a good idea to parallelize an operation just like it figures out when it's a good time to run the garbage collector?

The answer is that the runtime doesn't know enough about the function to make an informed decision on whether parallelization might change the program flow. Because of their properties, pure functions can always be applied in parallel, but the runtime doesn't know whether the function being applied is pure.

Meaning and types of concurrency

Concurrency is the general concept of having several things going on at the same time. More formally, concurrency is when a program initiates a task before another one has completed so that different tasks are executed in overlapping time windows. There are several scenarios in which concurrency can occur:

- *Asynchrony*—Your program performs *non-blocking* operations. For example, it can initiate a request for a remote resource via HTTP and then go on to do some other task while it waits to receive the response. It's a bit like when you send an email and then go on with your life without waiting for a response.
- *Parallelism*—Your program leverages the hardware of multicore machines to execute tasks at the same time by breaking up work into tasks, each of which is executed on a separate core. It's a bit like singing in the shower: you're actually doing two things at exactly the same time.
- *Multithreading*—A software implementation that allows different threads to execute concurrently. A multithreaded program appears to be doing several things at the same time even when it's running on a single-core machine. This is a bit like chatting with different people through various IM windows, although you're actually switching back and forth. The net result is that you're having multiple conversations at the same time.

Doing several things at the same time can boost performance. It also means that the order of execution isn't guaranteed, so concurrency can be the source of difficult problems, most notably when multiple tasks concurrently try to update some shared mutable state. (In later chapters, you'll see how FP addresses this by avoiding a shared mutable state altogether.)

3.2.2 *Parallelizing impure functions*

You've seen that you could successfully apply the pure `ToSentenceCase` in parallel. Let's see what happens if you naively apply the impure `PrependCounter` function in parallel:

```
list.AsParallel().Select(PrependCounter).ToList()
```

If you now create a list with a million items and format it with the naively parallelized formatter, you'll find that the last item in the list will be prepended not with 1,000,000, but with a smaller number. If you've downloaded the code samples, you can try it for yourself by running

```
cd Examples
dotnet build
dotnet run NaivePar
```

The output will end with something like

```
932335. Item999998
932336. Item999999
932337. Item1000000
```

Because `PrependCounter` increments the `counter` variable, the parallel version will have multiple threads reading and updating the counter, as figure 3.4 shows. As is well known, `++` is not an atomic operation, and because there's no locking in place, we'll lose some of the updates and end up with an incorrect result.

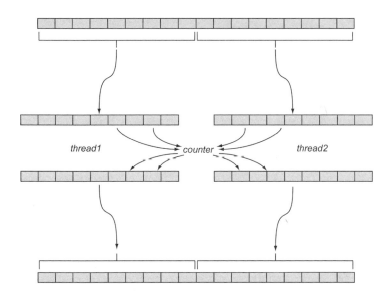

Figure 3.4 When processing the list in parallel, multiple threads access the counter concurrently.

This will sound familiar if you have some multithreading experience. Because multiple processes are reading and writing to the counter at the same time, some of the updates are lost. Of course, you could fix this by using a lock or the `Interlocked` class when incrementing the counter. But this would entail a performance hit, wiping out some of the gains made by parallelizing the computation. Furthermore, locking is an imperative construct that we'd rather avoid when coding functionally.

Let's summarize. Unlike pure functions, whose application can be parallelized by default, impure functions don't parallelize out of the box. And because parallel execution is nondeterministic, you may get some cases in which your result is correct and others in which it isn't (not the sort of bug you'd like to face).

Being aware of whether your functions are pure or not can help you understand these issues. Furthermore, if you develop with purity in mind, it's easier to parallelize the execution if you decide to do so.

3.2.3   *Avoiding state mutation*

One possible way to avoid the pitfalls of concurrent updates is to remove the problem at the source; don't use shared states to begin with. How this can be done varies with each scenario, but I'll show you a solution for the current scenario that enables us to format the list in parallel.

Let's go back to the drawing board and see if there's a sequential solution that doesn't involve mutation. What if, instead of updating a running counter, you generate a list of all the counter values you need and then pair items from the given list with items from the list of counters? For the list of integers, you can use Range, a convenience method on Enumerable, as the following listing demonstrates.

Listing 3.2   Generating a range of integers

```
Enumerable.Range(1, 3)
// => [1, 2, 3]
```

The operation of pairing two parallel lists is common in FP. It's called Zip. Zip takes two lists to pair up and a function to apply to each pair. The following listing shows an example.

Listing 3.3   Combining elements from parallel lists with Zip

```
Enumerable.Zip(
    new[] {1, 2, 3},
    new[] {"ichi", "ni", "san"},
    (number, name) => $"In Japanese, {number} is: {name}")

// => ["In Japanese, 1 is: ichi",
//     "In Japanese, 2 is: ni",
//     "In Japanese, 3 is: san"]
```

You can rewrite the list formatter using Range and Zip as the following listing shows.

Listing 3.4   List formatter refactored to use pure functions only

```
using static System.Linq.Enumerable;

static class ListFormatter
{
    public static List<string> Format(List<string> list)
```

```
    {
        var left = list.Select(StringExt.ToSentenceCase);
        var right = Range(1, list.Count);
        var zipped = Zip(left, right, (s, i) => $"{i}. {s}");
        return zipped.ToList();
    }
}
```

Here you use the list with `ToSentenceCase` applied to it as the left side of `Zip`. The right side is constructed with `Range`. The third argument to `Zip` is the pairing function: what to do with each pair of items. Because `Zip` can be used as an extension method, you can write the `Format` method using a more fluent syntax:

```
public static List<string> Format(List<string> list)
    => list
        .Select(StringExt.ToSentenceCase)
        .Zip(Range(1, list.Count), (s, i) => $"{i}. {s}")
        .ToList();
```

After this refactoring, `Format` is pure and can safely be made static. But what about making it parallel? That's a piece of cake because PLINQ offers an implementation of `Zip` that works with parallel queries. The following listing provides a parallel implementation of the list formatter.

Listing 3.5   A pure implementation that executes in parallel

```
using static System.Linq.ParallelEnumerable;          ◁─┐  Uses Range exposed by
                                                         │  ParallelEnumerable
static class ListFormatter
{
    public static List<string> Format(List<string> list)
        => list.AsParallel()                                ◁─┐  Turns the original data
            .Select(StringExt.ToSentenceCase)                  │  source into a parallel query
            .Zip(Range(1, list.Count), (s, i) => $"{i}. {s}")
            .ToList();
}
```

This is almost identical to the sequential version; there are only two differences. First, `AsParallel` is used to turn the given list into a `ParallelQuery` so that everything after that is done in parallel. Second, the change in `using static` has the effect that `Range` now refers to the implementation defined in `ParallelEnumerable` (this returns a `ParallelQuery`, which is what the parallel version of `Zip` expects). The rest is the same as the sequential version, and the parallel version of `Format` is still a pure function.

In this scenario, it was possible to enable parallel execution by removing state updates altogether, but this isn't always the case, nor is it always this easy. But the ideas you've seen so far put you in a better position when tackling issues related to parallelism and, more generally, concurrency.

The case for static methods

When all variables required within a method are provided as input (or are statically available), you can define the method as static. This chapter contains several examples of refactoring instance methods to static methods.

You may feel uneasy about this, especially if (like me) you've seen programs become difficult to test and maintain because of the inordinate use of static classes. Static methods can cause problems if they do either of the following:

- *Mutate static fields*—These are effectively the most global variables. They can be updated from any code that has visibility of the static class, causing coupling and unpredictable behavior.
- *Perform I/O*—In this case, it's testability that's jeopardized. If method A depends on the I/O behavior of static method B, it's not possible to unit test A.

Note that both of these cases imply an impure function. On the other hand, when a function is pure, it can safely be marked as static. As a general guideline

- Make pure functions static
- Avoid mutable static fields
- Avoid directly calling static methods that perform I/O

As you code more functionally, more of your functions will be pure. This means more of your code will potentially be in static classes without causing any of the problems associated with the abuse of static classes.

3.3 *Purity and testability*

In the previous section, you saw the relevance of purity in a concurrent scenario. Because the side effect had to do with state mutation, we could remove the mutation, and the resulting pure function could be run in parallel without problems.

Now we'll look at functions that perform I/O and how purity is relevant to unit testing. Unit tests have to be *repeatable* (if a test passes, it should do so irrespective of when it's run, on what machine, whether there's a connection, and so on). This is closely related to our requirement that pure functions be deterministic.

I'm aiming to leverage your knowledge of unit testing to help you understand the relevance of purity and also to dispel the notion that purity is only of a theoretical interest. Your manager may not care whether you write pure functions, but they're probably keen on good test coverage.

3.3.1 *Isolating I/O effects*

Unlike mutation, you can't avoid side effects related to I/O. Whereas mutation is an implementation detail, I/O is usually a requirement. Here are a few examples that help to clarify why functions that perform I/O can never be pure:

- A function that takes a URL and returns the resource at that URL yields a different result any time the remote resource changes, or it may throw an error if the connection is unavailable.

- A function that takes a file path and contents to be written to a file can throw an error if the directory doesn't exist or if the process hosting the program lacks write permissions.
- A function that returns the current time from the system clock returns a different result at any instant.

As you can see, any dependency on the external world gets in the way of function purity because the state of the world affects the function's return value. On the other hand, if your program is to do anything of use, there's no escaping the fact that some I/O is required. Even a purely mathematical program that just performs a computation must perform some I/O to communicate its result. Some of your code will have to be impure.

How can you reap the benefits of purity while satisfying the requirement to perform I/O? You *isolate* the pure, computational parts of your programs from the I/O. In this way, you minimize the footprint of I/O and reap the benefits of purity for the pure part of the program. For example, consider the following code:

```
using static System.Console;

WriteLine("Enter your name:");
var name = ReadLine();
WriteLine($"Hello {name}");
```

This trivial program mixes I/O with logic that could be captured in a pure function, as follows:

```
static string GreetingFor(string name) => $"Hello {name}";
```

In some real-world programs, separating logic from I/O is relatively simple. For example, take a document format converter like Pandoc, which can be used to convert a file from, say, Markdown to PDF. When you execute Pandoc, it performs the steps shown in figure 3.5.

The computational part of the program, which performs the format conversion, can be made entirely of pure functions. The impure functions that perform I/O can call the pure functions that perform the translation, but the functions that perform the translation can't call any function that performs I/O, or they will also become impure.

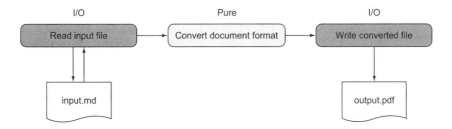

Figure 3.5 A program where I/O can easily be isolated. The core logic performing format conversion can be kept pure.

Most Line of Business (LOB) applications have a more complex structure in terms of I/O, so isolating the purely computational parts of the program from I/O is quite a challenge. Next, I'll introduce a business scenario we'll use throughout the book, and we'll see how we can test some validation that performs I/O.

3.3.2   *A business validation scenario*

Imagine you're writing some code for an online banking application. Your client is the Bank of Codeland (BOC); the BOC's customers can use a web or mobile device to make money transfers. Before booking a transfer, the server has to validate the request, as figure 3.6 shows.

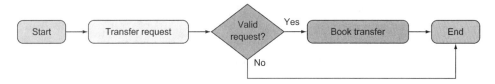

Figure 3.6   Business scenario: validating a transfer request

Let's assume that the user's request to make a transfer is represented by a `MakeTransfer` command. A *command* is a simple data transfer object (DTO) that the client sends the server, encapsulating details about the action it wants to be performed. The following listing shows our call to `MakeTransfer`.

Listing 3.6   A DTO representing a request to make a money transfer

```
public abstract record Command(DateTime Timestamp);

public record MakeTransfer
(
    Guid DebitedAccountId,            Identifies the
                                      sender's account

    string Beneficiary,               Details about the
    string Iban,                      beneficiary's account
    string Bic,

    DateTime Date,
    decimal Amount,                   Details about the transfer
    string Reference,

    DateTime Timestamp = default
)
    : Command(Timestamp)
{                                              We'll use this for testing when you don't
    internal static MakeTransfer Dummy         need all the properties to be populated.
        => new(default, default, default
            , default, default, default, default);
}
```

The properties of a `MakeTransfer` are populated by deserializing the client's request, except for the `Timestamp`, which needs to be set by the server. An initial `default` value is therefore declared. When unit testing, we'll have to populate the object manually, so having a `Dummy` instance allows you to only populate the properties relevant to the test, as you'll see in a moment.

Validation in this scenario can be quite complex. For the purposes of this explanation, we'll only look at the following validation:

- The `Date` field, representing the date on which the transfer should be executed, should not be past.
- The BIC code, a standard identifier for the beneficiary's bank, should be valid.

We'll start with an OO design. (In chapter 9, I show a more thoroughly functional approach to this scenario.) Following the single-responsibility principle, we'll write one class for each particular validation. Let's draft a simple interface that all these validator classes will implement:

```
public interface IValidator<T>
{
    bool IsValid(T t);
}
```

Now that we have our domain-specific abstractions in place, let's start with a basic implementation. The next listing shows how this is done.

Listing 3.7 Implementing validation rules

```
using System.Text.RegularExpressions;

public class BicFormatValidator : IValidator<MakeTransfer>
{
    static readonly Regex regex = new Regex("^[A-Z]{6}[A-Z1-9]{5}$");

    public bool IsValid(MakeTransfer transfer)
        => regex.IsMatch(transfer.Bic);
}

public class DateNotPastValidator : IValidator<MakeTransfer>
{
    public bool IsValid(MakeTransfer transfer)
        => (DateTime.UtcNow.Date <= transfer.Date.Date);
}
```

That was fairly easy. Is the logic in `BicFormatValidator` pure? Yes, because there are no side effects and the result of `IsValid` is deterministic. What about `DateNotPastValidator`? In this case, the result of `IsValid` depends on the current date, so clearly, the answer is no! What kind of side effect are we facing here? It's I/O: `DateTime.UtcNow` queries the system clock, which is outside the context of the program.

Functions that perform I/O are difficult to test. For example, consider the following test:

```
[Test]
public void WhenTransferDateIsFuture_ThenValidationPasses()
{
    var sut = new DateNotPastValidator();          ◁─┐  sut stands for
    var transfer = MakeTransfer.Dummy with            │  "structure under test."
    {
        Date = new DateTime(2021, 3, 12)   ◁─┐  This date used to be
    };                                        │  in the future!

    var actual = sut.IsValid(transfer);
    Assert.AreEqual(true, actual);
}
```

This test creates a MakeTransfer command to make a transfer on 2021-03-12. (If you're unfamiliar with the with expression syntax used in the example, I'll discuss this in section 11.3.) It then asserts that the command should pass the date-not-past validation.

The test passes as I'm writing this, but it will fail by the time you're reading it, unless you're running it on a machine where the clock is set before 2021-03-12. Because the implementation relies on the system clock, the test is not repeatable.

Let's take a step back and see why testing pure functions is fundamentally easier than testing impure ones. Then, in section 3.4, we'll come back to this example and see how we can bring DateNotPastValidator under test.

3.3.3 *Why testing impure functions is hard*

When you write unit tests, what are you testing? A unit, of course, but what's a unit exactly? Whatever unit you're testing is a function *or can be viewed as one*.

Unit tests need to be isolated (no I/O) and repeatable (you always get the same result, given the same inputs). These properties are guaranteed when you use pure functions. When you're testing a pure function, testing is easy: you just give it an input and verify that the output is as expected (as figure 3.7 illustrated).

If you use the standard Arrange Act Assert (AAA) pattern in your unit tests and the unit you're testing is a pure function, then the arrange step consists of defining the

Figure 3.7   Testing a pure function is easy: you simply provide inputs and verify that the outputs are as expected.

input values, the act step is the function invocation, and the assert step consists of checking that the output is as expected.[5] If you do this for a representative set of input values, you can be confident that the function works as intended.

If, on the other hand, the unit you're testing is an *impure* function, its behavior depends not only on its inputs but, possibly, also on the state of the program (any mutable state that's not local to the function under test) and the state of the world (anything outside the context of your program). Furthermore, the function's side effects can lead to a new state of the program and the world: for example,

- The date validator depends on the state of the world, specifically the current time.
- A void-returning method that sends an email has no explicit output to assert against, but it results in a new state of the world.
- A method that sets a non-local variable results in a new state of the program.

As a result, you could view an impure function as a pure function that takes as input its arguments, along with the current state of the program and the world, and returns its outputs, along with a new state of the program and the world. Figure 3.8 shows this process.

Figure 3.8 Testing an impure function. You need to set up and assert against more than just the function inputs and output.

Another way to look at this is that an impure function has implicit inputs other than its arguments or implicit outputs other than its return value or both.

How does this affect testing? Well, in the case of an impure function, the arrange stage must not only provide the explicit inputs to the function under test, but must additionally set up a representation of the state of the program and the world. Similarly, the assert stage must not only check the result, but also that the expected changes have occurred in the state of the program and the world. This is summarized in table 3.2.

---

[5] AAA is a ubiquitous pattern for structuring the code in unit tests. According to this pattern, a test consists of three steps: *arrange* prepares any prerequisites, *act* performs the operation being tested, and *assert* runs assertions against the obtained result.

Table 3.2 **Unit testing from a functional perspective**

AAA pattern	Functional perspective
Arrange	Sets up the (explicit and implicit) inputs to the function under test
Act	Evaluates the function under test
Assert	Verifies the correctness of the (explicit and implicit) output

Again, we should distinguish between different kinds of side effects with respect to testing:

- Setting the state of the program and checking that it's updated makes for brittle tests and breaks encapsulation.
- The state of the world can be represented by using stubs that create an artificial world in which the test runs.

It's hard work, but the technique is well understood. We'll look at this next.

3.4   *Testing code that performs I/O*

In this section, you'll see how we can bring code that depends on I/O operations under test. I'll show you different approaches to *dependency injection*, contrasting the mainstream OO approach with a more functional approach.

To demonstrate this, let's go back to the impure validation in `DateNotPastValidator` and see how we can refactor the code to make it testable. Here's a reminder of the code:

```
public class DateNotPastValidator : IValidator<MakeTransfer>
{
    public bool IsValid(MakeTransfer transfer)
        => (DateTime.UtcNow.Date <= transfer.Date.Date);
}
```

The problem is that because `DateTime.UtcNow` accesses the system clock, it's not possible to write tests that are guaranteed to behave consistently.[6] Let's see how we can address this.

3.4.1   *Object-oriented dependency injection*

The mainstream technique for testing code that depends on I/O operations is to abstract these operations in an interface and to use a deterministic implementation in the tests. If you're already familiar with this approach, skip to section 3.4.2.

---

[6] You could try writing a test that reads from the system clock when populating the input `MakeTransfer`. This may work in most cases, but there is a small window around midnight during which, when arranging the inputs for the test, the date is different than the date when `IsValid` is called. You're not, in fact, guaranteed consistency after all. Furthermore, we need an approach that will work with any I/O operation, not just accessing the clock.

This *interface-based approach* to dependency injection is considered a best practice, but I've come to think of it as an anti-pattern. This is because of the amount of boiler-plate it entails. It involves the following steps, which we'll look at in greater detail in the following sections:

1 Define an interface that abstracts the I/O operations performed by the code you want to bring under test and put the impure implementation in a class that implements that interface.

2 In the class under test, require the interface in the constructor, store it in a field, and consume it as needed.

3 Create and inject a stubbed implementation for the purposes of unit testing.

4 Introduce some bootstrapping logic so that the impure implementation is provided at run time when the class under test is instantiated.

ABSTRACTING I/O WITH AN INTERFACE

Instead of calling `DateTime.UtcNow` directly, you abstract access to the system clock. That is, you define an interface and an implementation that performs the desired I/O like this:

```
public interface IDateTimeService
{
    DateTime UtcNow { get; }        ◁── Encapsulates the impure
}                                        behavior in an interface

public class DefaultDateTimeService : IDateTimeService
{
    public DateTime UtcNow => DateTime.UtcNow;    ◁── Provides a default
}                                                     implementation
```

CONSUMING THE INTERFACE

You then refactor the date validator to consume this interface instead of accessing the system clock directly. The validator's behavior now *depends* on the interface of which an instance should be injected (usually in the constructor). The following listing shows how to do this.

Listing 3.8 Refactoring a class to consume an interface

```
public class DateNotPastValidator : IValidator<MakeTransfer>
{
    private readonly IDateTimeService dateService;

    public DateNotPastValidator
        (IDateTimeService dateService)        ◁── Injects the interface
    {                                              in the constructor
        this.dateService = dateService;
    }

    public bool IsValid(MakeTransfer transfer)
        => dateService.UtcNow.Date <= transfer.Date.Date;    ◁── Validation now depends
}                                                                on the interface.
```

Let's look at the refactored `IsValid` method: is it a pure function? Well, the answer is, it *depends*! It depends, of course, on the implementation of `IDateTimeService` that's injected:

- When running normally, you'll compose your objects so that you get the real *impure* implementation that checks the system clock.
- When running unit tests, you'll inject a fake *pure* implementation that does something predictable, such as always returning the same `DateTime`, enabling you to write tests that are repeatable.

INJECT A STUB WHEN TESTING

The following listing shows how you can write tests using this approach.

Listing 3.9   Testing by injecting a predictable implementation

```
public class DateNotPastValidatorTest
{
    static DateTime presentDate = new DateTime(2021, 3, 12);

    private class FakeDateTimeService : IDateTimeService    ⟵  Provides a pure, fake
    {                                                          implementation
        public DateTime UtcNow => presentDate;
    }

    [Test]
    public void WhenTransferDateIsPast_ThenValidationFails()
    {
        var svc = new FakeDateTimeService();
        var sut = new DateNotPastValidator(svc);      ⟵  Injects
        var transfer = MakeTransfer.Dummy with            the fake
        {
            Date = presentDate.AddDays(-1)
        };
        Assert.AreEqual(false, sut.IsValid(transfer));
    }
}
```

That is, we create a stub, a *fake* implementation that, unlike the real one, has a deterministic result.

SETTING UP THE DEPENDENCIES

We're still not done because we need to provide `DateNotPastValidator` with the `IDateTimeService` it depends on at run time. This can be done in a variety of ways, both manually and with the help of a framework, depending on the complexity of your program and your technologies of choice.[7] In an ASP.NET application, it may end up looking like this:

---

[7] Manually composing all classes in a complex application can become quite a chore. To mitigate this, some frameworks allow you to declare what implementations to use for any interface that's required. These are called IoC containers, where IoC stands for *inversion of control*.

```
public void ConfigureServices(IServiceCollection services)
{
   services.AddTransient<IDateTimeService, DefaultDateTimeService>();
   services.AddTransient<DateNotPastValidator>();
}
```

This code registers the real, impure implementation `DefaultDateTimeService`, associating it with the `IDateTimeService` interface. As a result, when a `DateNotPast-Validator` is required, ASP.NET sees that it needs an `IDateTimeService` in the constructor and provides it an instance of `DefaultDateTimeService`.

PITFALLS OF THE INTERFACE-BASED APPROACH

Unit tests are so valuable that developers gladly put up with all this effort, even for something as simple as `DateTime.UtcNow`. One of the least desirable effects of using the interface-based approach systematically is the explosion in the number of interfaces because you must define an interface for every component that has an I/O element.

Most applications are developed with an interface for every service, even when only one concrete implementation is envisaged. These are called *header interfaces*, and they're not what interfaces were initially designed for (a common contract with several different implementations), but they're used across the board. You end up with more files, more indirection, more assemblies, and code that's difficult to navigate.

Avoiding trivial constructors

One of the issues of refactoring a class to consume an interface (shown in listing 3.8) is the need to define a trivial constructor. All that this constructor does is store its input arguments in class fields. In a complex enough application, this creates a lot of boilerplate.

Many languages spare you such ceremony by having *primary constructors*. This feature is not available for classes, but since C# 9, you can use records instead. The code in listing 3.8 could be refactored as follows:

```
public record DateNotPastValidator(IDateTimeService DateService)
   : IValidator<MakeTransfer>
{
   private IDateTimeService DateService { get; } = DateService;

   public bool IsValid(MakeTransfer request)
      => DateService.UtcNow.Date <= request.Date.Date;
}
```

The positional record syntax automatically generates a constructor into which you can inject the required `IDateTimeService` and a public property called `DateService`. If you feel that the generated property pollutes the class's public API, you can explicitly specify that the property should be private. The preceding code shows how to do this.

3.4.2 *Testability without so much boilerplate*

I've discussed the pitfalls of the interface-based approach to dependency injection. In this subsection, I'll show you some simpler alternatives. Namely, instead of consuming an interface, the code under test can consume a function or, sometimes, simply a value.

PUSHING THE PURE BOUNDARY OUTWARDS

Can we get rid of the whole problem and make everything pure? No, we're required to check the current date. This is an operation with a nondeterministic result. But sometimes, we can push the boundaries of pure code. For instance, what if you rewrote the date validator as in the following listing?

Listing 3.10 Injecting a specific value, not an interface, making `IsValid` pure

```
public record DateNotPastValidator(DateTime Today)
    : IValidator<MakeTransfer>
{
    public bool IsValid(MakeTransfer transfer)
        => Today <= transfer.Date.Date;
}
```

Instead of injecting an interface, exposing some method you can invoke, we inject a *value*. Now the implementation of `IsValid` is pure! You've effectively pushed the side effect of reading the current date outward to the code instantiating the validator. To set up the creation of this validator, you might use some code like this:

```
public void ConfigureServices(IServiceCollection services)
{
    services.AddTransient<DateNotPastValidator>
        (_ => new DateNotPastValidator(DateTime.UtcNow.Date));
}
```

Without going into detail, this code defines a function to be called whenever a `Date-NotPastValidator` is required, and within this function, the current date creates the new instance. Note that this requires `DateNotPastValidator` to be transient; we have a new instance created when one is needed to validate an incoming request. This is a reasonable behavior in this case.

Consuming a value rather than a method that performs I/O is an easy win, making more of your code pure and, thus, easily testable. This approach works well when your logic depends on, say, configurations that are stored in a file or environment-specific settings. But things are not always this easy, so let's move on to a more general solution.

INJECTING FUNCTIONS AS DEPENDENCIES

Imagine that when a `MakeTransfer` request is received, a list of several validators, each enforcing a different rule, is created. If one validation fails, the request fails, and the subsequent validators will not be called.

Furthermore, imagine that querying the system clock is expensive (it isn't, but most I/O operations are). You don't want to do that every time the validator is created, but only when it's actually used. You can achieve this by injecting a function, rather than a value, which the validator calls as needed:

```
public record DateNotPastValidator(Func<DateTime> Clock)
   : IValidator<MakeTransfer>
{
   public bool IsValid(MakeTransfer transfer)
      => Clock().Date <= transfer.Date.Date;
}
```

I've called the injected function `Clock`, because what's a clock if not a function you can call to get the current time? The implementation of `IsValid` now performs no side effects *other than* those performed by `Clock`, so it can easily be tested by injecting a "broken clock":

```
readonly DateTime today = new(2021, 3, 12);

[Test]
public void WhenTransferDateIsToday_ThenValidatorPasses()
{
   var sut = new DateNotPastValidator(() => today);
   var transfer = MakeTransfer.Dummy with { Date = today };

   Assert.AreEqual(true, sut.IsValid(transfer));
}
```

On the other hand, when creating the validator, you'll pass a function that actually queries the system clock, as follows:

```
public void ConfigureServices(IServiceCollection services)
{
   services.AddSingleton<DateNotPastValidator>
      (_ => new DateNotPastValidator(() => DateTime.UtcNow.Date));
}
```

Notice that because the function that returns the current date is now called by the validator, it's no longer required to have the validator be short-lived. You could use it as a singleton as I showed in the preceding snippet.

This solution ticks all the boxes: the validator can now be tested deterministically, no I/O will be performed unless required, and we don't need to define any unnecessary interfaces or trivial classes. We'll pursue this approach further in chapter 9.

INJECTING A DELEGATE FOR MORE CLARITY

If you go down the route of injecting a function, you could consider going the extra mile. You can define a delegate rather than simply using a `Func`:

```
public delegate DateTime Clock();

public record DateNotPastValidator(Clock Clock)
   : IValidator<MakeTransfer>
{
   public bool IsValid(MakeTransfer transfer)
      => Clock().Date <= transfer.Date.Date;
}
```

The code for testing remains identical; in the setup, you can potentially gain in clarity by just registering a `Clock`. Once that's done, the framework knows to use that when the validator that requires a `Clock` is created:

```
public void ConfigureServices(IServiceCollection services)
{
   services.AddTransient<Clock>(_ => () => DateTime.UtcNow);
   services.AddTransient<DateNotPastValidator>();
}
```

Parameterized unit tests

Regardless of what approach you use to bring `DateNotPastValidator` under test, you can use parameterized unit tests. Parameterized tests allow you to test your code with a variety of input values. They tend to be more functional because they make you think in terms of inputs and outputs. For example, the following shows how you can test that the date-not-past validation works in a variety of cases:

```
[TestCase(+1, ExpectedResult = true)]
[TestCase( 0, ExpectedResult = true)]
[TestCase(-1, ExpectedResult = false)]
public bool WhenTransferDateIsPast_ThenValidatorFails(int offset)
{
   var sut = new DateNotPastValidator(() => presentDate);
   var transfer = MakeTransfer.Dummy with
   {
      Date = presentDate.AddDays(offset)
   };
   return sut.IsValid(transfer);
}
```

This code uses NUnit's `TestCase` attribute to effectively run three tests: a transfer requested to take place today (relatively to a hard-coded date), yesterday, and tomorrow. The XUnit testing framework has the `Theory` and `InlineData` attributes that allow you to do the same thing, whereas in MSTest, it's called `DataRow`.

Parameterized tests have the advantage that you can test a variety of scenarios just by tweaking the parameter values. Should a client be able to request a transfer for a date that's more than one year in the future? If not, you can add a test to verify this with a single line:

```
[TestCase(+366, ExpectedResult = false)]
```

Notice that the test method now is itself a function: it maps the given parameter values to an output that NUnit can check. In fact, it's a pure function, given that assertions (which throw exceptions) have been pushed out of the test method and are performed by the testing framework.

A parameterized test is essentially just an adapter for the function under test. In this example, the test creates an artificial state of the world with a hard-coded present date. It then maps the test's input parameter (the offset between the present date and the requested transfer date) to a suitably populated `MakeTransfer` object, which is given as input to the function under test.

3.5 *Purity and the evolution of computing*

I hope that this chapter has made the concept of function purity less mysterious and has shown why extending the footprint of pure code is a worthwhile objective. This improves the maintainability, performance, and testability of your code.

The evolution of software and hardware also has important consequences for how we think about purity. Our systems are increasingly distributed, so the I/O part of our programs is increasingly important. With microservices architectures becoming mainstream, our programs consist less of doing computation and more of delegating computation to other services, which they communicate with via I/O.

This increase in I/O requirements means purity is harder to achieve. But it also means increased requirements for asynchronous I/O. As you've seen, purity helps you deal with concurrent scenarios, which include dealing with asynchronous messages.

Hardware evolution is also important: CPUs aren't getting faster at the same pace as before, so hardware manufacturers are moving toward combining multiple processors and cores. Parallelization is becoming the main road to computing speed, so there's a need to write programs that can be parallelized well. Indeed, the move toward multicore machines is one of the main reasons for the renewed interest we're currently seeing in FP.

Exercises

Write a console app that calculates a user's Body Mass Index (BMI):

1 Prompt the user for their height in meters and weight in kilograms.
2 Calculate the BMI as weight / height^2.
3 Output a message: underweight (BMI < 18.5), overweight (BMI >= 25), or healthy.
4 Structure your code so that pure and impure parts are separate.
5 Unit test the pure parts.
6 Unit test the overall workflow using the function-based approach to abstract away the reading from and writing to the console.

Because most of this chapter was devoted to seeing the concept of purity in practice, I encourage you to investigate, applying the techniques we discussed to some code you're presently working on. You can learn something new while getting paid for it!

1 Find a place where you're doing some non-trivial operation based on a list (search for `foreach`). See if the operation can be parallelized; if not, see if you can extract a pure part of the operation and parallelize that part.
2 Search for uses of `DateTime.Now` or `DateTime.UtcNow` in your codebase. If that area isn't under test, bring it under test using both the interface-based approach and the function-based approach described in this chapter.
3 Look for other areas of your code where you're relying on an impure dependency that has no transitive dependencies. The obvious candidates are static

classes such as `ConfigurationManager` or `Environment` that cross the application boundary. Try to apply the function-based testing pattern.

Summary

- Compared to mathematical functions, programming functions are more difficult to reason about because their output may depend on variables other than their input arguments.
- Side effects include state mutation, throwing exceptions, and I/O.
- Functions without side effects are called *pure*. These functions do nothing other than return a value that depends solely on their input arguments.
- Pure functions can be more readily optimized and tested than impure ones, and they can be used more reliably in concurrent scenarios. You should prefer pure functions whenever possible.
- Unlike other side effects, I/O can't be avoided, but you can still isolate the parts of your application that perform I/O in order to reduce the footprint of impure code.

Part 2

Core techniques

In this part, we'll look at some of the most common techniques used in FP. You'll see how simple constructs and techniques enable you to solve problems with succinct, elegant, and readable code.

Chapter 4 deals with principles for designing types and function signatures—things you thought you knew, but you'll see them in a new light when looking at them from a functional perspective.

Chapter 5 shows you the reason and implementation for the Option type, a staple of FP that is not only useful in itself but will guide you in understanding many subsequent concepts throughout the book.

Chapter 6 introduces some of the core functions of FP: Map, Bind, ForEach, and Where. These functions provide the basic tools for interacting with the most common data structures in FP.

Chapter 7 shows how functions can be chained into pipelines that capture the workflows of your program. It then widens the scope to developing a whole use case in a functional style.

By the end of part 2, you'll have a good feel for what a program written in a functional style looks like. You'll also be able to apply FP ideas and constructs in your own code—on a small scale—creating islands of functional code within a sea of OO code.

Designing function
signatures and types

This chapter covers
- Designing good function signatures
- Fine-grained control over the inputs to a function
- Using `Unit` as a more flexible alternative to `void`

The principles we've covered so far define FP in general, regardless of whether you're programming in a statically typed language like C# or a dynamically typed language like JavaScript. In this chapter, you'll learn some functional techniques that are specific to statically typed languages. Having functions and their arguments typed opens up a whole set of interesting considerations..

Functions are the building blocks of a functional program, so getting the function signature right is paramount. And because a function signature is defined in terms of the types of its inputs and outputs, getting those types right is just as important. Type design and function signature design are really two faces of the same coin.

You may think that after years of defining classes and interfaces, you know how to design your types and functions. But it turns out that FP brings a number of interesting concepts to the table that can help you increase the robustness of your programs and the usability of your APIs.

4.1   Designing function signatures

A function's signature tells you the types of its inputs and outputs; if the function is named, it also includes the function's name. As you code more functionally, you'll find yourself looking at function signatures more often. Defining function signatures is an important step in your development process, often the first thing you do as you approach a problem.

I'll start by introducing a notation for function signatures that's standard in the FP community. We'll use it throughout the book.

4.1.1   Writing functions signatures with arrow notation

In FP, function signatures are usually expressed in *arrow notation*. There's great benefit to learning it because you'll find it in books, articles, and blogs on FP: it's the lingua franca used by functional programmers from different languages.

Let's say we have a function f from `int` to `string`; it takes an `int` as input and yields a `string` as output. We'll notate the signature like this:

```
f : int → string
```

In English, you'd read that as f has type of `int` to `string` or f takes an `int` and yields a `string`. In C#, a function with this signature is assignable to `Func<int, string>`.

You'll probably agree that the arrow notation is more readable than the C# type, and that's why we'll use it when discussing signatures. When we have no input or no output (`void` or `Unit`), we'll indicate this with `()`.

Let's look at some examples. Table 4.1 shows function types expressed in arrow notation side by side with the corresponding C# delegate type and an example implementation of a function that has the given signature in lambda notation.

Table 4.1   Expressing function signatures with arrow notation

Function signature	C# type	Example
`int → string`	`Func<int, string>`	`(int i) => i.ToString()`
`() → string`	`Func<string>`	`() => "hello"`
`int → ()`	`Action<int>`	`(int i) => WriteLine($"gimme {i}")`
`() → ()`	`Action`	`() => WriteLine("Hello World!")`
`(int, int) → int`	`Func<int, int, int>`	`(int a, int b) => a + b`

The last example in table 4.1 shows multiple input arguments: we just group them with parentheses. (Parentheses indicate tuples, so in fact, we're notating a binary function as a unary function whose input argument is a binary tuple.)

Now, let's move on to more complex signatures, namely those of HOFs. Let's start with the following method (from listing 2.10) that takes a `string` and a function from `IDbConnection` to R and returns an R:

```
static R Connect<R>(string connStr, Func<IDbConnection, R> func)
    => // ...
```

How would you notate this signature? The second argument is itself a function, so it can be notated as `IDbConnection → R`. The HOF's signature is notated as follows:

```
(string, (IDbConnection → R)) → R
```

And this is the corresponding C# type:

```
Func<string, Func<IDbConnection, R>, R>
```

The arrow syntax is slightly more lightweight and is more readable, especially as the complexity of the signature increases.

4.1.2 *How informative is a signature?*

Some function signatures are more expressive than others, by which I mean that they give us more information about what the function is doing, what inputs are permissible, and what outputs we can expect. The signature `() → ()`, for example, gives us no information at all: it may print some text, increment a counter, launch a spaceship . . . who knows? On the other hand, consider this signature:

```
(IEnumerable<T>, (T → bool)) → IEnumerable<T>
```

Take a minute and see if you can guess what a function with this signature does. Of course, you can't really know for sure without seeing the actual implementation, but you can make an educated guess. The function returns a list of `T`'s and takes a list of `T`'s, as well as a second argument, which is a function from `T` to `bool`, a *predicate* on `T`.

It's reasonable to assume that the function uses the predicate on `T` to filter the elements in the list. In short, it's a filtering function. Indeed, this is exactly the signature of `Enumerable.Where`. Let's look at another example:

```
(IEnumerable<A>, IEnumerable<B>, ((A, B) → C)) → IEnumerable<C>
```

Can you guess what the function does? It returns a sequence of `C`'s and takes a sequence of `A`'s, a sequence of `B`'s, and a function that computes a `C` from an `A` and a `B`. It's reasonable to assume that this function applies the computation to elements from the two input sequences, returning a third sequence with the computed results. This function could be the `Enumerable.Zip` function, which we discussed in section 3.2.3.

These last two signatures are so expressive that you can make a good guess at the implementation, which is a desirable trait. When you write an API, you want it to be clear, and if the signature goes hand in hand with good naming in expressing the intent of the function, all the better.

Of course, there are limits to how much a function signature can express. For instance, `Enumerable.TakeWhile`, a function that traverses a given sequence, yielding all elements as long as a given predicate evaluates to true, has the same signature as `Enumerable.Where`. This makes sense because `TakeWhile` can also be viewed as a filtering function, but one that works differently than `Where`.

In summary, some signatures are more expressive than others. As you develop your APIs, make your signatures as expressive as possible—this facilitates the consumption of your APIs and adds robustness to your programs.

4.2   *Capturing data with data objects*

Functions and data are like the two sides of a coin: functions consume and produce data. A good API needs functions with clear signatures and well-designed data types to represent the inputs and outputs of these functions. In FP (unlike OOP), it's natural to draw a separation between logic and data:

- Logic is encoded in functions.
- Data is captured with data objects, which are used as inputs and outputs of these functions.

In this section, we'll look at some basic ideas for designing data objects. We'll then move on to the somewhat more abstract concepts of representing the absence of data (section 4.3) or the possible absence of data (chapter 5).

Imagine that you're in the business of life insurance. You need to write a function that calculates a customer's risk profile based on their age. The risk profile will be captured with an enum:

```
enum Risk { Low, Medium, High }
```

You're pair programming with David, a trainee who comes from a dynamically typed language, and he has a stab at implementing the function. He runs it in the REPL with a few inputs to see that it works as expected:

```
Risk CalculateRiskProfile(dynamic age)
   => (age < 60) ? Risk.Low : Risk.Medium;

CalculateRiskProfile(30) // => Low
CalculateRiskProfile(70) // => Medium
```

Although the implementation does seem to work when given reasonable inputs, you're surprised by David's choice of dynamic as the argument type. You show him that his implementation allows client code to invoke the function with a string, causing a run-time error:

```
CalculateRiskProfile("Hello")
// => runtime error: Operator '<' cannot be applied to operands
 of type 'string' and 'int'
```

You explain to David that you can tell the compiler what type of input your function expects, so that invalid inputs can be ruled out. You rewrite the function, taking an int as the type of the input argument:

```
Risk CalculateRiskProfile(int age)
   => (age < 60) ? Risk.Low : Risk.Medium;
```

```
CalculateRiskProfile("Hello")
// => compiler error: cannot convert from 'string' to 'int'
```

Is there still room for improvement?

4.2.1 *Primitive types are often not specific enough*

As you keep testing your function, you find that the implementation still allows for invalid inputs:

```
CalculateRiskProfile(-1000) // => Low
CalculateRiskProfile(10000) // => Medium
```

Clearly, these are not valid values for a customer's age. What's a valid age, anyway? You have a word with the business to clarify this, and they indicate that a reasonable value for an age must be positive and less than 120. Your first instinct is to add some validation to your function—if the given age is outside of the valid range, throw an exception:

```
Risk CalculateRiskProfile(int age)
{
    if (age < 0 || 120 <= age)
        throw new ArgumentException($"{age} is not a valid age");

    return (age < 60) ? Risk.Low : Risk.Medium;
}

CalculateRiskProfile(10000)
// => runtime error: 10000 is not a valid age
```

As you type this, you're thinking that this is rather annoying:

- You'll have to write additional unit tests for the cases in which validation fails.
- There are other areas of the application where an age is expected, so you're probably going to need this validation there as well. This may lead to some code duplication.

Duplication is usually a sign that separation of concerns has been broken: the CalculateRiskProfile function, which should only concern itself with the calculation, now also concerns itself with validation. Is there a better way?

4.2.2 *Constraining inputs with custom types*

In the meantime, your colleague Frida, who comes from a statically typed functional language, joins the session. She looks at your code so far and finds that the problem lies in your use of int to represent age. She comments, "You can tell the compiler what type of input your function expects so that invalid inputs can be ruled out."

David listens in amazement because those were the very words you patronized him with a few moments earlier. You're not sure what she means exactly, so she starts to implement Age as a custom type that can only represent a valid value for an age as in the following listing.

> ### Listing 4.1 A custom type that can only be instantiated with a valid value

```
public struct Age
{
   public int Value { get; }

   public Age(int value)
   {
      if (!IsValid(value))
         throw new ArgumentException($"{value} is not a valid age");

      Value = value;
   }

   private static bool IsValid(int age)
      => 0 <= age && age < 120;
}
```

This implementation still uses an `int` as the underlying representation for an age, but the constructor ensures that the `Age` type can only be instantiated with a valid value.

This is a good example of functional thinking: the `Age` type is created precisely to represent the domain of the `CalculateRiskProfile` function. This can now be rewritten as follows:

```
Risk CalculateRiskProfile(Age age)
   => (age.Value < 60) ? Risk.Low : Risk.Medium;
```

This new implementation has several advantages:

- You're guaranteeing that only valid values can be given.
- `CalculateRiskProfile` no longer causes run-time errors.
- The concern of validating the age value is captured in the constructor of the `Age` type, removing the need for duplicating validation wherever an age is processed.

You're still throwing an exception in the `Age` constructor, but we'll remedy that in section 5.4.3. There's still some room for improvement, however.

In the preceding implementation, we used `Value` to extract the underlying value of the age, so we're still comparing two integers. There are a couple of problems with that:

- Reading the `Value` property not only creates a bit of noise, but it also means that the client code knows about the internal representation of `Age`, which you might want to change in the future.
- Because you're performing integer comparison, you're also not protected if, say, someone accidentally changes the threshold value of 60 to 600, which is a valid `int` but not a valid `Age`.

You can address these issues by modifying the definition of `Age`, as the following listing shows.

> ### Listing 4.2 Encapsulating the internal representation of the age

```
public class Age
{
    private int Value { get; }          ⟵── Keeps the internal
                                              representation private

    public static bool operator <(Age l, Age r)    ⟵┐ Logic for comparing an
        => l.Value < r.Value;                        │ Age with another Age
    public static bool operator >(Age l, Age r)
        => l.Value > r.Value;

    public static bool operator <(Age l, int r)    ⟵┐ For ease of use, makes it
        => l < new Age(r);                           │ possible to compare an Age
    public static bool operator >(Age l, int r)      │ with an int; the int is first
        => l > new Age(r);                           │ converted into an Age.
}
```

Now the internal representation of an age is encapsulated, and the logic for comparison is within the Age class. You can rewrite your function as follows:

```
Risk CalculateRiskProfile(Age age)
    => (age < 60) ? Risk.Low : Risk.Medium;
```

What happens now is that a new Age is constructed from the value 60 so that the usual validation is applied. (If this throws a run-time error, that's fine because it indicates a developer error; more about this in chapter 8.) When the input age is then compared, this comparison happens in the Age class, using the comparison operators you've defined. Overall, the code is just as readable as before, but more robust.

In summary, primitive types are often used too liberally (this has become known as *primitive obsession*). If you need to constrain the inputs of your functions, it's usually better to define a custom type. This follows the idea of making invalid state unrepresentable. In the preceding example, you can't represent an age outside of the valid bounds.

The new implementation of CalculateRiskProfile is identical to its original implementation, except for the input type, which is now Age, and this ensures the validity of the data and makes the function signature more explicit. A functional programmer might say that now the function is *honest*. What does that mean?

4.2.3 *Writing honest functions*

You might hear functional programmers talk about *honest* or *dishonest* functions. An honest function is simply one that does what it says on the tin: it honors its signature—*always*. For instance, consider the function we ended up with in section 4.2.2:

```
Risk CalculateRiskProfile(Age age)
    => (age < 60) => Risk.Low : Risk.Medium;
```

Its signature is Age → Risk, which declares, "Give me an Age, and I will give you back a Risk." Indeed, there's no other possible outcome.[1] This function behaves as a

---

[1] There is, however, the possibility of hardware failure, of the program running out of memory, and so on, but these are not intrinsic to the function implementation.

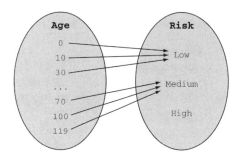

Figure 4.1 An honest function does exactly what the signature says: it maps all possible values of the input type(s) to a valid value of the output type. This makes the behavior of your functions predictable and your program more robust.

mathematical function, mapping each element from the domain to an element of the codomain, as figure 4.1 shows.

Compare this to the previous implementation, which looked like this:

```
Risk CalculateRiskProfile(int age)
{
    if (age < 0 || 120 <= age)
        throw new ArgumentException($"{age} is not a valid age");

    return (age < 60) ? Risk.Low : Risk.Medium;
}
```

Remember, a signature is a contract. The signature int → Risk says, "Give me an int (*any* of the 2³² possible values for int), and I'll return a Risk." But the implementation doesn't abide by its signature, throwing an ArgumentException for what it considers invalid input (see figure 4.2).

That means this function is *dishonest*—what it *really* should say is "Give me an int, and I *may* return a Risk, or I *may* throw an exception instead." Sometimes there are legitimate reasons why a computation can fail, but in this example, constraining the function input so that the function always returns a valid value is a much cleaner solution.

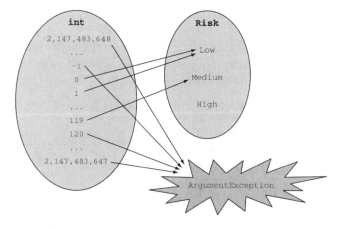

Figure 4.2 A dishonest function can have an outcome that isn't accounted for in the signature.

In summary, a function is honest if its behavior can be predicted by its signature:

- It returns a value of the declared type.
- It doesn't throw exceptions.
- It never returns `null`.

Note that these requirements are less stringent and less formal than function purity. Notably, a function that performs I/O can still be honest. In this case, its return type should typically convey that the function may fail or take a long time (for example, by returning its result wrapped in an `Exceptional` or a `Task`, which I'll discuss in chapters 8 and 16, respectively.)

4.2.4 *Composing values into complex data objects*

You might require more data to fine-tune the implementation of your calculation of health risk. For instance, women statistically live longer than men, so you may want to account for this:

```
enum Gender { Female, Male }

Risk CalculateRiskProfile(Age age, Gender gender)
{
    var threshold = (gender == Gender.Female) ? 62 : 60;
    return (age < threshold) ? Risk.Low : Risk.Medium;
}
```

The signature of the function thus defined is as follows:

```
(Age, Gender) → Risk
```

How many possible input values are there? Well, there are 2 possible values for `Gender` in this admittedly simplistic model and 120 values for `Age`, so in total, there are 2 × 120 = 240 possible inputs. Notice that if you define a tuple of `Age` and `Gender`, 240 tuples are possible. The same is true if you define a type to hold that same data like this:

```
readonly record struct HealthData
{
    Age Age;
    Gender Gender;
};
```

Whether you call a binary function that accepts an `Age` and a `Gender`, or a unary function that takes a `HealthData`, 240 distinct inputs are possible. They're just packaged up a bit differently.

Earlier I said that types represent sets, so the `Age` type represents a set of 120 elements, and `Gender`, a set of 2 elements. What about more complex types such as `HealthData`, which is defined in terms of the former two?

Essentially, creating an instance of `HealthData` is equivalent to taking all the possible combinations of the two sets, `Age` and `Gender` (a Cartesian product), and picking one element. More generally, every time you add a field to a type (or a tuple), you're

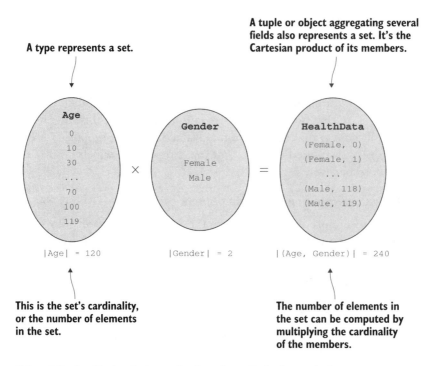

A type represents a set.

A tuple or object aggregating several fields also represents a set. It's the Cartesian product of its members.

This is the set's cardinality, or the number of elements in the set.

The number of elements in the set can be computed by multiplying the cardinality of the members.

Figure 4.3   An object or tuple can be viewed as a Cartesian product.

creating a Cartesian product and adding a dimension to the space of possible values of the object, as figure 4.3 illustrates.

For this reason, in type theory, types that are defined by aggregating other types (whether in a tuple, a record, a struct or a class) are called *product types*. In contrast, you have *sum types*. For instance, if types A and B are the two only concrete implementations of C, then

$$|C| = |A| + |B|$$

The number of possible C's is the *sum* of all possible A's and all possible B's. (Sum types are also known as *union types*, *discriminated unions*, and a number of other names.)

This concludes our brief foray into data object design. The main takeaway is that you should model your data objects in a way that gives you fine control over the range of inputs that your functions will need to handle. Counting the number of possible instances can bring clarity. Once you have control over these simple types, it's easy to aggregate them into more complex data objects. Now, let's move on to the simplest type of all: the empty tuple or Unit.

4.3   *Modeling the absence of data with Unit*

We've discussed how to represent data; what about when there is no data to represent? Many functions are called for their side effects and return void. But void doesn't play well with many functional techniques, so in this section, I'll introduce Unit, a type that we can use to represent the absence of data without the problems of void.

4.3.1 *Why void isn't ideal*

Let me start by illustrating why void is less than ideal. In section 2.1.2, we covered the all-purpose Func and Action delegate families. If they're so all-purpose, why do we need two of them? Why can't we use Func<Void> to represent a function that returns nothing just like we use Func<string> to represent a function that returns a string? The problem is that although the framework has the System.Void type and the void keyword to represent *no return value*, Void receives special treatment by the compiler and can't therefore be used as a return type. (In fact, it can't be used at all from C# code.)

Let's see why this can be a problem in practice. Say you need to gain some insight as to how long certain operations take, and to do so, you write a HOF that starts a stopwatch, runs the given function, and stops the stopwatch, printing out some diagnostic information. This is a typical example of the setup/teardown scenario I demonstrated in section 2.3. Here's the implementation:

```
public static class Instrumentation
{
    public static T Time<T>(string op, Func<T> f)
    {
        var sw = new Stopwatch();
        sw.Start();

        T t = f();

        sw.Stop();
        Console.WriteLine($"{op} took {sw.ElapsedMilliseconds}ms");
        return t;
    }
}
```

If you wanted to read the contents of a file and log how long the operation takes, you could use this function:

```
var contents = Instrumentation.Time("reading from file.txt"
    , () => File.ReadAllText("file.txt"));
```

It would be quite natural to want to use this with a void-returning function. For example, you might want to time how long it takes to *write* to a file, so you'd like to write this:

```
Instrumentation.Time("writing to file.txt"
    , () => File.AppendAllText("file.txt", "New content", Encoding.UTF8));
```

The problem is that AppendAllText returns void, so it can't be represented as a Func. To make the preceding code work, you need to add an overload of Instrumentation.Time that takes an Action:

```
public static void Time(string op, Action act)
{
```

```
var sw = new Stopwatch();
sw.Start();

act();

sw.Stop();

Console.WriteLine($"{op} took {sw.ElapsedMilliseconds}ms");
}
```

This is terrible! You have to duplicate the entire implementation just because of the incompatibility between the Func and Action delegates. (A similar dichotomy exists in the world of asynchronous operations between Task and Task<T>.) How can you avoid this?

4.3.2 *Bridging the gap between Action and Func*

If you're going to use functional programming, it's useful to have a different representation for *no return value*. Instead of using void, which is a special language construct, we'll use a special value, the empty tuple (also called Unit). The empty tuple has no members, so it can only have one possible value. Because it contains no information whatsoever, that's as good as no value.

The empty tuple is available in the System namespace. Uninspiringly, it's called ValueTuple, but I'll follow the FP convention of calling it Unit:[2]

```
using Unit = System.ValueTuple;
```

Technically, void and Unit differ in that

- void is a type that represents an empty set; as such, it's not possible to create an instance of it.
- Unit represents a set with a single value; as such, any instance of Unit is equivalent to any other and, therefore, carries no information.

If you have a HOF that takes a Func but you want to use it with an Action, how can you go about this? In chapter 2, I introduced the idea that you can write *adapter* functions to modify existing functions to suit your needs. In this case, you want a way to easily convert an Action into a Func<Unit>. The next listing provides the definition of the ToFunc function, which does just that. It is included in my functional library, LaYumba .Functional, which I developed to support the teaching in this book.

Listing 4.3 Converting Action into Func<Unit>

```
using Unit = System.ValueTuple;          ⟵┐ Aliases the empty
                                          │ tuple as Unit
namespace LaYumba.Functional;    ⟵┐ This file-scoped namespace
                                  │ includes all of the following code.
```

---

[2] Until recently, functional libraries have tended to define their own Unit type as a struct with no members. The obvious downside is that these custom implementations aren't compatible, so I would call for library developers to adopt the nullary ValueTuple as the standard representation for Unit.

```
public static class ActionExt
{
    public static Func<Unit> ToFunc
        (this Action action)
        => () => { action(); return default; };

    public static Func<T, Unit> ToFunc<T>
        (this Action<T> action)
        => (t) => { action(t); return default; };

    // more overloads for Action's with more arguments...
}
```

Adapter functions that convert an `Action` into a `Unit`-returning `Func`

When you call `ToFunc` with a given `Action`, you get back a `Func<Unit>`. This is a function that when invoked runs the `Action` and returns `Unit`.

TIP This listing includes a *file-scoped namespace*, a feature introduced in C# 10 to reduce indentation. The declared namespace applies to the contents of the file.

With this in place, you can expand the `Instrumentation` class with a method that accepts an `Action`, converts it into a `Func<Unit>`, and calls the existing overload that works with any `Func<T>`. The following listing shows this approach.

Listing 4.4 HOFs that take a `Func` or an `Action` without duplication

```
using LaYumba.Functional;
using Unit = System.ValueTuple;

public static class Instrumentation
{
    public static void Time(string op, Action act)
        => Time<Unit>(op, act.ToFunc());

    public static T Time<T>(string op, Func<T> f)
        => // same as before...
}
```

Includes an overload that takes an `Action`

Converts the `Action` to a `Func<Unit>` and passes it to the overload taking a `Func<T>`

As you can see, this enables you to avoid duplicating any logic in the implementation of `Time`. You must still expose the overload taking an `Action`. But given the constraints of the language, this is the best compromise for handling both `Action` and `Func`.

While you may not be fully sold on `Unit` based on this example alone, you'll see more examples in this book where `Unit` and `ToFunc` are needed to take advantage of functional techniques. In summary,

- Use void to indicate the absence of data, meaning that your function is only called for side effects and returns no information.
- Use `Unit` as an alternative, more flexible representation when there's a need for consistency in the handling of `Func` and `Action`.

NOTE C# 7 introduced tuple notation, allowing you to write, say, (1, "hello") to represent a binary tuple, so logically you'd expect to be able to write (1) for a unary tuple, and () for the nullary tuple. Unfortunately, because of how parentheses work in C# syntax, this is not possible: only tuples with two or more elements can be written using parentheses. We'll therefore stick with Unit in our C# code and () when using arrow notation. For example, I'll notate a Func<int, Unit> as int → ().

Summary

- Make your function signatures as specific as possible. This makes them easier to consume and less error-prone.
- Make your functions honest. An honest function always does what its signature says, and given an input of the expected type, it yields an output of the expected type—no Exceptions, no nulls.
- Use custom types rather than ad hoc validation code to constrain the input values of a function.
- Use Unit as an alternative to void when you need a more flexible representation for functions that return no data.

Modeling the possible absence of data

This chapter covers

- Using `Option` to represent the possible absence of data
- Understanding why `null` is a terrible idea
- Whether you should use C# 8 nullable reference types

In chapter 4, I introduced you to the idea that types should precisely represent the data they encapsulate in order to write expressive function signatures. One particularly thorny issue is that of representing data that may not be available. For instance, when you register on a website, you typically have to provide your email address, but other details like your age and gender are optional. The website owner may want to process and analyze this data *if it's available.*

"Wait a minute," you're probably thinking, "don't we use `null` for this?" I'll discuss `null` in section 5.5, but for the first part of this chapter, you could just pretend that `null` doesn't exist and that we have to come up with a way to represent the possible absence of data.

When coding functionally, you never use `null`—*ever.* Instead, FP uses the `Option` type to represent optionality. I hope to show you that `Option` provides a much more robust and expressive representation. If you've never heard of Option before, I ask you to suspend judgment, as the added value of Option may not be clear until you see it used in the next couple of chapters.

5.1 *The bad APIs you use every day*

The problem of representing the possible absence of data isn't handled gracefully in .NET libraries. Imagine you go for a job interview and are given the following quiz:

Question: What does this program print?

```
using System;
using System.Collections.Generic;
using System.Collections.Specialized;
using static System.Console;

class IndexerIdiosyncracy
{
    public static void Main()
    {
        try
        {
            var empty = new NameValueCollection();
            var green = empty["green"];              ❶
            WriteLine("green!");

            var alsoEmpty = new Dictionary<string, string>();
            var blue = alsoEmpty["blue"];            ❷
            WriteLine("blue!");
        }
        catch (Exception ex)
        {
            WriteLine(ex.GetType().Name);
        }
    }
}
```

Take a moment to read through the code. Note that NameValueCollection is simply a map from string to string.[1] Then, write down what you think the program prints (make sure nobody's looking). Now, how much would you be willing to bet that you got the right answer? If you're like me and have a nagging feeling that as a programmer you should really be concerned with other things than these annoying details, the rest of this section will help you see why the problem lies with the APIs themselves and not with your lack of knowledge.

The code uses indexers to retrieve items from two empty collections, so both operations fail. Indexers are, of course, just normal functions—the [] syntax is just sugar—so both indexers are functions of type string → string and both are dishonest. Why do I say *dishonest?*

---

[1] In the early days of .NET, NameValueCollection was used quite frequently because it was common to use ConfigurationManager.AppSettings to get configuration settings from a .config file. This was superseded by the more recent configuration providers, so you may not encounter NameValueCollection often, even though it's still part of .NET.

The NameValueCollection indexer ❶ returns null if a key isn't present. It's somewhat open to debate whether null is actually a string, but I tend to say no.[2] You give the indexer a perfectly valid input string, and it returns the useless null value—not what the signature claims.

The Dictionary indexer ❷ throws a KeyNotFoundException, so it's a function that says, "Give me a string, and I'll return you a string," when it should actually say, "Give me a string, and I *may* return you a string, or I may throw an exception instead."

To add insult to injury, the two indexers are dishonest in inconsistent ways. Now that you know this, it's easy to see that the program prints:

```
green!
KeyNotFoundException
```

The interface exposed by two different associative collections in .NET is inconsistent. Who'd have thought? And the only way to find out is by looking at the documentation (boring) or stumbling on a bug (worse). Let's look at the functional approach to representing the possible absence of data.

5.2 An introduction to the Option type

Option is essentially a container that wraps a value . . . or no value. It's like a box that *may* contain a thing, or it could be empty. The symbolic definition for Option is as follows:

```
Option<T> = None | Some(T)
```

Let's see what that means. T is a type parameter (the type of the inner value), so an Option<int> may contain an int. The | sign means *or*, so the definition says that an Option<T> can be one of two things:

- None—A special value indicating the absence of a value. If the Option has no inner value, we say that *the Option is None.*
- Some(T)—A container that wraps a value of type T. If the Option has an inner value, we say that *the Option is Some.*

(In case you're wondering, in Option<T>, I use angle brackets to indicate that T is a type parameter; in Some(T), I use parentheses to indicate that Some is a function that takes a T and returns an Option<T>, wrapping the given value.)

In terms of sets, Option<T> is the *union* of the set Some(T) with the singleton set None (see figure 5.1). Option is a good example of a sum type, which we discussed in section 4.2.4.

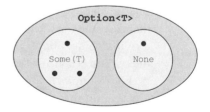

Figure 5.1 Option<T> **is the union of the set** Some<T> **with the singleton set** None.

---

[2] In fact, the language specification itself says so: if you assign null to a variable as in string s = null;, then s is string evaluates to false.

If `bool` has two possible values, then `Some<bool>` also has two possible values, but `Option<bool>` has three possible values because it also includes `None`. Similarly, `Option<DayOfWeek>` has eight possible values, and so on.

We'll look at implementing `Option` in the next subsection, but first, let's take a look at its basic usage so you're familiar with the API. I recommend you follow along in the REPL, but you'll need a bit of setup, and that's described in the following sidebar.

Using the `LaYumba.Functional` library in the REPL

I developed my own functional library, `LaYumba.Functional`, to support the teaching of many of the techniques in this book. It would be useful for you to play with the constructs included in `LaYumba.Functional` in the REPL. This requires you to import it in the REPL:

1 If you haven't done so already, download and compile the code samples from https://github.com/la-yumba/functional-csharp-code-2.

2 Reference the `LaYumba.Functional` library in your REPL. Just how this works depends on your setup. On my system (using the C# Interactive window in Visual Studio with the code samples solution open), I can do so by typing the following:

```
#r "functional-csharp-code-2\LaYumba.Functional\bin\Debug\net6.0\
➥ LaYumba.Functional.dll"
```

3 Type the following imports into the REPL:

```
using LaYumba.Functional;
using static LaYumba.Functional.F;
```

Once you're set up, you can create some `Options`:

```
Option<string> _ = None;          ⊲— Creates a None
```

```
Option<string> john = Some("John");   ⊲— Creates a Some
```

That was easy! Now that you know how to create `Options`, how can you interact with them? At the most basic level, you can do so with `Match`, a method that performs pattern matching. Simply put, it allows you to run different code depending on whether the `Option` is `None` or `Some`.

For example, if you have an optional name, you can write a function that returns a greeting for that name or a general-purpose message if no name is given. Type the following into the REPL:

```
string Greet(Option<string> greetee)
   => greetee.Match(                        If greetee is None, Match
      None: () => "Sorry, who?",    ⊲—      evaluates this function.
      Some: (name) => $"Hello, {name}");   ⊲┐ If greetee is Some, Match
                                            │ evaluates this function, passing
Greet(Some("John")) // => "Hello, John"     │ it greetee's inner value.

Greet(None) // => "Sorry, who?"
```

As you can see, Match takes two functions: the first one says what to do in the None case; the second, what to do in the Some case. In the Some case, the function is given the inner value of the Option.

In the preceding call to Match, the named arguments None: and Some: are used for extra clarity. It's possible to omit those:

```
string greet(Option<string> greetee)
   => greetee.Match
   (
       () => "Sorry, who?",
       (name) => $"Hello, {name}"
   );
```

In general, I omit them because the empty parens () in the first lambda already suggest an empty container (that is, an Option in the None state), whereas the parens with an argument inside, (name), suggest a container with a value inside. (The parens are optional in the Some case, as with any unary lambda, but I keep them here to maintain this graphic analogy.)

If this is all a bit confusing right now, don't worry; things will fall into place as we go along. For now, these are the things to remember:

1 Use Some(value) to wrap a value into an Option.
2 Use None to create an empty Option.
3 Use Match to run some code depending on the state of the Option.

For now, you can think of None as a replacement for null, and Match as a replacement for a null check. You'll see in subsequent sections why using Option is actually preferable to null, and why, eventually, you won't need to use Match very often.

5.3 Implementing Option

Feel free to skip to section 5.4 or skim over this section on first reading. To start with, it's important that you understand enough to be able to *use* Option. But if you'd like to see what's under the hood, in this section, I'll show you the techniques I used in the implementation of Option that I included in LaYumba.Functional. This is both to show you that there's little magic involved and to show you ways to work around some limitations of the C# type system. You might like to type this code into an empty project as you follow along.

5.3.1 An idealized implementation of Option

In many typed functional languages, Option can be defined with a one-liner along these lines:

```
type Option t = None | Some t
```

The closest equivalent in C# is the following:

```
interface Option<T> { }
record None : Option<T>;
record Some<T>(T Value) : Option<T>;
```

That is, we define `Option<T>` as a *marker* interface and then provide minimal implementations for `None` and `Some<T>`, saying that each of them is a valid `Option<T>`. `Some<T>` contains a `T`, and `None` contains nothing.

Here we already run into a problem: because `None` does not actually contain a `T`, we'd like to say that `None` is a valid `Option<T>` regardless of what type `T` eventually resolves to. Unfortunately, the C# compiler does not allow this, so in order to make the code compile, we need to provide a generic parameter for `None` as well.

```
record None<T> : Option<T>;
```

We now have a basic, working implementation.

5.3.2 *Consuming an Option*

Next, we want to write code that consumes an `Option` using pattern matching. Ideally, I'd like it to look like this:

```
string Greet(Option<string> greetee)
   => greetee switch
   {
      None => "Sorry, who?",
      Some(name) => $"Hello, {name}"
   };
```

Unfortunately, this does not compile. If we are to satisfy the syntax for pattern matching in C#, we need to rewrite the code as follows:

```
string Greet(Option<string> greetee)
   => greetee switch
   {
      None<string> => "Sorry, who?",
      Some<string>(var name) => $"Hello, {name}"
   };
```

This is definitely less elegant (imagine if you have a long type name instead of `string`), but at least it compiles. It does, however, generate a compiler warning, saying that "the switch expression does not handle all possible values of its input type." This is because, in theory, some other implementation of `Option<string>` could exist, and the `switch` expression in our example does not cater to this. Unfortunately, there is no way to tell C# that we never want anything other than `Some` and `None` to implement `Option`.

We can mitigate both issues by defining our own adapter function `Match` that includes a *discard pattern*. This allows us to perform exhaustive pattern matching and gives us an interface that's easy to consume:

```
static R Match<T, R>(this Option<T> opt, Func<R> None, Func<T, R> Some)
   => opt switch
   {
      None<T> => None(),
      Some<T>(var t) => Some(t),
      _ => throw new ArgumentException("Option must be None or Some")
   };
```

Then we can consume an `Option` like this:

```
string Greet(Option<string> greetee)
   => greetee.Match
   (
      None: () => "Sorry, who?",
      Some: (name) => $"Hello, {name}"
   );
```

Now we have an elegant, concise way to consume an `Option`. (Notice that we also need an overload of `Match` that takes two actions, allowing us to *do something* depending on the state of the `Option`. This can easily be done following the approach described in section 4.3.2.)

5.3.3 *Creating a None*

Let's move on to creating `Options`. To explicitly create a `None`—say, for testing that `Greet` works with `None`—we have to write this:

```
var greeting = Greet(new None<string>());
```

This is not nice. I particularly dislike that we have to specify the `string` parameter: when calling a method, we'd like to have type inference resolve our generic parameters. What we need, ideally, is a value that can be converted to a `None<T>`, regardless of the type of `T`.

While you can't do this with inheritance, it turns out you can do it with type conversion. To achieve this, we need to define a dedicated, non-generic type, `NoneType`:

```
struct NoneType { }
```

Next, we change `Option<T>` to include implicit conversion from `NoneType` to `None<T>`:

```
abstract record Option<T>
{
   public static implicit operator Option<T>(NoneType _)
      => new None<T>();
}
```

This effectively tells the runtime that an instance of `NoneType` can be used where an `Option<T>` is expected and instructs the runtime to convert the `NoneType` to a `None<T>`. Finally, we include a convenience field called `None` that stores a `NoneType`:

```
public static readonly NoneType None = default;
```

You can now create a `None<T>` by simply typing `None`:

```
Greet(None) // => "Sorry, who?"
```

Much better! Note that this assumes that the `None` field is in scope, which can be achieved with `using static`.

In the previous snippet, `None` returns a `NoneType`. Seeing that `Greet` expects an `Option<string>`, the runtime calls the implicit conversion we defined in `Option<T>`, which yields a None<string>. When all is said and done, you can forget that the None-Type exists and just code knowing that None returns a None<T> for the expected T.

5.3.4   *Creating a Some*

Now for creating a Some. First, because Some indicates the presence of a value, it should *not* to be possible to wrap a null into a Some. To do this, instead of relying on the automatic methods generated for records by the compiler, we'll explicitly define the constructor:

```
record Some<T> : Option<T>
{
    private T Value { get; }

    public Some(T value)
        => Value = value ?? throw new ArgumentNullException();

    public void Deconstruct(out T value)
        => value = Value;
}
```

Here I also made the Option's inner value private so that it can only be accessed when the Option is deconstructed in pattern matching. We can then define a convenience function, Some, that wraps a given value into a Some:

```
public static Option<T> Some<T>(T t) => new Some<T>(t);
```

With this in place, we can create a Some like so:

```
Greet(Some("John")) // => "Hello, John"
```

Now we have nice, clean syntax for creating both a None and a Some. To put the icing on the cake, I'm also going to define an implicit conversion from T to Option<T>:

```
abstract record Option<T>
{
    public static implicit operator Option<T>(T value)
        => value is null ? new None<T>() : new Some<T>(value);
}
```

This means that a T can be used where an Option<T> is expected and will automatically be wrapped into a Some<T>—unless it's null, in which case it will be a None<T>. This snippet saves us from explicitly calling Some:

```
Greet(None)    // => "Sorry, who?"
Greet("John") // => "Hello, John"
```

It also allows us to trivially convert a function that returns null to one that returns an Option:

```
var empty = new NameValueCollection();
Option<string> green = empty["green"];

green // => None
```

5.3.5 *Optimizing the Option implementation*

For a number of reasons, in my `LaYumba.Functional` library, I've chosen to use a slightly different approach and define `Option` as in the following listing.

> **Listing 5.1   An implementation of `Option` optimized for C#**

```
public struct Option<T>
{
    readonly T? value;              The value wrapped
    readonly bool isSome;           by a Some
                                                    Indicates whether the
                                                    Option is Some or None

    internal Option(T value)
    {                                               Constructs an Option
        this.value = value ?? throw new ArgumentNullException();
        this.isSome = true;                         in the Some state
    }

    public static implicit operator Option<T>(NoneType _)   Constructs an Option
        => default;                                         in the None state

    public static implicit operator Option<T>(T value)
        => value is null ? None : Some(value);      Once an Option is
                                                    constructed, the only
    public R Match<R>(Func<R> None, Func<T, R> Some)  way to interact with
        => isSome ? Some(value!) : None();            it is with Match.
}
```

In this implementation, instead of using different types, I use *state* (namely, the `isSome` flag) to indicate whether the `Option` is `Some` or `None`. I'm providing a single constructor that creates an `Option` in the `Some` state. That's because I've defined `Option` as a struct, and structs have an implicit parameterless constructor that initializes all fields to their default values. In this case, the `isSome` flag is initialized to `false`, indicating that the `Option` is `None`. This implementation has several advantages:

- Performance is better because structs are allocated on the stack.
- Being a struct, an `Option` cannot be `null`.
- The `default` value of an `Option` is `None` (with records, it was `null`).

Everything else (the `NoneType`, implicit conversion, and the interface of `Match`) is the same as discussed previously. Finally, I've defined the `Some` function and the `None` value in the `F` class, which allows you to easily create `Option`s:

```
namespace LaYumba.Functional;

public static partial class F
{
    public static Option<T> Some<T>(T value) => new Option<T>(value);
    public static NoneType None => default;
}
```

Now that you have seen all the pieces of the puzzle, take another look at the example I showed earlier. It should be clearer now:

```
using LaYumba.Functional;
using static LaYumba.Functional.F;

string Greet(Option<string> greetee)
   => greetee.Match
   (
      None: () => "Sorry, who?",
      Some: (name) => $"Hello, {name}"
   );

Greet(Some("John")) // => "Hello, John"

Greet(None) // => "Sorry, who?"
```

As you've seen, there are different possible ways to implement Option in C#. I've chosen this particular implementation because it allows the cleanest API from the perspective of client code. But Option is a concept, not a particular implementation, so don't be alarmed if you see a different implementation in another library or tutorial.[3] It will still have the defining features of an Option:

- A value None that indicates the absence of a value
- A function Some that wraps a value, indicating the presence of a value
- A way to execute code depending on whether a value is present (in our case, Match)

Option is also called Maybe

Different functional frameworks use varying terminology to express similar concepts. A common synonym for Option is Maybe, with the Some and None states called Just and Nothing, respectively.

Such naming inconsistencies are unfortunately quite common in FP, and this doesn't help in the learning process. In this book, I'll try to present the most common synonyms for each pattern or technique and then stick with one name. From now on, I'll stick to Option. Just know that if you run across Maybe (say, in a JavaScript or Haskell library), it's the same concept.

Let's now look at some practical scenarios in which you can use Option.

5.4   *Option as the natural result type of partial functions*

We've discussed how functions map elements from one set to another and how types represent these sets. There's an important distinction to make between total and partial functions:

---

[3] For example, the popular mocking framework NSubstitute includes an implementation of Option.

- *Total functions*—Mappings that are defined for *every* element of the domain
- *Partial functions*—Mappings that are defined for *some* but not all elements of the domain

Partial functions are problematic because it's not clear what the function should do when given an input for which it can't compute a result. The Option type offers a perfect solution to model such cases: if the function is defined for the given input, it returns a Some wrapping the result; otherwise, it returns None. Let's look at some common use cases in which we can use this approach.

5.4.1 Parsing strings

Imagine a function that parses a string representation of an integer. You could model this as a function of type string → int. This is clearly a partial function because not all strings are valid representations of integers. In fact, there are infinitely many strings that can't be mapped to an int.

You can provide a safer representation of parsing by having the parser function return an Option<int>. This will be None if the given string can't be parsed, as figure 5.2 illustrates.

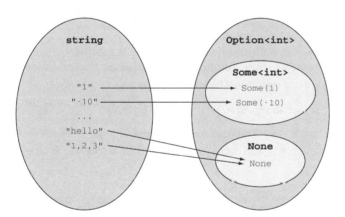

Figure 5.2 Using Option to convey that parsing is a partial function. For input strings that provide valid representation of an integer, the parsing function wraps the parsed int into a Some. Otherwise, it returns None.

A parser function with the signature string → int is partial, and it's not clear from the signature what will happen if you supply a string that can't be converted to an int. On the other hand, a parser function with signature string → Option<int> is total because, for any given string, it returns a valid Option<int>. Here's an implementation that uses a BCL method to do the grunt work but exposes an Option-based API:

```
public static class Int
{
   public static Option<int> Parse(string s)
      => int.TryParse(s, out int result)
         ? Some(result) : None;
}
```

The helper functions in this subsection are included in LaYumba.Functional. You can try them out in the REPL:

```
Int.Parse("10")    // => Some(10)
Int.Parse("hello") // => None
```

Similar methods are defined to parse strings into other commonly used types like doubles and dates and, more generally, to convert data in one form to another, more restrictive form.

5.4.2   *Looking up data in a collection*

In section 5.1, I showed you that some collections expose an API that's neither honest nor consistent in representing the absence of data. The gist was as follows:

```
new NameValueCollection()["green"]
// => null

new Dictionary<string, string>()["blue"]
// => runtime error: KeyNotFoundException
```

The fundamental problem is the following. An associative collection maps keys to values and can, therefore, be seen as a function of type TKey → TValue. But there's no guarantee that the collection contains a value for every possible key, so looking up a value is a partial function.

A better, more explicit way to model the retrieval of a value is by returning an Option. It's possible to write adapter functions that expose an Option-based API, and I generally name these Option-returning functions Lookup:

```
Lookup : (NameValueCollection, string) → Option<string>
```

Lookup takes a NameValueCollection and a string (the key) and returns a Some wrapping the value if the key exists and None otherwise. The following listing shows the implementation.

Listing 5.2   Changing a null-returning function to return an Option

```
public static Option<string> Lookup
    (this NameValueCollection collection, string key)
    => collection[key];
```

That's it! The expression collection[key] is of type string, whereas the declared return value is Option<string>, so the string value will be implicitly converted into an Option<string>, with null being replaced by None. With minimal effort, we've gone from a null-based API to an Option-based API.

Here's an overload of Lookup that takes an IDictionary. The signature is similar:

```
Lookup : (IDictionary<K, T>, K) → Option<T>
```

We can implement the Lookup function as follows:

```
public static Option<T> Lookup<K, T>(this IDictionary<K, T> dict, K key)
    => dict.TryGetValue(key, out T value) ? Some(value) : None;
```

We now have an honest, clear, and consistent API to query both collections:

```
new NameValueCollection().Lookup("green")
// => None

new Dictionary<string, string>().Lookup("blue")
// => None
```

No more `KeyNotFoundException` or `NullReferenceException` because you asked for a key that wasn't present in the collection. We can apply the same approach when querying other data structures.

5.4.3 *The smart constructor pattern*

In section 4.2.2, we defined the `Age` type, a type more restrictive than `int`, in that not all `int`s represent a valid age. You can, again, model this with `Option`, as figure 5.3 shows.

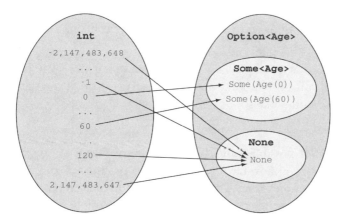

Figure 5.3 Converting from int to Age can also be modeled with Option.

If you need to create an `Age` from an `int`, instead of calling the constructor, which has to throw an exception if it's unable to create a valid instance, you can define a function that returns `Some` or `None` to indicate the successful creation of an `Age`. This is known as a *smart constructor*: it's smart in the sense that it's aware of some rules and can prevent the construction of an invalid object. The following listing shows this approach.

Listing 5.3   Implementing a smart constructor for `Age`

```
public struct Age
{
    private int Value { get; }

    public static Option<Age> Create(int age)      ◁─┐ A smart constructor
        => IsValid(age) ? Some(new Age(age)) : None;    returning an Option
```

```
private Age(int value)
   => Value = value;

private static bool IsValid(int age)
   => 0 <= age && age < 120;
}
```

◁— The constructor should now
be marked as `private`.

If you now need to obtain an `Age` from an `int`, you'll get an `Option<Age>`, which forces you to account for the failure case.

5.5 *Dealing with null*

At the beginning of this chapter, I asked you to pretend there was no `null` in C# and that we had to come up with a way to represent optional values. Truly functional languages don't have `null` and model optional values with the `Option` type. However, some of the most popular programming languages, including C#, not only allow for `null`, but use it as the default value for all reference types. In this section, I'll show you why this is a problem and how it can be tackled.

5.5.1 *Why null is such a terrible idea*

Let's look at some of the reasons why `null` causes so many problems.

SLOPPY DATA MODELING

In section 4.2.4, you saw that the tuple (`Age`, `Gender`) has $(120 \times 2) = 240$ possible values. The same is true if you store those two values in a struct. Now, if you define a class or record to hold these values like so

```
record HealthData(Age age, Gender Gender);
```

then there are actually 241 possible values because reference types can be `null`. If you refactor `Age` to be a class, you now have 121 possible values for `Age` and 243 possible values for `HealthData`! Not only is `null` polluting the mathematical representation of the data, but we also have to write code to handle all those possible values.

AMBIGUOUS FUNCTION SIGNATURES

You may have heard that the `NullReferenceException` is the single most common source of bugs. But why is it so common? The answer lies, I believe, in a fundamental ambiguity:

- Because reference types are `null` by default, your program may encounter a `null` as a result of a programming error, where a required value was simply not initialized.
- Other times, `null` is considered a legal value; for example, the authors of `NameValueCollection` decided it was OK to represent that a key is not present by returning `null`.

Because there is no way to declare whether a `null` value is deliberate or the result of a programming error (at least before C# 8's nullable reference types, which I'll discuss in section 5.5.3), you're often in doubt as to how to treat a `null` value. Should you allow for null? Should you throw an `ArgumentNullException`? Should you let the `NullReferenceException` bubble up? Essentially, every function that accepts or returns a reference type is ambiguous because it's unclear whether a null value is a legal input or output.

DEFENSIVE NULL-CHECKING

The ambiguity between legal and unintentional `null`s does not only cause bugs. It has another effect, which may be even more damaging: it leads to defensive programming. To prevent the lurking `NullReferenceException`, developers litter their code with `null` checks and assertions against `null` arguments. While there is a case for using these assertions (see section 5.5.4), if used throughout the codebase, they create a lot of noise.

5.5.2 *Gaining robustness by using Option instead of null*

The main step to address these problems is to *never* use `null` as a legal value. Instead, use `Option` to represent optional values. This way, any occurrence of `null` is the result of a programming error. (This means that you never need to check for `null`; just let the `NullReferenceException` bubble up.) Let's see an example.

Imagine you have a form on your website that allows people to subscribe to a newsletter. A user enters his name and email, and this causes the instantiation of a `Subscriber`, which is then persisted to the database. `Subscriber` is defined as follows:

```
public record Subscriber
(
    string Name,
    string Email
);
```

When it's time to send out the newsletter, a custom greeting is computed for the subscriber, which is prepended to the body of the newsletter:

```
public string GreetingFor(Subscriber subscriber)
    => $"Dear {subscriber.Name.ToUpper()},";
```

This all works fine. `Name` can't be `null` because it's a required field in the signup form, and it's not nullable in the database.

Some months later, the rate at which new subscribers sign up drops, so the business decides to lower the barrier to entry by no longer requiring new subscribers to enter their name. The name field is removed from the form, and the database is modified accordingly.

This should be considered a *breaking change* because it's not possible to make the same assumptions about the data any more. And yet, the code still happily compiles. When time comes for the newsletter to be sent, `GreetingFor` throws an exception when it receives a `Subscriber` without a `Name`.

By this time, the person responsible for making the name optional in the database may be on a different team than the person maintaining the code that sends out the newsletter. The code may be in different repositories. In short, it may not be simple to look up all the usages of Name. Instead, it's better to explicitly indicate that Name is now optional. That is, Subscriber should be changed to

```
public record Subscriber
(
    Option<string> Name,        Name is now explicitly
    string Email                marked as optional.
);
```

This not only clearly conveys the fact that a value for Name may not be available, it causes GreetingFor to no longer compile. GreetingFor and any other code that was accessing the Name property will have to be modified to take into account the possibility of the value being absent. For example, you might modify it like so:

```
public string GreetingFor(Subscriber subscriber)
    => subscriber.Name.Match
    (
        () => "Dear Subscriber,",
        (name) => $"Dear {name.ToUpper()},"
    );
```

By using Option, you're forcing the users of your API to handle the case in which no data is available. This places greater demands on the client code, but it effectively removes the possibility of a NullReferenceException occurring.

Changing a string to an Option<string> is a breaking change: in this way, you're trading run-time errors for compile-time errors, thus making a compiling application more robust.

5.5.3 Non-nullable reference types?

It has become widely accepted that having nullable types is a flaw in the language design. This is somewhat confirmed by the fact that so many releases of C# have introduced new syntax for dealing with null, gradually making the language more complex but without ever solving the problem at the root.

The most radical effort to take a stab at the problem has been made in C# 8 by introducing a feature called *nullable reference types* (NRT). The name may seem odd, given that reference types were always nullable in C#; the point is that the feature allows you to mark the types you intend to be nullable, and the compiler keeps track of how you access instances of those types. For example, NRT allows you to write

```
#nullable enable              Enables the NRT feature
                              in the code that follows
public record Subscriber
(
    string? Name,             A nullable
                              field
    string Email              A non-nullable
);                            field
```

This allows you to be explicit in your declarations on which values can be `null`. Furthermore, if you dereference `Name` without a `null` check, you'll get a compiler warning telling you that `Name` may be `null`:

```
#nullable enable

public string GreetingFor(Subscriber subscriber)
    => $"Dear {subscriber.Name.ToUpper()},";

// => CS8602 Dereference of a possibly null reference
```

On the face of it, you might think this feature supersedes `Option`, and to a certain extent, it does. When you look deeper, however, you'll find a few problems:

- You need to explicitly opt into the feature by adding the `Nullable` element to your project file (or adding the `#nullable` directive in your files as shown previously).
- Even when you've opted into NRT at project level, it's still possible to override this within a file by using the `#nullable disable` directive. This means that you cannot reason about code in isolation: you now need to look in different places to see whether a `string` is nullable or not.
- The compiler warnings only appear if both the nullable value declaration and the code where the value is dereferenced are in a NRT-enabled context, again making it difficult to reason about code in isolation.
- Unless you're treating warnings as errors, your code will still compile after changing, say, `string` to `string?`, which is, therefore, not a breaking change and will go unnoticed in a codebase with lots of warnings.
- The compiler can't always keep track of the `null` checks you've made along the way. For example,

```
public string GreetingFor(Subscriber subscriber)       ◁── Checks that
    => IsValid(subscriber)                                  subscriber.Name
        ? $"Dear {subscriber.Name.ToUpper()},"             is not null
        : "Dear Subscriber";                       ◁── Still warns that you may
                                                       be dereferencing a null
```

  results in a compiler warning even if `IsValid` checks that `Name` is not `null`. To fix this, you have to learn an obscure set of attributes to keep the compiler from warning you about these *false positives*.[4]

- Fields that are *not* marked as nullable can still end up being `null` (for example, when deserializing an object):

```
#nullable enable

var json = @"{""Name"":""Enrico"", ""Email"":null}";
var subscriber = JsonSerializer.Deserialize<Subscriber>(json);

if (subscriber is not null)
    WriteLine(subscriber.Email.ToLower());
// => throws NullReferenceException
```

---

[4] For more details, see http://mng.bz/10XQ.

- The feature doesn't allow you to deal with optionality in a way that is uniform between value and reference types. Despite the syntactic similarity between, say, `int?` and `string?`, they are completely different: `int?` is shorthand for `Nullable<int>`, so we have a structure wrapping the `int`, somewhat similarly to `Option`. On the other hand, `string?` is an annotation telling the compiler that the value could be `null`.

Notice that none of those limitations apply when using the `Option` type. Overall, despite my initial excitement as NRT was being developed, I'm now inclined to find it's too little, too late. It seems that the language team set out with a bold agenda for this feature, but then watered it down to allow users to migrate their existing code-bases to C# 8 without too much effort.

If you're working on a team that embraces NRT and opts to use it everywhere, or if in a few years' time adoption becomes ubiquitous, then NRT will certainly add value. But at the time of writing, if you're working on a variety of projects and consuming a variety of libraries, not all of which use NRT throughout, I don't see NRT bringing a real benefit.

5.5.4   *Bulletproof against NullReferenceException*

Given all that we discussed previously, in my opinion the most robust approach to prevent `null` values from wreaking havoc is as follows. Firstly

- If you're using C# 8, enable NRT. This helps to ensure that required values are always initialized. More importantly, it conveys intent to consumers of your code that also have NRT enabled.
- For optional values, use `Option<T>` rather than `T?`.

This means that, inside the boundaries of your code, you can be confident that no value is ever `null`. You should have no `null` checks nor throw any `ArgumentNullException`.

Secondly, identify the boundaries of your code. This includes

- Public methods exposed by libraries that you intend to publish or share across projects
- Web APIs
- Listeners to messages from message brokers or persisted queues

In those boundaries, prevent `null` values from seeping in

- For required values
  - Throw an `ArgumentNullException`.
  - Return a response with a status code of 400 (Bad Request).
  - Reject the message.
- For optional values, convert `null` values into `Options`:
  - In C#, this can be done trivially with implicit conversion.
  - If your boundary involves deserializing data sent in another format, you can add the conversion logic to your formatter.

Thirdly, where you consume .NET or third-party libraries, you also need to prevent null from seeping in. You saw an example of how to do this in listing 5.2, where we defined the Option-returning Lookup method on NameValueCollection.

Converting JSON null to C# Option

For convenience, my LaYumba.Functional library includes a formatter that works with .NET's System.Text.Json and illustrates how null in JSON objects can be translated into C# Option and back. Here's an example of how to use it:

```
using System.Text.Json;
using LaYumba.Functional.Serialization.Json;

record Person
(
   string FirstName,
   Option<string> MiddleName,
   string LastName
);

JsonSerializerOptions ops = new()
{
   Converters = { new OptionConverter() }
};

var json = @"{""FirstName"":""Virginia"",
   ""MiddleName"":null, ""LastName"":""Woolf""}";
var deserialized = JsonSerializer.Deserialize<Person>(json, ops);

deserialized.MiddleName // => None

json = @"{""FirstName"":""Edgar"",
   ""MiddleName"":""Allan"", ""LastName"":""Poe""}";
deserialized = JsonSerializer.Deserialize<Person>(json, ops);

deserialized.MiddleName // => Some("Allan")
```

In summary, Option should be your default choice when representing a value that's, well, optional. Use it in your data objects to model the fact that a property may not be set and in your functions to indicate the possibility that a suitable value may not be returned. Apart from reducing the chance of a NullReferenceException, this will enrich your model and make your code more self-documenting. Using Option in your function signature is one way of attaining the overarching recommendation of chapter 4: designing function signatures that are honest and highly descriptive of what the caller can expect.

In upcoming chapters, we'll look at how to work effectively with Options. Although Match is the basic way of interacting with an Option, we'll build a rich, high-level API starting in the next chapter. Option will be your friend, not only when you use it in your programs, but also as a simple structure through which I'll illustrate many FP concepts.

Exercises

1 Write a generic `Parse` function that takes a string and parses it as a value of an enum. It should be usable as follows:

```
Enum.Parse<DayOfWeek>("Friday")  // => Some(DayOfWeek.Friday)

Enum.Parse<DayOfWeek>("Freeday") // => None
```

2 Write a `Lookup` function that takes an `IEnumerable` and a predicate and returns the first element in the `IEnumerable` that matches the predicate or `None`, if no matching element is found. Write its signature in arrow notation:

```
bool isOdd(int i) => i % 2 == 1;

new List<int>().Lookup(isOdd)     // => None
new List<int> { 1 }.Lookup(isOdd) // => Some(1)
```

3 Write a type `Email` that wraps an underlying string, enforcing that it's in a valid format. Ensure that you include the following:

    – A smart constructor
    – Implicit conversion to string so that it can easily be used with the typical API for sending emails

4 Take a look at the extension methods defined on `IEnumerable` in `System.LINQ.Enumerable`.[5] Which ones could potentially return nothing or throw some kind of not-found exception and would, therefore, be good candidates for returning an `Option<T>` instead?

Summary

- Use the `Option` type to express the possible absence of a value. An `Option` can be in one of two states:
    – `None`, indicating the absence of a value
    – `Some`, a simple container wrapping a non-null value

- To execute code conditionally, depending on the state of an `Option`, use `Match` with the functions you'd like to evaluate in the `None` and `Some` cases.

- Use `Option` as a return value when a function cannot guarantee a valid output for all possible inputs including
    – Looking up values in collections
    – Creating objects requiring validation (smart constructors)

- Identify the boundaries of your code and prevent any `null` values from seeping in:
    – Enforce required values.
    – Convert optional values to `Option`.

---

[5] See the Microsoft documentation of enumerable methods: http://mng.bz/PXd8.

Patterns in functional programming

This chapter covers

- The core functions: `Return`, `Map`, `Bind`, `Where`, and `ForEach`
- Introducing functors and monads
- Working at different levels of abstraction

A pattern is a solution that can be applied to solve a variety of problems. The patterns we'll discuss in this chapter are simply functions: functions that are so ubiquitous when coding functionally that they can be seen as the *core functions* of FP.

You're probably familiar with some of these functions like `Where` and `Select` (which is equivalent to `Map`), having used them with `IEnumerable`. But you'll see that the same operations can be applied to other structures, hence establishing a pattern. I'll illustrate this with `Option` in this chapter; other structures will follow in coming chapters.

As usual, I suggest you type along in the REPL and see how these core functions can be used. (You'll need to import the `LaYumba.Functional` library as shown in the sidebar "Using the `LaYumba.Functional` library in the REPL" in chapter 5.)

6.1   *Applying a function to a structure's inner values*

The first core function we'll look at is Map. It takes a structure and a function and applies the function to the inner value(s) of the structure.[1] Let's start with the familiar case in which the structure in question is an IEnumerable.

6.1.1   *Mapping a function onto a sequence*

An implementation of Map for IEnumerable can be written as follows.

Listing 6.1   Applying a function to each element of the given IEnumerable

```
public static IEnumerable<R> Map<T, R>
   (this IEnumerable<T> ts, Func<T, R> f)
{
   foreach (var t in ts)
      yield return f(t);
}
```

Map maps a list of T's to a list of R's by applying a function T → R to each element in the source list. Notice that in this implementation, the results are packaged into an IEnumerable as a result of using the yield return statement.

> **NOTE**   In FP, it's normal to use variable names like t for a value of type T, ts for a collection of T's, and f (g, h, and so on) for a function. You can use more descriptive names when coding for more specific scenarios, but when a function is as general as Map, where you really know nothing about the value t or the function f, variables have correspondingly general names.

Graphically, Map can be illustrated as in figure 6.1.

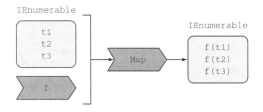

Figure 6.1   Mapping a function over an IEnumerable. This operation yields a list containing the result of applying the given function to each item in the source list.

Let's look at a simple usage:

```
using static System.Linq.Enumerable;
using LaYumba.Functional;

var triple = (int x) => x * 3;

Range(1, 3).Map(triple);
// => [3, 6, 9]
```

---

[1] The *inner value(s)* are also known as *bound values*.

Maybe you recognized that this is exactly the behavior you get when you call LINQ's `Select` method. Indeed, `Map` can be defined in terms of `Select`:

```
public static IEnumerable<R> Map<T, R>
   (this IEnumerable<T> ts, Func<T, R> f)
   => ts.Select(f);
```

This is potentially more efficient because LINQ's implementation of `Select` is optimized for some specific implementations of `IEnumerable`. The point is that I'm going to use the name `Map` rather than `Select` because `Map` is the standard terminology in FP, but you should consider `Map` and `Select` synonyms.

6.1.2 *Mapping a function onto an Option*

Now let's see how `Map` can be defined for a different structure: `Option`. Just like mapping a function onto a list abstracts away how the list is structured or implemented, how many items it contains, and how the function is applied to each element, similarly for an `Option` we want to apply a function to its inner value, without the need to know about the state or the implementation details of `Option`. The signature of `Map` for `IEnumerable` is

```
(IEnumerable<T>, (T → R)) → IEnumerable<R>
```

To get the signature of `Map` for `Option`, let's simply follow the pattern and replace `IEnumerable` with `Option`:

```
(Option<T>, (T → R)) → Option<R>
```

This signature says that `Map` is given

- An `Option` that *may* contain a `T`
- A function from `T` to `R`

It must return an `Option` that *may* contain an `R`. Can you think of an implementation? Let's see:

- If the given `Option` is `None`, then there is no `T` available and no way to compute an `R`: all you can do is return `None`.
- On the other hand, if the `Option` is `Some`, then its inner value is a `T`, so you can apply the given function to it, obtaining an `R`, which you can then wrap in a `Some`.

Hence, we can define `Map` as the following listing demonstrates. This is also represented in figure 6.2.

> **Listing 6.2   Definition of `Map` for `Option`**

```
public static Option<R> Map<T, R>
(
    this Option<T> optT,
    Func<T, R> f
)
```

```
=> optT.Match
(
    () => None,
    (t) => Some(f(t))
);
```

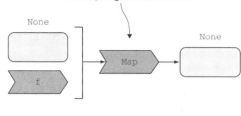

**If the given Option is
None, Map returns None.**

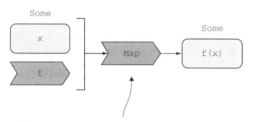

**Figure 6.2 Mapping a
function over an Option**

**If the given Option is Some, Map applies f
to its inner value and wraps the result in a Some.**

Intuitively, it can be useful to think of Option as a special kind of list that can either be empty (None) or contain exactly one value (Some). If you look at it in this light, it becomes clear that the implementations of Map for Option and IEnumerable are consistent: the given function gets applied to *all* inner values of the structure. Let's look at a simple example:

```
var greet = (string name) => $"hello, {name}";

Option<string> empty   = None;
Option<string> optJohn = Some("John");

empty.Map(greet);   // => None
optJohn.Map(greet); // => Some("hello, John")
```

Here's a real-life analogy: you have a lovely old aunt whose specialty is making apple pies (figure 6.3). She hates to go shopping, but boy, does she love baking pies (single responsibility principle).

You often drop a basket of apples outside her door on your way to work, and in the evening, you'll find a basket of freshly made pies! Your aunt also has a sense of humor, so if you get smart and leave an empty basket by her door, you'll find an empty basket in return.

In this analogy, the basket represents Option. The apples are its inner value, and your aunt's cooking skills are the function that gets applied to the apples. Map is the

Figure 6.3 Your aunt bakes the pie, but only if the apples are in the basket!

process of unboxing the apples, giving them to your aunt for processing, and reboxing the baked pie. Here's how this example would play out in code:

```
record Apples();
record ApplePie(Apples Apples);

var makePie = (Apples apples) => new ApplePie(apples);

Option<Apples> full  = Some(new Apples());
Option<Apples> empty = None;

full.Map(makePie)  // => Some(ApplePie)
empty.Map(makePie) // => None
```

6.1.3 *How Option raises the level of abstraction*

A really important thing to realize is that `Option` abstracts away the question of whether a value is present or not. If you directly apply a function to a value, you have to somehow ensure that the value is available. Instead, if you `Map` that function onto an `Option`, you don't really care whether the value is there or not—`Map` applies the function or not, as appropriate.

This may not be fully clear at this point, but it will become so as you proceed through the book. For now, let's see if I can illustrate this idea. In chapter 4, we defined a function that would calculate `Risk` based on `Age` as follows:

```
Risk CalculateRiskProfile(Age age)
   => (age < 60) ? Risk.Low : Risk.Medium;
```

Now, assume you're doing a survey where people volunteer some personal information and receive some statistics. Survey takers are modeled with a `Subject` class defined as follows:

```
record Subject
(
    Option<Age> Age,
    Option<Gender> Gender,
    // many more fields...
);
```

Some fields like `Age` are modeled as optional because survey takers can choose whether or not to disclose this information. This is how you'd compute the `Risk` of a particular `Subject`:

```
Option<Risk> RiskOf(Subject subject)
    => subject.Age.Map(CalculateRiskProfile);
```

Because `Risk` is based on the subject's age, which is optional, the computed `Risk` is also optional. You don't have to worry about whether the `Age` is there or not; instead, you can map the function that computes risk regardless, and allow the optionality to propagate by returning the result as an `Option`. Next, let's look at `Map` in a more general light.

6.1.4 *Introducing functors*

You've seen that `Map` is a function that follows a precise pattern, and that it's used to apply a function to the inner value(s) of a structure such as an `IEnumerable` or an `Option`. It can be defined for many other data structures including sets, dictionaries, trees, and more.

Let's generalize the pattern. Let `C<T>` indicate a generic *container* that wraps some inner value(s) of type `T`. Then the signature of `Map` can be generalized as follows:

```
Map : (C<T>, (T → R)) → C<R>
```

`Map` can be defined as a function that takes a container `C<T>` and a function *f* of type `(T → R)`. It returns a container `C<R>` that wraps the value(s) resulting from applying *f* to the container's inner value(s).

In FP, a type for which such a `Map` function is defined is called a *functor*.[2] `IEnumerable` and `Option` are functors, as you've just seen, and you'll meet many more in the book.

For practical purposes, we can say that anything that has a reasonable implementation of `Map` is a functor. But what's a reasonable implementation? Essentially, `Map` should apply a function to the container's inner value(s) and, equally important, it should do *nothing else*—`Map` should have no side effects.[3]

---

[2] Unfortunately, the term *functor* has different connotations depending on the context. In mathematics, it identifies the function that is being mapped; in programming, it's the container over which you can map the function.

[3] This is not the official definition, but it's essentially equivalent.

> ### Why is functor not an interface?
>
> If both `Option` and `IEnumerable` support the `Map` operation, why are we not capturing this with an interface? Indeed, it would be nice to do so, but unfortunately, it's not possible in C#. To illustrate why, let's try to define such an interface:
>
> ```
> interface Functor<F<>, T>
> {
>    F<R> Map<R>(Func<T, R> f);
> }
>
> public struct Option<T> : Functor<Option, T>
> {
>    public Option<R> Map<R>(Func<T, R> f) => // ...
> }
> ```
>
> This doesn't compile: we can't use `F<>` as a type variable because unlike `T`, it doesn't indicate a type but rather a *kind*: a type that's, in turn, parameterized with a generic type. And it's not enough for `Map` to return a `Functor`. It must return a functor of the same kind as the current instance.
>
> Other languages (including Haskell and Scala) support so-called *higher-kinded types*, so it's possible to represent these more general interfaces with *type classes*, but in C# (and even F#), we must content ourselves with a lesser level of abstraction and follow a pattern-based approach.[a]
>
> ---
>
> [a] It's possible to use the C# type system creatively and find a representation analogous to type classes, but the resulting code is rather intricate and, therefore, not suitable for the intent of this book.

6.2 Performing side effects with ForEach

In chapter 4, we discussed the dichotomy between `Func` and `Action`. We have this problem again with `Map`: `Map` takes a `Func`, so what do we do if we want to perform an `Action` for each value in a given structure? You may know that `List<T>` has a `ForEach` method that takes an `Action<T>`, which it invokes for each item in the list:

```
using static System.Console;

new List<int> { 1, 2, 3 }.ForEach(Write);
// prints: 123
```

This is essentially what we want. Let's generalize this so we can call `ForEach` on any `IEnumerable`:

```
using System.Collections.Immutable;
using Unit = System.ValueTuple;

public static IEnumerable<Unit> ForEach<T>
   (this IEnumerable<T> ts, Action<T> action)
   => ts.Map(action.ToFunc()).ToImmutableList();
```

The code changes the `Action` to a `Unit`-returning function and then relies on the implementation of `Map`. This only creates a lazily evaluated sequence of `Unit`s. Here we actually want the side effects to be performed; hence, the call to `ToImmutableList`. The usage is, unsurprisingly, like this:

```
Enumerable.Range(1, 5).ForEach(Write);
// prints: 12345
```

Now, let's see the definition of `ForEach` for `Option`. This is defined trivially in terms of `Map`, using the `ToFunc` function that converts an `Action` into a `Func`:[4]

```
public static Option<Unit> ForEach<T>
   (this Option<T> opt, Action<T> action)
   => Map(opt, action.ToFunc());
```

The `ForEach` name can be slightly counterintuitive—remember, an `Option` has at most one inner value, so the given action is invoked exactly once (if the `Option` is `Some`) or never (if it's `None`). Here's an example of using `ForEach` to apply an `Action` to an `Option`:

```
var opt = Some("John");

opt.ForEach(name => WriteLine($"Hello {name}"));
// prints: Hello John
```

However, remember from chapter 3 that we should aim to separate pure logic from side effects. We should use `Map` for logic and `ForEach` for side effects, so it would be preferable to rewrite the preceding code as follows:

```
opt.Map(name => $"Hello {name}")
   .ForEach(WriteLine);
```

> **TIP** Make the scope of the `Action` that you apply with `ForEach` as small as possible: use `Map` for data transformations and `ForEach` for side effects. This follows the general FP idea of avoiding side effects if possible and isolating them otherwise.

Take a moment to experiment in the REPL and see that `Map` and `ForEach` can be used with both `IEnumerable` and `Option`. Here's an example:

```
using static System.Console;
using String = LaYumba.Functional.String;

Option<string> name = Some("Enrico");

name
   .Map(String.ToUpper)
   .ForEach(WriteLine);
```

---

[4] You might ask yourself, "Why not just add an overload for `Map` that takes an `Action`?" The problem is that in this case, the compiler fails to resolve to the right overload when we call `Map` without specifying its generic arguments. The reason for this is fairly technical: overload resolution doesn't take into account output parameters, so it can't distinguish between `Func<T, R>` and `Action<T>` when it comes to overload resolution. The price to pay for such an overload would be to always specify generic arguments when calling `Map`, again causing noise. In short, the best solution is to introduce a dedicated `ForEach` method.

```
// prints: ENRICO

IEnumerable<string> names = new[] { "Constance", "Albert" };

names
   .Map(String.ToUpper)
   .ForEach(WriteLine);

// prints: CONSTANCE
//         ALBERT
```

Notice that you can use the same patterns, whether you're working with `Option` or `IEnumerable`. Isn't that nice? You can now view both `Option` and `IEnumerable` as *specialized containers,* and you have a set of core functions that allow you to interact with them. If you're presented with a new kind of container, and `Map` or `ForEach` are defined, you'll probably have a good idea of what they do because you recognize the pattern.

> **NOTE** In the preceding code, I used `LaYumba.Functional.String`, a class that exposes some commonly used functionality of `System.String` through static methods. This allows me to refer to `String.ToUpper` as a function without the need to specify the instance on which the `ToUpper` instance method acts as in: `s => s.ToUpper()`.

In summary, `ForEach` is similar to `Map`, but it takes an `Action` rather than a function, so it's used to perform side effects. Let's move on to the next core function.

6.3 Chaining functions with Bind

`Bind` is another important function, similar to `Map` but slightly more complex. I'll introduce the need for `Bind` with an example.

Suppose you want a simple program that reads the user's age from the console and prints out some related message. You also want error handling: the age should be valid!

Remember, in the last chapter, we defined `Int.Parse` to parse a string as an `int`. We also defined `Age.Create`, a smart constructor that creates an `Age` instance from the given `int`. Both functions return an `Option`:

```
Int.Parse : string → Option<int>
Age.Create : int → Option<Age>
```

Let's see what happens if we combine them with `Map`:

```
string input = Prompt("Please enter your age:");

Option<int> optI = Int.Parse(input);
Option<Option<Age>> ageOpt = optI.Map(i => Age.Create(i));
```

As you can see, we have a problem! We end up with a nested value: `Option` of `Option` of Age. . . . How are we going to work with that?

6.3.1 *Combining Option-returning functions*

It's in such scenarios that Bind is handy. For Option, this is the signature of Bind:

```
Option.Bind : (Option<T>, (T → Option<R>)) → Option<R>
```

Bind takes an Option and an Option-returning function and applies the function to the inner value of the Option. The following listing shows the implementation.

Listing 6.3 Implementation of Bind and Map for Option

```
public static Option<R> Bind<T, R>
(
    this Option<T> optT,
    Func<T, Option<R>> f                ◁──┐ Bind takes an
)                                          │ Option-returning function.
=> optT.Match
(
    () => None,
    (t) => f(t)
);

public static Option<R> Map<T, R>
(
    this Option<T> optT,
    Func<T, R> f                        ◁──┐ Map takes a
)                                          │ regular function.
=> optT.Match
(
    () => None,
    (t) => Some(f(t))
);
```

The preceding listing replicates the definition of Map so that you can see how similar these are. Simply put, the None case always returns None so that the given function won't be applied. The Some case does apply the function; however, unlike Map, there's no need to package the result into an Option because f already returns an Option.

Now let's see how we can put Bind to work in the example of parsing a string representing a person's age. The following listing shows this representation.

Listing 6.4 Using Bind to compose two functions that return an Option

```
Func<string, Option<Age>> parseAge = s
    => Int.Parse(s).Bind(Age.Create);

parseAge("26");          // => Some(26)
parseAge("notAnAge");    // => None
parseAge("180");         // => None
```

The function parseAge uses Bind to combine Int.Parse (which returns an Option<int>) and Age.Create (which returns an Option<Age>). As a result, parseAge combines the check that the string represents a valid integer and the check that the integer is a valid age value.

Let's now see this in the context of a simple program that reads an age from the console and prints out a related message:

```
WriteLine($"Only {ReadAge()}! That's young!");

static Age ReadAge()
   => ParseAge(Prompt("Please enter your age")).Match
   ( () => ReadAge(), (age) => age );        ◁─┐ Recursively calls itself as
                                                │ long as parsing the age fails
static Option<Age> ParseAge(string s)
   => Int.Parse(s).Bind(Age.Create);         ◁─┐ Combines parsing a string as an int
                                                │ and creating an Age from the int
static string Prompt(string msg)
{
   WriteLine(msg);
   return ReadLine();
}
```

Here's a sample interaction with this program (user inputs are shown in bold):

```
Please enter your age
> hello
Please enter your age
> 500
Please enter your age
> 45
Only 45! That's young!
```

Now let's see how Bind works with IEnumerable.

6.3.2 *Flattening nested lists with Bind*

You've just seen how you can use Bind to avoid having nested Options. The same idea applies to lists. But what are nested lists? Two-dimensional lists! We need a function that will apply a list-returning function to a list. But rather than returning a two-dimensional list, it should flatten the result into a one-dimensional list.

Remember that Map loops over a given IEnumerable and applies a function to each element. Bind is similar, but with a nested loop because applying the *bound* function also yields an IEnumerable. The resulting list is flattened to a one-dimensional list. It's probably easier to see this in code:

```
public static IEnumerable<R> Bind<T, R>
   (this IEnumerable<T> ts, Func<T, IEnumerable<R>> f)
{
   foreach (T t in ts)
      foreach (R r in f(t))
         yield return r;
}
```

If you're intimately familiar with LINQ, you'll recognize that this implementation is virtually identical to SelectMany. For IEnumerable, Bind and SelectMany are identical. Again, in this book, I'll use the name Bind because it's standard in FP-speak.

Let's see it in action with an example. Suppose you have a list of neighbors, and each neighbor has a list of pets. You want a list of all pets in the neighborhood:

```
using Pet = System.String;

record Neighbor(string Name, IEnumerable<Pet> Pets);

var neighbors = new Neighbor[]
{
    new (Name: "John", Pets: new Pet[] {"Fluffy", "Thor"}),
    new (Name: "Tim",  Pets: new Pet[] {}),
    new (Name: "Carl", Pets: new Pet[] {"Sybil"}),
};

IEnumerable<IEnumerable<Pet>> nested = neighbors.Map(n => n.Pets);
// => [["Fluffy", "Thor"], [], ["Sybil"]]

IEnumerable<Pet> flat = neighbors.Bind(n => n.Pets);
// => ["Fluffy", "Thor", "Sybil"]
```

Notice how using `Map` yields a nested `IEnumerable`, whereas `Bind` yields a flat `IEnumerable`. (Also notice that, whichever way you look at the results of the preceding example, `Bind` doesn't necessarily yield more items than `Map` does, which does make the choice of the name `SelectMany` seem rather odd.) Figure 6.4 shows a graphical representation of `Bind` for `IEnumerable`, particularized to the types and data in the neighborhood example.

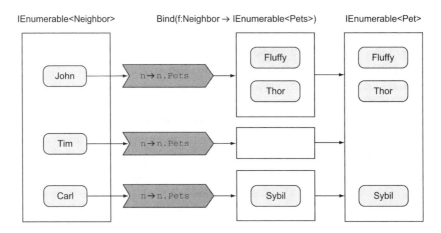

Figure 6.4   `Bind` **takes a source list and a function returning a list for each item of the source list. It returns a flat list, whereas `Map` returns a list of lists.**

As you can see, each function application yields an `IEnumerable`, and then the results for all applications are flattened into a single `IEnumerable`.

6.3.3 *Actually, it's called a monad*

Let's now generalize the pattern for Bind. If we use C<T> to indicate some structure that contains value(s) of type T, then Bind takes an instance of the container and a function with signature (T → C<R>) and returns a C<R>. The signature of Bind is always in this form:

```
Bind : (C<T>, (T → C<R>)) → C<R>
```

You saw that, for all practical purposes, functors are types for which a suitable Map function is defined, enabling you to apply a function to the functor's inner value(s). Similarly, *monads* are types for which a Bind function is defined, enabling you to effectively combine two (or more) monad-returning functions without ending up with a nested structure. You'll sometimes hear people talk of *monadic bind* to clarify that they're not just talking about some function called Bind, but about *the* Bind function that allows the type to be treated as a monad.

6.3.4 *The Return function*

In addition to the Bind function, monads must also have a Return function that *lifts* or *wraps* a normal value T into a monadic value C<T>. Somewhat confusingly, the Return function is usually not called "Return" but takes on a different name, depending on the structure in question. For Option, this is the Some function we defined in chapter 5.

What's the Return function for IEnumerable? Because there are many implementations of IEnumerable, there are many possible ways to create an IEnumerable. In my functional library, I have a suitable Return function for IEnumerable called List. To stick with functional principles, List returns an immutable list:

```
using System.Collections.Immutable;

public static IEnumerable<T> List<T>(params T[] items)
   => items.ToImmutableList();
```

The List function doesn't only satisfy the requirement of the Return function, allowing us to raise a simple T into an IEnumerable<T>. It also, thanks to the params arguments, gives us a nice shorthand syntax for initializing lists:

```
using static F;

var empty  = List<string>();            // => []
var single = List("Andrej");            // => ["Andrej"]
var many   = List("Karina", "Natasha"); // => ["Karina", "Natasha"]
```

To summarize, a monad is a type M<T> for which the following functions are defined:

```
Return : T → M<T>

Bind   : (M<T>, (T → M<R>)) → M<R>
```

There are certain properties that Bind and Return must observe for the type to be considered a "proper" monad; these are called the *monad laws*. To avoid overloading this chapter with theory, I'll postpone a discussion of the monad laws until section 10.3.

Suffice it to say, Return should only do the *minimal* amount of work required to lift a T into a M<T> and nothing else. It should be as dumb as possible.

6.3.5 *Relationship between functors and monads*

I said that functors are types for which Map is defined, whereas monads are types for which Return and Bind are defined. You've also seen that both Option and IEnumerable are functors *and* monads because all these functions are defined.

Two questions naturally arise: Is every monad also a functor? Is every functor also a monad? To answer the first question, let's take another look at the signatures of the core functions we've seen so far:

```
Map    : (C<T>, (T → R)) → C<R>

Bind   : (C<T>, (T → C<R>)) → C<R>

Return : T → C<T>
```

If you have an implementation of Bind and Return, you can implement Map in terms of these: the function T → R that Map takes as input can be turned into a function of type T → C<R> by composing it with Return. This function can, in turn, be given as input to Bind.

To convince yourself of this, I propose in the exercises that you implement Map in terms of Bind and Return. Although the implementation is correct, it may be suboptimal, so normally, Map is given its own implementation that doesn't rely on Bind. Still, this means that every monad is also a functor.

As for the second question, it turns out that the answer is *no*: not every functor is a monad. Bind can't be defined in terms of Map, so having an implementation of Map gives you no guarantee that a Bind function can be defined. For example, some kinds of trees support Map but not Bind. On the other hand, for most of the types we'll discuss in this book, both Map and Bind can be defined.

6.4 *Filtering values with Where*

In chapter 2, you saw several uses of Where to filter the values of an IEnumerable. It turns out that Where can also be defined for Option as the following listing illustrates.

Listing 6.5 Filtering the inner value of an `Option`

```
public static Option<T> Where<T>
(
    this Option<T> optT,
    Func<T, bool> pred
)
=> optT.Match
(
    () => None,
    (t) => pred(t) ? optT : None
);
```

Given an `Option` and a predicate, you get back `Some` if the given `Option` is `Some`, *and* its inner value satisfies the given predicate; otherwise, you get `None`. Again, if you think of `Option` as a list with at most one item, this makes sense. Here's a simple usage:

```
bool IsNatural(int i) => i >= 0;
Option<int> ToNatural(string s) => Int.Parse(s).Where(IsNatural);

ToNatural("2")     // => Some(2)
ToNatural("-2")    // => None
ToNatural("hello") // => None
```

Here we use `Int.Parse` (defined in section 5.4.1) that returns an `Option`, signaling whether the string has been correctly parsed as an `int`. We then use `Where` to additionally enforce that the value be positive.

This concludes our initial exploration of the core functions. You'll see a couple more as you progress through the book, but the functions described up to this point can take you a surprisingly long way, as you'll see in the next chapter.

The many names of the core functions

One of the hurdles of learning FP is that the same construct is given different names in different languages or libraries. This is true of the core functions, so I've included the following table to help you make sense of these synonyms when you encounter them elsewhere.

LaYumba.Functional	LINQ	Common synonyms
Map	Select	fMap, Project, Lift
Bind	SelectMany	FlatMap, Chain, Collect, Then
Where	Where	Filter
ForEach	n/a	Iter
Return	n/a	Pure

When writing this book and the `LaYumba.Functional` library, I had to decide which names to choose for these functions, and these choices are necessarily somewhat arbitrary. `ForEach` and `Where` are good names and standard in .NET, but `Select` and `SelectMany` would be poor names if used for functors or monads other than `IEnumerable`. I chose to use `Map` and `Bind`, which are more general, shorter, and standard in the FP literature.

6.5 Combining Option and IEnumerable with Bind

I've mentioned that one way to look at `Option` is as a special case of a list that can either be empty (`None`) or contain exactly one value (`Some`). You can express this in code by making it possible to convert an `Option` into an `IEnumerable` as follows:

```
public struct Option<T>
{
```

```
   public IEnumerable<T> AsEnumerable()
   {
      if (isSome) yield return value!;
   }
}
```

If the Option is Some, the resulting IEnumerable yields one item; if it's None, it yields no items. Functions that map between functors, such as AsEnumerable, are called *natural transformations* and are quite useful in practice.

IEnumerable is often used to store data, and Option skips a computation when a value isn't present, so their intent is usually different. Still, there are some cases in which it's useful to combine them. In some scenarios, you end up with an IEnumerable<Option<T>> (or vice versa, an Option<IEnumerable<T>>) and want to flatten it into an IEnumerable<T>.

For example, let's go back to the example of a survey, where each participant is modeled as a Subject. Because it's optional for participants to disclose their age, we model Subject.Age as an Option<Age>:

```
record Subject(Option<Age> Age);

IEnumerable<Subject> Population => new[]
{
   new Subject(Age.Create(33)),
   new Subject(None),                        ◁──┐ This person did not
   new Subject(Age.Create(37)),                 │ disclose their age.
};
```

You have the details of your participants stored in an IEnumerable<Subject>. Now suppose you need to compute the average age of the participants. How can you go about that? You can start by selecting all the values for Age:

```
IEnumerable<Option<Age>> optionalAges = Population.Map(p => p.Age);
// => [Some(Age(33)), None, Some(Age(37))]
```

If you use Map to select the age of the survey takers, you get a list of options. And because an Option can be viewed as a list, optionalAges can be viewed as a list of lists. To translate this intuition into code, let's add some overloads to Bind that convert the Option into an IEnumerable, so that Bind can be applied as though we were flattening a nested IEnumerable:

```
public static IEnumerable<R> Bind<T, R>
   (this IEnumerable<T> list, Func<T, Option<R>> func)
   => list.Bind(t => func(t).AsEnumerable());

public static IEnumerable<R> Bind<T, R>
   (this Option<T> opt, Func<T, IEnumerable<R>> func)
   => opt.AsEnumerable().Bind(func);
```

Even though according to FP theory Bind should only work on one type of container, the fact that an Option can always be *promoted* to the more general IEnumerable makes these overloads valid and quite useful in practice:

- We can use the first overload to get an IEnumerable<T>, where Map would give us an IEnumerable<Option<T>> as in the current survey example.
- We can use the second overload to get an IEnumerable<T>, where Map would give us an Option<IEnumerable<T>>.

In the survey scenario, we can now use Bind to filter out all the Nones and get a list of all the ages that were actually given:

```
var optionalAges = Population.Map(p => p.Age);
// => [Some(Age(33)), None, Some(Age(37))]

var statedAges = Population.Bind(p => p.Age);
// => [Age(33), Age(37)]

var averageAge = statedAges.Map(age => age.Value).Average();
// => 35
```

This allows us to take advantage of the flattening nature of Bind to filter out all the None cases. The preceding output shows the results of calling both Map and Bind so that you can compare the results.

6.6 *Coding at different levels of abstraction*

Abstraction (in English, not in OOP) means that specific features of different concrete things are removed in order for a general, common feature to emerge: a concept. For example, when you say, "You'll see a row of houses," or "Put your ducks in a row," the *row* concept removes anything that makes ducks differ from houses and only captures their spatial disposition.

Types like IEnumerable and Option have such a conceptual abstraction at their core: all specific features of their inner value(s) are abstracted away. These types only capture the ability to enumerate the values or the possible absence of a value, respectively. The same can be said for most generic types. Let's try to generalize this so that what you've learned for Option can help you understand other constructs that you'll see later in the book (and in other libraries).

6.6.1 *Regular vs. elevated values*

When you're dealing with a type like, say, IEnumerable<int> or Option<Employee>, you're coding at a higher level of abstraction than when dealing with a non-generic type like int or Employee. Let's divide the world of values we deal with into two categories:

- *Regular values*, which we'll call T. String, int, Neighbor, or DayOfWeek, are all examples of regular values.
- *Elevated values*, which we'll call A<T>. Option<int>, IEnumerable<string>, Func<Neighbor>, or Task<bool>, are all examples of elevated values.

Here, elevated values imply an abstraction of the corresponding regular types.[5] These abstractions are constructs that enable us to better work with and represent opera-

---

[5] Other authors refer to elevated values as wrapped, amplified values, and so on.

tions on the underlying types. More technically put, an *abstraction* is a way to add an effect to the underlying type.[6] Let's look at some examples:

- Option adds the effect of *optionality*, which is not a T but the *possibility* of a T.
- IEnumerable adds the effect of *aggregation*, which is not a T or two but a *sequence* of T's.
- Func adds the effect of *laziness*, which is not a T but a *computation* that can be evaluated to obtain a T.
- Task adds the effect of *asynchrony*, which is not a T but a *promise* that at some point you'll get a T.

As you can see from the preceding examples, things that are very different in nature can be considered abstractions, so there's little point in trying to fit the concept into a box. It's more interesting to see how these abstractions can be put to work.

Coming back to regular versus elevated values, you can visualize these different kinds of values as in figure 6.5. This diagram shows an example of a regular type, int, with some sample values and the corresponding abstraction A<int>, where A could be an arbitrary abstraction. The arrows that take a regular value and wrap it in a corresponding A represent the Return function.

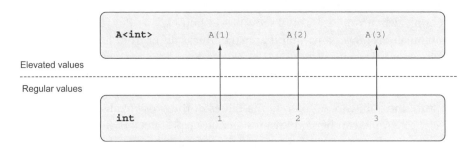

Figure 6.5 Return **lifts a regular into an elevated value.**

6.6.2 *Crossing levels of abstraction*

Now that we have this classification of types, we can classify functions accordingly. We have functions that remain within the same level of abstraction and functions that cross between levels of abstraction, as illustrated in figure 6.6.[7]

---

[6] In this context, *effect* has a completely different meaning and shouldn't be confused with *side effect*. This is unfortunate, but standard, terminology.

[7] This classification isn't exhaustive because you can envisage more categories where the application of a function would cause you to jump by several levels of abstraction or would take you from one type of abstraction to another. But these are probably the most usual kinds of functions you'll encounter, so the classification is still useful.

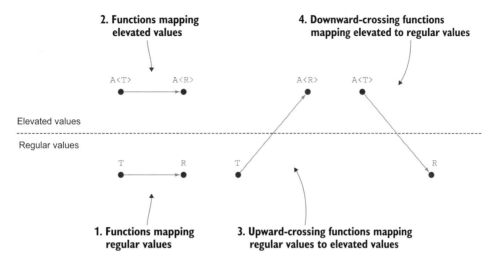

Figure 6.6   Functions classified in relation to levels of abstractions

Let's look at a few examples. The function `(int i) => i.ToString()` has signature `int → string`, so it maps one regular type to another and is clearly of the first kind.

The `Int.Parse` function we've been using has type `string → Option<int>`, so it's an upward-crossing function—the third kind. Scott Wlaschin calls these *world-crossing* functions because they go from the *world* of normal values `T` to the world of *elevated* values `E<T>` (extraterrestrial?).[8]

The `Return` function, which for any abstraction A has type `T → A<T>`, is a special case of an upward-crossing function that does nothing other than upward crossing. That's why I show `Return` as a vertical upward arrow and any other upward-crossing function as a diagonal arrow.

Functions of the second kind remain within the abstraction. For instance, the following function is a clear match:

```
(IEnumerable<int> ints) => ints.OrderBy(i => i)
```

Its signature is in the form `A<T> → A<R>`. But we should also include in this category any function in which we start with an `A<T>`, have some additional arguments, and ultimately end up with an `A<R>`. That is, any function whose application keeps us within the abstraction; its signature will be in the form `(A<T>, ...) → A<R>`. This includes many HOFs we've looked at, such as `Map`, `Bind`, `Where`, `OrderBy`, and others.

Finally, downward-crossing functions, in which we start with an elevated value and end up with a regular value, include `Average`, `Sum`, and `Count` for `IEnumerable` and `Match` for `Option`. Notice that, given an abstraction A, it's not always possible to define a downward counterpart to `Return`; there is often no vertical downward

---

[8] See Scott's "Understanding map and apply" article here: http://fsharpforfunandprofit.com/posts/elevated-world.

arrow. You can always lift an int into an Option<int>, but you can't *lower* an Option<int> to an int. What if it's None? Similarly, you can wrap a single Employee into an IEnumerable<Employee>, but there's no obvious way to reduce an IEnumerable<Employee> to a single Employee.

6.6.3 *Map vs. Bind, revisited*

Let's see how we can use this classification to better understand the difference between Map and Bind. Map takes an elevated value A<T> and a *regular* function T → R, and returns an elevated value of type A<R>, as figure 6.7 illustrates.

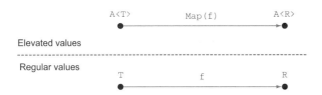

Figure 6.7 Map **in terms of regular vs. elevated values**

Bind also takes an elevated value A<T>, but then an *upward-crossing* function of type T → A<R>, and returns an elevated value of type A<R>, as figure 6.8 illustrates.

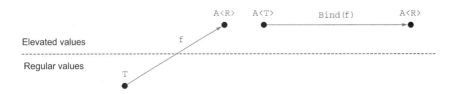

Figure 6.8 Bind **in terms of regular vs. elevated values**

The main difference is that Map takes a regular function, while Bind takes an upward-crossing function. If you use Map with an upward-crossing function of type T → A<R>, you'll end up with a nested value of type A<A<R>>. This is usually not the desired effect, and you should probably use Bind instead. Notice that both Map and Bind are in themselves functions that operate on elevated values because they both take an A<T> and yield an A<R>.

6.6.4 *Working at the right level of abstraction*

This idea of working at different levels of abstraction is important. If you always deal with regular values, you'll probably be stuck with low-level operations, such as for loops, null checks, and so on. Working at such a low level of abstraction is inefficient and error-prone. There's a definite sweet spot when working within one abstraction, as in the following snippet (from chapter 1):

```
Enumerable.Range(1, 100).
   Where(i => i % 20 == 0).
   OrderBy(i => -i).
   Select(i => $"{i}%")
 // => ["100%", "80%", "60%", "40%", "20%"]
```

Once you've used `Range` to go from regular values to an `IEnumerable<int>`, all following computations stay within the `IEnumerable` abstraction. That is, staying within one abstraction gives you the ability to nicely compose several operations—something we'll delve into in the next chapter.

There's also the danger of going too deep if you're dealing with values in the form `A<B<C<D<T>>>>`, where each level adds an abstraction and it's difficult to deal with the deeply buried `T`. This is something I'll address in chapter 17.

In this chapter, you've seen the implementation of some core functions for working with `Option` and `IEnumerable`. Although the implementations are simple, you've seen how this has given us a rich API for working with `Option`, just as you're used to with `IEnumerable`. Several common operations can be defined for both `Option` and `IEnumerable`—patterns that apply to different kinds of structures. With this API in place and a better understanding of the core functions of FP, you're ready to tackle more complex scenarios.

Exercises

1 Implement `Map` for `ISet<T>` and `IDictionary<K, T>`. (Tip: start by writing down the signature in arrow notation.)

2 Implement `Map` for `Option` and `IEnumerable` in terms of `Bind` and `Return`.

3 Use `Bind` and an `Option`-returning `Lookup` function as defined in section 5.4.2 to implement `GetWorkPermit` (shown in the following code snippet). Then enrich the implementation so that `GetWorkPermit` returns `None` if the work permit has expired.

4 Use `Bind` to implement `AverageYearsWorkedAtTheCompany` (shown in the following code snippet). Only employees who have left should be included:

```
Option<WorkPermit> GetWorkPermit(Dictionary<string, Employee> employees
   , string employeeId) => // your implementation here...

double AverageYearsWorkedAtTheCompany(List<Employee> employees)
   => // your implementation here...

public record Employee
(
   string Id,
   Option<WorkPermit> WorkPermit,
```

```
    DateTime JoinedOn,
    Option<DateTime> LeftOn
);

public record WorkPermit
(
    string Number,
    DateTime Expiry
);
```

Summary

- Structures like Option<T> and IEnumerable<T> can be seen as containers or abstractions, allowing you to work more effectively with the underlying values of type T.
- You can distinguish between regular values (say, T) and elevated values (like Option<T> or IEnumerable<T>).
- The core functions of FP that allow you to work effectively with elevated values include
  - Return, which takes a regular value and lifts it into an elevated value
  - Map, which applies a function to the inner value(s) of a structure and returns a new structure wrapping the result
  - ForEach, a side-effecting variant of Map, which takes an action that it performs for each of the container's inner values
  - Bind, which maps an Option-returning function onto an Option and flattens the result to avoid producing a nested Option, similarly for IEnumerable and other structures
  - Where, which filters the inner value(s) of a structure according to a given predicate
- Types for which Map is defined are called *functors*. Types for which Return and Bind are defined are called *monads*.

Designing programs
with function composition

7

This chapter covers

- Defining workflows with function composition and method chaining
- Writing functions that compose well
- An end-to-end example of handling server requests

Function composition is not only powerful and expressive but also pleasant to work with. It's used to some extent in any programming style, but in FP, it's used extensively. For example, have you noticed that when you use LINQ to work with lists, you can get a lot done with only a few lines of code? That's because LINQ is a functional API, designed with composition in mind.

In this chapter, we'll cover the basic concept and techniques of function composition and illustrate its use with LINQ. We'll also implement an end-to-end server-side workflow in which we'll use the Option API introduced in chapter 6. This example illustrates many of the ideas and benefits of the functional approach, so we'll end the chapter with a discussion of those.

7.1   *Function composition*

Let's start by reviewing function composition and how it relates to method chaining. Function composition is part of any programmer's implicit knowledge. It's a mathematical concept you learn in school and then use every day without thinking about it too much. Let's quickly brush up on the definition.

7.1.1   *Brushing up on function composition*

Given two functions, *f* and *g*, you can define a function *h* to be the composition of those two functions, notated as follows:

$$h = f \cdot g$$

Applying *h* to a value *x* is the same as applying *g* to *x* and then applying *f* to the result:

$$h(x) = (f \cdot g)(x) = f(g(x))$$

For example, say you want to get an email address for someone working at Manning. You can have a function calculate the local part (identifying the person) and another append the domain:

```
record Person(string FirstName, string LastName);

static string AbbreviateName(Person p)
   => Abbreviate(p.FirstName) + Abbreviate(p.LastName);

static string AppendDomain(string localPart)
   => $"{localPart}@manning.com";

static string Abbreviate(string s)
   => s.Substring(0, Math.Min(2, s.Length)).ToLower();
```

AbbreviateName and AppendDomain are two functions that you can compose to get a new function that yields the Manning email for my hypothetical collaborator. Take a look at the following listing.

Listing 7.1   Defining a function as the composition of two existing functions

```
Func<Person, string> emailFor =
   p => AppendDomain(AbbreviateName(p));        ◁─┐  emailFor composes AppendDomain
                                                  │  with AbbreviateName.
var joe = new Person("Joe", "Bloggs");
var email = emailFor(joe);

email // => jobl@manning.com
```

There are a couple of things worth noting. First, you can only compose functions with matching types: if you're composing (*f · g*), the output of *g* must be assignable to the input type of *f*.

Second, in function composition, functions appear in the reverse order in which they're performed, so *f · g* is sometimes read as "*f* after *g*." For example, in AppendDomain(AbbreviateName(p)), you *first* execute the rightmost function and then the one to its left. This is not ideal for readability, especially if you want to compose several functions.

C# doesn't have any special syntactic support for function composition, and although you could define a HOF `Compose` to compose two or more functions, this doesn't improve readability. This is why in C# it's best to resort to method chaining instead.

7.1.2 Method chaining

The method chaining syntax (that is, chaining the invocation of several methods with the `.` operator) provides a more readable way of achieving function composition in C#. Given an expression, you can chain to it any method that's defined as an instance or extension method on the type of the expression. For instance, the previous example would need to be modified as follows:

```
static string AbbreviateName(this Person p)        ◁──┐
    => Abbreviate(p.FirstName) + Abbreviate(p.LastName);   The this keyword makes
                                                           this an extension method
static string AppendDomain(this string localPart)  ◁──┘
    => $"{localPart}@manning.com";
```

You can now chain these methods to obtain the email for the person. The following listing shows this approach.

Listing 7.2 Using method chaining syntax to compose functions

```
var joe = new Person("Joe", "Bloggs");
var email = joe.AbbreviateName().AppendDomain();

email // => jobl@manning.com
```

Notice that now the extension methods appear in the order in which they will be executed. This significantly improves readability, especially as the complexity of the workflow increases (longer method names, additional parameters, more methods to be chained), and it's why method chaining is the preferable way of achieving function composition in C#.

A common misconception about extension methods

Extension methods are called with the `.` operator, like instance methods, yet the semantics are different from instance methods. For example, suppose you define a type `Circle` like this:

```
record Circle(Point Center, double Radius);
record Point(double X, double Y);
```

If you now define methods `Move` and `Scale` as instance methods on `Circle`, that implies that a `Circle` *knows* how to move/scale itself or *is responsible for* moving itself. That's an OO way of seeing things.

(continued)

In FP, on the other hand, we would put this logic into functions that are separate from the data they act on (more on this in section 11.4). For example, take a look at the following:

```
                            ┌─ A module of functions
                            │  for working with circles
static class Geometry  ◁────┘
{
    static Circle Move(this Circle c, double x, double y) => new
    (
        Center: new Point(c.Center.X + x, c.Center.Y + y), ◁──┐ Yields a circle
        Radius: c.Radius                                      │ that was moved
    );

    static Circle Scale(this Circle c, double factor) => new
    (
        Center: c.Center,
        Radius: c.Radius * factor    ◁──┐ Yields a circle
    );                                  │ that was scaled
}
```

The fact that we define `Move` and `Scale` as extension methods allows us to call them like this:

```
Circle Modify(this Circle c)
    => c
        .Move(10, 10)
        .Scale(2)
```

This is equivalent to but more readable than the corresponding invocation without the extension method syntax:

```
Circle Modify(this Circle c)
    => Scale(Move(c, 10, 10), 2)
```

Developers steeped in OOP tend to treat extension methods as though they were instance methods; e.g., just because `Move` marks the given circle with the `this` modifier, they tend to feel that `Move` *belongs* to `Circle` or that a `Circle` therefore *knows* or *is responsible for* moving itself.

This is a misconception you should leave behind. In the current example, you should think of `Move` and `Scale` simply as functions that process the given data; the fact that we're using them as extension methods is purely for readability.

7.1.3 *Composition in the elevated world*

Function composition is so important that it should also hold in the world of elevated values. Let's stay with the current example of determining a person's email address, but now we have an `Option<Person>` as a starting value. You would assume that the following holds:

```
Func<Person, string> emailFor =              ┌─ emailFor is composed of Append-
    p => AppendDomain(AbbreviateName(p));  ◁─┘ Domain with AbbreviateName.
```

```
var opt = Some(new Person("Joe", "Bloggs"));

var a = opt.Map(emailFor);

var b = opt.Map(AbbreviateName)
           .Map(AppendDomain);

a.Equals(b) // => true
```

Maps the composed functions

Maps `AbbreviateName` and `AppendDomain` in separate steps

Whether you map `AbbreviateName` and `AppendDomain` in separate steps or map their composition `emailFor` in a single step, the result shouldn't change. You should be able to safely refactor between these two forms.

More generally, if $h = f \cdot g$, then mapping h onto a functor should be equivalent to mapping g over that functor and then mapping f over the result. This should hold for any functor and for any pair of functions—it's one of the *functor laws*, so any implementation of `Map` should observe it.[1]

If this sounds complicated, that's probably because it describes something that you intuitively feel should always obviously hold. Indeed, it's not easy to break this law, but you could come up with a mischievous functor that, say, keeps an inner counter of how many times `Map` is applied (or otherwise changes its state with every call to `Map`), and then the preceding wouldn't hold because b would have a greater inner count than a.

Simply put, `Map` should apply a function to the functor's inner value(s) and do nothing else so that function composition holds when working with functors just as it does with normal values. The beauty of this is that you can use any functional library in any programming language and use any functor with confidence that a refactoring such as changing between a and b in the preceding snippet will be safe.

7.2 *Thinking in terms of data flow*

You can write entire programs with function composition. Each function somehow processes its input, and the output becomes the input to the following function. When you do this, you start to look at your program in terms of data flow: the program is just a set of functions, and data flows through the program through one function and into the next. Figure 7.1 illustrates a linear flow—the simplest and most useful kind.

Figure 7.1   Data flowing through a sequence of functions

7.2.1 *Using LINQ's composable API*

In the previous example, we made the `AbbreviateName` and `AppendDomain` methods chainable by making them extension methods. This is also the approach taken in the design of LINQ, and if you look at `System.Linq.Enumerable`, you'll see that it

---

[1]   There's a second, even simpler functor law: if you `Map` the identity function $(x \rightarrow x)$ over a functor f, the resulting functor is identical to f. Simply put, the identity function should hold in the elevated world of functors.

contains dozens of extension methods for working with `IEnumerable`. Let's look at an example of composing functions with LINQ.

Imagine that, given a population, you want to find the average earnings of the richest quartile (that is, the richest 25% of people in the target population). You could write something like the following listing.

Listing 7.3   Defining a query by chaining methods in `Linq.Enumerable`

```
record Person(decimal Earnings);

static decimal AverageEarningsOfRichestQuartile(List<Person> population)
   => population
      .OrderByDescending(p => p.Earnings)
      .Take(population.Count / 4)
      .Select(p => p.Earnings)
      .Average();
```

Notice how cleanly you can write this query using LINQ (compared to, say, writing the same query imperatively with control flow statements). You may have some sense that internally the code will iterate over the list and that `Take` will have an `if` check to only yield the requested number of items, but you don't really care. Instead, you can lay out your function calls in the form of a flat workflow—a linear sequence of instructions:

1. Sort the population (richest at the top).
2. Only take the top 25%.
3. Take each person's earnings.
4. Compute their average.

Notice how similar the code is to the workflow description. Let's look at it in terms of data flow: you can see the `AverageEarningsOfRichestQuartile` function as a simple program. Its input is a `List<Person>`, and the output is a `decimal`.

Furthermore, `AverageEarningsOfRichestQuartile` is effectively the composition of four functions, so that the input data flows through four transformative steps and is, thus, stepwise transformed into the output value as figure 7.2 shows.

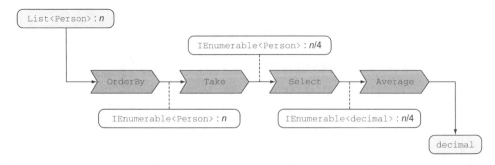

Figure 7.2   Data flow through the `AverageEarningsOfRichestQuartile` function

The first function, `OrderByDescending`, preserves the type of the data and yields a population sorted by earnings. The second step also preserves the type of the data but changes the cardinality: if the input population is composed of n people, `Take` now only yields $n/4$ people. `Select` preserves the cardinality but changes the type to a list of `decimal`s, and `Average` again changes the type to return a single `decimal` value.[2]

Let's try to generalize this idea of data flow so that it applies not only to queries on `IEnumerable` but to data in general. When something of interest happens in your program (a request, a mouse click, or simply your program being started), you can think of that something as *input*. That input, which is data, then goes through a series of transformations as the data flows through a sequence of functions in your program.

7.2.2 *Writing functions that compose well*

The simple `AverageEarningsOfRichestQuartile` function shown in listing 7.3 demonstrates how the design of the LINQ library allows you to compose general-purpose functions into specific queries. There are some properties that make some functions more composable than others:[3]

- *Pure*—If your function has side effects, it's less reusable.
- *Chainable*—A `this` argument (implicit on instance methods and explicit on extension methods) makes it possible to compose through chaining.
- *General*—The more specific the function, the fewer cases where it's useful to compose it.
- *Shape-preserving*—The function preserves the shape of the structure, so if it takes an `IEnumerable`, it returns an `IEnumerable`, and so on.

And, naturally, functions are more composable than actions. Because an `Action` has no output value, it's a dead end, so it can only come at the end of a pipeline.

Notice that the LINQ functions we've used all score 100% based on these criteria, with the exception of `Average`, which is not shape-preserving. Also note that the core functions we defined in the `Option` API do well.

How composable is `AverageEarningsOfRichestQuartile`? Well, about 40%: it's pure, and it has an output value, but it's not an extension method, and it's extremely specific. To demonstrate this, look at some code that consumes the function as part of a unit test:

```
[TestCase(ExpectedResult = 75000)]
public decimal AverageEarningsOfRichestQuartile()
{
    var population = Range(1, 8)
        .Select(i => new Person(Earnings: i * 10000))
        .ToList();
```

---

[2] Average also causes the whole chain of methods to be evaluated because it's the only "greedy" method in the chain.

[3] These are general guidelines. It will always be possible to compose functions that don't have these properties, but in practice, these properties are good indicators of how easy and useful it will be to compose those functions.

```
    return PopulationStatistics
        .AverageEarningsOfRichestQuartile(population);
}
```

The test passes, but the code also shows that `AverageEarningsOfRichestQuartile` doesn't share the qualities of the LINQ methods it's composed of: it's not chainable, and it's so specific that you'd hardly hope to reuse it. Let's change that:

1 Split it into two more general functions: `AverageEarnings` (so you can query the average earnings for any segment of the population) and `RichestQuartile` (after all, there are many other properties of the richest quartile you may be interested in).

2 Make them extension methods so they can be chained:

```
static decimal AverageEarnings(this IEnumerable<Person> pop)
    => pop.Average(p => p.Earnings);

static IEnumerable<Person> RichestQuartile(this IEnumerable<Person> pop)
    => pop.OrderByDescending(p => p.Earnings)
        .Take(pop.Count / 4);
```

Notice how easy it was to do this refactoring! This is because of the compositional nature of the function we refactored: the new functions just compose fewer of the original building blocks. (If you had an implementation of the same logic with `for` and `if` statements, the refactoring would probably not have been as easy.) You can now rewrite the test as follows:

```
[TestCase(ExpectedResult = 75000)]
public decimal AverageEarningsOfRichestQuartile()
    => SamplePopulation
        .RichestQuartile()
        .AverageEarnings();

List<Person> SamplePopulation
    => Range(1, 8)
        .Select(i => new Person(Earnings: i * 10000))
        .ToList();
```

You can see how much more readable the test is now. By refactoring to smaller functions and to the extension method syntax, you've created more composable functions and a more readable interface.

> **TIP** If you compose two pure functions, the resulting function is also pure, giving you all the benefits discussed in chapter 3. As a result, libraries consisting mainly of pure, composable functions (like LINQ) tend to be powerful and pleasant to use.

In this section, you've seen how LINQ provides (among many other things) a set of readily composable functions that work effectively with `IEnumerable`. Next, we'll see how we can use declarative, flat workflows when working with `Option`. Let's start by clarifying what we mean by workflows and why they matter.

7.3   *Programming workflows*

Workflows are a powerful way of understanding and expressing application requirements. A *workflow* is a meaningful sequence of operations leading to a desired result. For example, a cooking recipe describes the workflow for preparing a dish.

Workflows can be effectively modeled through function composition. Each operation in the workflow can be performed by a function, and these functions can be composed into *function pipelines* that perform the workflow, just as you saw in the previous example involving data flowing through different transformations in a LINQ query.

We're now going to look at a more complex workflow of a server processing a command. The scenario is that of a user requesting to make a money transfer through the Bank of Codeland (BOC) online banking application. We're only concentrating on the server side, so the workflow is kicked off when the server receives a request to make a transfer. We can write a specification for the workflow as follows:

1 Validate the requested transfer.
2 Load the account.
3 If the account has sufficient funds, debit the amount from the account.
4 Persist the changes to the account.
5 Wire the funds via the SWIFT network.[4]

7.3.1   *A simple workflow for validation*

The entire money transfer workflow is fairly complex, so to get us started, let's simplify it as follows:

1 Validate the requested transfer.
2 Book the transfer (all subsequent steps).

Let's say that all the steps following validation are part of the subworkflow of actually booking the transfer, which should only be triggered if validation passes (see figure 7.3).

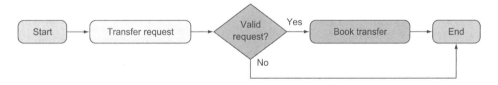

Figure 7.3   Example workflow: validating a request before processing it

Let's take a stab at implementing this high-level workflow. Assume that the server uses ASP.NET Core to expose an HTTP API and that it's set up so that requests are authenticated and routed to the appropriate MVC controller (in section 9.5.3, I'll show you

---

4 SWIFT is an interbank network; as far as we're concerned, it's just a third-party application with which we need to communicate.

how to build Web APIs without the need for controllers), making it the entry point for implementing the workflow:

```
using Microsoft.AspNetCore.Mvc;

public class MakeTransferController : ControllerBase
{
   IValidator<MakeTransfer> validator;

   [HttpPost, Route("api/MakeTransfer")]
   public void MakeTransfer
      ([FromBody] MakeTransfer transfer)
   {
      if (validator.IsValid(transfer))
         Book(transfer);
   }

   void Book(MakeTransfer transfer)
      => // actually book the transfer...
}
```

POST **requests to this route are routed to this method.**

Deserializes the request body into a MakeTransfer

The details about the requested transfer are captured in a MakeTransfer type, which is sent in the body of the user's request. Validation is delegated to a service on which the controller depends, which implements this interface:

```
public interface IValidator<T>
{
   bool IsValid(T t);
}
```

Now to the interesting part, the workflow itself:

```
public void MakeTransfer([FromBody] MakeTransfer transfer)
{
   if (validator.IsValid(transfer))
      Book(transfer);
}

void Book(MakeTransfer transfer)
   => // actually book the transfer...
```

That's the imperative approach of explicit control flow. I'm always wary of using ifs: a single if may look harmless, but if you start allowing one if, nothing is keeping you from having dozens of nested ifs as additional requirements come in, and the complexity that ensues is what makes applications error-prone and difficult to reason about. Next, we'll look at how to use function composition instead.

7.3.2 *Refactoring with data flow in mind*

Remember that idea we had about data flowing through various functions? Let's try to think of the transfer request as data flowing through validation and into the Book method that performs the transfer. Figure 7.4 shows how this would look.

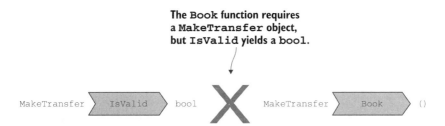

Figure 7.4   Viewing validation as a step in the data flow

There's a bit of a problem with types: `IsValid` returns a Boolean, whereas `Book` requires a `MakeTransfer` object, so these two functions don't compose, as figure 7.5 illustrates.

The `Book` function requires a `MakeTransfer` object, but `IsValid` yields a `bool`.

Figure 7.5   A type mismatch preventing function composition

Furthermore, we need to ensure that the request data flows through the validation and into `Book` *only* if it passes validation. This is where `Option` can help us: we can use `None` to represent an invalid transfer request and `Some<MakeTransfer>` for a valid one.

Notice that, in doing so, we're expanding the meaning we give to `Option`. We interpret `Some` not just to indicate the presence of data, but also the presence of *valid* data, just like we do in the smart constructor pattern. We can now rewrite the controller method as the following listing demonstrates.

Listing 7.4   Using `Option` to represent passing/failing validation

```
public void MakeTransfer([FromBody] MakeTransfer transfer)
   => Some(transfer)
       .Where(validator.IsValid)
       .ForEach(Book);

void Book(MakeTransfer transfer)
   => // actually book the transfer...
```

We lift the transfer data into an `Option` and apply the `IsValid` predicate with `Where`; this yields a `None` if validation fails, in which case, `Book` won't be called. In this example, `Where` is the highly composable function that allows us to glue everything together. This style may be unfamiliar, but it's actually very readable: "Keep the transfer if it's valid, then book it."

7.3.3   *Composition leads to greater flexibility*

Once you have a workflow in place, it becomes easy to make changes, such as adding a step to the workflow. Suppose you want to normalize the request before validating it so that things like whitespace and casing don't cause validation to fail.

How would you go about it? You need to define a function that performs the new step and then integrate it into your workflow. The following listing shows how to do this.

```
public void MakeTransfer([FromBody] MakeTransfer transfer)
   => Some(transfer)
      .Map(Normalize)
      .Where(validator.IsValid)            ◁──┐ Plugs a new step
      .ForEach(Book);                          │ into the workflow

MakeTransfer Normalize(MakeTransfer request) => // ...
```

More generally, if you have a business workflow, you should aim to express it by composing a set of functions, where *each function represents a step in the workflow,* and their composition represents the workflow itself. Figure 7.6 shows this one-to-one translation from steps in the workflow to functions in a pipeline.

Figure 7.6 Modeling a linear workflow with function composition

To be precise, in this case we're not composing these functions directly—as you've seen, the signatures don't allow this—but rather as arguments to the HOFs defined in Option, as figure 7.7 shows.

Figure 7.7 The Option API helps us compose existing functions.

Next, let's see how we can implement the rest of the workflow.

7.4   *An introduction to functional domain modeling*

Domain modeling means creating a representation for the entities and behaviors specific to the business domain in question. In this case, we need a representation for the bank account from which the transferred funds will be debited. We'll look at domain modeling in more detail in chapter 11, but it's good to see the fundamentals in the current scenario.

Let's start with a ridiculously simplistic representation of a bank account that just captures the account balance. This is enough to illustrate the fundamental differences between the OO and functional approaches. The following listing shows how an OO implementation could look.

Listing 7.6 In OOP, objects capture both data and behavior

```
public class Account
{
    public decimal Balance { get; private set; }

    public Account(decimal balance) { Balance = balance; }

    public void Debit(decimal amount)
    {
        if (Balance < amount)
            throw new InvalidOperationException("Insufficient funds");

        Balance -= amount;
    }
}
```

In OOP, data and behavior live in the same object, and methods in the object can typically modify the object's state. By contrast, in FP data is captured with "dumb" data objects while behavior is encoded in functions, so we'll separate the two. We'll use an `AccountState` object that only contains state and a static `Account` class that contains functions for interacting with an account.

More importantly, notice how the preceding implementation of `Debit` is full of side effects: exceptions if business validation fails and state mutation. Instead, we're going to make `Debit` a pure function. Instead of modifying the existing instance, we'll return a new `AccountState` with the new balance.

What about avoiding the debit if the funds on the account are insufficient? Well, by now you should have learned the trick! Use `None` to signal an invalid state and skip the following computations! The following listing provides a functional counterpart to the code in listing 7.6.

Listing 7.7 FP separates data and behavior

```
public record AccountState(decimal Balance);      ◁─┐ An immutable record,
                                                     │ only containing data
public static class Account   ◁─┤ Only contains pure logic
{
    public static Option<AccountState> Debit
        (this AccountState current, decimal amount)
        => (current.Balance < amount)               ┌ None here signals that the
            ? None                          ◁─┘     │ debit operation failed.
            : Some(new AccountState(current.Balance - amount));   ◁─┐
}
                                               Some wraps the new state of the
                                               account as a result of the operation.
```

Notice how the OO implementation of Debit in listing 7.6 isn't composable: it has side effects and returns void. The functional counterpart in listing 7.7 is completely different: it's a pure function and returns a value, which can be used as input to the next function in the chain. Next, we'll integrate this into the end-to-end workflow.

7.5   *An end-to-end server-side workflow*

Now that we have the main workflow skeleton and our simple domain model in place, we're ready to complete the end-to-end workflow. We still need to implement the Book function, which should do the following:

- Load the account.
- If the account has sufficient funds, debit the amount from the account.
- Persist the changes to the account.
- Wire the funds via the SWIFT network.

Let's define two services that capture DB and SWIFT access:

```
public interface IRepository<T>
{
   Option<T> Get(Guid id);
   void Save(Guid id, T t);
}

interface ISwiftService
{
   void Wire(MakeTransfer transfer, AccountState account);
}
```

Using these interfaces is still an OO pattern, but let's stick to it for now (you'll see how to use *just* functions in chapter 9). Note that IRepository.Get returns an Option to acknowledge the fact that there's no guarantee that an item will be found for any given Guid. The following listing displays the fully implemented controller, including the Book method that was missing until now.

Listing 7.8   Implementation of the end-to-end workflow in the controller

```
public class MakeTransferController : ControllerBase
{
   IValidator<MakeTransfer> validator;
   IRepository<AccountState> accounts;
   ISwiftService swift;

   public void MakeTransfer([FromBody] MakeTransfer transfer)
      => Some(transfer)
         .Map(Normalize)
         .Where(validator.IsValid)
         .ForEach(Book);

   void Book(MakeTransfer transfer)
      => accounts.Get(transfer.DebitedAccountId)
         .Bind(account => account.Debit(transfer.Amount))
```

```
      .ForEach(account =>
        {
          accounts.Save(transfer.DebitedAccountId, account);
          swift.Wire(transfer, account);
        });
}
```

Let's look at the newly added `Book` method. Notice that `accounts.Get` returns an `Option` (in case no account was found with the given ID), and `Debit` also returns an `Option` (in case there were insufficient funds). Therefore, we compose these two operations with `Bind`. Finally, we use `ForEach` to perform the side effects we need: saving the account with the new balance and wiring the funds to SWIFT.

There are a couple of obvious shortcomings in the overall solution. First, we're effectively using `Option` to stop the computation if something goes wrong along the way, but we're not giving any feedback to the user as to whether the request was successful or why. In chapter 8, you'll see how to remedy this with `Either` and related structures; this allows you to capture error details without fundamentally altering the approach shown here.

Another problem is that saving the account and wiring the funds should be done atomically: if the process fails in the middle, we could have debited the funds without sending them to SWIFT. Solutions to this issue tend to be infrastructure-specific and aren't specific to FP.[5] Now that I've come clean about what's missing, let's discuss the good bits.

7.5.1 Expressions vs. statements

Something that should stand out when you look at the controller in listing 7.8 is that there are no `if` statements, no `for` statements, and so forth. In fact, there are practically *no statements* at all!

One fundamental difference between the functional and imperative style is that imperative code relies on statements; functional code relies on expressions. (For a refresher on how these differ, see the "Expressions, statements, declarations" sidebar.) In essence, expressions have a value; statements don't. While expressions such as function calls *can* have side effects, statements *only* have side effects, so they don't compose.

If you create workflows by composing functions as we have, side effects naturally gravitate towards the end of the workflow: functions like `ForEach` don't have a useful return value, so that's where the pipeline ends. This helps to isolate side effects, even visually.

---

[5] This problem is difficult and fairly common in distributed architectures. If you're storing the accounts in a database, you could be tempted to open a DB transaction, save the account within the transaction, wire the funds, and only commit once that's done. This still leaves you unprotected if the process dies after wiring the funds but before committing the transaction. A thorough solution is to atomically create a single task, representing both operations, and have a process that performs both and removes the task only when *both* have successfully been carried out. This means that any of the operations are potentially performed more than once so provisions need to be made for the operations to be idempotent. A reference text on these sorts of problems and solutions is *Enterprise Integration Patterns* by Gregor Hohpe and Bobby Woolf (Addison-Wesley, 2004).

The idea of programming without using statements can seem quite foreign at first, but as the code in this and previous chapters demonstrates, it's perfectly feasible in C#. Notice that the only statements are the two within the last ForEach. This is fine because we want to have two side effects—there's no point hiding that.

I recommend you try coding using just expressions. It doesn't guarantee good design, but it certainly promotes better design.

Expressions, statements, declarations

Expressions include anything that produces a value such as these:

- Literals such as 123 or "something"
- Variables such as *x*
- Operators and operands such as a || b, b ? x : y or new object()

Expressions can be used wherever a value is expected; for example, as arguments in function invocations or as return values of a function.

Statements are instructions to the program, such as assignments, conditionals (if/else), loops, and so on.

Invocations are considered expressions if they produce a value, for example "hello".ToUpper() or Math.Sqrt(Math.Abs(n) + m). They're considered statements if they don't; that is, if the method being invoked returns void.

Declarations (of classes, methods, fields, and so on) are often considered statements but for the purpose of this discussion are best thought of as a category in their own right. Whether you prefer statements or expressions, declarations are equally necessary, so they're best left out of the statements versus expressions argument.

7.5.2   *Declarative vs. imperative*

When we prefer expressions to statements, our code becomes more declarative. It declares what's being computed rather than instructing the computer on which specific operations to carry out. In other words, it's higher-level and closer to the way in which we communicate with other human beings. For example, the top-level workflow in our controller reads as follows:

```
=> Some(transfer)
   .Map(Normalize)
   .Where(validator.IsValid)
   .ForEach(Book);
```

Discounting things like Map and Where, which essentially act as glue between the operations, this reads much like the verbal, bullet-point definition of the workflow. This means the code is closer to the spoken language and, hence, easier to understand and to maintain. Let's contrast the imperative and declarative styles in table 7.1.

Table 7.1 Comparing the imperative and declarative styles

Imperative	Declarative
Tells the computer what to do (for example, "Add this item to this list").	Tells the computer what you want (for example, "Give me all the items that match a condition").
Relies mainly on statements.	Relies mainly on expressions.
Side effects are ubiquitous.	Side effects naturally gravitate toward the end of the expression evaluation.[a]
Statements can be readily translated into machine instructions.	There is more indirection (hence, potentially more optimizations) in the process of translating expressions to machine instructions.

[a] This is because side-effecting functions don't normally return a value that can be used in further evaluation.

Another thing worth pointing out is that, because declarative code is higher-level, it's hard to look at the implementation and see that it works without the confidence of unit tests. This is actually a good thing: it's much better to convince yourself through unit tests than to rely on the false confidence of looking at the code and seeing that it looks like it's doing the right thing.

7.5.3 *The functional take on layering*

The implementation we've looked at sheds some light on a natural way to structure applications with function composition. In any reasonably complex application, we tend to introduce some form of *layering*, distinguishing a hierarchy of high- to low-level components where the highest-level components are entry points into the application (in our example, the controller), and the lowest are exit points (in our example, the repository and SWIFT service).

Unfortunately, I've worked on many projects where layering is more of a curse than a blessing, as you need to traverse several layers for any operation. This is because there's a tendency to structure invocations between layers, as in figure 7.8.

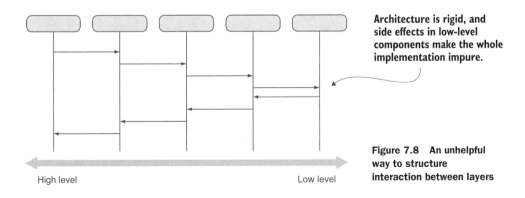

Architecture is rigid, and side effects in low-level components make the whole implementation impure.

High level   Low level

Figure 7.8 An unhelpful way to structure interaction between layers

In this approach, there's an implicit assumption that a layer should only call into an immediately adjacent layer. This makes the architecture rigid. Furthermore, it means that the whole implementation will be impure: because the lowest-level components have side effects (they typically access the DB or external APIs), everything above is also impure—a function that calls an impure function is itself impure.

In the approach demonstrated in this chapter, the interaction between layers looks more like figure 7.9.

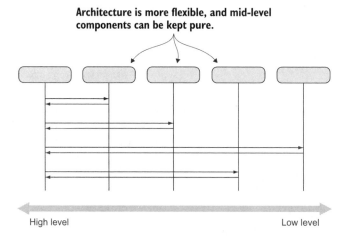

Architecture is more flexible, and mid-level components can be kept pure.

High level   Low level

Figure 7.9   A top-level workflow composing functions exposed by lower-level components

A higher-level component can depend on any lower-level component but not vice versa. This is a more flexible and effective approach to layering. In our example, there's a top-level workflow that composes functions exposed by lower-level components. There are a couple of advantages here:

- *You get a clear, synthetic overview of the workflow within the top-level component.* This doesn't preclude you from defining subworkflows within a lower-level component.
- *Mid-level components can be pure.* In our example, the interaction between components looks like figure 7.10.

As you can see, the domain representation can (and should!) consist of pure functions only because there's no interaction with lower-level components; there's only computation of a result based on inputs. The same could be true of other functionality like validation (depending on what the validation consists of). Therefore, this approach helps you to isolate side effects and facilitates testing. Because the domain model and other mid-level components are pure functions, they can easily be tested without the need for mocks.

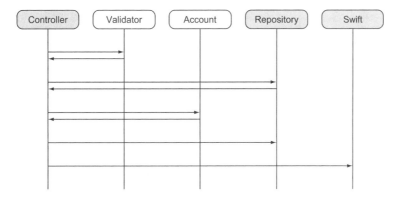

Figure 7.10 Mid-level components can be pure.

Exercises

1 Without looking at any code or documentation, write the type of the functions
   OrderBy, Take, and Average, which were used to implement AverageEarnings-
   OfRichestQuartile.

2 Check your answer with the MSDN documentation: http://mng.bz/MvwD.
   How is Average different?

3 Implement a general-purpose Compose function that takes two unary functions
   and returns the composition of the two.

Summary

- Function composition means combining two or more functions into a new
  function, and it's widely used in FP.
- In C#, the extension method syntax allows you to use function composition by
  chaining methods.
- Functions lend themselves to being composed if they are pure, chainable, and
  shape-preserving.
- Workflows are sequences of operations that can be effectively expressed in your
  programs through function pipelines: one function for each step of the work-
  flow with the output of each function fed into the next.
- The LINQ library has a rich set of easily composable functions to work with
  IEnumerables, and you can use it as inspiration to write your own APIs.
- Functional code prefers expressions over statements, unlike imperative code.
- Relying on expressions leads to your code becoming more declarative and,
  hence, more readable.

Part 3

Functional designs

In this part, we'll widen our focus to designing entire applications or tackling cross-cutting concerns with a functional approach.

Chapter 8 discusses the functional take on validation and error handling.

Chapter 9 shows how you can modularize and compose an application with functions only, using techniques like partial application and the powerful Aggregate function (fold).

Chapter 10 discusses another core function, Apply. It also teaches you about implementing the LINQ query pattern and compares some functional patterns like applicatives and monads. Chapter 10 also introduces a technique called property-based testing, which verifies that your code observes certain properties by throwing random data at it.

Chapter 11 discusses the functional approach to representing state, identity, and change through immutable data objects, while chapter 12 discusses immutable data structures. These principles can be applied not only to in-memory data but also at the database level, and this is shown in chapter 13.

By the end of part 3, you'll have acquired a set of tools enabling you to effectively tackle many common scenarios using an end-to-end functional approach.

Functional error handling

Error handling is an important part of our applications. It's also one aspect in which the functional and imperative programming styles differ starkly:

- *Imperative programming uses special statements like* `throw` *and* `try-catch`, *which disrupt the normal program flow.* This introduces side effects as discussed in section 3.1.1.
- *Functional programming strives to minimize side effects, so throwing exceptions is generally avoided.* Instead, if an operation can fail, it should return a representation of its outcome, including an indication of success or failure, as well as its result (if successful) or some error data otherwise. In other words, errors in FP are just *payload*.

There are lots of problems with the imperative, exception-based approach. It has been said that `throw` has similar semantics to `goto`, and this begs the question of

139

why imperative programmers have banished goto but not throw.[1] There's also a lot of confusion around when to use exceptions and when to use other error-handling techniques.[2] I feel that the functional approach brings a lot more clarity to the complex area of error handling, and I hope to convince you of this through the examples in this chapter.

We'll look at how the functional approach can be put into practice and how you can use the function signature to declare that the function can fail—namely, by returning a type that includes error information in its payload. Errors can then be consumed in the calling function just like any other value.

8.1   A safer way to represent outcomes

In previous chapters, you saw that you could use Option not only to represent the absence of a value but also the absence of a *valid* value. You can use Some to signal that everything went OK and None to signal that something went wrong. In other words, functional error handling can sometimes be satisfactorily achieved by using the Option type. Here are a couple of examples:

- *Parsing a string into a number*—Return None to indicate that the given string wasn't a valid representation for a number.
- *Retrieving an item from a collection*—Return None to indicate that no suitable item was found.

In scenarios like these, there's really only one way for the function to fail to compute a valid result and that's represented with None. Functions that return Option<T> rather than just T are acknowledging in their signature that the operation may fail. One way to look at it is that, along with the result T, they return some extra payload (namely, the isSome flag in our implementation of Option) that signals success or failure.

What if there are several ways in which an operation could fail? What if, for instance, the BOC application receives a complex request, such as a request to make a money transfer? Surely the user would need to know not only whether the transfer was successfully booked but also, in case of failure, the reason(s) for failure.

In such scenarios, Option is too limited because it doesn't convey any details about why an operation has failed. Accordingly, we'll need a richer way to represent outcomes—one that includes information about what exactly has gone wrong.

8.1.1   Capturing error details with Either

A classic functional approach to this problem is to use the Either type that, in the context of an operation with two possible outcomes, captures details about the outcome that has taken place. By convention, the two possible outcomes are indicated

---

[1] In fact, I think throw is much worse than goto. The latter at least jumps to a well-defined location; with throw, you don't really know what code will execute next unless you explore all possible paths into the code where throw occurs.

[2] These include returning a special value indicating an error or returning an object representing the outcome of the operation, which is the approach I'll pursue in this chapter.

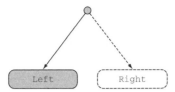

Figure 8.1 `Either` **represents one of two possible outcomes. It indicates that a computation could potentially result in a** `Left` **or a** `Right`**. The image depicts an example in which the left branch is taken.**

with `Left` and `Right` (as figure 8.1 shows), likening the `Either`-producing operation to a *fork*: things can go one way or another.

Although `Left` and `Right` can be seen in a neutral light, by far the most common use of `Either` is to represent the outcome of an operation that may fail, in which case, `Left` is used to indicate failure and `Right` to indicate success. So, remember this:

- `Right` = all right
- `Left` = something wrong

In this biased acceptation, `Either` is just like an `Option` that has been enriched with some data about the error. An `Option` can be in the `None` or `Some` state, and `Either` can similarly be in the `Left` or `Right` state, as summarized in table 8.1.

Table 8.1 `Option` **and** `Either` **can both represent possible failure.**

	Failure	Success
`Option<T>`	`None`	`Some<T>`
`Either<L, R>`	`Left<L>`	`Right<R>`

If `Option` can be symbolically defined as

`Option<T> = None | Some(T)`

then `Either` can similarly be defined like this:

`Either<L, R> = Left(L) | Right(R)`

Notice that `Either` has two generic parameters. It can be in one of two states:

- `Left(L)` wraps a value of type `L`, capturing details about the error.
- `Right(R)` wraps a value of type `R`, representing a successful result.

Let's see how an `Option`-based interface can differ from an `Either`-based one. Imagine you're doing some DIY and go to the store to get a tool you need. If the item isn't available, an `Option`-based shopkeeper would just say, "Sorry, it's not available"—and that would be it. An `Either`-based shopkeeper would give you more information such as, "We're out of stock until next week," or "This product has been discontinued"; you could then base further decisions on this information.

What about a deceiving shopkeeper who, having run out of stock, will sell you a product that looks just like the one you're after but which will explode in your face when you put it to use? That's the exception-throwing interface as figure 8.2 depicts.

Figure 8.2   Which shop would you prefer as a client?

Because the definition of Either is so similar to Option, it can be implemented using the same techniques. In my LaYumba.Functional library, I have defined a type Left<L> that wraps an L and can be implicitly converted to an Either<L, R> for any type R. Similarly for Right<R>. For convenience, values of type L and R are also implicitly convertible to Either<L, R>.

You can see the full implementation in the code samples, but I won't include it here because there's nothing new about the implementation of Option, compared to what was discussed in section 5.3. Instead, let's play around with Either in the REPL. As usual, you need to start by referencing LaYumba.Functional:

```
#r "functional-csharp-code-2\LaYumba.Functional\bin\Debug\net6.0\
➥ LaYumba.Functional.dll"

using LaYumba.Functional;
using static LaYumba.Functional.F;
```

Now create some Eithers:

```
Right(12)
// => Right(12)          ◁⎤ Creates an Either
                          ⎦ in the Right state

Left("oops")
// => Left("oops")       ◁⎤ Creates an Either
                          ⎦ in the Left state
```

That was easy! You use the Right function to wrap, say, an int into a Right<int>, which is implicitly convertible into an Either<L, int> for any L (this is similar to how I used the NoneType for creating Options in the None state) and similarly for Left.

Now, let's write a function that uses `Match` to compute a different value depending on the state of an `Either`:

```
string Render(Either<string, double> val)
   => val.Match
   (
      Left: l => $"Invalid value: {l}",
      Right: r => $"The result is: {r}"
   );

Render(Right(12d))
// => "The result is: 12"

Render(Left("oops"))
// => "Invalid value: oops"
```

Now that you know how to create and consume an `Either`, let's look at a slightly more interesting example. Imagine a function that performs a simple calculation:

$$f(x, y) \rightarrow sqrt(x / y)$$

For the calculation to be performed correctly, we need to ensure that y is nonzero and that the ratio x/y is non-negative. If one of these conditions isn't met, we'd like to know which one. So the calculation returns, let's say, a `double` in the happy path and a `string` with an error message otherwise. That means the return type of this function should be `Either<string, double>`—remember, the successful type is the one on the right. The following listing shows the implementation.

> **Listing 8.1 Capturing error details with `Either`**

```
using static System.Math;

Either<string, double> Calc(double x, double y)
{
   if (y == 0) return "y cannot be 0";

   if (x != 0 && Sign(x) != Sign(y))
      return "x / y cannot be negative";

   return Sqrt(x / y);
}
```

The signature of `Calc` clearly declares that it will return a structure, wrapping as either a string or a double. Indeed, the implementation returns either a string (an error message) or a double (the result of the computation). In either case, the returned value is implicitly converted into a suitably populated `Either`. Let's test it out in the REPL:

```
Calc(3, 0)   // => Left("y cannot be 0")
Calc(-3, 3)  // => Left("x / y cannot be negative")
Calc(-3, -3) // => Right(1)
```

Because `Either` is so similar to `Option`, you might guess that the core functions you've seen in relation to `Option` will have counterparts for `Either`. Let's find out.

8.1.2 *Core functions for working with Either*

As with Option, we can define Map, ForEach, and Bind in terms of Match. Because the Left case is used to signal failure, the computation is skipped in the Left case:

```
public static Either<L, RR> Map<L, R, RR>
(
    this Either<L, R> either,
    Func<R, RR> f
)
=> either.Match<Either<L, RR>>
(
    l => Left(l),
    r => Right(f(r))
);

public static Either<L, Unit> ForEach<L, R>
    (this Either<L, R> either, Action<R> act)
    => Map(either, act.ToFunc());

public static Either<L, RR> Bind<L, R, RR>
(
    this Either<L, R> either,
    Func<R, Either<L, RR>> f
)
=> either.Match
(
    l => Left(l),
    r => f(r)
);
```

In the Left case, the computation is skipped and the Left value is passed along.

There are a couple of things to point out here. In all cases, the function is applied *only* if the Either is Right.[3] This means that if we think of Either as a fork, then when we take the left path, we miss out on all the computations that lie ahead.

Also notice that when you use Map and Bind, the R type changes: just as Option<T> is a functor on T, Either<L, R> is a functor on R, meaning that you can use Map to apply functions to R. The L type, on the other hand, remains the same.

What about Where? Remember, you can call Where with a predicate and filter out the inner value of an Option if it fails to satisfy the predicate:

```
Option<int> three = Some(3);

three.Where(i => i % 2 == 0) // => None
three.Where(i => i % 2 != 0) // => Some(3)
```

With Either, you can't do that. Failure to meet a condition should yield a Left, but because Where takes a predicate and a predicate only returns a Boolean, there's no

---

[3] This is what's called a *biased* implementation of Either. There are also different, *unbiased* implementations of Either that aren't used to represent error/success disjunctions but two equally valid paths. In practice, the biased implementations are much more widely used.

value of type L available if the predicate fails. It's probably easiest to see this if you try to implement Where for Either:

```
public static Either<L, R> Where<L, R>
(
  this Either<L, R> either,
  Func<R, bool> predicate
)
=> either.Match
(
   l => Left(l),
   r => predicate(r)
     : Right(r)
     ? Left(/* now what? I don't have an L */)
);
```

As you can see, if the Either is Right but its inner value doesn't satisfy the predicate, you should return a Left. There is, however, no available value of type L with which you could populate a Left.

You've just learned that Where is less general than Map and Bind: it can only be defined for structures where a zero value exists (such as an empty sequence for IEnumerable or None for Option). There's no zero value for Either<L, R> because L is an arbitrary type. You can only cause an Either to fail by explicitly creating a Left or by calling Bind with a function that may return a suitable L value. You'll see this in practice in the next example, where I'll show you an Option-based implementation and an Either-based one side by side.

8.1.3 Comparing Option and Either

Imagine we're modeling a recruitment process. We'll start with an Option based implementation in which Some(Candidate) represents a candidate that has passed the interview process so far, whereas None represents rejection. The following listing shows this implementation.

Listing 8.2 Option-based implementation modeling the recruitment process

```
Func<Candidate, bool> IsEligible;
Func<Candidate, Option<Candidate>> TechTest;
Func<Candidate, Option<Candidate>> Interview;

Option<Candidate> Recruit(Candidate c)
   => Some(c)
      .Where(IsEligible)
      .Bind(TechTest)
      .Bind(Interview);
```

The recruitment process consists of a technical test first and then an interview. Fail the test and the interview won't take place. But even prior to the test, we'll check that the candidate is eligible. With Option, we can apply the IsEligible predicate with Where so that if the candidate isn't eligible, the subsequent steps won't take place.

Now imagine that HR isn't happy to just know whether a candidate has passed or not; they also want to know the reasons for the rejection because this information allows them to refine the recruitment process. We can refactor to an `Either`-based implementation, capturing the reasons for rejection with a `Rejection` object as in the following listing. The `Right` type is a `Candidate` as before, and the `Left` type is `Rejection`.

Listing 8.3   An equivalent `Either`-based implementation

```
Func<Candidate, bool> IsEligible;
Func<Candidate, Either<Rejection, Candidate>> TechTest;
Func<Candidate, Either<Rejection, Candidate>> Interview;

Either<Rejection, Candidate> CheckEligibility(Candidate c)      ◁──┐ Turns the predicate
{                                                                   │ into an Either-
    if (IsEligible(c)) return c;                                    │ returning function
    else return new Rejection("Not eligible");
}

Either<Rejection, Candidate> Recruit(Candidate c)
    => Right(c)
        .Bind(CheckEligibility)     ◁──┐ Applies CheckEligibility
        .Bind(TechTest)                │ using Bind
        .Bind(Interview);
```

We now need to be more explicit about failing the `IsEligible` test, so we turn this predicate into an `Either`-returning function, `CheckEligibility`. This provides a suitable `Left` value (the `Rejection`) for when the predicate isn't passed. We can now compose `CheckEligibility` into the workflow using `Bind`.

Notice that the `Either`-based implementation is more verbose. This makes sense because we choose `Either` when we need to be explicit about failure conditions.

8.2 *Chaining operations that may fail*

`Either` lends itself particularly well to representing a chain of operations where any operation may cause a deviation from the happy path. For example, once every so often, you prepare your boyfriend or girlfriend's favorite dish. The workflow may look like this:

```
   o WakeUpEarly
  / \
L   R ShopForIngredients
   / \
  L   R CookRecipe
     / \
    L   R EnjoyTogether
```

At each step of the way, something can go wrong: you could oversleep, you could wake up to stormy weather that prevents you from getting to the shops, you could get distracted and let everything burn. . . . In short, only if *everything* goes well do you get to a happy meal together (see figure 8.3).

Figure 8.3 If everything goes according to plan . . .

Using `Either`, we can model the preceding workflow. The following listing shows how to implement this.

Listing 8.4 Using `Bind` to chain several `Either`-returning functions

```
Func<Either<Reason, Unit>> WakeUpEarly;
Func<Either<Reason, Ingredients>> ShopForIngredients;
Func<Ingredients, Either<Reason, Food>> CookRecipe;

Action<Food> EnjoyTogether;
Action<Reason> ComplainAbout;
Action OrderPizza;

WakeUpEarly()
   .Bind(_ => ShopForIngredients())
   .Bind(CookRecipe)
   .Match
   (
      Right: dish => EnjoyTogether(dish),
      Left: reason =>
      {
         ComplainAbout(reason);
         OrderPizza();
      }
   );
```

Remember from the definition of `Bind` that if the state is `Left`, the `Left` value just gets passed along. In the preceding listing, when we say `ComplainAbout(reason)`, the reason is whatever failed in *any* of the previous steps: if we failed to wake up, `ComplainAbout` receives the reason for that; likewise, if we failed to shop, and so on.

The previous tree-like diagram is a correct, logical representation of the workflow. Figure 8.4 shows another way to look at it, which is closer to the implementation details.

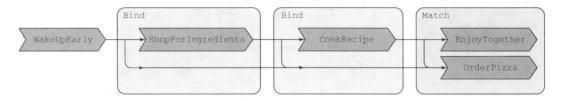

Figure 8.4   Chaining `Either`-returning functions

Each function returns a two-part structure, the `Either`, and is chained with the next function via `Bind`. F# evangelist Scott Wlaschin likens a workflow obtained by chaining several `Either`-returning functions to a two-track system:[4]

- There's a *main track* (the happy path), going from R1 to Rn.
- There's an auxiliary, *parallel track*, on the `Left` side.
- If you're on the `Right` track, with each function application, you will either proceed along the `Right` track or be diverted to the `Left` track.
- Once you're on the `Left` track, you stay on it until the end of the road.
- `Match` is the end of the road, where the disjunction of the parallel tracks takes place.

Although the "favorite dish" example is rather frivolous, it's representative of many programming scenarios. For example, imagine a stateless server that, upon receiving a request, must perform the following steps:

1 Validate the request
2 Load the model from the DB
3 Make changes to the model
4 Persist changes

Any of these operations could potentially fail, and failure at any step should prevent the workflow from continuing. Furthermore, the response should potentially include details about the success or failure of the requested operation, alerting the client as appropriate. Next, we'll look at using `Either` in such a scenario.

8.3   *Validation: A perfect use case for Either*

Let's revisit the scenario of requesting a money transfer, but in this case, we'll address a simplified scenario in which a client explicitly requests a transfer to be carried out on some future date. The application should do the following:

1 Validate the request
2 Store the transfer details for future execution
3 Return a response with an indication of success or details of any failure

---

[4] I encourage you to look at his "Railway Oriented Programming" article and video conference available on his site at http://fsharpforfunandprofit.com/rop/.

We can model the fact that the operation may fail with `Either`. If the transfer request is successfully stored, there's no meaningful data to return to the client, so the `Right` type parameter will be `Unit`. What should the `Left` type be?

8.3.1 Choosing a suitable representation for errors

Let's look at a few types you could use to capture error details. You saw that when applying functions to `Either` via `Map` or `Bind`, the `Right` type changes, but the `Left` type remains the same. So once you choose a type for `Left`, this type remains the same throughout the workflow.

I've used `string` in some of the previous examples, but this seems limiting; you might want to add more structured details about the errors. What about `Exception`? It's a base class that can be extended with arbitrarily rich subtypes. Here, however, the semantics are wrong: `Exception` denotes that something exceptional has occurred. Instead, here we're coding for errors that are "business as usual."

I've included a simple base `Error` type in the next listing, exposing just a `Message` property. You can extend this for specific errors.

Listing 8.5 A base class for representing failure

```
namespace LaYumba.Functional;

public record Error(string Message);
```

Although, strictly speaking, the representation of `Error` is part of the domain, this is a general enough requirement that I've added the type to my functional library. My recommended approach is to create *one type for each type of error*. For example, the next listing provides some error types we'll need in order to represent some cases of failed validation.

Listing 8.6 Distinct types capture details about specific errors

```
namespace Boc.Domain;

public sealed record InvalidBicError()
    : Error("The beneficiary's BIC/SWIFT code is invalid");

public sealed record TransferDateIsPastError()
    : Error("Transfer date cannot be in the past");
```

And, for convenience, we'll add a static class, `Errors`. It contains factory functions for creating specific `Errors`:

```
public static class Errors
{
    public static Error InvalidBic
        => new InvalidBicError();

    public static Error TransferDateIsPast
        => new TransferDateIsPastError();
}
```

This is a trick that will help us keep the code where the business decisions are made cleaner, as you'll see in a moment. It also provides good documentation: Errors effectively gives you an overview of all the specific errors defined for the domain.

8.3.2   Defining an Either-based API

Let's assume that the details about the transfer request are captured in a DTO of type MakeTransfer (see listing 3.6): this is what we receive from the client, and it's the input data for our workflow. We can also establish that the workflow should return an Either<Error, Unit> when there's no data (in case of success) or an Error with details (in case of failure). That means the main function we need to implement to perform this workflow has this signature:

```
MakeTransfer → Either<Error, Unit>
```

We're now ready to introduce a skeleton of the implementation:

```
public class MakeTransferController : ControllerBase
{
   [HttpPost, Route("transfers/book")]
   public void MakeTransfer([FromBody] MakeTransfer request)
      => Handle(request);

   Either<Error, Unit> Handle(MakeTransfer cmd)
      => Validate(cmd)              Uses Bind to chain two
         .Bind(Save);               operations that may fail

   Either<Error, MakeTransfer> Validate(MakeTransfer cmd)    Uses Either to
      => // TODO: add validation...                          acknowledge that
                                                             validation may fail

   Either<Error, Unit> Save(MakeTransfer cmd)
      => // TODO: save the request...
}                                   Uses Either to acknowledge that
                                    persisting the request may fail
```

The Handle method defines the high-level workflow: first validate, then persist. Both Validate and Save return an Either to acknowledge that the operation may fail. Also note that the return type of Validate is Either<Error, MakeTransfer>. That is, we need the MakeTransfer command on the right side so that the transfer data is available and can be piped to Save. Next, let's add some validation.

8.3.3   Adding validation logic

Let's start by validating a couple of simple conditions about the request:

- The date for the transfer should be in the future.
- The provided BIC code should be in the right format.[5]

You've already seen the logic for this validation in section 3.3.2. However, back then we wrote functions that returned a Boolean, indicating whether the MakeTransfer was valid. Now, we want to return an Either to capture details of what validation failed.

---

[5] The BIC code, also known as SWIFT code, is a standard identifier for a bank branch.

We can have a function perform each validation. The typical scheme will be as follows:

```
Regex bicRegex = new Regex("[A-Z]{11}");

Either<Error, MakeTransfer> ValidateBic(MakeTransfer transfer)
   => bicRegex.IsMatch(transfer.Bic)
       ? transfer
       : Errors.InvalidBic;
```

Failure: the error is wrapped in an `Either` in the `Left` state.

Success: the original request is wrapped in an `Either` in the `Right` state.

That is, each validator function takes a request as input and returns *either* the (validated) command *or* the appropriate error.

Each validation function is a world-crossing function (going from a normal value, `MakeTransfer`, to an elevated value, `Either<Error, MakeTransfer>`), so we can combine several of these functions using `Bind`. The following listing shows how to do this.

Listing 8.7   Chaining several validation functions with `Bind`

```
DateTime now;
Regex bicRegex = new Regex("[A-Z]{11}");

Either<Error, Unit> Handle(MakeTransfer transfer)
   => Right(transfer)
       .Bind(ValidateBic)
       .Bind(ValidateDate)
       .Bind(Save);

Either<Error, MakeTransfer> ValidateBic(MakeTransfer transfer)
   => bicRegex.IsMatch(transfer.Bic)
       ? transfer
       : Errors.InvalidBic;

Either<Error, MakeTransfer> ValidateDate(MakeTransfer transfer)
   => transfer.Date.Date > now.Date
       ? transfer
       : Errors.TransferDateIsPast;

Either<Error, Unit> Save(MakeTransfer cmd) => //...
```

Lifts the command into an `Either`

Applies all subsequent operations that can fail with `Bind`

In summary, use `Either` to acknowledge that *an* operation may fail and `Bind` to chain *several* operations that may fail.

Now that our workflow nicely captures the possibility of failure with `Either`, how do we relay this information, say, to the HTTP client that made the request? We'll look at this next.

8.4   *Representing outcomes to client applications*

You've now seen quite a few use cases for `Option` and `Either`. Both types can be seen as representing outcomes: in the case of `Option`, `None` can signify failure; in the case of `Either`, it's `Left`. We've defined `Option` and `Either` as C# types, but in this section, you'll see how you can translate them for the outside world.

Although we've defined `Match` for both types, we've used it quite rarely, relying instead on `Map`, `Bind`, and `Where` to define workflows. Remember, the *key difference* here is that the latter work "within the abstraction" (you start with, say, `Option<T>` and end up with an `Option<R>`). `Match`, on the other hand, allows you to "leave the abstraction" (you start with `Option<T>` and end up with an `R`). Figure 8.5 shows this process.

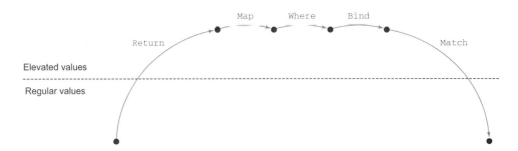

Figure 8.5   With `Option` and `Either`, `Match` is used to leave the abstraction.

As a general rule, once you've introduced an abstraction like `Option`, it's best to stick with it as long as possible. What does *as long as possible* mean? Ideally, it means that you'll leave the abstract world when you cross application boundaries.

It's good practice to design applications with some separation between the application core (which contains services and domain logic) and an outer layer (which contains a set of adapters through which your application interacts with the outside world). You can see your application as an orange, where the skin is composed of a layer of adapters, as figure 8.6 shows.

Abstractions such as `Option` and `Either` are useful within the application core, but they may not translate well to the message contract expected by the interacting applications. Thus, the outer layer is where you need to leave the abstraction and translate to the representation expected by your client applications.

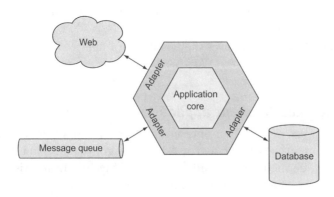

Figure 8.6   The outer layer of an application consists of adapters.

8.4.1   Exposing an Option-like interface

Imagine an API that, given a *ticker* (an identifier for a stock or other financial instrument, such as AAPL, GOOG, or MSFT), returns details about the requested financial instrument. Within the application core, you've implemented a function that does this; its signature is

```
GetDetails : string → Option<InstrumentDetails>
```

You can't know whether the string given as a ticker actually identifies an existing instrument, so you've used `Option` to model this. Next, let's expose this data to the outer world. You can do this by defining an endpoint on an ASP.NET MVC controller.

The API returns, let's say, JSON over HTTP (a format and protocol that doesn't deal in `Options`), so the controller needs to act as an adapter that can translate `Option` into something that's supported by that protocol. Namely, if no instrument exists for the given ticker, we'll return an HTTP response with a code of 404 (Not Found) as the following listing shows.

Listing 8.8   Translating None to status code 404

```
using Microsoft.AspNet.Mvc;

public class InstrumentsController : ControllerBase
{
    [HttpGet, Route("api/instruments/{ticker}/details")]
    public IActionResult GetInstrumentDetails(string ticker)
        => GetDetails(ticker)
          .Match<IActionResult>
           (
              () => NotFound(),          ←──┤ Maps None
              (result) => Ok(result)     ←─┐  to a 404
           );                               └ Maps Some
                                              to a 200
    Option<InstrumentDetails> GetDetails(string ticker) => //
}
```

Note that because `NotFound` and `Ok`, which are inherited from `ControllerBase`, return different implementations of `IActionResult`, we must explicitly declare `IActionResult` as a type parameter for `Match`.

> **Point-free style**
>
> The body of `GetInstrumentDetails` can be written more tersely:
>
> ```
> => getInstrumentDetails(ticker)
>    .Match<IActionResult>
>    (
>       None: NotFound,
>       Some: Ok
>    );
> ```

You've now seen how you can take a workflow modeled with an Option-based interface and expose it through an HTTP API. Next, let's see an Either-based interface.

8.4.2   *Exposing an Either-like interface*

Just like with Option, once you've lifted your value to the elevated world of Either, it's best to stay there until the end of the workflow. But all good things must come to an end, so at some point, you'll need to leave your application domain and expose a representation of your Either to the external world.

Let's go back to the banking scenario we looked at in this chapter—that of a request from a client to book a transfer on a future date. Our core functionality returns an Either<Error, Unit>, and we must translate that to, say, JSON over HTTP.

One approach is similar to what we just looked at for Option: we can use HTTP status code 400 to signal that we received a bad request. The following listing demonstrates this approach.

Listing 8.9   Translating Left to status code 400

```
public class MakeTransferController : ControllerBase
{
   [HttpPost, Route("api/transfers/future")]
   public IActionResult MakeTransfer([FromBody] MakeTransfer transfer)
      => Handle(transfer).Match<IActionResult>
      (
         Left: BadRequest,
         Right: _ => Ok()
      );

   Either<Error, Unit> Handle(MakeTransfer transfer) => // ...
}
```

This works. The only downside is that the convention of how business validation relates to HTTP error codes is shaky. Some people will argue that 400 signals a *syntactically* incorrect request and not a *semantically* incorrect request, as is the case here.

In situations of concurrency, a request that was valid at the time it was sent may no longer be valid by the time the server receives it (for example, the account balance may have gone down). Does a 400 convey this?

Instead of trying to figure out which HTTP status code best suits a particular error scenario, another approach is to return a representation of the outcome in the response. We'll explore this option next.

8.4.3 Returning a result DTO

This approach involves always returning a successful status code (because, at a low level, the response was correctly received and processed), along with an arbitrarily rich representation of the outcome in the response body. The following listing shows a simple data transfer object (DTO) representing the result of processing the request, including its left and right components.

Listing 8.10 DTO representing the outcome serialized in the response

```
public record ResultDto<T>
{
   public bool Succeeded { get; }
   public bool Failed => !Succeeded;

   public T Data { get; }
   public Error Error { get; }

   internal ResultDto(T data) => (Succeeded, Data) = (true, data);
   internal ResultDto(Error error) => Error = error;
}
```

This `ResultDto` is similar to `Either`. But unlike `Either`, whose internal values are only accessible via higher-order functions, the DTO exposes them for easy serialization and access on the client side. We can then define a utility function that translates an `Either` to a `ResultDto`:

```
public static ResultDto<T> ToResult<T>(this Either<Error, T> either)
   => either.Match
   (
      Left: error => new ResultDto<T>(error),
      Right: data => new ResultDto<T>(data)
   );
```

Now we can just expose the `Result` in our API method. The next listing shows how to do this.

Listing 8.11 Returning error details as part of a successful response payload

```
public class MakeTransferController : ControllerBase
{
   Func<MakeTransfer, Either<Error, Unit>> makeTransfer;

   [HttpPost, Route("api/transfers/future")]
   public ResultDto<Unit> MakeTransfer([FromBody] MakeTransfer transfer)
      => makeTransfer(transfer).ToResult();
}
```

Overall, this approach means less code in your endpoints. More importantly, it means you're not relying on the idiosyncrasies of the HTTP protocol in your representation of results but can, instead, create the structure that best suits you to represent whatever you choose to see as `Left`.

In the end, both approaches are viable and both are used in APIs in the wild. Which approach you choose has more to do with API design than with FP. The point is that you'll generally have to make some choices when exposing to client applications outcomes that you can model with Either in your application.

I've illustrated "lowering" values from abstractions through the example of an HTTP API because this is such a common requirement, but the concepts don't change if you expose another kind of endpoint. In summary, use Match if you're in the skin of the orange; stay with the juicy abstractions within the core of the orange.

8.5 *Variations on the Either theme*

Either takes us a long way toward functional error handling. In contrast to exceptions, which cause the program to "jump" out of its normal execution flow and into an exception-handling block somewhere up the stack, Either maintains the normal program execution flow and, instead, returns a representation of the outcome.

There's a lot to like about Either. There are also some possible objections:

- Bind doesn't change the Left type, so how you compose functions that return an Either with a different Left type?
- Always having to specify two generic arguments makes the code too verbose.
- The names Either, Left, and Right are too cryptic. Can't we have something more user-friendly?

In this section, I'll address these concerns. You'll see how they can be mitigated with some variations on the Either theme.

8.5.1 *Changing between different error representations*

As you saw, Map and Bind allow you to change the R type but not the L type. Although having a homogeneous representation for errors is preferable, it may not always be possible. What if you write a library where the L type is always Error, and someone else writes a library where it's always string? How can you to integrate the two?

It turns out this can be resolved simply with an overload of Map, which allows you to apply a function to the left value *as well as* the right one. This overload takes an Either<L, R> and then not one but two functions: one of type (L → LL), which is applied to the left value (if present), and another one of type (R → RR), which is applied to the right value,

```
public static Either<LL, RR> Map<L, LL, R, RR>
(
    this Either<L, R> either,
    Func<L, LL> Left,
    Func<R, RR> Right
)
=> either.Match<Either<LL, RR>>
(
    l => F.Left(Left(l)),
    r => F.Right(Right(r))
);
```

This variation of `Map` allows you to arbitrarily change both types so that you can interoperate between functions where the `L` types are different.[6] Here's an example:

```
Either<string, double> Calc(double x, double y) //...          ◁─┐ L is
                                                                 │ string.
Either<Error, int> ToIntIfWhole(double d) //...        ◁─┐ L is
                                                         │ Error.
Either<Error, int> Run(double x, double y)
    => Calc(x, y)
        .Map
        (
           Left: msg => Error(msg),      ◁─┐ Translates from
           Right: d => d                    │ string to Error
        )
        .Bind(ToIntIfWhole);
```

If possible, it's best to avoid the noise and stick to a consistent representation for errors. Different representations, though, aren't a stumbling block.

8.5.2 *Specialized versions of Either*

Let's look at the other shortcomings of using `Either` in C#.

First, having two generic arguments adds noise to the code.[7] For example, imagine you want to capture multiple validation errors and, for this, you choose `IEnumerable<Error>` as your Left type. You'd end up with signatures that look like this:

```
public Either<IEnumerable<Error>, Rates> RefreshRates(string id) //...
```

You now have to read through three things (`Either`, `IEnumerable`, and `Error`) before you get to the most meaningful part—the desired return type `Rates`. Compared to signatures that say nothing about failure, which we discussed in section 4.2.3, it seems we've fallen into the opposite extreme.

Second, the names `Either`, `Left`, and `Right` are too abstract. Software development is complex enough, so we should opt for the most intuitive names possible.

Both issues can be addressed by using more specialized versions of `Either` that have a fixed type to represent failure (hence, a single generic parameter) and more user-friendly names. Note that such variations on `Either` are common but not standardized. You'll find a multitude of different libraries and tutorials that each have their own minor variations in terminology and behavior.

---

[6] Because there's no shortage of terminology in FP, functors for which a `Map` in this form is defined are called *bifunctors*. The idea is that functors have an inner value, whereas bifunctors have two (or one of two) inner values. Bifunctors can then have the functions `RightMap` (which is the same as `Map`), `LeftMap` (which maps a function onto the left value), and `BiMap` (which is identical to the overload of `Map` I've just shown).

[7] You can look at this as a shortcoming of `Either` or of C#'s type system. `Either` is successfully used in the ML languages where types can (nearly) always be inferred, so even complex generic types don't add any noise to the code. This is a classic example showing that although the principles of FP are language-independent, they need to be adapted based on the strengths and weaknesses of each particular language.

For this reason, I thought it best to first give you a thorough understanding of `Either`, which is ubiquitous and well established in the literature and will allow you to grasp any variations you may encounter. (You can then choose the representation that serves you best, or even implement your own type for representing outcomes if you're so inclined.)

`LaYumba.Functional` includes the following two variations for representing outcomes:

- `Validation<T>`—You can think of this as an `Either` that has been *particularized* to `IEnumerable<Error>`:

  ```
  Validation<T> = Invalid(IEnumerable<Error>) | Valid(T)
  ```

  `Validation` is like an `Either`, where the failure case is fixed to `IEnumerable<Error>`, making it possible to capture multiple validation errors.

- `Exceptional<T>`—Here, failure is fixed to `System.Exception`:

  ```
  Exceptional<T> = Exception | Success(T)
  ```

  `Exceptional` can be used as a bridge between an exception-based API and functional error handling.

Table 8.2 shows these variations side by side.

Table 8.2   Some particularized versions of `Either` and their state names

Type	Success case	Failure case	Failure type
`Either<L, R>`	`Right`	`Left`	`L`
`Validation<T>`	`Valid`	`Invalid`	`IEnumerable<Error>`
`Exceptional<T>`	`Success`	`Exception`	`Exception`

These new types have friendlier, more intuitive names than `Either`. And because the `Left` type is static, it won't clutter your method signatures. You'll see an example of using them next.

8.5.3   *Refactoring to Validation and Exceptional*

Let's go back to the scenario of a user booking a money transfer for future execution. Previously, we modeled the simple workflow that included validation and persistence (both of which could fail) with `Either`. Let's now see how the implementation would change by using the more specific `Validation` and `Exceptional` instead.

A function that performs validation should, naturally, yield a `Validation`. In our scenario, its type would be

```
Validate : MakeTransfer → Validation<MakeTransfer>
```

Because `Validation` is just like `Either`, particularized to the `Error` type, the implementation of the validation functions would be the same as in the previous `Either`-based implementation except for the change in signature. Here's an example:

```
DateTime now;

Validation<MakeTransfer> ValidateDate(MakeTransfer transfer)
   => transfer.Date.Date > now.Date
        ? transfer                               ⟵──┐  Wraps the command
        : Errors.TransferDateIsPast;  ⟵──┐          │  in a Validation in
              Wraps an Error in a Validation │          │  the Valid state
                      in the Invalid state ┘
```

In line with previous implementations, I've defined `Valid` as a function that takes a `T` and lifts it into a `Validation<T>` in the `Valid` state and similarly for `Invalid`, which takes one or more `Errors`. Implicit conversion is also defined, so in the previous example, you could omit the calls to `Valid` and `Invalid`.

BRIDGING BETWEEN AN EXCEPTION-BASED API AND FUNCTIONAL ERROR HANDLING

Next, let's look at persistence. Unlike validation, failure here would indicate a fault in the infrastructure or configuration or another technical error. We consider such errors exceptional, so we can model this with `Exceptional`:[8]

```
Save : MakeTransfer → Exceptional<Unit>
```

The following listing shows what the implementation of `Save` could look like.

Listing 8.12 Translating an Exception-based API to an Exceptional value

```
string connString;

Exceptional<Unit> Save(MakeTransfer transfer)      ⟵──┐  The return type acknowledges
{                                                      │  the possibility of an exception.
   try
   {
      ConnectionHelper.Connect(connString            ⟵──┐  The call to a third-party API
         , c => c.Execute("INSERT ...", transfer));       │  that throws an exception
   }                                                      │  is wrapped in a try.

   catch (Exception ex) { return ex; }   ⟵──┐  The exception will be implicitly converted
                                             │  and wrapped in an Exceptional
                                             │  in the Exception state.

   return Unit();    ⟵──┐  The returned Unit will be
}                       │  converted into an Exceptional
                        │  in the Success state.
```

---

[8] In this context, *exceptional* doesn't necessarily mean *occurring rarely*; it denotes a technical error as opposed to an error from the point of view of the business logic.

Notice that the scope of the try-catch is as small as possible: we want to catch any exceptions that may be raised when connecting to the database and immediately translate to the functional style, wrapping the result in an Exceptional. As usual, implicit conversion creates an appropriately initialized Exceptional. Notice also how this pattern allows us to go from a third-party exception-throwing API to a functional API, where errors are handled as payload and the possibility of errors is reflected in the return type.

FAILED VALIDATION VS. TECHNICAL ERRORS

Failed validation and technical errors should be handled differently. The nice thing about using Validation and Exceptional is that they have distinct semantic connotations:

- Validation denotes possible business rule violations.
- Exceptional denotes possible unexpected technical errors.

We'll now look at how using these different representations allows us to handle each case appropriately. We still need to combine validation and persistence, which is done in Handle here:

```
public class MakeTransferController : ControllerBase
{
    Validation<Exceptional<Unit>> Handle(MakeTransfer transfer)
        => Validate(transfer)                    Combines validation
            .Map(Save);                          and persistence

    Validation<MakeTransfer> Validate(MakeTransfer transfer)
        => ValidateBic(transfer)                         Top-level validation function
            .Bind(ValidateDate);                  combining various validation rules

    Validation<MakeTransfer> ValidateBic(MakeTransfer transfer) // ...
    Validation<MakeTransfer> ValidateDate(MakeTransfer transfer) // ...

    Exceptional<Unit> Save(MakeTransfer transfer) // ...
}
```

Because Validate returns a Validation, whereas Save returns an Exceptional, we can't compose these types with Bind. But that's OK: we can use Map instead and end up with the return type Validation<Exceptional<Unit>>. This is a nested type, expressing the fact that we're combining the *effect* of validation (we may get validation errors instead of the desired return value) with the *effect* of exception handling (even after validation passes, we may get an exception instead of the return value).[9]

As a result, Handle is acknowledging that the operation may fail for business reasons, as well as technical reasons by "stacking" the two monadic effects. Figure 8.7 illustrates how in both cases we express errors by including them as part of the payload.

To complete the end-to-end scenario, we need only add the entry point. This is where the controller receives a MakeTransfer command from the client, invokes

---

[9] Remember, these are monadic effects not side effects, but in FP-speak, they're simply called *effects*.

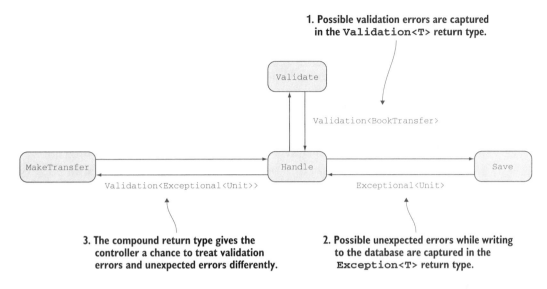

Figure 8.7 In functional error handling, errors are treated as part of the returned payload.

Handle as defined previously, and translates the resulting Validation<Exceptional-<Unit>> into a result to send back to the client. This is shown in the following listing.

Listing 8.13 Different treatments for validation and exceptional errors

```
public class MakeTransferController : ControllerBase
{
    ILogger<MakeTransferController> logger;

    [HttpPost, Route("api/transfers/book")]
    public IActionResult MakeTransfer([FromBody] MakeTransfer transfer)
        => Handle(transfer).Match
        (
            Invalid: BadRequest,
            Valid: result => result.Match
            (
                Exception: OnFaulted,
                Success: _ => Ok()
            )
        );

    IActionResult OnFaulted(Exception ex)
    {
        logger.LogError(ex.Message);
        return StatusCode(500, Errors.UnexpectedError);
    }

    Validation<Exceptional<Unit>> Handle(MakeTransfer transfer) //...
}
```

Unwraps the value inside the Validation

If validation fails, sends a 400

Unwraps the value inside the Exceptional

If persistence fails, sends a 500

Here we use two nested calls to Match to first unwrap the value inside the Validation and then the value inside the Exceptional:

- If validation fails, we send a 400, which includes the full details of the validation errors, so that the user can address them.
- If persistence fails, on the other hand, we don't want to send the details to the user. Instead, we return a 500 with a more generic error type (this is also a good place to log the exception).

As you can see, an explicit return type from each of the functions involved allows you to clearly distinguish and customize how you treat failures related to business rules versus those related to technical issues.

In summary, Either gives you an explicit, functional way to handle errors without introducing side effects, unlike throwing/catching exceptions. But as our relatively simple banking scenario illustrates, using specialized versions of Either, like Validation and Exceptional, leads to an even more expressive and readable implementation.

8.5.4 *Leaving exceptions behind?*

In this chapter, you've gained a solid understanding of the ideas behind functional error handling.[10] You may feel this is a radical departure from the exception-based approach and, indeed, it is!

I mentioned that throwing exceptions disrupts the normal program flow, introducing side effects. More pragmatically, it makes your code more difficult to maintain and reason about: if a function throws an exception, the only way to analyze the implications of this for the application is to follow all possible code paths into the function and then look for the first exception handler up the stack. With functional error handling, errors are just part of the return type of the function, so you can still reason about the function in isolation.

Having realized the detrimental effects of using exceptions, several younger programming languages such as Go, Elixir, and Elm have embraced the idea that errors should simply be treated as values so that equivalents to the throw and try-catch statements are used only rarely (Elixir) or are absent from the language altogether (Go, Elm). The fact that C# includes exceptions doesn't mean you need to use them for error handling; instead, you can use functional error handling within your application and use adapter functions to convert the outcomes of calls to exception-based APIs to something like Exceptional as shown previously.

Are there any cases in which exceptions are still useful? I believe so:

- *Developer errors*—For example, if you're trying to remove an item from an empty list or if you're passing a null value to a function that requires that value, it's OK for that function or for the list implementation to throw an exception. Such exceptions are never meant to be caught and handled in the calling code; they indicate that the application logic is wrong.

---

[10] We'll revisit error handling in part 3 in the context of laziness and asynchrony, but the fundamental aspects have all been covered in this chapter.

- *Configuration errors*—For example, if an application relies on a message bus to connect to other systems and can't effectively perform anything useful unless connected, failure to connect to the bus upon startup should result in an exception. The same applies if a critical piece of configuration like a database connection string is missing. These exceptions should only be thrown upon initialization and aren't meant to be caught (other than possibly in an outermost, application-wide handler), but should, rightly, cause the application to crash.

Exercises

1. Write a ToOption extension method to convert an Either into an Option; if present, the left value is thrown away. Then write a ToEither method to convert an Option into an Either with a suitable parameter that can be invoked to obtain the appropriate Left value if the Option is None. (Tip: start by writing the function signatures in arrow notation.)

2. Take a workflow where two or more functions that return an Option are chained using Bind. Then change the first of the functions to return an Either. This should cause compilation to fail. Either can be converted into an Option (as you saw in the previous exercise), so write extension overloads for Bind. That way, functions returning Either and Option can be chained with Bind, yielding an Option.

3. Write a function with the signature

   ```
   TryRun : (() → T) → Exceptional<T>
   ```

   which runs the given function in a try catch, returning an appropriately populated Exceptional.

4. Write a function with the signature

   ```
   Safely : ((() → R), (Exception → L)) → Either<L, R>
   ```

   which runs the given function in a try-catch, returning an appropriately populated Either.

Summary

- Use Either to represent the result of an operation with two different possible outcomes, typically success or failure. An Either can be in one of two states:
  - Left indicates failure and contains error information for an unsuccessful operation.
  - Right indicates success and contains the result of a successful operation.
- Interact with Either using the equivalents of the core functions already seen with Option:
  - Map and Bind apply the mapped/bound function *if* the Either is in the Right state; otherwise, they just pass along the Left value.
  - Match allows you to handle the Right and Left cases differently.

- Where is not readily applicable; if you want to filter out certain Right values according to a predicate, use Bind instead, providing a function that yields a suitable Left value if the predicate fails.

- Either is particularly useful for combining several validation functions with Bind or, more generally, for combining several operations, each of which can fail.

- Because Either is rather abstract and because of the syntactic overhead of its two generic arguments, in practice, it's better to use a particularized version of Either, such as Validation and Exceptional.

- When working with functors and monads, prefer using functions that stay within the abstraction, like Map and Bind. Use the downward-crossing Match function as little or as late as possible.

Structuring an
application with functions

This chapter covers

- Partial application and currying
- Getting around the limitations of method type inference
- Modularizing and composing an application
- Reducing lists to single values

Structuring a complex, real-world application is no easy task. There are entire books written on the subject, so this chapter by no means aims to provide a comprehensive view. We'll focus on the techniques that you can use to modularize and compose an application consisting entirely of functions and how the result compares to how this is usually done in OOP.

We'll get there gradually. First, you'll need to learn about a classic but fairly low-level functional technique called *partial application*. This technique allows you to write highly general functions whose behavior is parameterized and then supply those parameters, obtaining more specialized functions that have the parameters given so far "baked in."

165

We'll then look at how partial application can be used in practice to first specify configuration arguments that are available at startup and purely run-time arguments later as they're received. Finally, we'll look at how you can take the approach one step further and use partial application for dependency injection, to the point of composing an entire application out of functions, without losing any of the granularity or decoupling you'd expect when composing it with objects.

9.1   *Partial application: Supplying arguments piecemeal*

Imagine that you're having your house redecorated. Your interior designer, Ada, calls Fred, her trusted paint supplier, with details about the paint she intends to order and then sends Bruno, the decorator, to pick up the required amount of paint. Figure 9.1 illustrates this scenario.

Figure 9.1   Fred needs several pieces of information before he can provide the product. This information can be given at different points by Ada and Bruno.

Clearly, the shop needs to know both *what* the customer wants to buy and *how much* in order to fulfill the request, and in this case, the information is given at different points in time. Why? Well, it's Ada's responsibility to choose the color and brand (she wouldn't trust Bruno to remember her exact choice). Bruno, on the other hand, has the task of measuring the surface and calculating the amount of paint required. At this point, all required information is available, and Bruno can pick up the paint from the supplier.

What I've just described is a real-life analogy of partial application. In programming, this means giving a function its input arguments piecemeal. Just as in my real-life example, this has to do with *separation of concerns*: it may be best to provide the arguments that a function needs at different points in the application lifecycle and from different components.

Let's see this in code. The idea here is that you have a function that needs several pieces of information to do its work (analogous to Fred, the paint supplier). For instance, in the following listing, we have the function greet, which takes a general greeting and a name and produces a greeting personalized for the given name.

> **Listing 9.1** **A binary function mapped over a list**

```
using Name = System.String;
using Greeting = System.String;
using PersonalizedGreeting = System.String;

var greet = (Greeting gr, Name name) => $"{gr}, {name}";

Name[] names = { "Tristan", "Ivan" };

names.Map(n => greet("Hello", n)).ForEach(WriteLine);
// prints: Hello, Tristan
//         Hello, Ivan
```

TIP If you've never used partial application before, it's important that you type the examples in this section into the REPL to get a hands-on feel for how it works.

The using statements at the top of listing 9.1 allow us to attach some semantic meaning to specific uses of the string type, thus making the function signatures more meaningful. You could go the extra mile and define dedicated types (as discussed in chapter 4), thus ensuring that, say, a PersonalizedGreeting can't accidentally be given as input to the greet function. But for the present discussion, I'm not too worried about enforcing business rules—just about having meaningful, unequivocal signatures because we'll be looking at the signatures a lot. This is the signature of greet:

```
(Greeting, Name) → PersonalizedGreeting
```

We then have a list of names and map greet over the list to obtain a greeting for each name in the list. Notice that the greet function is always called with "Hello" as its first argument, whereas the second argument varies with each name in the list.

This feels slightly odd. We have a single general greeting and *n* different names, and we're repeating that one greeting *n* times. Somehow it seems we're repeating ourselves. Wouldn't it be better to fix the greeting to be "Hello" outside the scope of Map? This would express the fact that deciding on "Hello" as the greeting to use for all names is a more general decision and can be taken first. The function passed to Map would then only consume the name. How can we achieve this?

In listing 9.1, we can't do this because greet expects two arguments, and we're using "normal" function application; that is, we call greet with the two arguments it expects. (It's called *application* because we're applying the function greet to its arguments.)

We can solve this with partial application. The idea is to allow some code to decide on the general greeting and give it to greet as its first argument (the way Ada decides on the color). This will generate a new function with "Hello" already baked in as the greeting to use. Some other code can then invoke this function with the name of the person to greet.

There are a couple of ways to make this possible. You'll first see how to write a specific function in a way that supports partial application and then how to define a general `Apply` function that enables partial application for any given function.

9.1.1 *Manually enabling partial application*

One way to supply arguments independently would be to rewrite the `greet` function like so:

```
var greetWith = (Greeting gr) => (Name name) => $"{gr}, {name}";
```

This new function, `greetWith`, takes a single argument, the general greeting, and returns a new function of type `Name → PersonalizedGreeting`. Notice that when the function is called with its first argument, `gr`, this is captured in a closure and is, therefore, "remembered" until the returned function is called with the second argument, `name`. You'd use it like this:

```
var greetFormally = greetWith("Good evening");
names.Map(greetFormally).ForEach(WriteLine);
// prints: Good evening, Tristan
//         Good evening, Ivan
```

We've achieved our goal of fixing the greeting outside of the scope of `Map`. Notice that `greet` and `greetWith` rely on the same implementation, but their signatures are different. Let's compare them:

```
greet      : (Greeting, Name) → PersonalizedGreeting
greetWith : Greeting → (Name → PersonalizedGreeting)
```

`greet` takes two arguments and returns a value. In contrast, `greetWith` takes a single argument, a `Greeting`, and returns a function that, in turn, takes a `Name` to return a `PersonalizedGreeting`.

In fact, arrow notation is *right-associative*: everything to the right of an arrow is grouped. So the parentheses in the signature of `greetWith` are redundant, and the type of `greetWith` would normally be written as follows:

```
greetWith : Greeting → Name → PersonalizedGreeting
```

`greetWith` is said to be in *curried* form: all arguments are supplied one by one via function invocation.

Again, `greet` and `greetWith` rely on the same implementation. What changes is the signature and the fact that arguments are provided independently and are captured in closures. This is a good indicator that we should be able to do partial application mechanically without the need to rewrite the function. Let's look at how to do this next.

9.1.2 Generalizing partial application

As a more general alternative to the approach you've just seen with greetWith, we can define an adapter function that allows you to provide just one argument to a multi-argument function, producing a function that is waiting to receive the remaining arguments. The following snippet shows the definition of a general Apply function, providing a given value as the first argument to a given binary function:

```
public static Func<T2, R> Apply<T1, T2, R>
(
    this Func<T1, T2, R> f,                          A binary
    T1 t1                                            function
)                          A value for the
=> t2 => f(t1, t2);       first argument

                          Returns a unary function that takes the
                          second argument of the original function
```

Apply takes a binary function, *partially applies* it to the given argument, and returns a unary function accepting the second argument. The supplied input argument, t1, is captured in a closure, yielding a new function that calls the original function, f, when the second parameter is provided.

We can similarly define Apply for functions of greater arities. For example, here is Apply defined for a ternary function:

```
public static Func<T2, T3, R> Apply<T1, T2, T3, R>
(
    this Func<T1, T2, T3, R> f,
    T1 t1
)
=> (t2, t3) => f(t1, t2, t3);
```

This overload takes a ternary function and a value to use as the first argument. It yields a binary function waiting for the remaining two arguments. Similar overloads can be defined for functions of greater arity and are included in LaYumba.Functional.

Notice how expression-bodied methods and the lambda notation give us good syntactic support to define this sort of function transformation. This general definition of Apply means you need not manually create a function like greetWith. Instead, you can just use Apply to give the original greet function its first argument:

```
var greetInformally = greet.Apply("Hey");
names.Map(greetInformally).ForEach(WriteLine);
// prints: Hey, Tristan
//         Hey, Ivan
```

Whether you're using the manual approach or the general Apply function, you should be starting to see a pattern: we're starting with a general function (like greet) and using partial application to create a specialized version of this function (like greetInformally). This is now a unary function that can be passed around, and the code that uses it doesn't even need to be aware that this new function was partially applied. Figure 9.2 graphically summarizes the steps we've covered so far.

A binary function

The function is repeatedly called with a fixed value for its first argument.

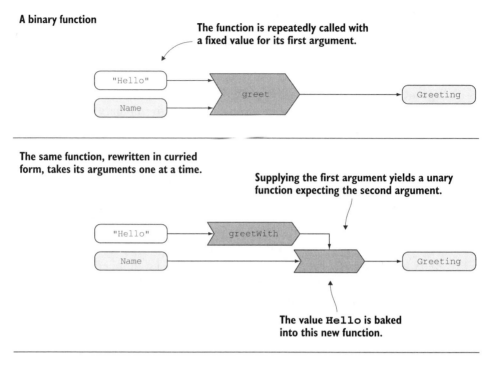

The same function, rewritten in curried form, takes its arguments one at a time.

Supplying the first argument yields a unary function expecting the second argument.

The value **Hello** is baked into this new function.

The same can be achieved using the original binary function and the general Apply function.

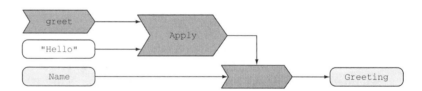

Figure 9.2 Comparing normal function application with partial application. Partial application allows you to supply arguments piecemeal to obtain functions that have those arguments built-in and are awaiting the following arguments. Partial application can be enabled manually or by using the general Apply function.

In summary, partial application is always about going from general to specific. It allows you to define general functions and then fine-tune their behavior by giving them arguments. Ultimately, writing such general functions ups the level of abstraction and potentially allows greater code reuse.

9.1.3 *Order of arguments matters*

The greet function shows what is generally a good order of arguments: the more general parameters, which are likely to be applied early in the life of the application, should come first, followed by the more specific parameters. We learn to say "Hello" early in life, but we keep meeting and greeting new people until we're old.

As a rule of thumb, if you think of a function as an operation, its arguments typically include the following:

- The data that the operation will affect. This is likely to be given late and should be left last.
- Some options that determine *how* the function will operate or dependencies that the function requires to do its work. These are likely to be determined early and should come first.

WARNING This order of parameters is sometimes in conflict with our desire to use extension methods: unfortunately, we can only mark the *first* of a method's parameters with the `this` modifier, although it may not be the most general parameter. In such cases, you have to make a choice on whether extension-method syntax or partial application is more desirable for your intended use.

Of course, it's not always easy to establish the best order for parameters. You'll shortly see how you can use partial application even if the order of parameters is wrong for your intended use.

In summary, whenever you have a multi-argument function and it's desirable to separate the responsibilities of supplying the different arguments it takes, you have a good case for using partial application. There is, however, one catch that we should iron out before proceeding to more practical uses of partial application. The catch has to do with type inference, and we'll tackle this next.

9.2 Overcoming the quirks of method resolution

So far, we've freely used methods, lambdas, and delegates to represent functions. To the compiler, however, these are all different things, and type inference for methods is not as good as we'd like it to be. Let's first see what happens when things go well, like when we use `Option.Map`:

```
Some(9.0).Map(Math.Sqrt) // => 3.0
```

Note that `Map` has two type parameters. If the compiler were unable to infer their types, we would have to write the preceding snippet like this:

```
Some(9.0).Map<double, double>(Math.Sqrt)
```

Here, the name `Math.Sqrt` identifies a method, and `Map` expects a delegate of type `Func<T, R>`. More technically, `Math.Sqrt` identifies a method group. Because of method overloading, there may be several methods with the same name. The compiler is smart enough to not only pick the right overload (in this case, there's only one), but also to infer the type arguments for `Map`.

This is all very well and good. It keeps us from having to convert between methods (or, alternatively, lambdas) and delegates, and from specifying the generic types, given that these can be inferred from the method signature. Unfortunately, for methods taking two or more arguments, all this goodness goes away.

Let's see what happens if we try to rewrite the `greet` function as a method. In the following listing, it's called `GreeterMethod`. Here's what we would like to write.

Listing 9.2   Type inference fails with multi-argument methods

```
PersonalizedGreeting GreeterMethod(Greeting gr, Name name)
    => $"{gr}, {name}";

Func<Name, PersonalizedGreeting> GreetWith(Greeting greeting)
    => GreeterMethod.Apply(greeting);
```

> If we write our greeting function as a method...

> ...then this expression does not compile.

Here we've written the greeter function as a method, and we now want a `GreetWith` method to partially apply it to a given greeting. Unfortunately, this code doesn't compile because the name `GreeterMethod` identifies a `MethodGroup`, whereas `Apply` expects a `Func`, and the compiler doesn't make the inference for us.

Type inference in local functions

C# 7 introduces *local functions* (functions that are declared within the scope of a method), but they should actually be called *local methods*. Internally, they're implemented as methods even though this gives no benefit (you can't overload them), so in terms of type inference, they have the same characteristics as normal methods.

If you want to use the generic `Apply` to supply arguments to a method, you have to use one of the forms in the following listing. You'll see that using multi-argument methods as arguments to HOFs requires messy syntax.

Listing 9.3   Multi-argument methods as arguments to HOFs

```
PersonalizedGreeting GreeterMethod(Greeting gr, Name name)
    => $"{gr}, {name}";

Func<Name, PersonalizedGreeting> GreetWith_1(Greeting greeting)
    => FuncExt.Apply<Greeting, Name, PersonalizedGreeting>
         (GreeterMethod, greeting);
```

> Foregoes extension method syntax and provides all generic arguments explicitly

```
Func<Name, PersonalizedGreeting> GreetWith_2(Greeting greeting)
    => new Func<Greeting, Name, PersonalizedGreeting>(GreeterMethod)
         .Apply(greeting);
```

> Explicitly converts the method to a `Func` before calling `Apply`

I personally find the syntactic noise in both cases unacceptable. Note that these issues are specific to *method* resolution. They go away if you use delegates (think `Func`) instead.

The following listing shows different ways to create a delegate, which you can then use with `Apply`.

Listing 9.4 Different ways of obtaining a delegate instance

```
public class TypeInference_Delegate
{
    readonly string separator = ", ";

    // 1. field
    readonly Func<Greeting, Name, PersonalizedGreeting> GreeterField
        = (gr, name) => $"{gr}, {name}";

    // 2. property
    Func<Greeting, Name, PersonalizedGreeting> GreeterProperty
        => (gr, name) => $"{gr}{separator}{name}";

    // 3. factory
    Func<Greeting, T, PersonalizedGreeting> GreeterFactory<T>()
        => (gr, t) => $"{gr}{separator}{t}";
}
```

Declaration and initialization of a delegate field; note that you can't reference `separator` here.

A getter-only property has its body introduced by `=>`.

A method that acts as a factory of functions can have generic parameters.

Let's briefly discuss these options. Declaring a delegate field would seem the most natural option. Unfortunately, it's not very powerful. For example, if you combine declaration and initialization as shown in listing 9.4, you can't reference any instance variables like `separator` in the delegate body. Also, because fields can be reassigned (something we certainly don't want to do in this case), you should mark the delegate as readonly.

Alternatively, you can expose the delegate through a property instead. In the class exposing the delegate, this amounts to just replacing `=` with `=>` to declare a getter-only property. From the point of view of the calling code, this change is completely transparent.

But the most powerful way is to have a *factory method*: a method that's there just to create the delegate you want. The big difference here is that you can also have generic parameters, which isn't possible with fields or properties.

Whichever way you obtain a delegate instance, type resolution will work fine, so that in all cases, you can supply the first argument like so:

```
GreeterField.Apply("Hi");
GreeterProperty.Apply("Hi");
GreeterFactory<Name>().Apply("Hi");
```

The takeaway from this section is that if you want to use HOFs that take multi-argument functions as arguments, it's sometimes best to move away from using methods and write `Func`s instead (or methods that return `Func`s). While less idiomatic than methods, `Func`s save you the syntactic overhead of explicitly specifying type arguments, making the code much more readable.

Now that you know about partial application, let's move on to a related concept: currying. It's a technique that assumes and arguably simplifies partial application.

9.3   *Curried functions: Optimized for partial application*

Named after mathematician Haskell Curry, *currying* is the process of transforming an *n*-ary function *f* that takes the arguments *t1*, *t2*,..., *tn* into a unary function that takes *t1* and yields a new function that takes *t2*, and so on, ultimately returning the same result as *f* once the arguments have all been given. In other words, an *n*-ary function with this signature

```
(T1, T2, ..., Tn) → R
```

when curried, has this signature:

```
T1 → T2 → ... → Tn → R
```

You've seen an example of this in the first section of this chapter. Here's a reminder:

```
var greet = (Greeting gr, Name name) => $"{gr}, {name}";

var greetWith = (Greeting gr) => (Name name) => $"{gr}, {name}";
```

I mentioned that `greetWith` is like `greet` but in curried form. Indeed, compare the signatures:

```
greet     : (Greeting, Name) → PersonalizedGreeting
greetWith : Greeting → Name → PersonalizedGreeting
```

This means that you could call the curried `greetWith` function like so:

```
greetWith("hello")("world") // => "hello, world"
```

This is two function invocations, and it's effectively the same as calling `greet` with two arguments. Of course, if you're going to pass in all the parameters at the same time, this is pointless. But it becomes useful when you're interested in partial application. If a function is curried, partial application is achieved simply by invoking the function:

```
var greetFormally = greetWith("Good evening");
names.Map(greetFormally).ForEach(WriteLine);
// prints: Good evening, Tristan
//         Good evening, Ivan
```

A function can be written in curried form like `greetWith` here; this is called *manual currying*. Alternatively, it's possible to define generic functions that will take an *n*-ary function and curry it. For binary and ternary functions, `Curry` looks like this:

```
public static Func<T1, Func<T2, R>> Curry<T1, T2, R>
   (this Func<T1, T2, R> f)
   => t1 => t2 => f(t1, t2);

public static Func<T1, Func<T2, Func<T3, R>>> Curry<T1, T2, T3, R>
   (this Func<T1, T2, T3, R> f)
```

```
=> t1 => t2 => t3 => f(t1, t2, t3);
```

Similar overloads can be defined for functions of other arities. As an exercise, write the signatures of the preceding functions in arrow notation. Let's look at how we could use such a generic `Curry` function to curry the `greet` function:

```
var greetWith = greet.Curry();
var greetNostalgically = greetWith("Arrivederci");

names.Map(greetNostalgically).ForEach(WriteLine);
// prints: Arrivederci, Tristan
//         Arrivederci, Ivan
```

Of course, if you want to use the generic `Curry` function, the same caveats about method resolution apply as with `Apply`.

Partial application and currying are closely related yet distinct concepts, and this is often confusing when you're introduced to them. Let's spell out the differences:

- *Partial application*—You give a function fewer arguments than the function expects, obtaining a function that's particularized with the values of the arguments given so far.
- *Currying*—You don't give any arguments; you just transform an *n*-ary function into a unary function to which arguments can be successively given to eventually get the same result as the original function.

As you can see, currying doesn't really *do* anything; rather, it optimizes a function for partial application. You can do partial application without currying as we did previously in this chapter with the use of the generic `Apply` functions. On the other hand, currying by itself is pointless: you curry a function (or write a function in curried form) so that you can more easily use partial application.

Partial application is so commonly used in FP that in many functional languages all functions are curried by default. For this reason, function signatures in arrow notation are given in curried form in the FP literature, like this:

```
T1 → T2 → ... → Tn → R
```

> **IMPORTANT** In the rest of the book, I'll always use the curried notation even for functions that aren't, in fact, curried.

Even though functions aren't curried by default in C#, you can still take advantage of partial application, allowing you to write highly general and, hence, widely reusable functions by parameterizing their behavior. You can then use partial application to create the more specific functions that you'll require from time to time. As you've seen so far, you can achieve this in different ways:

- By writing functions in curried form
- By currying functions with `Curry` and then invoking the curried function with subsequent arguments
- By supplying arguments one by one with `Apply`

Which technique you use is a matter of taste, although I personally find that using `Apply` is the most intuitive.

9.4   *Creating a partial-application-friendly API*

Now that you've seen the basic mechanism of partial application and how to work around poor type inference by using `Func`s instead of methods, we can move on to a more complex scenario in which we'll use a third-party library and realistic real-world requirements.

One good scenario for partial application is when a function requires some configuration that's available at startup and doesn't change, along with transient arguments that vary with every invocation. In such cases, a bootstrapping component can supply the configuration arguments, obtaining a specialized function that only expects invocation-specific arguments. This can then be given to the final consumer of the functionality, which is thus freed from having to know anything about the configuration.

In this section, we'll look at such an example: that of accessing a SQL database. Imagine an application that, like most, needs to perform a number of queries against a database. Let's think about this in terms of partial application. Imagine a general function for retrieving data:

- It can be particularized to query a specific database.
- It can be further particularized to retrieve objects of a given type.
- It can be further particularized with a given query and parameters.

Let's explore this through a simple example. Suppose we want to load an `Employee` by ID or to search for `Employees` by last name. These operations can be captured by functions with the following signatures:

```
lookupEmployee           : Guid → Option<Employee>
findEmployeesByLastName : string → IEnumerable<Employee>
```

Implementing these functions is our high-level goal. At a low level, we're going to use the Dapper library to query a SQL Server database.[1] For retrieving data, Dapper exposes the `Query` method with the following signature:

```
public static IEnumerable<T> Query<T>
(
    this IDbConnection conn,
    string sqlQuery,
    object param = null,
    SqlTransaction tran = null,
    bool buffered = true
)
```

---

[1] Dapper is a lightweight ORM that has gained a lot of popularity for being fast and simple to use; we used it first in chapter 2. It's available on GitHub at https://github.com/StackExchange/dapper-dot-net, and you can find more documentation there.

Table 9.1 describes the arguments we need to provide when calling `Query`, including the type parameter `T`. In this example, we'll disregard the last two parameters, which are optional.

Table 9.1 Arguments to Dapper's `Query` method

T	The type that should be populated from the data returned by the query. In our case, this will be `Employee` (Dapper automatically maps columns to fields).
conn	The connection to the database (notice that `Query` is an extension method on the connection but that doesn't matter as far as partial application is concerned).
sqlQuery	This is a template for the SQL query you want to execute, such as `"SELECT * FROM EMPLOYEES WHERE ID = @Id"` (notice the `@Id` placeholder).
param	An object whose properties are used to populate the placeholders in the `sqlQuery`. For instance, the preceding query needs the provided object to include a field called `Id`, whose value will be evaluated and rendered in the `sqlQuery` instead of `@Id`.

This is a great example of order of parameters because the connection and the SQL query can be applied as part of the application setup, whereas the `param` object will be specific to each call to `Query`. Right?

Err . . . well, actually, wrong! SQL connections are lightweight objects and should be obtained and disposed of whenever a query is performed. In fact, as you may remember from chapter 2, the standard use of Dapper's API follows this pattern:

```
const string sql = "SELECT 1";

using (var conn = new SqlConnection(connString))
{
    conn.Open();
    var result = conn.Query(sql);
}
```

This means our first parameter, the connection, is less general than the second parameter, the SQL template. But all is not lost. Remember, if you don't like the API you have, you can change it! That's what adapter functions are for.[2]

In the rest of this section, we'll write an API that better supports partial application in order to create specialized functions that retrieve the data we're interested in.

9.4.1 *Types as documentation*

While the DB connection must be short lived, the connection string which is used to create a connection typically doesn't change during the application's lifetime. It can be read from configuration when the application starts, and it never changes thereafter. The connection string would therefore be the most general parameter taken by a function that retrieves data.

---

[2] We discussed adapter functions in chapter 2: if you don't like the signature of a function, you can change it by defining a function that calls another and exposes an interface better suited to your needs.

Let's apply an idea introduced in section 4.2 (namely, that we can use types to make our code more expressive) and create a dedicated type for connection strings. The following listing shows this approach.

Listing 9.5 A custom type for connection strings

```
public record ConnectionString(string Value)
{
   public static implicit operator string(ConnectionString c) => c.Value;
   public static implicit operator ConnectionString(string s) => new (s);
}
```

When a string is not just a string but a DB connection string, we'll wrap it in a ConnectionString. This can be done trivially through implicit conversion. For example, on startup, we can populate it from configuration like so:

```
ConnectionString connString = configuration
   .GetSection("ConnectionString").Value;
```

The same thinking applies to the SQL template, so I've also defined a SqlTemplate type along the same lines. Most statically typed functional languages let you define custom types in terms of built-in types with a one-liner like this:

```
type ConnectionString = string
type SqlTemplate = string
```

In C#, it's a bit more laborious but still worth the effort. First, it makes your function signatures more intention-revealing: you're using types to document what your function does. For example, a function can declare that it depends on a connection string as in the following listing.

Listing 9.6 Making function signatures more explicit with custom types

```
public Option<Employee> lookupEmployee
   (ConnectionString conn, Guid id) => //...
```

This is much more explicit than depending on a string. The second benefit is that you can now define extension methods on ConnectionString, which wouldn't make sense on string. You'll see this next.

9.4.2 *Particularizing the data access function*

Now that we've looked at representing and acquiring a connection string, let's look at the remaining data needed to perform the DB query, from general to specific:

- The type of data we want to retrieve (such as Employee)
- The SQL query template (such as "SELECT * FROM EMPLOYEES WHERE ID = @Id")
- The param object that we'll use to render the SQL template (such as new { Id = "123" })

Now comes the crux of the solution. We can define an extension method on `ConnectionString` that takes the parameters we need as in the following listing.

Listing 9.7 An adapter function that's better suited for partial application

```
using Dapper;
using static ConnectionHelper;

public static class ConnectionStringExt
{
    public static Func<object, IEnumerable<T>> Retrieve<T>
    (
        this ConnectionString connStr,        These values are available
        SqlTemplate sql                       on application startup.
    )
    => param                                         ◁─┐ This value changes
    => Connect(connStr, conn => conn.Query<T>(sql, param));    with each query.
}
```

Notice that we're relying on `ConnectionHelper.Connect`, which we implemented in section 2.3 and which internally takes care of opening and disposing the connection. It doesn't matter if you don't remember the implementation details; just notice that here the most general parameter (the connection string, which will not change throughout the lifetime of the application) comes as the first parameter, whereas the DB connection itself is short-lived, and a new instance will be created by `Connect` with every query. This is the signature of the preceding method:

```
Retrieve<T> : (ConnectionString, SqlTemplate) → object → IEnumerable<T>
```

The function takes a connection string and a SQL template. These values are known when the application starts, so they can be given by a component that reads the configuration to `Retrieve` at startup. The result is a function that is still waiting to receive a final parameter: an object with the SQL query parameters. Such a function can be given to the component that handles incoming requests made by a client, for example. Hopefully, you now see how partial application relates to separation of concerns.

The following listing shows how `Retrieve` can be particularized to implement the functions we need.

Listing 9.8 Supplying arguments to get a function of the desired signature

```
ConnectionString conn = configuration
    .GetSection("ConnectionString").Value;

SqlTemplate sel = "SELECT * FROM EMPLOYEES"
    , sqlById = $"{sel} WHERE ID = @Id"
    , sqlByName = $"{sel} WHERE LASTNAME = @LastName";

// queryById : object → IEnumerable<Employee>            The connection string
var queryById = conn.Retrieve<Employee>(sqlById);    ◁─┘ and SQL query are fixed.
```

```
// queryByLastName : object → IEnumerable<Employee>
var queryByLastName = conn.Retrieve<Employee>(sqlByName);     ◁─┐  The connection string
                                                                 │  and SQL query are fixed.
// lookupEmployee : Guid → Option<Employee>
Option<Employee> lookupEmployee(Guid id)                      ◁─┐
   => queryById(new { Id = id }).SingleOrDefault();             │  The functions
                                                                 │  we set out to
// findEmployeesByLastName : string → IEnumerable<Employee>     │  implement
IEnumerable<Employee> findEmployeesByLastName(string lastName) ◁─┘
   => queryByLastName(new { LastName = lastName });
```

Here we define `queryById` and `queryByLastName` by particularizing the previously defined `Retrieve` method. We now have two unary functions that expect a `param` object, which wraps values that are used to replace the placeholder in the `SqlTemplate`.

All that's left to do is to define `lookupEmployee` and `findEmployeesByLastName` with the signatures we set out to expose at the beginning of the section. These act as adapter functions that translate their input argument to a suitably populated `param` object.

> **NOTE** It would be nice to be able to give `Retrieve` the connection string and obtain a function that can then be parameterized by the type of data returned. After all, we're going to use the same connection string for retrieving `Employees` as for any other entities. Unfortunately, C# doesn't allow us to defer the resolution of generic type arguments.

In this example, you saw how we started with an extremely general function for running any query against any SQL database and ended up with highly specialized functions. Note that we didn't explicitly use `Curry` or `Apply`; instead, `Retrieve` is defined in such a way that the arguments can be given piecemeal.

9.5 *Modularizing and composing an application*

As applications grow, we need to modularize them and break them down into components. For instance, in chapter 8, you saw an end-to-end example of handling a request to book a transfer. We put all the code in the controller, and by the end, the list of members in the controller looked like that shown in the following listing.

Listing 9.9 **A controller with too many responsibilities?**

```
public class MakeTransferController : ControllerBase
{
   DateTime now;
   static readonly Regex regex = new Regex("^[A-Z]{6}[A-Z1-9]{5}$");
   string connString;
   ILogger<MakeTransferController> logger;

   public IActionResult MakeTransfer([FromBody] MakeTransfer request)

   IActionResult OnFaulted(Exception ex)

   Validation<Exceptional<Unit>> Handle(MakeTransfer request)

   Validation<MakeTransfer> Validate(MakeTransfer cmd)
```

```
    Validation<MakeTransfer> ValidateBic(MakeTransfer cmd)
    Validation<MakeTransfer> ValidateDate(MakeTransfer cmd)

    Exceptional<Unit> Save(MakeTransfer transfer)
}
```

If this were a real-world banking application, you'd have not two but dozens of rules for checking the validity of the transfer request. You'd also have functionality to deal with identity and session management, instrumentation, and so on. In short, the controller would quickly become too big, and you'd need to break it down into separate components with more discrete responsibilities. This makes your code more modular and more manageable.

The other big drive for modularity is code reuse: logic for, say, session management or authorization could be required by several controllers and should, therefore, be placed in a separate component. Once you've broken up an application into components, you need to compose it back together so that all required components can collaborate at run time.

In this section, we'll look at how to deal with modularity and how the OO and functional approaches differ in this respect. We'll illustrate this by refactoring `MakeTransferController`.

9.5.1 Modularity in OOP

Modularity in OOP is usually obtained by assigning responsibilities to different classes and capturing these responsibilities with interfaces. For instance, you might define an `IValidator` interface for validation and an `IRepository` for persistence as the following listing displays.

Listing 9.10 Interfaces in OOP capture the components' responsibilities

```
public interface IValidator<T>
{
    Validation<T> Validate(T request);
}

public interface IRepository<T>
{
    Option<T> Lookup(Guid id);
    Exceptional<Unit> Save(T entity);
}
```

The controller would then depend on these interfaces in order to do its work as figure 9.3 shows.

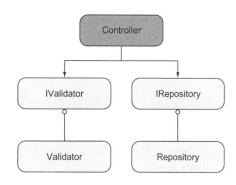

Figure 9.3 In OO design, higher-level components, like `Controller`, consume lower-level components, like `Repository`, via interfaces.

This follows a pattern called *dependency inversion*, according to which a higher-level component (such as the controller) doesn't consume lower-level components directly but rather through abstractions, which is usually understood to mean interfaces that the lower-level components (such as the validators and repository) implement.[3] There are a couple of benefits to this approach:

- *Decoupling*—You can swap out the repository implementation, changing it from writing to a database to writing to a queue, and this wouldn't impact the controller. You'd only need to change how the two are wired.
- *Testability*—You can unit test the handler without hitting the database by injecting a fake IRepository.

There's also a rather high cost associated with dependency inversion:

- There's an explosion in the number of interfaces, adding boilerplate and making the code difficult to navigate.
- The bootstrapping logic to compose the application is often far from trivial.
- Building fake implementations for testability can be complex.

To manage this extra complexity, third-party frameworks are often used; namely, IoC containers and mocking frameworks. If we follow this approach, the implementation of the controller ends up looking like what you see in the following listing.

Listing 9.11   Functional in the small and OO in the large

```
public class MakeTransferController : ControllerBase
{
    IValidator<MakeTransfer> validator;          Dependencies are objects.
    IRepository<MakeTransfer> repository;

    public MakeTransferController(IValidator<MakeTransfer> validator
        , IRepository<MakeTransfer> repository)
    {
        this.validator = validator;              Dependencies are injected
        this.repository = repository;            in the constructor.
    }

    [HttpPost, Route("api/transfers/book")]
    public IActionResult TransferOn([FromBody] MakeTransfer transfer)
        => validator.Validate(transfer)
            .Map(repository.Save)                 Consumes dependencies
            .Match
            (
                Invalid: BadRequest,
```

---

[3] Note that there's a difference between dependency injection and dependency inversion. *Dependency injection* is far more general: it means you're injecting something that a class, method, or function requires. For example, if you inject a concrete implementation, a primitive value, or a configuration object, you're using dependency injection but not dependency inversion. *Dependency inversion* relies on dependency injection, but the opposite is not true.

```
            Valid: result => result.Match<IActionResult>
            (
                Exception: _ => StatusCode(500, Errors.UnexpectedError),
                Success: _ => Ok()
            )
        );
}
```

You could say that the preceding implementation is functional in the small and OO in the large. The main components (controller, validator, repository) are indeed objects, and the program behavior is encoded in methods on these objects. On the other hand, many functional concepts are then used in the implementation of the methods and in defining their signatures.

This approach of using functional techniques within an overall OO software architecture is a perfectly valid way to integrate FP with OOP. It's also possible to push the functional approach so that all behavior is captured in functions. You'll see this next.

9.5.2 Modularity in FP

If the fundamental units of OOP are objects, in FP they're functions. Modularity in FP is achieved by assigning responsibilities to functions, which are then combined using function composition. In a functional approach, we don't define interfaces because function signatures already provide all the interface we need.

For instance, in chapter 3, you saw that a validator class that needs to know the current time doesn't need to depend on a service, but can just depend on a function that returns the current time. The following listing provides a reminder.

Listing 9.12 Injecting functions as dependencies

```
public record DateNotPastValidator(Func<DateTime> Clock)
    : IValidator<MakeTransfer>
{
    public Validation<MakeTransfer> Validate(MakeTransfer transfer)
        => transfer.Date.Date < Clock().Date
            ? Errors.TransferDateIsPast
            : Valid(transfer);
}
```

After all, what is a clock if not a function that you can invoke to get the current time? But let's take this one step further: Why would you even need the IValidator interface in the first place? After all, what is a validator if not a function that you can call to find out if a given object is valid? Let's instead use a delegate to represent validation:

```
// Validator<T> : T → Validation<T>
public delegate Validation<T> Validator<T>(T t);
```

If we follow this approach, MakeTransferController depends not on an IValidator object but on a Validator function. To implement a Validator, you don't need to have an object storing dependencies as fields; instead, dependencies can be passed as function arguments, as the next listing shows.

Listing 9.13 Passing dependencies as function arguments

```
public static Validator<MakeTransfer> DateNotPast(Func<DateTime> clock)
   => transfer
   => transfer.Date.Date < clock().Date
      ? Errors.TransferDateIsPast
      : Valid(transfer);
```

Here, `DateNotPast` is a HOF that takes a function `clock` (the dependency it needs in order to know the current date) and returns a function of type `Validator`. Notice how this approach spares you the whole ceremony of creating interfaces, injecting them in the constructor, and storing them in fields.

Let's see how you would create a `Validator`. When bootstrapping the application, you'd give `DateNotPast` a function that reads from the system clock:

```
Validator<MakeTransfer> val = DateNotPast(() => DateTime.UtcNow());
```

For testing purposes, however, you can provide a `clock` that returns a constant date:

```
var uut = DateNotPast(() => new DateTime(2020, 20, 10));
```

Notice that this is, in fact, partial application: `DateNotPast` is a binary function (in curried form) that needs a clock and a `MakeTransfer` to compute its result. You supply the first argument when composing the application (or in the *arrange* phase of a unit test) and the second argument when processing an incoming request (or in the *act* phase of a unit test).

Apart from the validator, `MakeTransferController` also needs a dependency to persist the `MakeTransfer` request data. If we're going to use functions, we can represent this with the following signature:

```
MakeTransfer → Exceptional<Unit>
```

Again, we can create such a function by starting with a general function that writes to the DB with this signature:

```
TryExecute : ConnectionString → SqlTemplate → object → Exceptional<Unit>
```

We can then parameterize it with a connection string from the configuration and a SQL template with the command we want to execute. This is similar to the `Retrieve` function you saw in section 9.3, so I'll omit the full details here. Our controller implementation will now look like this:

```
public class MakeTransferController : ControllerBase
{
   Validator<MakeTransfer> validate;
   Func<MakeTransfer, Exceptional<Unit>> save;
```

```
[HttpPost, Route("api/transfers/book")]
public IActionResult MakeTransfer([FromBody] MakeTransfer cmd)
   => validate(cmd).Map(save).Match( //...
}
```

If we take this approach to its logical conclusion, we should question why we need a controller at all when all the logic we're using could be captured in a function of type:

```
MakeTransfer → IResult
```

This is a function that takes a `MakeTransfer` command, deserialized from the body of the HTTP request, and returns an `IResult`, which ASP.NET uses to populate the HTTP response appropriately. More precisely, the function also needs to take in the `validate` and `save` functions it depends on. The following listing shows this approach.

Listing 9.14 The top-level function of our use case

```
using static Microsoft.AspNetCore.Http.Results;        ◁——  Defines the functions Ok,
                                                             BadRequest, etc., which
                                                             populate an IResult
static Func<MakeTransfer, IResult> HandleSaveTransfer
(
   Validator<MakeTransfer> validate,                    Dependencies required
   Func<MakeTransfer, Exceptional<Unit>> save           to handle the command
)
=> transfer                                   ◁——  The command that is
=> validate(transfer).Map(save).Match              received by the API
   (
      Invalid: err => BadRequest(err),
      Valid: result => result.Match
      (
         Exception: _ => StatusCode(StatusCodes.Status500InternalServerError),
         Success: _ => Ok()
      )
   );
```

This is pretty much the same as our `MakeTransferController` method with a couple of differences:

- *Dependencies are not stored in fields but are functions passed as parameters.* We expect that `validate` and `save` are given when the application starts, resulting in a function that takes a `MakeTransfer`, which is called with each incoming request.
- *The code uses functions like* `OK` *and* `BadRequest` *to populate an* `IResult`. These are exposed as static methods in `Microsoft.AspNetCore.Http.Results`. In contrast, the previous implementation (listing 9.11) used equally named methods inherited from `ControllerBase`.

We now need to register this function to actually be called when a client sends an HTTP request to the corresponding route. Let's do that next.

9.5.3   *Mapping functions to API endpoints*

You could think of a Web API as a function that takes an HTTP request as input and yields an HTTP response as output. How would such a function work? It would look at the request's route and pass the request to a corresponding function, so, a collection of functions, one for each API endpoint. Conceptually, it's easy to conceive of an API as a set of functions. For a long time, however, translating this idea into practice using ASP.NET has been impractical because ASP.NET favored MVC controllers as the way to create Web APIs.

This has changed completely with .NET 6, which includes *minimal APIs*, a feature allowing you to simply map functions to API endpoints. This represents a huge shift! For years, we've had functional features in C# but were somewhat inhibited in their use by OO frameworks, including ASP.NET. Minimal APIs allow you to start building in a functional style from the ground up.

> **TIP** If you cannot use .NET 6, you can still build Web APIs in a functional style by using a package called Feather HTTP. Feather HTTP was the first incarnation of what has since become .NET 6 minimal APIs. See https://github.com/featherhttp/framework for up-to-date instructions on how to reference Feather HTTP.

Using minimal APIs, you can configure a Web API with just a few lines of code.

Listing 9.15   Configuring a minimal Web API

```
using Microsoft.AspNetCore.Builder;

var app = WebApplication.Create();          ⟵┘ Creates a web application

app.MapGet("/", () => "Hello World!");      ⟵┘ Configures an endpoint

await app.RunAsync();                       ⟵┘ Starts listening for requests
```

As you can see, you just create a `WebApplication` and then use `MapGet`, `MapPost`, and so on, providing a route and the function that should handle requests on that route. This is in line with the micro web frameworks that are so popular in other languages.

Top-level statements

The previous listing uses *top-level statements*, a feature introduced in C# 9. You can have a single file containing loose statements, and this will serve as the entry point for your application (previously these statements would have been wrapped in `Program.Main`).

If you're writing a minimal API, it makes sense to have your API configuration in your entry-point file, potentially using top-level statements. In this file, you can map all your application's endpoints to functions defined in other files in your project.

The following listing shows another, slightly more complex, endpoint. This one receives a `Todo` object and saves it to a database.

Listing 9.16 Configuring a POST request

```
app.MapPost("/todos", async
    (
        [FromServices] TodoDbContext db,       ◁──┐ This dependency
                                                   must be registered.
        Todo todo          ◁───┐ The deserialized
    ) =>                       │ request body
    {
        await db.Todos.AddAsync(todo);    │ Writes to the DB
        await db.SaveChangesAsync();       │

        return new StatusCodeResult(204);   ◁──┐ Populates
    });                                        │ the response
```

As you can see, minimal APIs offer all the perks available in MVC controllers (dependency injection, deserialization, handling asynchronous processing, etc.) with less ceremony. Similarly, in our BOC application, we can simply plug the handler defined in listing 9.14 into the `WebApplication`. The application's entry point will then look like this:

```
var app = WebApplication.Create();
var handleSaveTransfer = ConfigureSaveTransferHandler(app.Configuration);

app.MapPost("/Transfer/Future", handleSaveTransfer);

await app.RunAsync();
```

All that is left to do is to implement `ConfigureSaveTransferHandler`, where we set up the dependencies that will be used in our `MakeTransfer` handler. The following listing shows this setup.

Listing 9.17 Wiring up the functions needed for a use case

```
static Func<MakeTransfer, IResult>
    ConfigureSaveTransferHandler(IConfiguration config)
{
    ConnectionString connString
        = config.GetSection("ConnectionString").Value;
    SqlTemplate InsertTransferSql = "INSERT ...";
                                                         │ Sets up
    var save = connString.TryExecute(InsertTransferSql);  ◁──┘ persistence

    var validate = DateNotPast(() => DateTime.UtcNow);   ◁── Sets up validation

    return HandleSaveTransfer(validate, save);   ◁──┐ Combines the two into
}                                                    │ the main workflow
```

Here we wire up the various pieces: we give our general `TryExecute` all the parameters it needs to be able to save a `MakeTransfer` to the DB when required; we give `DateNot-Past` a clock; and, finally, we give both resulting functions to the main function in our logic (listing 9.14).

That's it! You can see how we were able to build a whole use case using just functions: no interfaces, no repositories—just functions (a function for saving data, a function for validating, a function for combining both in the handling of a request). When you look at it, it's actually pretty clean and simple.

We still simplistically only apply one validation rule, but we'll cater for several rules in section 9.6. First, let's discuss how the OO and the functional approach stack up in this example.

9.5.4   *Comparing the two approaches*

In the functional approach I just demonstrated, all dependencies are injected as functions. Notice that with this approach, you still have the benefits associated with dependency inversion:

- *Decoupling*—A function knows nothing about the implementation details of the functions it consumes.
- *Testability*—When testing any of these functions, you can simply pass it functions that return a predictable result.

You also mitigate some of the problems associated with dependency inversion in its OOP version:

- You don't need to define any interfaces.
- This makes testing easier because you don't need to set up fakes.

For example, the following listing shows a test for the use case we developed in this section. Note that when dependencies are functions, unit tests can be written without fakes.

Listing 9.18   A unit test without fakes

```
[Test]
public void WhenValid_AndSaveSucceeds_ThenResponseIsOk()
{
   var handler = HandleSaveTransfer
   (
      validate: transfer => Valid(transfer),          Injects functions that return
      save: _ => Exceptional(Unit())                  a predictable result
   );

   var result = controller.MakeTransfer(MakeTransfer.Dummy);

   Assert.AreEqual(typeof(OkResult), result.GetType());
}
```

So far, the functional approach seems preferable. There's also another difference to point out. In the OO implementation (listing 9.10), the controller depends on an IRepository interface defined as follows:

```
public interface IRepository<T>
{
   Option<T> Lookup(Guid id);
   Exceptional<Unit> Save(T entity);
}
```

But notice that the controller only uses the Save method. This violates the *interface segregation principle* (ISP), which states that clients shouldn't depend on methods they don't use. The idea is that just because you're trusting your 15-year-old child with your house keys, that doesn't mean they should have your car keys as well. The IRepository interface should actually be broken up into two single-method interfaces, and the controller should depend on a smaller interface like this:

```
public interface ISaveToRepository<T>
{
   Exceptional<Unit> Save(T entity);
}
```

This further increases the number of interfaces in the application. If you push the ISP hard enough, you'll end up with a prevalence of single-method interfaces that convey the same information as a function signature, ultimately making it simpler to just inject functions as in the functional approach.

(Of course, if the controller did require both a function to read and to write, then in the functional style, we'd have to inject two functions, increasing the number of dependencies. As usual, the functional style is more explicit.)

To complete the implementation of this use case, we need to cater for not one, but many validation rules. In OOP, you could use a composite validator that implements IValidator and internally uses a list of specific IValidators. But we want to do this in a functional style and have a Validator function that internally combines the rules of many Validators. We'll look at this next, but in order to do so, we must first take a step back and look at a general pattern for reducing a list of values to a single value.

9.6 Reducing a list to a single value

Reducing a list of values into a single value is a common operation, but one we haven't discussed so far. In FP-speak, this operation is called *fold* or *reduce*, and these are the names you'll encounter in most languages or libraries and in the FP literature. Characteristically, LINQ uses a different name: Aggregate. If you're already familiar with Aggregate, you can skip the next subsection.

9.6.1 LINQ's Aggregate method

Note that most of the functions we've used so far with IEnumerable also return an IEnumerable. For example, Map takes a list of *n* things and returns another list of *n* things, possibly of a different type. `Where` and `Bind` also stay within the abstraction; they take an `IEnumerable` and return an `IEnumerable`, although the quantity and the type of the elements may change.

`Aggregate` is different from these functions in that it takes a list of *n* things and returns exactly one thing (just like the SQL aggregate functions `COUNT`, `SUM`, and `AVERAGE`, which you may be familiar with).

Given an `IEnumerable<T>`, `Aggregate` takes an initial value, called an *accumulator* (or *seed*), and a *reducer* function (a binary function accepting the accumulator and an element in the list and returning the new value for the accumulator). `Aggregate` then traverses the list, applying the function to the current value of the accumulator and each element in the list. The signature for `Aggregate` is

```
IEnumerable<T> → Acc → (Acc → T → Acc) → Acc
```

For example, you could have a list of lemons and aggregate it into a glass of lemon juice. The accumulator would be an empty glass, and this is what you get back if the list of lemons is empty. The reducer function takes a glass and a single lemon and returns a glass with the lemon squeezed into it. Given these arguments, `Aggregate` traverses the list, squeezing each lemon into the glass, finally returning the glass with juice from all the lemons.

Figure 9.4 shows it graphically. If the list is empty, `Aggregate` returns the given accumulator, *acc*. If it contains one item, t_0, it returns the result of applying *f* to *acc* and t_0; let's call this value acc_1. If it contains more items, it will compute acc_1 and then apply *f* to acc_1 and t_1 to obtain acc_2, and so on, finally returning acc_N as a result: *acc* can be seen as an initial value on top of which all values in the list are applied using the given function.

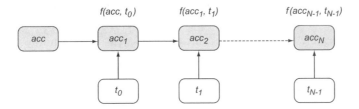

Figure 9.4   Reducing a list to a single value with `Aggregate`

The `Sum` function (available in its own right in LINQ) is a special case of `Aggregate`. What's the sum of all the numbers in an empty list? Naturally, 0! That's our accumulator value. The binary function is just addition, so we can express `Sum` as the next listing shows.

Listing 9.19   Sum as a special case of `Aggregate`

```
Range(1, 5).Aggregate(0, (acc, i) => acc + i) // => 15
```

Notice that this expands to the following:

```
((((0 + 1) + 2) + 3) + 4) + 5
```

More generally, `ts.Aggregate(acc, f)` expands to

```
f(f(f(f(acc, t0), t1), t2), ... tn)
```

`Count` can also be seen as a special case of `Aggregate`:

```
Range(1, 5).Aggregate(0, (count, _) => count + 1) // => 5
```

Notice that the type of the accumulator isn't necessarily the type of the list items. For example, let's say that we have a list of things, and we want to add them to a tree. The type in our list would be, say, `T`, and the type of the accumulator would be `Tree<T>`. The following listing shows how we could start with an empty tree as an accumulator and add each item as we traverse the list.

> **Listing 9.20 Using `Aggregate` to create a tree of all items in a list**

```
Range(1, 5).Aggregate(Tree<int>.Empty, (tree, i) => tree.Insert(i))
```

In this example, I'm assuming that `tree.Insert(i)` returns a tree with the newly inserted value.

`Aggregate` is such a powerful method that it's possible to implement `Map`, `Where`, and `Bind` in terms of `Aggregate` (something I suggest as an exercise). There's also a less general overload that doesn't take an accumulator argument but uses the first element of the list as accumulator. The signature for this overload is

```
IEnumerable<T> → (T → T → T) → T
```

When using this overload, the result type is the same as the type of the elements in the list, and the list can't be empty.

9.6.2 *Aggregating validation results*

Now that you know how to reduce a list of values to a single value, let's apply this knowledge and see how we can reduce a list of validators to a single validator. To do this, we'll need to implement a function with type

```
IEnumerable<Validator<T>> → Validator<T>
```

Notice that because `Validator` is itself a function type, the preceding type expands to this:

```
IEnumerable<T → Validation<T>> → T → Validation<T>
```

First of all, we need to decide how we want the combined validation to work:

- *Fail fast*—If validation should be optimized for efficiency, the combined validation should fail as soon as one validator fails, thus minimizing the use of resources. This is a good approach if you're validating a request made programmatically from an application.
- *Harvest errors*—You may want to identify all the rules that have been violated so that they can be fixed prior to making another request. This is a better approach when validating a request made by a user through a form.

The fail-fast strategy is easier to implement: every validator returns a `Validation`, and `Validation` exposes a `Bind` function that only applies the bound function if the state is `Valid` (just like `Option` and `Either`), so we can use `Aggregate` to traverse the list of validators and `Bind` each validator to the running result. The following listing shows this approach.

Listing 9.21   Using `Aggregate` to apply all validators in a list

```
public static Validator<T> FailFast<T>
   (IEnumerable<Validator<T>> validators)
   => t
   => validators.Aggregate(Valid(t)
      , (acc, validator) => acc.Bind(_ => validator(t)));
```

Notice that the `FailFast` function takes a list of `Validators` and returns a `Validator`: a function that expects an object of type `T` to validate. On receiving the valid `t`, it traverses the list of validators using `Valid(t)` as accumulator (if the list of validators is empty, then `t` is valid) and applies each validator in the list to the accumulator with `Bind`. Conceptually, the call to `Aggregate` expands as follows:

```
Valid(t)
   .Bind(validators[0]))
   .Bind(validators[1]))
   ...
   .Bind(validators[n - 1]));
```

Because of how `Bind` is defined for `Validation`, when a validator fails, the subsequent validators will be skipped, and the whole validation fails.

Not all validation is equally expensive. For instance, validating that the BIC code is well-formed with a regular expression (as shown in listing 8.7) is cheap. Suppose that you also need to ensure that the given BIC code identifies an existing bank branch. This might involve a DB lookup or a remote call to a service with a list of valid codes, which is clearly more expensive.

To ensure that overall validation is efficient, you need to order the list of validators accordingly. In this case, you'd need to apply the (cheap) regular expression validation first and only then the (expensive) remote lookup.

9.6.3   *Harvesting validation errors*

The opposite approach is to prioritize *completeness*, including the details of *all* failing validations. In this case, you don't want failure to prevent further computation; on the contrary, you want to ensure that all the validators run and that all errors, if any, are harvested. This is useful if, say, you're validating a form with lots of fields, and you want the user to see everything they need to fix in order to make a valid submission. The following listing shows how we could rewrite the method that combines the different validators.

Listing 9.22 Collecting errors from all validators that fail

```
public static Validator<T> HarvestErrors<T>
  (IEnumerable<Validator<T>> validators)
  => t =>
{
  var errors = validators              Runs all validators
    .Map(validate => validate(t))  ◁──┘ independently
    .Bind(v => v.Match(                        Collects
       Invalid: errs => Some(errs),  ◁──────── validation errors
       Valid: _ => None))   ◁──┐
    .ToList();                 │ Disregards
                                 passed validation
  return errors.Count == 0  ◁──┐
    ? Valid(t)                 │ If there were no errors, the
    : Invalid(errors.Flatten());  overall validation passes.
};
```

Here, instead of using Aggregate, we use Map to map the list of validators to the results of running the validators on the object to be validated. This ensures that all validators are called independently, and we end up with an IEnumerable of Validations.

We're then interested in harvesting all the errors. To do this, we use Option. We map Invalids to a Some wrapping the errors and Valids to None. Remember from chapter 6 that Bind can be used to filter Nones from a list of Options, and that's what we're doing here to obtain a list of all errors. Because each Invalid contains a list of errors, errors is actually a list of lists. In case of failure, we need to flatten it into a one-dimensional list and use it to populate an Invalid. If there were no errors, we return the object being validated, wrapped in a Valid.[4]

Exercises

1 Partial application with a binary arithmetic function:

  – Write a function, Remainder, that calculates the remainder of integer division (and works for negative input values!). Notice how the expected order of parameters isn't the one that's most likely to be required by partial application (you're more likely to partially apply the divisor).

  – Write an ApplyR function that gives the rightmost parameter to a given binary function. (Try to do so without looking at the implementation for Apply.) Write the signature of ApplyR in arrow notation, both in curried and non-curried forms.

  – Use ApplyR to create a function that returns the remainder of dividing any number by 5.

  – Write an overload of ApplyR that gives the rightmost argument to a ternary function.

---

[4] There's actually a simpler way to accomplish this using applicatives and traverse, tools we haven't covered yet. You'll see this in chapter 15.

2   Ternary functions:
   – Define a `PhoneNumber` class with three fields: number type (home, mobile . . .), country code ('it', 'uk' . . .), and number. `CountryCode` should be a custom type with implicit conversion to and from `string`.
   – Define a ternary function that creates a new number, given values for these fields. What's the signature of your factory function?
   – Use partial application to create a binary function that creates a UK number and then again to create a unary function that creates a UK mobile.

3   Functions everywhere: you may still have a feeling that objects are ultimately more powerful than functions. Surely a logger object should expose methods for related operations such as `Debug`, `Info`, and `Error`? To see that this is not necessarily so, challenge yourself to write a simple logging mechanism (logging to the console is fine) that doesn't require any classes or structs. You should still be able to inject a `Log` value into a consumer class or function, exposing the operations `Debug`, `Info`, and `Error`, like so:

```
void ConsumeLog(Log log)
   => log.Info("look! no classes!");
```

4   Open exercise: in your day-to-day coding, start paying more attention to the signatures of the functions you write and consume. Does the order of arguments make sense; do they go from general to specific? Is there some argument that you always invoke with the same value so that you could partially apply it? Do you sometimes write similar variations of the same code, and could these be generalized into a parameterized function?

5   Implement `Map`, `Where`, and `Bind` for `IEnumerable` in terms of `Aggregate`.

Summary

- Partial application means giving a function its arguments piecemeal, effectively creating a more specialized function with each argument given.
- Currying means changing the signature of a function so that it will take its arguments one at a time.
- Partial application enables you to write highly general functions by parameterizing their behavior and then supplying arguments to obtain increasingly specialized functions.
- The order of arguments matters: you give the leftmost argument first so that a function should declare its arguments from general to specific.
- When working with multi-argument functions in C#, method resolution can be problematic and lead to syntactic overhead. This can be overcome by relying on `Func`s rather than on methods.
- You can inject the dependencies required by your functions by declaring them as arguments. This allows you to compose your application entirely of functions without compromising on the separation of concerns, decoupling, and testability.

Working effectively with
multi-argument functions

10

This chapter covers

- Using multi-argument functions with elevated types
- Using LINQ syntax with any monadic type
- Fundamentals of property-based testing

The main goal of this chapter is to teach you to use multi-argument functions in the world of *effectful* types, so the "effectively" in the title is also a pun! Remember from section 6.6.1, effectful types are types such as `Option` (which adds the effect of optionality), `Exceptional` (exception handling), `IEnumerable` (aggregation), and others. In part 3, you'll see several more effects related to state, laziness, and asynchrony.

As you code more functionally, you'll come to rely heavily on these effects. You probably already use `IEnumerable` a lot. If you embrace the fact that types like `Option` and some variation of `Either` add robustness to your programs, you'll soon be dealing in elevated types in much of your code.

Although you've seen the power of core functions like `Map` and `Bind`, there's an important technique you haven't seen yet: how to integrate multi-argument functions in your workflows, given that `Map` and `Bind` both take unary functions.

It turns out that there are two possible approaches: the applicative and monadic approaches. We'll first look at the applicative approach, which uses the Apply function (a core function you haven't seen yet). We'll then revisit monads, and you'll see how you can use Bind with multi-argument functions and how LINQ syntax can be helpful in this area. We'll then compare the two approaches and see why both can be useful in different cases. Along the way, I'll also present some of the theory related to monads and applicatives, and I'll introduce a technique for unit testing called *property-based testing*.

10.1 *Function application in the elevated world*

In this section, I'll introduce the *applicative* approach, which relies on the definition of a new function, Apply, that performs function application in the elevated world. Apply, like Map and Bind, is one of the core functions in FP.

To warm up, start the REPL and import the LaYumba.Functional library as usual. Then, type the following:

```
var doubl = (int i) => i * 2;

Some(3).Map(doubl) // => Some(6)
```

So far, nothing new: you have a number wrapped in an Option, and you can apply the unary function doubl to it with Map. Now, say you have a *binary* function like multiplication, and you have two numbers, each wrapped in an Option. How can you apply the function to its arguments?

Here's the key concept: currying (which was covered in chapter 9) allows you to turn any *n*-ary function into a unary function that, when given its argument, returns a *(n–1)*-ary function. This means you can use Map with any function as long as it's curried! Let's see this in practice as the following listing shows.

Listing 10.1 Mapping a curried function onto an `Option`

```
var multiply = (int x) => (int y) => x * y;

var multBy3 = Some(3).Map(multiply);
// => Some(y => 3 * y))
```

Remember, when you Map a function onto an Option, Map extracts the value in the Option and applies the given function to it. In the preceding listing, Map extracts the value 3 from Option and feeds it to the multiply function: 3 replaces the variable x, yielding the function y => 3 * y. Let's look at the types:

```
multiply             : int → int → int
Some(3)              : Option<int>
Some(3).Map(multiply) : Option<int → int>
```

When you map a multi-argument function, the function is partially applied to the argument wrapped in the Option. Let's look at this from a more general point of view. Here's the signature of Map for a functor F:

```
Map : F<T> → (T → R) → F<R>
```

Now imagine that the type of R happens to be T1 → T2, so R is actually a function. In that case, the signature expands to

```
F<T> → (T → T1 → T2) → F<T1 → T2>
```

But look at the second argument: T → T1 → T2. That's a binary function in curried form. This means that you can use Map with functions of any arity! In order to free the caller from having to curry functions, my functional library includes overloads of Map that accept functions of various arities and takes care of currying: for example,

```
public static Option<Func<T2, R>> Map<T1, T2, R>
   (this Option<T1> opt, Func<T1, T2, R> func)
   => opt.Map(func.Curry());
```

As a result, the code in the following listing also works.

Listing 10.2 Mapping a binary function onto an `Option`

```
var multiply = (int x, int y) => x * y;

var multBy3 = Some(3).Map(multiply);
multBy3 // => Some(y => 3 * y))
```

Now that you know you can effectively use Map with multi-argument functions, let's look at the resulting value. This is something you've not seen before: an elevated function, which is a function wrapped in an elevated type, as figure 10.1 illustrates.

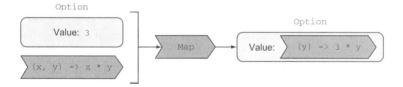

Figure 10.1 Mapping a binary function onto an `Option` yields a unary function wrapped in an `Option`.

There's nothing special about an elevated function. Functions are values, so it's simply another value wrapped in one of the usual containers.

And yet, how do you deal with an elevated value that's a function? Now that you have a unary function wrapped in an `Option`, how do you supply it its second argument? And what if the second argument is also wrapped in an `Option`? A crude approach would be to explicitly unwrap both values and then apply the function to the argument like this:

```
var multiply = (int x, int y) => x * y;

Option<int> optX = Some(3)
          , optY = Some(4);
```

```
var result = optX.Map(multiply).Match
(
    () => None,
    (f) => optY.Match
    (
        () => None,
        (y) => Some(f(y))
    )
);

result // => Some(12)
```

This code isn't nice. It leaves the elevated world of `Option` to apply the function, only to lift the result back up into an `Option`. Is it possible to abstract this and integrate multi-argument functions in a workflow without leaving the elevated world? This is indeed what the `Apply` function does, and we'll look at it next.

10.1.1 *Understanding applicatives*

Before we look at defining `Apply` for elevated values, let's briefly review the `Apply` function we defined in chapter 9, which performs partial application in the world of regular values. We defined various overloads for `Apply` that take an *n*-ary function and an argument and return the result of applying the function to the argument. The signatures are in the form

```
Apply : (T → R) → T → R
Apply : (T1 → T2 → R) → T1 → (T2 → R)
Apply : (T1 → T2 → T3 → R) → T1 → (T2 → T3 → R)
```

These signatures say, "Give me a function and a value, and I'll give you the result of applying the function to the value," whether that's the function's return value or the partially applied function.

In the elevated world, we need to define overloads of `Apply` where the input and output values are wrapped in elevated types. In general, for any functor `A` for which `Apply` can be defined, the signatures of `Apply` will be in the form

```
Apply : A<T → R> → A<T> → A<R>
Apply : A<T1 → T2 → R> → A<T1> → A<T2 → R>
Apply : A<T1 → T2 → T3 → R> → A<T1> → A<T2 → T3 → R>
```

It's just like the regular `Apply`, but in the elevated world, it says, "Give me a function wrapped in an `A` and a value wrapped in an `A`, and I'll give you the result of applying the function to the value also wrapped in an `A`, of course." This is illustrated in figure 10.2.

An implementation of `Apply` must unwrap the function, unwrap the value, apply the function to the value, and wrap the result back up. When we define a suitable implementation of `Apply` for a functor `A`, this is called an *applicative functor* (or simply an *applicative*). The following listing shows how `Apply` is defined for `Option`, thus making `Option` an applicative.

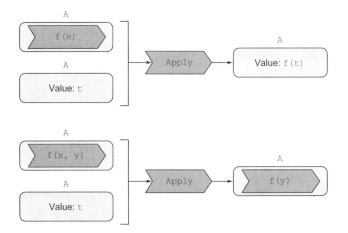

Figure 10.2 `Apply` performs function application in the elevated world.

Listing 10.3   Implementation of `Apply` for `Option`

```
public static Option<R> Apply<T, R>
(
    this Option<Func<T, R>> optF,
    Option<T> optT
)
=> optF.Match
(
    () => None,
    (f) => optT.Match
    (
        () => None,
        (t) => Some(f(t))          Only applies the wrapped function to the
    )                              wrapped value if both Options are Some
);

public static Option<Func<T2, R>> Apply<T1, T2, R>
(
    this Option<Func<T1, T2, R>> optF,
    Option<T1> optT                       Curries the wrapped function and
)                                         calls the overload that takes an
=> Apply(optF.Map(F.Curry), optT);        Option wrapping a unary function
```

The first overload is the important one. It takes a unary function wrapped in an `Option` and an argument to that function, also wrapped in an `Option`. The implementation returns `Some` only if both inputs are `Some` and `None` in all other cases.

As usual, overloads are required for the various arities of the wrapped functions. We can define those in terms of the unary version as the second overload demonstrates.

Now that the low-level details of wrapping and unwrapping are taken care of, let's see how you can use `Apply` with a binary function:

```
var multiply = (int x, int y) => x * y;

Some(3).Map(multiply).Apply(Some(4));
// => Some(12)
```

```
Some(3).Map(multiply).Apply(None);
// => None
```

In short, if you have a function wrapped in a container, `Apply` allows you to supply arguments to it. Let's take this idea one step further.

10.1.2 Lifting functions

In the examples so far, you've seen functions lifted into a container by mapping a multi-argument function onto an elevated value like this:

```
Some(3).Map(multiply)
```

Alternatively, you could lift a function into a container by simply using the container's `Return` function as with any other value. After all, the wrapped function doesn't care *how* it gets there, so you can write this:

```
Some(multiply)         ◁─┐  Lifts the function
   .Apply(Some(3))        └─ into an Option
   .Apply(Some(4))      │  Supplies arguments
                        │  with Apply

// => Some(12)
```

This can be generalized to functions of any arity. And, as usual, you get the safety of `Option` so that if any value along the way is `None`, the final result is also `None`:

```
Some(multiply)
   .Apply(None)
   .Apply(Some(4))
// => None
```

As you can see, there are two distinct but equivalent ways of evaluating a binary function in the elevated world. You can see these side by side in table 10.1.

Table 10.1 Two equivalent ways to achieve function application in the elevated world

Map the function, then `Apply`.	Lift the function, then `Apply`.

`Some(3)`
`   .Map(multiply)`
`   .Apply(Some(4))`
	`Some(multiply)`
	`   .Apply(Some(3))`
	`   .Apply(Some(4))`

The second way (first lifting the function with `Return` and then applying arguments) is more readable and more intuitive because it's similar to partial application in the world of regular values, as table 10.2 shows.

Table 10.2 Partial application in the worlds of regular and elevated values

Partial application with regular values	Partial application with elevated values
| ```
multiply
   .Apply(3)
   .Apply(4)

   // => 12
``` | ```
Some(multiply)
   .Apply(Some(3))
   .Apply(Some(4))

   // => Some(12)
``` |

Whether you obtain the function by using `Map` or lifting it with `Return` doesn't matter in terms of the resulting functor. This is a requirement, and it will hold if the applicative is correctly implemented. It's sometimes called the *applicative law.*[1]

10.1.3 An introduction to property-based testing

Can we write some unit tests to prove that the functions we've been using to work with `Option` satisfy the applicative law? There's a specific technique for this sort of testing (testing that an implementation satisfies certain laws or properties). It's called *property-based testing*, and a supporting framework called FsCheck is available for doing property-based testing in .NET.[2]

Property-based tests are parameterized unit tests whose assertions should hold for *any* possible value of the parameters. You write a parameterized test and then let a framework, such as FsCheck, repeatedly run the test with a large set of randomly generated parameter values.

It's easiest to understand this with an example. The following listing shows what a property test for the applicative law could look like.

Listing 10.4 A property-based test illustrating the applicative law

```
using FsCheck.Xunit;
using Xunit;

Func<int, int, int> multiply = (i, j) => i * j;

[Property]          ⟵── Marks a property-based test
void ApplicativeLawHolds(int a, int b)      ⟵┐ FsCheck randomly generates a large
{                                            │ set of input values to run the test with.
    var first = Some(multiply)
        .Apply(Some(a))
        .Apply(Some(b));
```

---

[1] In reality, there are four laws that correct implementations of `Apply` and `Return` must satisfy; these essentially hold that the identity function, function composition, and function application work in the applicative world as they do in the normal world. The applicative law I refer to in the text holds as a consequence of these, and it's more important than the underlying four laws in terms of refactoring and practical use. I won't discuss the four laws in detail here, but if you want to learn more, you can see the documentation for the applicative module in Haskell at http://mng.bz/AOBx. In addition, you can view property-based tests illustrating the applicative laws in the code samples, LaYumba.Functional.Tests/Option/ApplicativeLaws.cs.

[2] FsCheck is written in F# and is available freely (https://github.com/fscheck/FsCheck). Like many similar frameworks written for other languages, it's a port from Haskell's QuickCheck.

```
    var second = Some(a)
        .Map(multiply)
        .Apply(Some(b));

    Assert.Equal(first, second);
}
```

If you look at the signature of the test method, you'll see that it's parameterized with two int values. But unlike the parameterized tests discussed in the sidebar on "Parameterized unit tests" in chapter 3, here we're not providing any values for the parameters. Instead, we're just decorating the test method with the Property attribute defined in FsCheck.Xunit.[3] When you run your tests, FsCheck randomly generates a large number of input values and runs the test with these values.[4] This frees you from having to come up with sample inputs and gives you much better confidence that edge cases are covered.

This test passes, but we're taking ints as parameters and lifting them into Options, so it only illustrates the behavior with Options in the Some state. We should also test what happens with None. The signature of our test method should really be

```
void ApplicativeLawHolds(Option<int> a, Option<int> b)
```

We'd also ideally like FsCheck to randomly generate Options in the Some or None state and feed them to the test.

If we try to run this, FsCheck will complain that it doesn't know how to randomly generate an Option<int>. Fortunately, we can teach FsCheck how to do this as the following listing demonstrates.

> **Listing 10.5   Teaching FsCheck to create an arbitrary Option**

```
static class ArbitraryOption
{
    public static Arbitrary<Option<T>> Option<T>()
    {
        var gen = from isSome in Arb.Generate<bool>()
                  from val in Arb.Generate<T>()
                  select isSome && val != null ? Some(val) : None;
        return gen.ToArbitrary();
    }
}
```

FsCheck knows how to generate primitive types such as bool and int, so generating an Option<int> should be easy: generate a random bool and then a random int; if the bool is false, return None; otherwise, wrap the generated int into a Some. This is the essential meaning of the preceding code—don't worry about the exact details at this point.

---

[3] This also has the effect of integrating the property-based tests with your testing framework: when you run your tests with dotnet test, all property-based tests are run, as well as the regular unit tests. An FsCheck.NUnit package also exists, exposing the Property attribute for NUnit.

[4] By default, FsCheck generates 100 values, but you can customize the number and range of input values. If you start using property-based testing seriously, being able to fine-tune the parameters with which the values are generated becomes quite important.

Now we just need to instruct FsCheck to look into the `ArbitraryOption` class when a random `Option<T>`, is required. The following listing shows how to do this.

```
[Property(Arbitrary = new[] { typeof(ArbitraryOption) })]
void ApplicativeLawHolds(Option<int> a, Option<int> b)
    => Assert.Equal
    (
        Some(multiply).Apply(a).Apply(b),
        a.Map(multiply).Apply(b)
    );
```

Sure enough, FsCheck is now able to randomly generate the inputs to this test, which passes and beautifully illustrates the applicative law. Does it *prove* that our implementation always satisfies the applicative law? Not entirely, because it only tests that the property holds for the `multiply` function, whereas the law should hold for *any* function. Unfortunately, unlike with numbers and other values, it's impossible to randomly generate a meaningful set of functions. But this sort of property-based test still gives us good confidence—certainly better than a unit test, even a parameterized one.

> **Real-world property-based testing**
>
> Property-based testing is not just for theoretical stuff but can be effectively applied to LOB (Line of Business) applications. When you have an invariant, you can write property tests to capture it.
>
> Here's a really simple example: if you have a randomly populated shopping cart, and you remove a random number of items from it, the total of the modified cart must always be less than or equal to the total of the original cart. You can start with such apparently trivial properties and keep adding properties until they capture the essence of your model.
>
> This is demonstrated nicely in Scott Wlaschin's "Choosing properties for property-based testing" article, available at http://mng.bz/ZxOA.

Now that we've covered the mechanics of the `Apply` function, let's compare applicatives with the other patterns we've previously discussed. Once that's done, we'll look at applicatives in action with a more concrete example and at how they compare, especially to monads.

10.2   Functors, applicatives, and monads

Let's recap three important patterns you've seen so far: functors, applicatives, and monads.[5] Remember that functors are defined by an implementation of `Map`, monads

---

[5]   As pointed out in chapter 6, in the "Why is functor not an interface?" sidebar, some languages like Haskell allow you to capture these patterns with *type classes*, which are akin to interfaces but more powerful. The C# type system doesn't support these generic abstractions, so you can't idiomatically capture `Map` or `Bind` in an interface.

by an implementation of `Bind` and `Return`, and applicatives by an implementation of `Apply` and `Return` as table 10.3 shows.

Table 10.3   Summary of the core functions for functors, applicatives, and monads

Pattern	Required functions	Signature
Functor	Map	F<T> → (T → R) → F<R>
Applicative	Return	T → A<T>
	Apply	A< (T → R) > → A<T> → A<R>
Monad	Return	T → M<T>
	Bind	M<T> → (T → M<R>) → M<R>

First, why is `Return` a requirement for monads and applicatives but not for functors? You need a way to somehow put a value `T` into a functor `F<T>`; otherwise, you couldn't create anything on which to `Map` a function. The point, really, is that the functor laws (the properties that `Map` should observe) don't rely on a definition of `Return`, whereas the monad and applicative laws do. This is then mostly a technicality.

More interestingly, you may be wondering what the relationship is between these three patterns. In chapter 7, you saw that monads are more powerful than functors. Applicatives are also more powerful than functors because you can define `Map` in terms of `Return` and `Apply`. `Map` takes an elevated value and a regular function, so you can lift the function using `Return` and then apply it to the elevated value using `Apply`. For `Option`, that looks like this:

```
public static Option<R> Map<T, R>
   (this Option<T> opt, Func<T, R> f)
   => Some(f).Apply(opt);
```

The implementation for any other applicative would be the same, using the relevant `Return` function instead of `Some`.

Finally, monads are more powerful than applicatives because you can define `Apply` in terms of `Bind` and `Return` like so:

```
public static Option<R> Apply<T, R>
(
    this Option<Func<T, R>> optF,
    Option<T> optT
)
=> optT.Bind(t => optF.Bind(f => Some(f(t))));
```

This enables us to establish a hierarchy in which functor is the most general pattern and applicative sits between functor and monad. Figure 10.3 shows these relationships.

You can read this as a class diagram: if functor were an interface, applicative would extend it. Furthermore, in chapter 9, I discussed the *fold* function, or `Aggregate` as it's called in LINQ, which is the most powerful of them all because you can define `Bind` in terms of it. *Foldables* (things for which *fold* can be defined) are more powerful than monads.

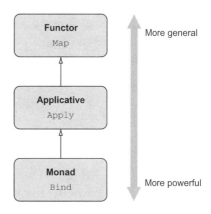

Figure 10.3   Relationship of functors, applicatives, and monads

Applicatives aren't as commonly used as functors and monads, so why even bother? It turns out that although `Apply` can be defined in terms of `Bind`, it generally receives its own implementation, both for efficiency and because `Apply` can include interesting behavior that's lost when you define `Apply` in terms of `Bind`. In this book, I'll show two monads for which the implementation of `Apply` has such interesting behavior: `Validation` (later in this chapter) and `Task` (in chapter 16).

Next, let's go back to the topic of monads to see how you can use `Bind` with multi-argument functions.

10.3   *The monad laws*

I'll now discuss the monad laws as promised in chapter 6, where I first introduced the term *monad*. If you're not interested in the theory, skip to section 10.3.4.

Remember, a monad is a type `M` for which the following functions are defined:

- `Return`—Takes a regular value of type `T` and lifts it into a monadic value of type `M<T>`
- `Bind`—Takes a monadic value `m` and a world-crossing function `f`; extracts from `m` its inner value(s) `t` and applies `f` to it

`Return` and `Bind` should have the following three properties:

1. Right identity
2. Left identity
3. Associativity

For the present discussion, we're mostly interested in the third law, *associativity*, but the first two are simple enough that we can cover them too.

10.3.1   *Right identity*

The property of *right identity* states that if you `Bind` the `Return` function onto a monadic value `m`, you end up with `m`. In other words, the following should hold:

```
m == m.Bind(Return)
```

If you look at the preceding equation, on the right side, `Bind` unwraps the value inside `m` and applies `Return`, which lifts it back up. It's not surprising that the net effect should be nought. The next listing shows a test that proves that right identity holds for the `Option` type.

Listing 10.7   A property-based test for right identity

```
[Property(Arbitrary = new[] { typeof(ArbitraryOption) })]
void RightIdentityHolds(Option<object> m)
    => Assert.Equal
    (
        m,
        m.Bind(Some)
    );
```

10.3.2 *Left identity*

The property of *left identity* states that if you first use `Return` to lift a t and then `Bind` a function f over the result, that should be equivalent to applying f to t:

```
Return(t).Bind(f)  ==  f(t)
```

If you look at this equation, on the left side you're lifting t with `Return` and then `Bind` extracts it before feeding it to f. This law states that this lifting and extracting should have no side effects, and it should also not affect t in any way. The next listing shows a test that proves that left identity holds for `IEnumerable`.

Listing 10.8   A property-based test for left identity

```
Func<int, IEnumerable<int>> f = i => Range(0, i);

[Property] void LeftIdentityHolds(int t)
    => Assert.Equal
    (
        f(t),
        List(t).Bind(f)
    );
```

Taken together, left and right identity ensure that the lifting operation performed in `Return` and the unwrapping that occurs as part of `Bind` are neutral operations that have no side effects and don't distort the value of t or the behavior of f, regardless of whether this wrapping and unwrapping happens before (left) or after (right) a value is lifted into the monad. We could write a monad that, say, internally keeps a count of how many times `Bind` is called, or includes some other side effect. That would violate this property.

In simpler words, `Return` should be *as dumb as possible*: no side effects, no conditional logic, no acting upon the given t; only the minimal work required to satisfy the signature T → C<T>.

Let's look at a counterexample. The following property-based test supposedly illustrates left identity for `Option`:

```
Func<string, Option<string>> f = s => Some($"Hello {s}");

[Property] void LeftIdentityHolds(string t)
    => Assert.Equal
    (
```

```
        f(t),
        Some(t).Bind(f)
);
```

It turns out that the preceding property fails when the value of t is null. This is because our implementation of Some is too smart and throws an exception if given null, whereas this particular function, f, is null-tolerant and yields Some("Hello ").

If you wanted left identity to hold for any value including null, you'd need to change the implementation of Some to lift null into a Some. But this would *not* be a good idea because then Some would indicate the presence of data when, in fact, there is none. This is a case in which practicality trumps theory.[6]

10.3.3 Associativity

Let's now move on to the third law, which is the most meaningful for our present discussion. I'll start with a reminder of what associativity means for addition: if you need to add more than two numbers, it doesn't matter how you group them. That is, for any numbers a, b, and c, the following is true:

```
(a + b) + c  ==  a + (b + c)
```

Bind can also be thought of as a binary operator and can be indicated with the symbol >>= so that instead of m.Bind(f), you can symbolically write m >>= f, where m indicates a monadic value and f a world-crossing function. The symbol >>= is a fairly standard notation for Bind, and it's supposed to graphically reflect what Bind does: extract the inner value of the left operand and feed it to the function that's the right operand.

It turns out that Bind is also associative in some sense. You should be able to write the following equation:

```
(m >>= f) >>= g == m >>= (f >>= g)
```

Let's look at the left side. Here you compute the first Bind operation and then you use the resulting monadic value as input to the next Bind operation. This would expand to m.Bind(f).Bind(g), which is how we normally use Bind.

Let's now look at the right side. As it's written, it's syntactically wrong: (f >>= g) doesn't work because >>= expects the left operand to be a monadic value, whereas f is a function. But note that f can be expanded to its lambda form, x ? f(x), so you can rewrite the right side as follows:

```
m >>= (x => f(x) >>= g)
```

The associativity of Bind can be then summarized with this equation:

```
(m >>= f) >>= g  ==  m >>= (x => f(x) >>= g)
```

Or, if you prefer, the following:

```
m.Bind(f).Bind(g)  ==  m.Bind(x => f(x).Bind(g))
```

---

[6] Of course, in a functional language, you wouldn't have null in the first place, so you wouldn't be in this conundrum.

The following listing shows how you could translate this into code. It shows a property-based test illustrating that the associative property holds for my implementation of `Option`.

Listing 10.9 A property-based test showing `Bind` associativity for `Option`

```
using Double = LaYumba.Functional.Double;              ◁──┐  Exposes an Option-returning
                                                           │  Parse function
Func<double, Option<double>> safeSqrt = d
   => d < 0 ? None : Some(Math.Sqrt(d));

[Property(Arbitrary = new[] { typeof(ArbitraryOption) })]
void AssociativityHolds(Option<string> m)
   => Assert.Equal
   (
      m.Bind(Double.Parse).Bind(safeSqrt),
      m.Bind(x => Double.Parse(x).Bind(safeSqrt))
   );
```

When we associate to the left as in `m.Bind(f).Bind(g)`, that gives the more readable syntax (the one we've used so far). But if we associate to the right and expand g to its lambda form, we get this:

```
m.Bind(x => f(x).Bind(y => g(y)))
```

The interesting thing is that here g has visibility not only of y but also of x. This is what enables you to integrate multi-argument functions in a monadic flow (by which I mean a workflow chaining several operations with `Bind`). We'll look at this next.

10.3.4 *Using Bind with multi-argument functions*

Let's look at how calling `Bind` inside a previous call to `Bind` allows you to integrate multi-argument functions. For instance, imagine multiplication where both arguments are wrapped in an `Option` because they must be parsed from strings. In this example, `Int.Parse` takes a string and returns an `Option<int>`:

```
static Option<int> MultiplicationWithBind(string strX, string strY)
   => Int.Parse(strX)
      .Bind(x => Int.Parse(strY)
         .Bind<int, int>(y => multiply(x, y)));
```

That works, but it's not at all readable. Imagine if you had a function taking three or more arguments! The nested calls to `Bind` make the code difficult to read, so you certainly wouldn't want to write or maintain code like this. The applicative syntax you saw in section 10.1.2 was much clearer. It turns out that there's a much better syntax for writing nested applications of `Bind`. That syntax is called *LINQ*.

10.4 *Improving readability by using LINQ with any monad*

Depending on the context, the name LINQ is used to indicate different things:

- It can simply refer to the `System.Linq` library.

- It can indicate a special SQL-like syntax that can be used to express queries on various kinds of data. In fact, LINQ stands for *Language-Integrated Query*.

Naturally, these two are linked, and they were both introduced in tandem in C# 3. So far, all usages of the LINQ library you've seen in this book have used normal method invocation, but sometimes using the LINQ syntax can result in more readable queries. For example, type the two expressions in table 10.4 into the REPL to see that they're equivalent.

Table 10.4 LINQ is a dedicated syntax for expressing queries.

Normal method invocation	LINQ expression
```Enumerable.Range(1, 100). Where(i => i % 20 == 0). OrderBy(i => -i). Select(i => $"{i}%")```	```from i in Enumerable.Range(1, 100) where i % 20 == 0 orderby -i select $"{i}%"```

These two expressions aren't just equivalent in the sense that they produce the same result; they actually compile to the same code. When the C# compiler finds a LINQ expression, it translates its clauses to method calls in a pattern-based way—you'll see what this means in more detail in a moment.

   This means that it's possible for you to implement the query pattern for your own types and work with them using LINQ syntax, which can significantly improve readability. Next, we'll look at implementing the query pattern for `Option`.

10.4.1 Using LINQ with arbitrary functors

The simplest LINQ queries have single `from` and `select` clauses, and they resolve to the `Select` method. For example, here's a simple query using a range as a data source:

```
using System.Linq;
using static System.Linq.Enumerable;

from x in Range(1, 4)
select x * 2;
// => [2, 4, 6, 8]
```

`Range(1, 4)` yields a sequence with the values `[1, 2, 3, 4]`, and this is the data source for the LINQ expression. We then create a *projection* by mapping each item `x` in the data source to `x * 2` to produce the result. What happens under the hood?

   Given a LINQ expression like the preceding one, the compiler looks at the type of the data source (in this case, `Range(1, 4)` has type `RangeIterator`) and then looks for an instance or extension method called `Select`. The compiler uses its normal strategy for method resolution, prioritizing the most specific match in scope, which in this case is `Enumerable.Select`, defined as an extension method on `IEnumerable`.

   In table 10.5, you can see the LINQ expression and its translation side by side. Notice how the lambda given to `Select` combines the identifier `x` in the `from` clause and the selector expression `x * 2` in the `select` clause.

Table 10.5   A LINQ expression with a single `from` clause and its interpretation

`from x in Range(1, 4)` `select x * 2`	`Range(1, 4).` `    Select(x => x * 2)`

Remember from chapter 6 that `Select` is the LINQ equivalent for the operation more commonly known in FP as `Map`. LINQ's pattern-based approach means that you can define `Select` for any type you please, and the compiler will use it whenever it finds that type as the data source of a LINQ query. Let's do that for `Option`:

```
public static Option<R> Select<T, R>
   (this Option<T> opt, Func<T, R> f)
   => opt.Map(f);
```

The preceding code effectively just aliases `Map` with `Select`, which is the name that the compiler looks for. That's all you need to be able to use an `Option` inside a simple LINQ expression! Here are some examples:

```
from x in Some(12)
select x * 2
// => Some(24)

from x in (Option<int>)None
select x * 2
// => None

(from x in Some(1) select x * 2) == Some(1).Map(x => x * 2)
// => true
```

In summary, you can use LINQ queries with a single `from` clause with any functor by providing a suitable `Select` method. Of course, for such simple queries, the LINQ notation isn't really beneficial; standard method invocation even saves you a couple of keystrokes. Let's see what happens with more complex queries.

10.4.2 *Using LINQ with arbitrary monads*

Let's look at queries with multiple `from` clauses—queries that combine data from multiple data sources. Here's an example:

```
var chars = new[] { 'a', 'b', 'c' };
var ints = new [] { 2, 3 };

from c in chars
from i in ints
select (c, i)
// => [(a, 2), (a, 3), (b, 2), (b, 3), (c, 2), (c, 3)]
```

As you can see, this is somewhat analogous to a nested loop over the two data sources, which we discussed in section 6.3.2 when looking at `Bind` for `IEnumerable`. Indeed, you could write an equivalent expression using `Map` and `Bind` as follows:

```
chars
   .Bind(c => ints
      .Map(i => (c, i)));
```

Or, equivalently, using the standard LINQ method names (`Select` instead of `Map` and `SelectMany` instead of `Bind`):

```
chars
   .SelectMany(c => ints
      .Select(i => (c, i)));
```

Notice that you can construct a result that includes data from both sources because you close over the variable c.

You might guess that when multiple `from` clauses are present in a query, they're interpreted with the corresponding calls to `SelectMany`. Your guess would be correct, but there's a twist. For performance reasons, the compiler doesn't perform the preceding translation, translating instead to an overload of `SelectMany` with a different signature:

```
public static IEnumerable<RR>
SelectMany<T, R, RR>
(
   this IEnumerable<T> source,
   Func<T, IEnumerable<R>> bind,
   Func<T, R, RR> project
)
{
   foreach (T t in source)
      foreach (R r in bind(t))
         yield return project(t, r);
}
```

That means this LINQ query

```
from c in chars
from i in ints
select (c, i)
```

will actually be translated as

```
chars.SelectMany(c => ints, (c, i) => (c, i))
```

The following listing shows both the plain vanilla implementation of `SelectMany` (which has the same signature as `Bind`) and the extended overload (which will be used when a query with two `from` clauses is translated into method calls).

Listing 10.10   The two overloads of `SelectMany` required by LINQ

```
public static IEnumerable<R> SelectMany<T, R>      ◁──  Plain vanilla SelectMany,
(                                                        equivalent to Bind.
   this IEnumerable<T> source,
   Func<T, IEnumerable<R>> func
)
{
   foreach (T t in source)
      foreach (R r in func(t))
         yield return r;
}
```

```
public static IEnumerable<RR> SelectMany<T, R, RR>          ◁──┐  Extended overload of
(                                                                SelectMany (used when
   this IEnumerable<T> source,                                   translating a query with
   Func<T, IEnumerable<R>> bind,                                 two from clauses)
   Func<T, R, RR> project
)
{
   foreach (T t in source)
      foreach (R r in bind(t))
         yield return project(t, r);
}
```

Compare the signatures. You'll see that the second overload is obtained by "squashing" the plain vanilla `SelectMany` with a call to a selector function; not the usual selector in the form T→R, but a selector that takes two input arguments (one for each data source).

The advantage is that with this more elaborate overload of `SelectMany`, there's no longer any need to nest one lambda inside another, improving performance.[7]

The extended `SelectMany` is more complex than the plain vanilla version we identified with the monadic `Bind`, but it's still functionally equivalent to a combination of `Bind` and `Select`. This means we can define a reasonable implementation of the LINQ-flavored `SelectMany` for any monad. Let's see it for `Option`:

```
public static Option<RR> SelectMany<T, R, RR>
(
   this Option<T> opt,
   Func<T, Option<R>> bind,
   Func<T, R, RR> project
)
=> opt.Match
(
   () => None,
   (t) => bind(t).Match
   (
      () => None,
      (r) => Some(project(t, r))
   )
);
```

If you write an expression with three or more `from` clauses, the compiler also requires the plain vanilla version of `SelectMany`—the one with the same signature as `Bind`. Therefore, both overloads of `SelectMany` need to be defined to satisfy the LINQ query pattern.

You can now write LINQ queries on `Option`s with multiple `from` clauses. For example, here's a simple program that prompts the user for two integers and computes their sum, using the `Option`-returning function `Int.Parse` to validate that the inputs are valid integers:

---

[7] The designers of LINQ noticed that performance deteriorated rapidly as several `from` clauses were used in a query.

```
WriteLine("Enter first addend:");
var s1 = ReadLine();

WriteLine("Enter second addend:");
var s2 = ReadLine();

var result = from a in Int.Parse(s1)
             from b in Int.Parse(s2)
             select a + b;

WriteLine(result.Match
(
    None: () => "Please enter 2 valid integers",
    Some: (r) => $"{s1} + {s2} = {r}"
));
```

The following listing shows how the LINQ query from the preceding example compares with alternative ways to write the same expression.

Listing 10.11 Different ways to add two optional integers

```
// 1. using LINQ query
from a in Int.Parse(s1)
from b in Int.Parse(s2)
select a + b

// 2. normal method invocation
Int.Parse(s1)
   .Bind(a => Int.Parse(s2)
     .Map(b => a + b))

// 3. the method invocation that the LINQ query will be converted to
Int.Parse(s1)
   .SelectMany(a => Int.Parse(s2)
     , (a, b) => a + b)

// 4. using Apply
Some(new Func<int, int, int>((a, b) => a + b))
   .Apply(Int.Parse(s1)
   .Apply(Int.Parse(s2))
```

There's little doubt that LINQ provides the most readable syntax in this scenario. Apply compares particularly poorly because you must specify that you want your projection function to be used as a Func.[8] You may find it unfamiliar to use the SQL-ish LINQ syntax to do something that has nothing to do with querying a data source, but this use is perfectly legitimate. LINQ expressions simply provide a convenient syntax for working with monads, and they were modeled after equivalent constructs in functional languages.[9]

---

[8] This is because lambda expressions can be used to represent Expressions as well as Funcs.

[9] For instance, do blocks in Haskell or for comprehensions in Scala.

10.4.3 *The LINQ clauses let, where, and others*

In addition to the `from` and `select` clauses you've seen so far, LINQ provides a few other clauses. The `let` clause is useful for storing the results of intermediate computations. For example, let's look at the program in the following listing, which calculates the hypotenuse of a right triangle, having prompted the user for the lengths of the legs.

Listing 10.12 Using the `let` clause with `Option`

```
using Double = LaYumba.Functional.Double;        ◁────┐  Exposes an Option-returning
                                                       │  Parse function
string s1 = Prompt("First leg:")        ◁────┐
    , s2 = Prompt("Second leg:");            │  Assume Prompt is a convenience function
                                                that reads user input from the console
var result = from a in Double.Parse(s1)
             let aa = a * a               ◁────┐
             from b in Double.Parse(s2)        │  A let clause allows you to
             let bb = b * b               ◁────┘  store intermediate results.
             select Math.Sqrt(aa + bb);

WriteLine(result.Match
(
    () => "Please enter two valid numbers",
    (h) => $"The hypotenuse is {h}"
));
```

The `let` clause allows you to put a new variable, like `aa` in this example, within the scope of the LINQ expression. To do so, it relies on `Select`, so no extra work is needed to enable the use of `let`.[10]

One more clause you can use with `Option` is the `where` clause. This resolves to the `Where` method we've already defined, so no extra work is necessary in this case. For example, for the calculation of the hypotenuse, you should check not only that the user's inputs are valid numbers but also that they are positive. The following listing shows how to do this.

Listing 10.13 Using the `where` clause with `Option`

```
string s1 = Prompt("First leg:")
    , s2 = Prompt("Second leg:");

var result = from a in Double.Parse(s1)
             where a >= 0
             let aa = a * a

             from b in Double.Parse(s2)
             where b >= 0
             let bb = b * b
             select Math.Sqrt(aa + bb);
```

---

[10] `let` stores the newly computed result in a tuple along with the previous result.

```
WriteLine(result.Match
(
    () => "Please enter two valid, positive numbers",
    (h) => $"The hypotenuse is {h}"
));
```

As these examples show, the LINQ syntax allows you to concisely write queries that would be cumbersome to write as combinations of calls to the corresponding `Map`, `Bind`, and `Where` functions. LINQ also contains various other clauses such as `orderby`, which you've seen in a previous example. These clauses make sense for collections but have no counterpart in structures like `Option` and `Either`.

In summary, for any monad you can implement the LINQ query pattern by providing implementations for `Select` (`Map`), `SelectMany` (`Bind`), and the ternary overload to `SelectMany` you've seen. Some structures may have other operations that can be included in the query pattern, such as `Where` in the case of `Option`.

Now that you've seen how LINQ provides a lightweight syntax for using `Bind` with multi-argument functions, let's go back to comparing `Bind` and `Apply`, not just based on readability, but on actual functionality.

10.5 When to use Bind vs. Apply

LINQ provides a good syntax for using `Bind`, even with multi-argument functions—even better than using `Apply` with normal method invocation. Should we still care about `Apply`? It turns out that in some cases, `Apply` can have interesting behavior. One such case is validation; let's see why.

10.5.1 Validation with smart constructors

Consider the following implementation of a `PhoneNumber` class. Can you see anything wrong with it?

```
public record PhoneNumber
(
    string Type,
    string Country,
    long Nr
);
```

The answer should be staring you in the face: the types are wrong! This class allows you to create a `PhoneNumber` with, say, `Type` equal to "green," `Country` equal to "fantasyland," and `Nr` equal to "•10."

You saw in chapter 4 how defining custom types enables you to ensure that invalid data can't creep into your system. Here's a definition of a `PhoneNumber` class that follows this philosophy:

```
public record PhoneNumber
{
    public NumberType Type { get; }
    public CountryCode Country { get; }
    public Number Nr { get; }
```

```
      public enum NumberType { Mobile, Home, Office }
      public struct Number { /* ... */ }
}

public class CountryCode { /* ... */ }
```

Now the three fields of a PhoneNumber all have specific types, which should ensure that only valid values can be represented. CountryCode may be used elsewhere in the application, but the remaining two types are specific to phone numbers, so they're defined inside the PhoneNumber class.

We still need to provide a way to construct a PhoneNumber. For that, we can define a private constructor and a public factory function, Create:

```
public record PhoneNumber
{
   public static Func<NumberType, CountryCode, Number, PhoneNumber>
   Create = (type, country, number)
      => new(type, country, number);

   PhoneNumber(NumberType type, CountryCode country, Number number)
   {
      Type = type;
      Country = country;
      Nr = number;
   }
}
```

Note that I've defined Create as a Func rather than using a constructor or a method to help out with type inference. This was discussed in section 9.2.

Now imagine we're given three strings as raw input, and based on them, we need to create a PhoneNumber. Each property can be validated independently, so we can define three smart constructors with the following signatures:

```
validCountryCode : string → Validation<CountryCode>
validNumberType  : string → Validation<PhoneNumber.NumberType>
validNumber      : string → Validation<PhoneNumber.Number>
```

The implementation details of these functions aren't important (see the code samples if you want to know more). The gist is that validCountryCode takes a string and returns a Validation in the Valid state only if the given string represents a valid CountryCode. The other two functions are similar.

10.5.2 *Harvesting errors with the applicative flow*

Given the three input strings, we can combine these three functions in the process of creating a PhoneNumber as the following listing shows. With the applicative flow, we can lift the PhoneNumber's factory function into a Valid and apply its three arguments.

Listing 10.14   Validation using an applicative flow

```
Validation<PhoneNumber> CreatePhoneNumber
   (string type, string countryCode, string number)        Lifts the factory function
   => Valid(PhoneNumber.Create)                             into a Validation
      .Apply(validNumberType(type))
      .Apply(validCountryCode(countryCode))       Supplies arguments, each of which
      .Apply(validNumber(number));                is also wrapped in a Validation
```

This function yields `Invalid` if *any* of the functions we use to validate the individual fields yields `Invalid`. Let's see its behavior, given a variety of different inputs:

```
CreatePhoneNumber("Mobile", "ch", "123456")
// => Valid(Mobile: (ch) 123456)

CreatePhoneNumber("Mobile", "xx", "123456")
// => Invalid([xx is not a valid country code])

CreatePhoneNumber("Mobile", "xx", "1")
// => Invalid([xx is not a valid country code, 1 is not a valid number])
```

The first expression shows the successful creation of a `PhoneNumber`. In the second, we pass an invalid country code and get a failure as expected. In the third case, both the country and number are invalid, and we get a validation with two errors (remember, the `Invalid` case of a `Validation` holds an `IEnumerable<Error>` precisely to capture multiple errors).

But how are the two errors, which are returned by different functions, harvested in the final result? This is due to the implementation of `Apply` for `Validation`. Check out the following listing.

Listing 10.15   Implementation of `Apply` for `Validation`

```
public static Validation<R> Apply<T, R>
(
   this Validation<Func<T, R>> valF,
   Validation<T> valT
)
=> valF.Match
(
   Valid: (f) => valT.Match
   (
      Valid: (t) => Valid(f(t)),          If both inputs are valid, the wrapped function is
      Invalid: (err) => Invalid(err)      applied to the wrapped argument, and the result
   ),                                      is lifted into a Validation in the Valid state.
   Invalid: (errF) => valT.Match
   (
      Valid: (_) => Invalid(errF),
      Invalid: (errT) => Invalid(errF.Concat(errT))     If both inputs have errors, a
   )                                                     Validation in the
);                                                       Invalid state is returned
                                                         that collects the errors
                                                         from both valF and valT.
```

As we'd expect, `Apply` applies the wrapped function to the wrapped argument only if both are valid. But, interestingly, if both are invalid, it returns an `Invalid` that combines errors from both arguments.

10.5.3 *Failing fast with the monadic flow*

The following listing demonstrates how to create a `PhoneNumber` using LINQ.

Listing 10.16 Validation using a monadic flow

```
Validation<PhoneNumber> CreatePhoneNumberM
    (string typeStr, string countryStr, string numberStr)
  => from type    in validNumberType(typeStr)
     from country in validCountryCode(countryStr)
     from number  in validNumber(numberStr)
     select PhoneNumber.Create(type, country, number);
```

Let's run this new version with the same test values as before:

```
CreatePhoneNumberM("Mobile", "ch", "123456")
// => Valid(Mobile: (ch) 123456)

CreatePhoneNumberM("Mobile", "xx", "123456")
// => Invalid([xx is not a valid country code])

CreatePhoneNumberM("Mobile", "xx", "1")
// => Invalid([xx is not a valid country code])
```

The first two cases work as before, but the third case is different: only the first validation error appears. To see why, let's look at how `Bind` is defined in the next listing (the LINQ query actually calls `SelectMany`, but this is implemented in terms of `Bind`).

Listing 10.17 Implementation of `Bind` for `Validation`

```
public static Validation<R> Bind<T, R>
(
    this Validation<T> val,
    Func<T, Validation<R>> f
)
=> val.Match
(
    Invalid: (err) => Invalid(err),
    Valid: (t) => f(t)
);
```

If the given monadic value is `Invalid`, the given function isn't evaluated. In this listing, `validCountryCode` returns `Invalid`, so `validNumber` is never called. Therefore, in the monadic version, we never get a chance to accumulate errors because any error along the way causes the subsequent functions to be bypassed. You can probably grasp the difference more clearly if we compare the signatures of `Apply` and `Bind`:

```
Apply : Validation<(T  → R)>  → Validation<T>  → Validation<R>
Bind  : Validation<T>  → (T  → Validation<R>)  → Validation<R>
```

With `Apply`, both arguments are of type `Validation`; the `Validations` and any possible errors they contain have already been evaluated independently prior to the call to `Apply`. Because errors from both arguments are present, it makes sense to collect them in the resulting value.

With `Bind`, only the first argument has type `Validation`. The second argument is a function that yields a `Validation`, but this hasn't been evaluated yet, so the implementation of `Bind` can avoid calling the function altogether if the first argument is `Invalid`.[11]

Hence, `Apply` is about combining two elevated values that are computed independently, whereas `Bind` is about sequencing computations that yield an elevated value. For this reason, the monadic flow allows short-circuiting: if an operation fails along the way, the following operations will be skipped.

I think what the case of `Validation` shows is that despite the apparent rigor of functional patterns and their laws, there's still room for designing elevated types in a way that suits the particular needs of a particular application. Given my implementation of `Validation` and the current scenario of creating a valid `PhoneNumber`, you'd use the monadic flow to fail fast but the applicative flow to harvest errors.

In summary, you've seen three ways to use multi-argument functions in the elevated world: the good, the bad, and the ugly. Nested calls to `Bind` are certainly the ugly and are best avoided. Which of the other two is good or bad depends on your requirements. If you have an implementation of `Apply` with some desirable behavior as you saw with `Validation`, use the applicative flow; otherwise, use the monadic flow with LINQ.

Exercises

1. Implement `Apply` for `Either` and `Exceptional`.
2. Implement the query pattern for `Either` and `Exceptional`. Try to write down the signatures for `Select` and `SelectMany` without looking at any examples. For the implementation, just follow the types—if it type checks, it's probably right!
3. Come up with a scenario in which various `Either`-returning operations are chained with `Bind`. (If you're short of ideas, you can use the "favorite dish" example from chapter 8.) Rewrite the code using a LINQ expression.

Summary

- You can use the `Apply` function to perform function application in an elevated world, such as the world of `Option`.
- Multi-argument functions can be lifted into an elevated world with `Return`; then you can supply arguments with `Apply`.
- Types for which `Apply` can be defined are called *applicatives*. Applicatives are more powerful than functors but less powerful than monads.

---

[11] Of course, you could provide an implementation of `Bind` that doesn't perform any such short-circuiting but always executes the bound function and collects any errors. This is possible, but it's counterintuitive because it breaks the behavior that we've come to expect from similar types like `Option` and `Either`.

- Because monads are more powerful, you can also use nested calls to `Bind`; to perform function application in an elevated world.
- LINQ provides a lightweight syntax for working with monads that reads better than nesting calls to `Bind`.
- To use LINQ with a custom type, you must implement the LINQ query pattern, particularly providing implementations of `Select` and `SelectMany` with appropriate signatures.
- For several monads, `Bind` has short-circuiting behavior (the given function won't be applied in some cases), but `Apply` doesn't (it's not given a function but rather an elevated value). For this reason, you can sometimes embed desirable behavior into applicatives, such as collecting validation errors in the case of `Validation`.
- FsCheck is a framework for property-based testing. It allows you to run a test with a large number of randomly generated inputs, giving high confidence that the test's assertions hold for any input.

Representing state and change

Greek philosopher Heraclitus said that we cannot step into the same river twice; the river constantly changes, so the river that was there a moment ago is no longer. Many programmers would disagree, objecting that it's the same river but its *state* has changed. Functional programmers try to stay true to Heraclitus's thinking and would create a new river with every observation.

Most programs are built to represent things and processes in the real world, and because the world constantly changes, programs must somehow represent that change. The question is *how* we represent change. Commercial applications written in the imperative style have state mutation at their core: objects represent entities in the business domain, and change in the world is modeled by mutating the state of these objects.

We'll start by looking at the weaknesses we introduce in our programs when we use mutation. We'll then see how we can avoid these problems at the source by representing change *without* using mutation and, more pragmatically, how to enforce immutability in C#. Finally, because much of our programs' data is stored in data structures, we'll introduce the concepts and techniques behind functional data structures, which are also immutable.

11.1   *The pitfalls of state mutation*

State mutation is when memory is updated in place, and an important problem with it is that concurrent access to a shared mutable state is unsafe. You've already seen examples demonstrating loss of information due to concurrent updates in chapters 1 and 3; let's now look at a more object-oriented scenario. Imagine a `Product` class with an `Inventory` field, representing the number of units in stock:

```
public class Product
{
    public int Inventory { get; private set; }
    public void ReplenishInventory(int units) => Inventory += units;
    public void ProcessSale(int units) => Inventory -= units;
}
```

If `Inventory` is mutable as this example shows, and you have concurrent threads updating its value, that can lead to *race conditions*, and the results can be unpredictable. Imagine that you have a thread replenishing the inventory, while another thread concurrently processes a sale, diminishing the inventory as figure 11.1 shows. If both threads read the value at the same time, and the thread with the sale has the last update, you'll end up with an overall decrease in inventory.

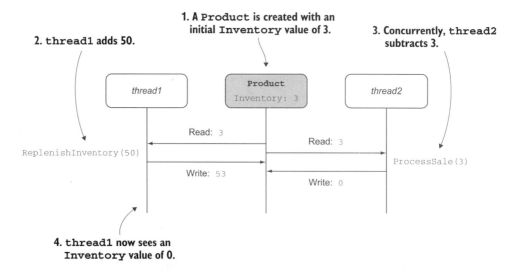

Figure 11.1   Loss of data as a result of concurrent updates. Both threads cause the `Inventory` value to be updated concurrently with the result that one of the updates is lost.

Not only has the update to replenish the inventory been lost, but the first thread now potentially faces a completely invalid state: a product that's just been replenished has zero inventory.

If you've done some basic multithreading, you're probably thinking, "Easy! You just need to wrap the updates to `Inventory` in a critical section using the `lock` statement." It turns out that this solution, which works for this simple case, can become the source of some difficult bugs as the complexity of the system increases. (A sale affects not only the inventory, but the sales order, the company balance sheet, and so on.)

If things can fail when a single variable is set, imagine when an update to an entity involves updating several fields. For example, imagine that when you update the inventory, you also set a flag indicating whether the product is low on inventory as the following listing shows.

Listing 11.1 Temporary inconsistency as a result of non-atomic updates

```
class Product
{
    int inventory;

    public bool IsLowOnInventory { get; private set; }

    public int Inventory
    {
        get => inventory;
        private set
        {
            inventory = value;                              At this point, the object can be in an
                                                            invalid state from the perspective of
                                                            any thread reading its properties.
            IsLowOnInventory = inventory <= 5;
        }
    }
}
```

This code defines an invariant: when `inventory` is 5 or less, then `IsLowOnInventory` must be true.

In a single-threaded setting, there aren't any problems with the preceding code. But in a multithreaded setting, a thread could be reading the state of this object just as another thread is performing the update in the window during which `Inventory` has been updated but `IsLowOnInventory` hasn't. (Notice that this window widens if the logic to compute `IsLowOnInventory` becomes more expensive.) During that window, the invariant can be broken, so the object would appear to be in an invalid state to the first thread. This will, of course, happen very rarely, and it will be nearly impossible to reproduce. This is part of the reason why bugs caused by race conditions are so hard to diagnose.

Indeed, race conditions are known to have caused some of the most spectacular failures in the software industry. If you have a system with concurrency and state mutation, it's impossible to prove that the system is free of race conditions.[1] In other words, if you want concurrency (and, given today's tendency toward multicore processors and distributed computing, you hardly have a choice) *and* strong guarantees of correctness, you simply must give up mutation.

Lack of safe concurrent access may be the biggest pitfall of a shared mutable state, but it's not the only one. Another problem is the risk of introducing *coupling*—a high degree of interdependence between different parts of your system. In figure 11.1, `Inventory` is *encapsulated*, meaning it can only be set from within the class, and according to OOP theory, that's supposed to give you a sense of comfort. But how many methods in the `Product` class can set the inventory value? How many code paths lead into these methods so that they ultimately affect the value of `Inventory`? How many parts of the application can get the same instance of the `Product` and rely on the value of `Inventory`, and how many will be affected if you introduce a new component that causes `Inventory` to change?

For a non-trivial application, it's difficult to answer these questions completely. This is why `inventory`, even though it's a private field and can be set only via a private setter, qualifies as a global mutable state; as far as we can tell, it could be mutated by any part of the program via public methods in the enclosing class. As a result, mutable state couples the behavior of the various components that read or update that state, making it difficult to reason about the behavior of the system as a whole.

Finally, shared mutable state implies *loss of purity*. As explained in chapter 3, mutating global state (remember, that's all state that's not local to a function, including private variables) constitutes a side effect. If you represent change in the world by mutating objects in your system, you lose the benefits of function purity. For these reasons, the functional paradigm discourages state mutation altogether.

> **NOTE**   In this chapter, you'll learn how to work with immutable data objects. That's an important technique, but keep in mind that it's not always sufficient to represent entities that change with time. Immutable data objects can represent the state of an entity at any given point in time, somewhat like a frame in a film, but to represent the entity itself, to get the full moving picture, you need a further abstraction that links those successive states together. We'll discuss techniques for accomplishing that in chapters 13, 15, 18, and 19.

Local mutation is OK

Not all state mutation is equally evil. Mutating local state (state that's only visible within the scope of a function) is inelegant but benign. For example, imagine the following function:

---

[1] The preceding examples refer to multithreading, but the same problems can arise if the source of concurrency is asynchrony or parallelism (these terms were described in the sidebar on the "Meaning and types of concurrency" in chapter 3).

```
int Sum(int[] ints)
{
    var result = 0;
    foreach (int i in ints) result += i;
    return result;
}
```

Although we're updating `result`, this isn't visible from outside the scope of the function. As a result, this implementation of `Sum` is actually a pure function: it has no *observable* side effects from the point of view of a calling function.

Naturally, this code is also low-level. You can normally achieve what you want with built-in functions like `Sum`, `Aggregate`, and so on. In practice, it's rare that you'll find a legitimate case for mutating local variables.

11.2 Understanding state, identity, and change

Let's look more closely at change and mutation.[2] By *change*, I mean change in the real world, such as when 50 units of stock become available for sale. *Mutation* means data is updated in place; as you saw in the `Product` class, when the `Inventory` value is updated, the previous value for `Inventory` is lost.

In FP, we represent change without mutation: values aren't updated in place. Instead, we create new instances that represent the data with the desired changes, as figure 11.2 shows. The fact that the current level of inventory is 53 doesn't obliterate the fact that it was previously 3.

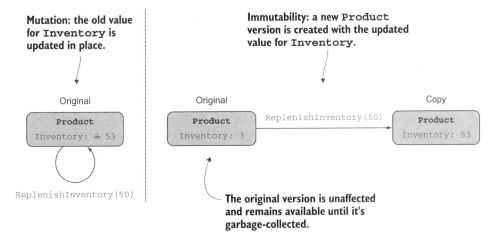

Figure 11.2   In FP, change can be represented by creating new versions of the data.

---

[2]   The fundamental techniques I discuss in this section are ubiquitous in FP, but the concepts and metaphors I use to explain them are largely inspired by Rich Hickey, the creator of the Clojure programming language.

In FP, we work with *immutable* values: once a value is initialized, it's never updated.

Wrapping your head around immutable objects

If you've always used mutation to represent change, creating replicas of objects when their properties are updated can seem counterintuitive. For example, consider this code:

```
record Product(int Inventory);

static Product ReplenishInventory(Guid id, int units)
{
    Product original = RetrieveProduct(id);
    Product updated = new Product(original.Inventory + units);
    return updated;
}
```

In this code, `Product` is immutable, so we represent new inventory becoming available by creating a new `Product` instance. You may feel awkward about this because now there are two competing `Product` instances in memory, only one of which accurately represents the real-world product.

Note that in this example, the `updated` instance is returned, while the `original` instance runs out of scope and will therefore be garbage-collected. In many cases, the obsolete instance will simply be "forgotten" rather than overwritten.

But there are cases in which you *do* want several views of an entity to coexist. For example, say your employer offers free shipping for orders that are over $40. You might like to have a view of the order before and after a user removes an item to warn them if they have just lost the right to free delivery. Or, an update may be part of an in-memory transaction, and you may want to revert to the previous state of the entity if the transaction fails.

The idea that only the latest or current view of the data is valuable is just a prejudice deriving from mainstream practice. When you give it up, many new possibilities appear.

To refine or redefine your intuition about change and mutation, it's useful to distinguish between things that change and things that don't.

11.2.1 *Some things never change*

There are some things that we think of as inherently immutable. For example, your age may change from 30 to 31, but the number 30 is still the number 30, and 31 is still 31.

This is modeled in the Base Class Library (BCL) in that *all primitive types are immutable*. What about more complex types? Dates are a good example. The third of March is still the third of March, even though you may change an appointment in your calendar from the third of March to the fourth. This is also reflected in the BCL in that types that are used to represent dates such as `DateTime` are immutable.[3] See this

---

[3] The creators of .NET took inspiration from Java, but in this case, they also learned from Java's mistakes (Java had mutable dates until Java 8).

for yourself by typing the following in the REPL (use `DateTime` instead of `DateOnly` if you don't have .NET 6):

```
var momsBirthday = new DateOnly(1966, 12, 13);
var johnsBirthday = momsBirthday;          ◁── John has the same
                                               birthday as Mom.
// some time goes by...

johnsBirthday = johnsBirthday.AddDays(1);  ◁── You realize that John's birthday
                                               is actually one day later.
johnsBirthday // => 14/12/1966
momsBirthday  // => 13/12/1966   ◁── Mom's birthday
                                     was not affected.
```

In the preceding example, we start by saying that Mom and John have the same birthday, so we assign the same value to `momsBirthday` and `johnsBirthday`. When we then use `AddDays` to create a later date and assign it to `johnsBirthday`, this leaves `momsBirthday` unaffected. In this example, we are doubly protected from mutating the date:

- Because `System.DateOnly` is a struct, it's copied upon assignment, so `momsBirthday` and `johnsBirthday` are different instances.
- Even if `DateOnly` were a class, so that `momsBirthday` and `johnsBirthday` pointed to the same instance, the behavior would still be the same because `AddDays` creates a new instance, leaving the underlying instance unaffected.

If, on the other hand, `DateOnly` were a mutable class and `AddDays` mutated the days of its instance, the value of `momsBirthday` would be updated as a result—or, rather, as a side effect—of updating `johnsBirthday`. (Imagine explaining to Mom that that's the reason for your belated birthday wishes.)

Immutable types in the .NET framework

Here are the most commonly used immutable types in .NET's Base Class Library:

- `DateTime, TimeSpan, DateTimeOffset, DateOnly, TimeOnly`
- `Delegate`
- `Guid`
- `Nullable<T>`
- `String`
- `Tuple<T1>, Tuple<T1, T2>, ...`
- `Uri`
- `Version`

Furthermore, all primitive types are immutable.

Now let's define a custom immutable type. Say we represent a `Circle` like so:

```
readonly record struct Circle(Point Center, double Radius);
```

You would probably agree that it makes no sense that a circle should ever grow or shrink because it's a completely abstract geometric entity. The preceding implementation reflects this by declaring the struct as `readonly`, which makes it immutable. This means that it will not be possible to update the values for Radius and Center; once created, the state of the circle can never change.[4]

> ### Structs should be immutable
>
> Notice that I've defined Circle as a value type. Because value types are copied when passed between functions, it makes sense that structs should be immutable. This isn't enforced by the compiler, so you *could* create a mutable struct. In fact, if you declare a record struct without the readonly modifier, you get a mutable struct.
>
> Unlike with classes, any changes you make to a mutable struct propagate down but not up the call stack, potentially leading to unexpected behavior. For this reason, I recommend you always stick to immutable structs, the only exceptions being warranted by proven performance requirements.

If you have a circle and you'd like a circle double the size, you can define functions to create a new circle based on an existing one. Here's an example:

```
static Circle Scale(this Circle c, double factor)
   => c with { Radius = c.Radius * factor };
```

OK, so far we haven't used mutation, and these examples are pretty intuitive. What do numbers, dates, and geometric entities have in common? Their value captures their identity: they are *value objects*. If you change the value of a date . . . well, it identifies a different date! The problems begin when we consider objects whose value and identity are different things. We'll look at this next.

11.2.2 *Representing change without mutation*

Many real-world entities change with time: your bank account, your calendar, your contacts list—all these things have a state that changes with time. Figure 11.3 illustrates this idea.

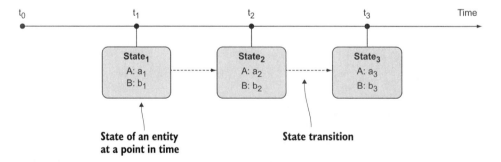

Figure 11.3   An entity whose state changes over time

---

[4] In reality, you can still mutate read-only variables by using reflection. But making a field read-only is a clear signal to any clients of your code that the field isn't meant to be mutated.

For such entities, their identity isn't captured by their value because their identity remains constant, whereas their value changes with time. Instead, their identity is associated with different states at different points in time. Your age may change, or your salary, but your identity doesn't. To represent such entities, programs must model not only an entity's state (that's the easy part), but the transitions from one state to another and often the association of an identity with the entity's current state.

We've discussed some reasons why mutation provides an imperfect mechanism for managing state transitions. In FP, states are not mutated; they're snapshots that, like the frames of a film, represent an evolving reality but are in themselves static.

11.3 *Using records to capture the state of domain entities*

To illustrate immutable data objects in C#, let's start working on `AccountState`, which we'll use to represent the state of a bank account in the BOC application. The following listing shows our model.

> **Listing 11.2 A simple model for the state of a bank account**

```
public enum AccountStatus
{ Requested, Active, Frozen, Dormant, Closed }

public record AccountState
(
   CurrencyCode Currency,
   AccountStatus Status = AccountStatus.Requested,
   decimal AllowedOverdraft = 0m,
   IEnumerable<Transaction> TransactionHistory = null
);

public record Transaction
(
   decimal Amount,
   string Description,
   DateTime Date
);
```

For brevity, I've omitted the definition of `CurrencyCode`, which simply wraps a string value such as EUR or USD similarly to the `ConnectionString` and `SqlTemplate` types we saw in section 9.4.1.

Because `AccountState` has several fields and not all may be meaningful all the time, I have provided some reasonable default values for all fields except the currency. To create an `AccountState`, all you really need is its currency:

```
var newAccount = new AccountState(Currency: "EUR");
```

This creates an `AccountState` with a default status of `Requested`. When you're ready to activate the account, you can do this by using a `with` expression:

```
public static AccountState Activate(this AccountState original)
   => original with { Status = AccountStatus.Active };
```

This creates a new instance of `AccountState`, populated with all the values from the original except for `Status`, which is set to the new value. The original object is still intact:

```
var original = new AccountState(Currency: "EUR");
var activated = original.Activate();

original.Status     // Requested
original.Currency   // "EUR"

activated.Status    // Active
activated.Currency  // "EUR"
```

Notice that you can use `with` expressions that set more than one property:

```
public static AccountState RedFlag(this AccountState original)
   => original with
   {
      Status = AccountStatus.Frozen,
      AllowedOverdraft = 0m
   };
```

Performance impact of using immutable objects

Working with immutable objects means that every time your data needs to change, you create a new, modified instance rather than mutating the object in place. "But isn't that terribly inefficient?" you may be thinking.

There is indeed a small performance penalty for creating modified copies, as well as for creating a greater number of objects that will eventually need to be garbage-collected. This is also why FP isn't practical in languages that lack automatic memory management.

But the performance impact is smaller than you might think because the modified instance is a *shallow copy* of the original. That is, objects referenced by the original object aren't copied; only the reference is copied. With the exception of the field being updated, the new object is a bitwise replica of the original.

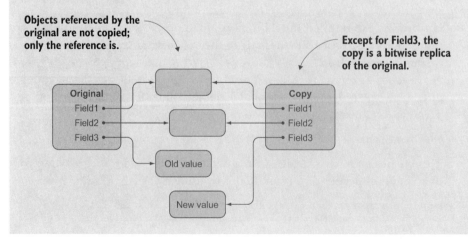

For example, when you create a new `AccountState` with an updated status, the list of transactions won't be copied. Instead, the new object references the original list of transactions. (This too should be immutable, so it's OK for different instances to share it.)

`with` expressions are fast. Of course, in-place updates are even faster, so there's a tradeoff between performance and safety. The performance penalty of creating shallow copies is likely to be negligible in the wide majority of cases. My advice is to put safety first and optimize later as needed.

Next, let's see how we can further improve this model.

11.3.1 *Fine-grained control on record initialization*

Have another look at the proposed definition of `AccountState` (replicated in the following snippet) and see if you can spot any potential problems with it:

```
public record AccountState
(
    CurrencyCode Currency,
    AccountStatus Status = AccountStatus.Requested,
    decimal AllowedOverdraft = 0m,
    IEnumerable<Transaction> TransactionHistory = null
);
```

There are in fact a couple of issues here. One thing that immediately stands out is the default value of `null` for the list of transactions. The reason for providing a default value is that when a new account is created, it will have no previous transactions, so it makes sense to have this as an optional parameter. But we also don't want `null` to potentially cause a `NullReferenceException`. Secondly, this record definition allows you to create an account by changing the currency of an existing account, like so:

```
var usdAccount = newAccount with { Currency = "USD" };
```

This makes no sense. Although the status of an account may go from, say, `Requested` to `Active`, once an account is opened with a given currency, that should never change. We'd like our model to represent this. Let's see how we can address both issues, starting with the latter.

READ-ONLY VS. INIT-ONLY PROPERTIES

When you use positional records, the compiler creates an *init-only auto property* for each parameter you declare. This is a property with a `get` and an `init` method; the latter is a setter that can only be called when the record instance is initialized. If we were to explicitly declare the `Currency` property as a public init-only auto property, just as the compiler would generate, it would look like this:

```
public record AccountState
(
    CurrencyCode Currency,
```

```
        AccountStatus Status = AccountStatus.Requested,
        decimal AllowedOverdraft = 0m,
        IEnumerable<Transaction> TransactionHistory = null
    )
    {

        public CurrencyCode Currency { get; init; } = Currency;
    }
```

The following listing breaks this down so that you can see what every bit means.

Listing 11.3   Explicitly defining a property in a positional record definition

```
public record AccountState(CurrencyCode Currency /*...*/)
{
                                                    ┌─ Currency here refers to
    public CurrencyCode Currency      ◁────────────┘  the name of the property.
    {
        get;                                    ◁──── ┌─ Gets the value
        init;          ◁──── ┌─ Allows the value to be set only │ of the property
    }                        │ upon record initialization
    =
    Currency;          ◁──── ┌─ Currency here refers to the constructor parameter; this means
                             │ that upon initialization the Currency property is set to the
}                            │ value provided for the Currency constructor parameter.
}
```

Introduces the property initializer (annotation pointing to `init;` and `=`)

When you use a `with` expression to create a modified version of a record, the runtime creates a clone of the original and then calls the init method of any properties for which you've provided new values. Now, writing the property explicitly allows us to override the compiler's defaults; in this case, we want to define the Currency property as a read-only auto property by removing the init method:

```
public CurrencyCode Currency { get; } = Currency;
```

Then a `with` expression attempting to create a modified version of an account with a different currency will not compile because there's no init method for setting the Currency of the copy.

   Immutable objects never change, so all properties of an immutable object must be either read-only or init-only:

- Use init-only properties if it makes sense to create a copy where a property is given an updated value.
- Use read-only properties otherwise.

As you've seen, the compiler-generated properties of positional records are init-only, so you need to explicitly declare them if you want them to be read-only.

INITIALIZING AN OPTIONAL LIST TO BE EMPTY

Now let's go back to the problem of TransactionHistory, which is initialized to be null when no value is passed to the constructor for AccountState. What we really want is to have an empty list as the default value, so ideally we'd like to write

```
public record AccountState
(
    // ...
    IEnumerable<Transaction> TransactionHistory
        = Enumerable.Empty<Transaction>()
);
```

But this doesn't compile because default values for optional arguments must be compile-time constants. The most concise solution is to explicitly define the Transaction-History property and use a property initializer, as the following listing shows.

Listing 11.4 Initializing a record with an empty list

```
public record AccountState
(
    CurrencyCode Currency,
    AccountStatus Status = AccountStatus.Requested,
    decimal AllowedOverdraft = 0m,
    IEnumerable<Transaction> TransactionHistory = null
)
{
    public IEnumerable<Transaction>
        TransactionHistory { get; init; }          Refers to the
        = TransactionHistory            ◁——┘      constructor parameter
            ?? Enumerable.Empty<Transaction>();   ◁——┐  Uses an empty list if the
}                                                     │  constructor was given null
```

While default values for method arguments must be compile-time constants, property initializers don't have this constraint. Therefore, we can include some logic in the property initializer. The previous code replaces the auto-generated property for TransactionHistory with an explicit declaration; it's essentially saying, "When a new AccountState is created, use the value given for the optional TransactionHistory constructor parameter to populate the TransactionHistory property, but use an empty list if it's null."

There are other possible approaches: you could explicitly define a constructor and have this logic in the constructor, or define a full property with a backing field and have this logic in the property's init method.

11.3.2 *Immutable all the way down*

There is one more tweak. For an object to be immutable, all its members must be immutable. If you look at the definition for AccountState, there's a catch. TransactionHistory is defined as an IEnumerable<Transaction>, and while Transaction is immutable, there are many mutable lists that implement IEnumerable. For example, consider the following code:

```
var mutableList = new List<Transaction>();

var account = new AccountState
(
```

```
    Currency: "EUR",
    TransactionHistory: mutableList
);

account.TransactionHistory.Count() // => 0

mutableList.Add(new(-1000, "Create trouble", DateTime.Now));

account.TransactionHistory.Count() // => 1
```

This code creates an `AccountState` with a mutable list; it then holds a reference to that list so that the list can still be mutated. As a result, we cannot say that our definition of `AccountState` is truly immutable.

There are two possible solutions. You could change the type definition, declaring `TransactionHistory` to be an `ImmutableList` rather than an `IEnumerable`. Alternatively, you could rewrite the property as the following listing shows.

Listing 11.5   Making a record immutable even if given a mutable list

```
using System.Collections.Immutable;

public record AccountState // ...
{
    public CurrencyCode Currency { get; } = Currency;

    public IEnumerable<Transaction> TransactionHistory { get; init; }
        = ImmutableList.CreateRange
            (TransactionHistory ?? Enumerable.Empty<Transaction>());
}
```

This code creates an `ImmutableList` from the given `IEnumerable`, thus making `AccountState` truly immutable.

> **TIP** If given an `ImmutableList`, `CreateRange` will just return it so that you don't incur any overhead by using this approach. Otherwise, it will create a defensive copy, ensuring that any subsequent mutation to the given list does not affect `AccountState`.

If an account has an immutable list of transactions, how do you add a transaction to the list? You don't. You create a new list that has the new transaction as well as all existing ones, and that will be part of a new `AccountState`. The following listing shows that adding a child to an immutable object involves the creation of a new parent object.

Listing 11.6   Adding a child to an immutable object

```
using LaYumba.Functional;                    ◁──┐  Includes Prepend as an extension
                                                 │  method on IEnumerable
public static AccountState Add
    (this AccountState account, Transaction trans)
    => account with
    {
```

```
TransactionHistory
    = account.TransactionHistory.Prepend(trans)   ◁──┐  A new IEnumerable,
};                                                    │  including existing values
                                                      │  and the one being added
```

Notice that in this particular case, we're *prepending* the transaction to the list. This is domain-specific; in most cases, you're interested in the latest transactions, so it's efficient to keep the latest ones at the front of the list.

Copying a list every time a single element is added or removed may sound terribly inefficient, but this isn't necessarily the case. We'll discuss why in chapter 12.

> **Hurdles to using C# records**
>
> In this section, you've seen how we could use records to great effect to define custom immutable data types. However, records are a recent feature in C#, so it's possible that you may encounter some hurdles when trying to adopt records.
>
> Specifically, if you use an object-relational mapper (including Entity Framework), which uses change tracking to see which objects have changed and need to be updated in the DB, or relies on an empty constructor and settable properties to populate objects, you may not be able to use records. Another stumbling block could be serialization. While System.Text.Json supports serializing records to and from JSON, other serializers may not support records yet. In this case, consider using immutability by convention (discussed in the appendix). I expect that in time records will gain popularity and will eventually be supported by all major libraries.

11.4 *Separating data and logic*

One of the ways in which FP reduces coupling in your applications, therefore making them simpler and easier to maintain, is that it naturally leads to a separation between data and logic. This is the approach we've been following in the preceding section:

- AccountState, which we defined in listing 11.2, only contains data.
- Business logic, such as activating an account or adding a transaction, is modeled through functions.

We can group all these functions into a static Account class, including logic for creating new and updated versions of AccountState, as the following listing demonstrates.

Listing 11.7 A static class that includes account-specific business logic

```
public static class Account
{
    public static AccountState Create(CurrencyCode ccy) => new(ccy);

    public static AccountState Activate(this AccountState account)
        => account with { Status = AccountStatus.Active };

    public static AccountState Add
        (this AccountState account, Transaction trans)
```

```
    => account with
    {
       TransactionHistory
          = account.TransactionHistory.Prepend(trans)
    };
}
```

`Account` is a static class for representing changes to an account, including a factory function. While `AccountState` represents the *state* of the account at a given time, the functions in `Account` represent *state transitions*. This is illustrated in figure 11.4.

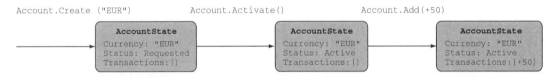

Figure 11.4   Representing state and logic related to an entity are separate concerns. In this example, `AccountState` captures the data representing an account, while `Account` is a collection of functions that model changes to an account.

When we write logic at a high level, we only rely on `Account`: for example,

```
var onDayOne = Account.Create("USD");
var onDayTwo = Account.Activate(onDayOne);
```

This means that FP allows you to treat representing state and representing state transitions as separate concerns. Also, business logic is higher-level compared to the data (`Account` depends on the lower-level `AccountState`).

Naming conventions

If you follow the approach of separating logic from data, you have to pick a naming convention to differentiate the data object from the class including the logic. Here, I used the entity name (`Account`) for the class containing the logic; this is because I like to have the best readability when referring to functions point-free: for example, `Account.Activate` in

```
Option<AccountState> Activate(Guid id)
   => GetAccount(id).Map(Account.Activate);
```

The more verbose `AccountState`, on the other hand, can often be omitted by using `var`. Other naming conventions are possible, of course. Pick what makes the most sense, and be consistent within your application.

`Account` is a class because C# syntax requires it (with the exception of top-level statements, you cannot declare methods or delegates outside of a class), but conceptually, it's just a grouping of related functions. This can be referred to as a *module*. These functions don't rely on any state in the enclosing class, so you can think of them as free-standing functions and of the class name as part of the namespace.

This separation between data (which is inert) and functions (which perform data transformations) is typical of FP. This is in stark contrast with OOP, where objects include both data and methods that mutate that data.

Separating data from logic results in simpler systems with less coupling that are, therefore, easier to understand and to maintain. It is also a logical choice when programming with distributed systems, where data structures need to be easy to serialize and pass between applications, while logic resides within those applications.

Data-oriented programming (DOP)

Several of the ideas I've discussed in this chapter are relevant to DOP, a paradigm that advocates separating logic from data as a means to decrease the complexity of an application. FP and DOP are distinct, but there is some overlap. The principles of DOP are

1. Separate logic from data entities.
2. Use immutable data.
3. Use generic structures to represent data entities.

FP also advocates using immutable data, and the use of immutable data and pure functions naturally leads to separating logic from data entities, as I demonstrated in this section. There is definitely some overlap between FP and DOP.

As for the third principle, DOP advocates using generic structures to represent data; for example, instead of defining an `AccountState` type with a `Currency` property, you would use a dictionary, mapping the value for the account's currency to the Currency key and similarly for other fields.[a] It turns out that you can represent data of any shape by using just lists, dictionaries, and primitives.

The main benefit of using generic structures to represent data is that you can handle data in a correspondingly general fashion; for example, given two snapshots of data of any shape, you can compare them and see what bits have changed. You can merge change sets and see if concurrent updates cause conflicts. That's pretty powerful.

The obvious drawback is that you lose type safety, so it's a bit of a hard sell for programmers who are used to working in statically typed languages like C#.

If you want to learn more about DOP, understand how separating logic and data simplifies life, and see why using generic structures to represent data entities can be worthwhile, see *Data-Oriented Programming* by Yehonathan Sharvit (Manning, 2021).

---

[a] If you wanted to follow this approach in C#, you would probably use the `dynamic` type for sugar-coating an underlying dictionary. This allows you to access field values with the dot notation.

Summary

- FP discourages state mutation, preventing several drawbacks associated with state mutation, such as lack of thread safety, coupling, and impurity:
  - Things that don't change are represented with immutable objects.
  - Things that change are also represented with immutable objects; these immutable snapshots represent an entity's state at a given point. Change is represented by creating a new snapshot with the desired changes.
- Use records to define custom immutable data types.
- For a type to be immutable, all its children, including lists and other data structures, must also be immutable.
- You can simplify your application and promote loose coupling by separating data from logic:
  - Use data objects (typically records) to encapsulate data.
  - Use functions (implemented as static methods within stateless static classes) to represent business logic.

A short introduction to functional data structures

In chapter 11, you saw how to create immutable objects. Particularly, section 11.1 showed the pitfalls of state mutation when concurrency is involved. These pitfalls become even more evident when dealing with collections. Because it takes longer to process a large collection than to update a single object, there are greater chances of a race conditions occurring (we saw an example of this in section 1.1.3).

Now that you know about immutable objects, let's look at some of the principles behind the design of immutable data structures. Note that the terms *functional* data structures and *immutable* data structures are used interchangeably in the

239

literature.[1] You'll see that the principles are the same: after all, objects are just ad hoc data structures.

If you commit to only working with immutable data, all data structures should also be immutable. For example, you should never add an element to a list by changing its structure, but rather create a new list with the desired changes.

This may initially cause you to raise your eyebrows: "To add an item to a list, I need to copy all existing elements into a new list along with the extra item? How inefficient is that?"

To give you an idea of why this isn't necessarily inefficient, let's look at some simple functional data structures. You'll see that adding a new element to a collection does yield a new collection, but this doesn't involve copying every item in the original collection.

> **NOTE** The implementations shown in this chapter are naive. They're helpful in understanding the basic concepts, but they're not for use in production. For real-world applications, use a proven library such as `System.Collections.Immutable`.

12.1 *The classic functional linked list*

We'll start with the classic functional linked list. While deceptively simple, this is the basic list you'll find in the core library of most functional languages. Symbolically, we can describe it as follows:

```
List<T> = Empty | Cons(T, List<T>)
```

In other words, a `List` of `T`'s can be one of two things:

- `Empty`—A special value representing the empty list
- `Cons`—A non-empty list *cons*-tructed from two values:
  - A single `T`, called the *head*, representing the first element in the list
  - Another `List` of `T`'s, called the *tail*, representing all the other elements

The tail can, in turn, be `Empty` or a `Cons` and so on. Thus, `List` is an example of a *recursive type*: a type that's defined in terms of itself. This is how with just two cases we can cater for lists of any length. For example, the structure of a list containing `["a", "b", "c"]` is as follows:

```
Cons("a", Cons("b", Cons("c", Empty)))
```

---

[1] Immutable data structures are also referred to as persistent data structures. The term *persistence* in this context doesn't indicate persistence onto some media but simply persistence in memory: the original data structure is unaffected by any operation that creates a new version, such as adding or removing elements. Furthermore, the term *persistent* applied to a data structure implies that it offers certain guarantees in terms of the running time of certain operations. Namely, operations should be just as efficient in a persistent data structure as in the corresponding mutable structure or at least be within the same order of magnitude. This goes deeper into data structure and algorithm design, so here I'll just stick with the terms *immutable/functional* data structures/collections.

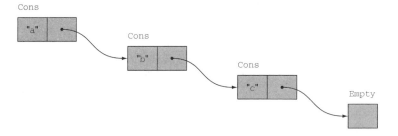

Figure 12.1 A linked list containing the values `["a", "b", "c"]`

It can be represented graphically as in figure 12.1, where each `Cons` is represented as a box with a value (the head) and a pointer to the rest of the list (the tail).

Let's look at how we can implement this in C#. These implementations are included in the `LaYumba.Functional.Data` project in the source repository. Here are the types I use to model a list:

```
namespace LaYumba.Functional.Data.LinkedList;

public abstract record List<T>;
internal sealed record Empty<T> : List<T>;
internal sealed record Cons<T>(T Head, List<T> Tail) : List<T>;
```

Note that only the `List` type is public. To interact with a `List`, I've defined a `Match` method that provides nice syntax for pattern matching:

```
public static R Match<T, R>
(
    this List<T> list,
    Func<R> Empty,
    Func<T, List<T>, R> Cons
)
=> list switch
{
    Empty<T> => Empty(),
    Cons<T>(var t, var ts) => Cons(t, ts),
    _ => throw new ArgumentException("List can only be Empty or Cons")
};
```

This is all similar to the idealized implementation for `Option` I showed in section 5.3: `Empty` has no members (like `None`), while `Cons` stores the list's elements. The `Match` method allows you to handle both cases, taking away some of the syntactical noise of the `switch` expression.

It turns out that you can define all commonly used list operations in terms of `Match`. For example, if you want to know the length of the list (as the following listing demonstrates), you'd use `Match`—the empty list obviously has length 0, whereas the non-empty list has the length of its tail plus 1.

Listing 12.1   Calculating the length of a list

```
public static int Length<T>(this List<T> list)
   => list.Match
   (
      () => 0,                          The first function given to Match
                                        handles the case of an empty list.
      (_, tail) => 1 + tail.Length()    The second function is given the head
   );                                   and tail of the list if it's not empty.
```

Notice how in the first function given to Match, the empty braces graphically suggest an empty list. In the second function, the arguments include the Cons's head and tail. In most cases, here we'll process the head and then rely on the list's recursive definition to recursively process the tail.

Finally, I've provided a few functions to create empty and populated lists. Creating the whole structure explicitly with new Cons("a", new Cons("b", ... would be tedious, so I've defined a few functions for initializing an empty or populated list. These are shown in the following listing.

Listing 12.2   Functions for initializing a list

```
public static class LinkedList
{
   public static List<T> List<T>()
      => new Empty<T>();            Creates an empty list

   public static List<T> List<T>(T h, List<T> t)
      => new Cons<T>(h, t);         Creates a non-empty
                                    list from a head and tail

   public static List<T> List<T>(params T[] items)
      => items.Reverse().Aggregate(List<T>()    Convenience method for creating a
         , (tail, head) => List(head, tail));   list with a few hard-coded elements
}
```

The first two functions simply call the constructors for Empty and Cons, respectively. The following function in the listing is a convenience list initializer. The params keyword already collects all the arguments into an array, so we just need to translate the array into a suitable combination of Empty and Cons. That's done with Aggregate, using Empty as the accumulator, and creating a Cons in the reducer function. Because List prepends the item to the list, we must reverse the parameters list first.

Now that you've seen all the building blocks, let's play with List in the REPL. You'll need to import the LaYumba.Functional.Data assembly:

```
#r "functional-csharp-code-2\LaYumba.Functional\bin\Debug\net6.0\
➡ LaYumba.Functional.Data.dll"
```

Here are some examples of how you can create lists in the REPL:

```
using LaYumba.Functional.Data.LinkedList;
using static LaYumba.Functional.Data.LinkedList.LinkedList;
```

```
var empty = List<string>();
// => []

var letters = List("a", "b");
// => [a, b]

var taxi = List("c", letters);
// => [c, a, b]
```

This code demonstrates how you can create a list, empty or prepopulated, and how you can create a Cons by adding a single item to an existing list.

12.1.1 *Common list operations*

Let's now look at how we can perform some common operations with this list, like those we've become accustomed to with IEnumerable. For example, here's Map:

```
public static List<R> Map<T, R>
(
    this List<T> list,
    Func<T, R> f
)
=> list.Match
(
    () => List<R>(),
    (t, ts) => List(f(t), ts.Map(f))
);
```

Map takes a list and a function to be mapped onto the list. It then uses pattern matching. If the list is empty, it returns an empty list; otherwise, it applies the function to the head and recursively maps the function onto the tail and returns the Cons of these two.

Here you see a common naming convention; when a Cons is deconstructed, its elements are often called t (singular, for the head) and ts (plural, for the tail), given that they are all of type T. (You'll see x and xs in languages where the generic type does not need to be named.)

If we had a list of integers and wanted the sum, we could implement this along the same lines:

```
public static int Sum(this List<int> list)
    => list.Match
    (
        () => 0,
        (head, tail) => head + tail.Sum()
    );
```

As you know from section 9.6, Sum is a special case of Aggregate. Let's see how we can implement the more generic Aggregate for List:

```
public static Acc Aggregate<T, Acc>
(
    this List<T> list,
    Acc acc,
```

```
      Func<Acc, T, Acc> f
)
=> list.Match
(
      () => acc,
      (t, ts) => Aggregate(ts, f(acc, t), f)
);
```

Again, we pattern match, and in the Cons case, we apply the reducer function f to the accumulator and the head. Then we recursively call Aggregate with the new accumulator and the tail of the list.

> **WARNING**   The implementations shown here aren't stack-safe. If the list is long enough, they'll cause a StackOverflowException.

Now that we've looked at how we can work with the linked list, let's see about operations that modify the list.

12.1.2 *Modifying an immutable list*

Let's say we want to add an item to an existing list (by which, naturally, I mean obtain a *new* list with an additional item). With a singly linked list, the natural approach is to add items at the front:

```
public static List<T> Add<T>(this List<T> list, T value)
    => List(value, list);
```

Given an existing list and a new value, we construct a new list with a new head. The head of the new list is a list node holding the new value and a pointer to the head of the original list. That's all! There's no need to copy all the elements, so we can add an element in constant time, creating just one new object. Here's an example of adding to our immutable linked list:

```
var fruit = List("pineapple", "banana");
// => ["pineapple", "banana"]

var tropicalMix = fruit.Add("kiwi");
// => ["kiwi", "pineapple", "banana"]

var yellowFruit = fruit.Add("lemon");
// => ["lemon", "pineapple", "banana"]
```

The fruit list is initialized with two items. We then add a third fruit to obtain a new list, tropicalMix. Because the list is immutable, our original fruit list hasn't changed and still contains two items. This is apparent because we can reuse it to create a new, modified version of the list containing just yellow fruit.

Figure 12.2 offers a graphical representation of the objects that are created in the preceding code and shows that the original fruit list is not altered (nor do its elements need to be copied) when creating new lists with an added item.

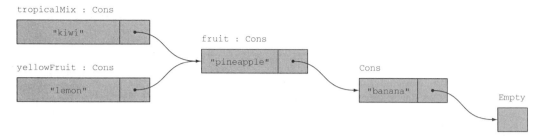

Figure 12.2 Adding an item to a list doesn't affect the original list.

Think what this means in terms of decoupling: when you have an immutable list (and more generally, an immutable object), you can expose it without ever having to worry about what some other component will do to the data. There's nothing they can do to the data at all!

What about removing an item? The singly linked list is biased to work well with the first item, so we'll remove the first item (the head) and return the rest of the list (the tail):

```
public static List<T> Tail<T>(this List<T> list)
    => list.Match
    (
        () => throw new IndexOutOfRangeException(),
        (_, tail) => tail
    );
```

Again, we can remove the first element from the list in constant time, without altering the original list. (Notice that this is one of very few places where throwing an exception is justified because calling `Tail` on an empty list is a developer error. If there's a chance of the list being empty, a correct implementation should use `Match` rather than calling `Tail`.)

You may find these examples rather limited because we've only interacted with the first element of the list. But, in practice, this can be used to cover quite a number of use cases. For example, it's a perfect starting point if you need a stack. Common operations like `Map` and `Where` would be $O(n)$ for a list of length n as with any other list.

You can define functions to insert or remove an element at index m, and these operations are $O(m)$ because they would require traversing m elements and creating m new `Cons` objects. If you need to append or remove from the end of a long list often (for example, if you need to implement a queue), you'd use a different data structure—all the data structures you're used to have immutable counterparts.

12.1.3 Destructuring any IEnumerable

Notice how we could define many useful operations on our simple linked list type in terms of pattern matching. This is because it's common to want different behavior for an empty list rather than for a non-empty list. Note that the non-empty case destructures the list into its head and tail.

A `Match` method with the same semantics can be defined to work for any `IEnumerable` and can be defined as follows:

```
public static Option<T> Head<T>(this IEnumerable<T> list)
{
    var enumerator = list.GetEnumerator();
    return enumerator.MoveNext()
        ? Some(enumerator.Current)
        : None;
}

public static R Match<T, R>
(
    this IEnumerable<T> list,
    Func<R> Empty,
    Func<T, IEnumerable<T>, R> Otherwise
)
=> list.Head().Match
(
    None: () => Empty(),
    Some: (head) => Otherwise(head, list.Skip(1))
);
```

Head returns None if the list is empty; otherwise, the head of the list wrapped in a Some.

Calls the Empty handler if the list is empty

Calls the Otherwise handler with the list's head and tail if it's not empty

This implementation of `Match` is included in `LaYumba.Functional`. You'll see how it can be useful in practice in chapter 13.

12.2   Binary trees

Trees are also common data structures. Most list implementations other than linked lists use trees as their underlying representation because this allows certain operations to be performed more efficiently. We'll just look at a basic binary tree, defined as follows:[2]

```
Tree<T> = Leaf(T) | Branch(Tree<T>, Tree<T>)
```

According to this definition, a tree can be a `Leaf`, which is a terminal node and contains a `T`, or it can be a `Branch`, which is a non-terminal node that contains two children or *subtrees*. These can, in turn, be leaves or branches and so on recursively. Like with `List`, I'll represent each case with a different type:

```
public abstract record Tree<T>;
internal record Leaf<T>(T Value) : Tree<T>;
internal record Branch<T>(Tree<T> Left, Tree<T> Right) : Tree<T>;
```

As you traverse a tree, you will want to execute different code for branches and for leaves and access the leaves' inner values. I'll define a `Match` method providing a pleasant API to perform pattern matching:

```
public static R Match<T, R>
(
    this Tree<T> tree,
```

---

[2] *Binary* here means that every branch has two subtrees.

```
      Func<T, R> Leaf,
      Func<Tree<T>, Tree<T>, R> Branch
   )
   => tree switch
   {
      Leaf<T>(T val) => Leaf(val),
      Branch<T>(var l, var r) => Branch(l, r),
      _ => throw new ArgumentException("{tree} is not a valid tree")
   };
```

You can now call `Match` as usual:

```
myTree.Match
(
   Leaf: t => $"It's a leaf containing '{t}'",
   Branch: (left, right) => "It's a branch"
);
```

I also have the typical factory functions `Leaf` and `Branch`, allowing you to create a tree in the REPL like this:

```
using static LaYumba.Functional.Data.BinaryTree.Tree;

Branch(
   Branch(Leaf(1), Leaf(2)),
   Leaf(3)
)
```

That would create a tree like this:

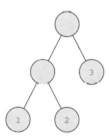

12.2.1 Common tree operations

Now let's look at some common operations. As with lists, we can define most operations in terms of pattern matching. For example, counting the number of values in a tree can be done as follows:

```
public static int Count<T>(this Tree<T> tree)
   => tree.Match
   (
      Leaf: _ => 1,
      Branch: (l, r) => l.Count() + r.Count()
   );
```

Trees also have *depth* (how many nodes you have to traverse to get from the root node to the furthest leaf) and, again, you can compute the depth using pattern matching:

```
public static int Depth<T>(this Tree<T> tree)
   => tree.Match
   (
      Leaf: _ => 0,
      Branch: (l, r) => 1 + Math.Max(l.Depth(), r.Depth())
   );
```

What about Map? Map should yield a new tree, isomorphic to the original one, with the mapped function applied to each value in the original tree, as figure 12.3 shows.

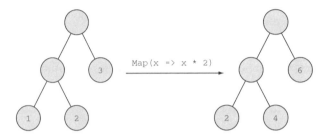

Figure 12.3   The Map function for a binary tree

Try to avoid looking at the following implementation and write down how you think Map might work:

```
public static Tree<R> Map<T, R>
(
   this Tree<T> tree,
   Func<T, R> f
)
=> tree.Match
(
   Leaf: t => Leaf(f(t)),
   Branch: (left, right) => Branch
   (
      Left: left.Map(f),
      Right: right.Map(f)
   )
);
```

To implement Map on a tree, you pattern match:

- If you have a leaf, then you extract its value, apply the function to the leaf, and wrap it in a new leaf.
- Otherwise, you create a new branch whose left and right subtrees are the result of mapping the function onto the original subtrees.

It's also reasonable to define an Aggregate function that reduces all the values in the tree to a single value:

```
public static Acc Aggregate<T, Acc>
(
    this Tree<T> tree,
    Acc acc,
    Func<Acc, T, Acc> f
)
=> tree.Match
(
    Leaf: t => f(acc, t),
    Branch: (l, r) =>
    {
        var leftAcc = l.Aggregate(acc, f);
        return r.Aggregate(leftAcc, f);
    }
);
```

12.2.2 *Structure sharing*

More interestingly, let's look at an operation that changes the structure of a tree, such as inserting an element. This can be done simply, as the following listing shows.

Listing 12.3 Adding a value to an immutable tree

```
public static Tree<T> Insert<T>
(
    this Tree<T> tree,
    T value
)
=> tree.Match
(
    Leaf: _ => Branch(tree, Leaf(value)),
    Branch: (l, r) => Branch(l, r.Insert(value))
);
```

As usual, the code uses pattern matching. If the tree is a leaf, it creates a branch whose two children are the leaf itself and a new leaf with the inserted value. If it's a branch, it inserts the new value into the right subtree.

For example, if you start with a tree containing {1, 2, 3, 7} and insert the value 9, the result would be as figure 12.4 shows. As you can see, the new tree shares large portions of its structure with the original tree. This is an example of the more general idea of *structure sharing*; the updated collection shares as much of its structure as possible with the original collection.

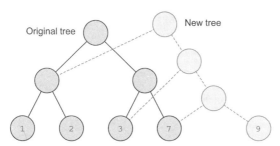

Figure 12.4 The tree with the added value shares parts of the structure with the original tree.

How many new items are created to insert an item into a tree? As many as it takes to reach a leaf. If you start with a balanced tree with n elements,[3] an insert involves the creation of log $n + 2$ objects, which is reasonable.[4]

Of course, the implementation in listing 12.3 would eventually lead to a very imbalanced tree because it always adds elements to the right. To guarantee efficient inserts, we'd need to refine the tree representation to include a self-balancing mechanism. This is certainly possible but beyond the scope of this introduction.

12.3 In conclusion

Developing efficient functional data structures is a vast and fascinating topic of which we've only scratched the surface. The reference book on the subject is *Purely Functional Data Structures* by Chris Okasaki (Cambridge University Press, 1999). Unfortunately, the code samples are in Standard ML. Nonetheless, in this section, you've gained some insight into the inner workings of functional data structures and the idea of structure sharing, which allows immutable data structures to be safe and to perform well.

Functional programs may incur some performance penalty for copying data rather than updating it in place, but imperative programs may have to introduce locking and defensive copies to ensure correctness. As a result, functional programs tend to perform better in many scenarios. For most practical applications, however, performance isn't the critical concern, but rather the greater reliability that you gain by embracing immutability.

Exercises

Lists:

1 Implement the following functions to work with the singly linked `List` defined in this chapter:
   - `InsertAt` inserts an item at the given index.
   - `RemoveAt` removes the item at the given index.
   - `TakeWhile` takes a predicate and traverses the list, yielding all items until it finds one that fails the predicate.
   - `DropWhile` works similarly but excludes all items at the front of the list.

2 What's the complexity of these four functions? How many new objects are required to create the new list?

3 `TakeWhile` and `DropWhile` are useful when working with a list that's sorted, and you'd like to get all items greater or smaller than some value. Write implementations that take an `IEnumerable` rather than a `List`.

---

[3] A tree is balanced if all paths from the root to a leaf have the same length or differ at most by one.

[4] The base of the log will be the arity of the tree (how many children each node has). A real-world implementation of a tree underlying a list representation may have an arity of 32 so that after inserting 1 million objects, your tree may still only have a depth of 4 levels.

Trees:

1 Is it possible to define `Bind` for the binary tree implementation shown in this chapter? If so, implement `Bind`; otherwise, explain why it's not possible. (Hint: start by writing the signature and then sketch a binary tree and how you could apply a tree-returning function to each value in the tree.)

2 Implement a `LabelTree` type where each node has a label of type `string` and a list of subtrees. This could be used to model a typical navigation tree or a category tree in a website.

3 Imagine you need to add localization to your navigation tree. You're given a `LabelTree` where the value of each label is a key, and a dictionary that maps keys to translations in one of the languages that your site must support. You need to compute the localized navigation/category tree. (Hint: define `Map` for `LabelTree`.)

4 Unit test the preceding implementation.

Summary

- In FP, collections should be immutable so that existing collections are never altered, but rather new collections are created with the desired changes.
- Immutable collections can be safe and efficient because an updated version shares much of its structure with the original collection without affecting it.

Event sourcing:
A functional
approach to persistence

In chapter 11, you saw that in FP we avoid mutating state, especially global state. Did I mention that the database is also state, so it too should be immutable? What? Yes, didn't you see this one coming? A database is, conceptually, just a data structure. Whether it's stored in memory or on disk is ultimately just an implementation detail.

You saw in chapter 12 how functional data structures, although immutable, can evolve: you can create new states or new views of any given structure that are built on but don't alter the original structure. This idea (which we explored with respect to objects, lists, and trees) naturally applies to in-memory data, as well as to stored data, and this is how our applications represent change without mutation, even at the database level.

There are currently two approaches to this idea of "append-only" data storage:

- *Assertion-based*—Treats the DB as an ever-growing collection of facts that are true at a given point in time
- *Event-based*—Treats the DB as an ever-growing collection of events that occur at given points in time

In both cases, data is never updated or deleted, only appended.[1] I'll compare these two approaches in more detail in section 13.4, but we'll spend most of this chapter discussing the event-based approach, usually referred to as *event sourcing* (ES). This is because it's easier to understand and to implement using various kinds of backing storage, and its adoption in the .NET community has been much wider.

13.1 Thinking functionally about data storage

A significant majority of server applications today are *stateless*: when they receive a request, they retrieve the required data from the database, do some processing, and persist the relevant changes (see figure 13.1).[2]

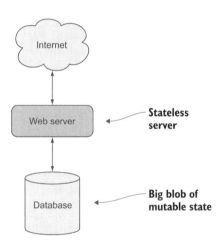

Indeed, the stateless server approach has proven effective precisely because state is such a major source of complexity. If you can get the data out of thin air (as it were) when you need it, then a lot of difficult problems go away. This is, in essence, what stateless servers do.

This also means that it's relatively easy to avoid state mutation in a stateless server: simply create new, updated versions of the data and persist those to the database. But we're fooling ourselves if we think that we're developing functionally if values in the DB are being updated or deleted in the process. When we develop an application with a CRUD approach (updating stored data in place), we're essentially using the DB as a big blob of global mutable state.

Figure 13.1   So-called stateless servers usually rely on a big blob of mutable data called the database.

13.1.1 Why data storage should be append-only

Relational databases have been in use for some 40 years. They were conceived in a time when disk space was scarce, so using those efficiently was paramount. Typically, only the current state was stored. When a customer changed address, the old address

---

[1] The traditional functions of a relational DB are the CRUD operations: create, read, update, and delete. The functional approach to data storage is CRA: create, read, append.

[2] Stateless servers are easy to scale: you can have countless instances, all of which can process requests interchangeably. By contrast, if a server is stateful and processes requests differently depending on its internal state, then you are limited to a single instance, or alternatively, you have to devise a mechanism to ensure that different instances behave consistently.

was overwritten with the new one—a mindset we still have today, even though it's now become completely obsolete.

Today, in the age of big data, the tables are turned: storage is cheap and data is valuable. Overwriting data is like throwing money out the window. Say that a customer removes an item from their shopping basket—what do you do? Do you delete a row in the database? If you do, you've just deleted valuable information that might be useful in determining why certain items aren't selling as expected. Maybe customers often abandon certain items mid-purchase and replace them with cheaper items from the suggestions list. If you delete the data, you can never run this sort of analysis.

This is why the idea of append-only storage has gained traction—never delete or overwrite any data and only append new data. (For example, think about the version control system you use to store your code. Does it overwrite existing code when you commit new changes?)

Append-only storage has another great virtue: it eliminates the problem of database contention. DB engines internally use locks to ensure that concurrent connections modifying the same fields don't conflict with each other. For instance, imagine you have an e-commerce site, and there's a rush of purchases for one particular product. If the inventory count for that product is modeled as a value in a DB cell that's updated as orders are placed, that puts contention on that cell, making database access inefficient. An append-only approach such as event sourcing eliminates this problem. Let's see what event sourcing looks like.

13.1.2 *Relax and forget about storing state*

An important idea we explored in chapter 11 was the relationship of states to entities. *States* are snapshots of an entity at a given time; conversely, an *entity* is a sequence of logically related states. *State transitions* cause a new state to be associated with the entity or, more intuitively, cause the entity to go from one state to the next.

State transitions are triggered by *events*; for example, your bank account is affected by events like deposits, withdrawals, bank charges, and so on. As a result, the state of your bank account changes, as figure 13.2 illustrates.

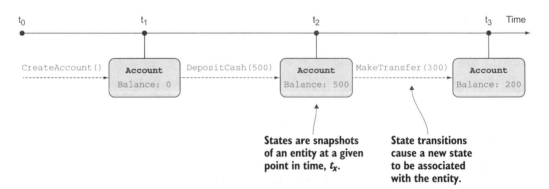

Figure 13.2   An entity can be viewed as a sequence of logically related states. The identity of the entity remains the same, but the state changes as the result of events that affect the entity's state.

As developers, we tend to be overly concerned with representing state. In fact, we often take it for granted that we *must* persist state. But this tacit assumption is unfounded: it's just the effect of relational databases being prevalent for half a century.

Typically, we use a relational database to only store the latest state of an entity, overwriting previous states. When we really need to know about the past, we often use history tables in which we store all snapshots. This approach is inefficient because we're duplicating all the data that hasn't changed between snapshots, and it's ineffective because we must run complicated logic to compare two states if we want to figure out what caused the changes.

Event sourcing (ES) turns things around: it shifts the focus from states to state transitions. Instead of storing data about the states, it stores data about the events. It's always possible to reconstruct the current state of an entity by replaying all the events that affected the entity.

Figure 13.3 shows the same information as figure 13.2, but the focus has changed. We don't want to focus on state: *state is secondary*. In fact, an entity's state is (literally) a function of its event history.

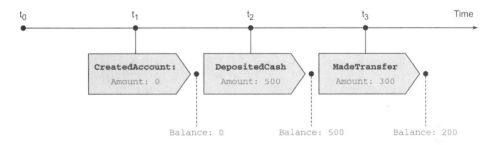

Figure 13.3 Event sourcing implies a shift of focus in thinking about entities. Instead of concentrating on an entity's state, we concentrate on the transitions that bring about the new state.

Given two successive states of an entity, it's difficult to figure out what event caused the transition. By contrast, given an entity's state and an event affecting that entity, it's easy to figure out the entity's new state. So in ES, we persist data that captures details about events, not states.

13.2 Event sourcing basics

Next, we'll look at how we can apply these ideas in practice, illustrating them through our BOC scenario. You'll see how

- *Events* are represented as simple, immutable data objects capturing the details of what happened.
- *States* are also represented as immutable data objects, although they may have a more complex structure than events, such as parent-child relationships.

- *State transitions* are represented as functions that take a state and an event and produce a new state.

Finally, you'll see how you can recreate an entity's state from its event history.

13.2.1 Representing events

Events are really simple, plain data objects that capture the minimum amount of information required to faithfully represent what happened. For example, the following listing shows some events that represent things that may affect a bank account.

Listing 13.1   Some events affecting a bank account

```
public abstract record Event
(
   Guid EntityId,                      Identifies the affected entity
   DateTime Timestamp                  (in this case, an account)
);

public record CreatedAccount
(
   Guid EntityId,
   DateTime Timestamp,
   CurrencyCode Currency
)
: Event(EntityId, Timestamp);

public record FrozeAccount
(
   Guid EntityId,
   DateTime Timestamp
)
: Event(EntityId, Timestamp);

public record DepositedCash
(
   Guid EntityId,
   DateTime Timestamp,
   decimal Amount,
   Guid BranchId
)
: Event(EntityId, Timestamp);

public record DebitedTransfer
(
   Guid EntityId,
   DateTime Timestamp,

   string Beneficiary,
   string Iban,
   string Bic,

   decimal DebitedAmount,
   string Reference
)
: Event(EntityId, Timestamp);
```

The preceding events are only a subset of the events that might affect an account (most obviously, we're missing cash withdrawals and credited transfers). But they're representative enough that with these examples, you can figure out how other events would be handled.

Events should be immutable: they represent things that happened in the past, and there's no changing the past. They are persisted to storage, so they must also be serializable.

13.2.2 Persisting events

If you look at the sample events in listing 13.1 with a view to persisting them to a DB, you'll immediately notice that all the events have a different structure (different fields), so you can't store them in a fixed-format structure like a relational table. There are various options for storing events. In order of decreasing event-orientation, you should consider using the following:

- A specialized event DB such as Event Store (https://geteventstore.com), which was designed specifically with event-sourced systems in mind.
- A document database such as Redis, MongoDB, and others. These storage systems make no assumptions about the structure of the data they store.
- A traditional relational DB such as SQL Server.

NOTE Whatever storage you use to persist your events is generally referred to as an *event store*. Don't confuse this with Event Store (always capitalized in this chapter), which is a specific product that includes an event store and much related functionality.

If you opt to store events in a relational DB, you'll need an events table with some header columns such as `EntityId` and `Timestamp`, which you'll need in order to query the event history of an entity (sorted and potentially filtered by timestamp). The event payload is serialized into a JSON string and stored into a wide column, as table 13.1 illustrates.

Table 13.1 Event data can be stored in a relational DB table.

EntityId	Timestamp	EventType	Data
abcd	2021-07-22 12:40	CreatedAccount	{ "Currency": "EUR" }
abcd	2021-07-30 13:25	DepositedCash	{ "Amount": 500, "BranchId": "BOCLHAYMCKT" }
abcd	2021-08-03 10:33	DebitedTransfer	{ "DebitedAmount": 300, "Beneficiary": "Rose Stephens", …}

All three storage options are viable; it depends on your requirements and existing infrastructure. If most of your data is already in a relational DB and you only want to event source some entities, then using that same DB may make sense because it would involve less operational overhead.

13.2.3 *Representing state*

We spent much of chapter 11 discussing how to represent state, so we're already in a pretty good position. But now we must ask the question, if we're using events for persistence, what exactly is the purpose of these states or snapshots? It turns out that we still need snapshots of the state of data entities for two completely independent purposes:

- *We need snapshots to make decisions on how to process commands.* For example, if the server receives a command to make a transfer and the account is frozen or has an insufficient balance, then it must reject the command.
- *We also need snapshots to display to clients.* I'll refer to these as *view models.*[3]

Let's deal with the first type of snapshot (we'll look at view models in section 13.3.4). We need a snapshot that captures *only* what we need in order to make decisions about how to handle commands. The following listing shows such an object that models the account state.

Listing 13.2   A simplified model of the entity state

```
public sealed record AccountState
(
    CurrencyCode Currency,
    AccountStatus Status = AccountStatus.Requested,
    decimal Balance = 0m,
    decimal AllowedOverdraft = 0m
);
```

You'll notice that this is somewhat simplified compared to the `AccountState` type discussed in chapter 11. Specifically, I don't have a list of transactions because I'm assuming that the current balance and the account status are enough to make decisions about how to handle any commands. Transactions may be shown to the user, but they're not required when processing commands.

13.2.4 *Representing state transitions*

Now let's see how states and events are combined in state transitions. Once you have a state and an event, you can compute the next state by applying the event to the state. This computation is called a *state transition*, and it's a function whose signature has this general form:

```
state → event → state
```

---

[3] Running complex analytics on data stored as events can be inefficient, so you may also decide to store snapshots for this reason. These snapshots are called *projections* and are updated as the events occur to make the data available for querying in an efficient format. They're not fundamentally different from view models (more precisely, you can think of a view model as a projection), so I won't deal with projections specifically in this book.

In other words, "Give me a state and an event, and I'll compute the new state after the event." Particularized for our scenario, this signature becomes

```
AccountState → Event → AccountState
```

Here, Event is the base class from which all our events derive, so an implementation must pattern match on the type of the event and then compute a new AccountState with the relevant changes.

There's also one special state transition, which is when an account is first created. In that case, we have an event but no prior state, so the signature is in this form:

```
event → state
```

The following listing shows the implementation for our scenario.

Listing 13.3 Modeling state transitions

```
public static class Account
{
    public static AccountState Create(CreatedAccount evt)    ⟵  CreatedAccount
        => new AccountState                                      is a special case
        (                                                        because there is no
            Currency: evt.Currency,                              prior state.
            Status: AccountStatus.Active
        );

    public static AccountState Apply
        (this AccountState acc, Event evt)        Makes the relevant transition
        => evt switch                        ⟵   depending on the type of the event
        {
            DepositedCash e
                => acc with { Balance = acc.Balance + e.Amount },

            DebitedTransfer e
                => acc with { Balance = acc.Balance - e.DebitedAmount },

            FrozeAccount
                => acc with { Status = AccountStatus.Frozen },

            _ => throw new InvalidOperationException()   ⟵  The discard pattern matches
        };                                                   any events for which
}                                                            processing is not defined.
```

The first method is the special case of creation: it takes a CreatedAccount event and creates a new AccountState populated with values from the event. To simplify things, let's assume that an account can be set to Active as soon as it's created.

The Apply method is the more general formulation of a state transition, and it will process all other types of events by pattern matching on the event type. If the event is FrozeAccount, we return a new state that has status Frozen; if the event is Deposited-Cash, we increase the balance accordingly and so on. In a real application, you'd have many more types of events here.

Unrestricted inheritance and the discard pattern

The `switch` expression in listing 13.3 includes the obligatory *discard pattern*, catering for any events that don't match any of the patterns specified explicitly. It's obligatory in the sense that if you omit it, you'll get a compiler warning: without the discard pattern, the compiler cannot assume that the pattern matching is exhaustive. `Event` could have other subclasses, even ones defined in other assemblies, compiled separately.

It's wise to always throw an exception if the discard pattern matches. If you introduce a new type of event and forget to define how to handle it, you want the code to fail.

Most statically typed functional languages take a different approach to sum types: when you define a sum type, you also define all possible subtypes. For example, you can say that a `List` can be `Empty` or `Cons` *and nothing else*. The fact that it's not possible to restrict inheritance in this way in C# has lead me to define `Match` methods for most of the sum types in this book.

In languages where you can exhaustively specify the possible cases of a sum type, pattern matching becomes even more powerful. The compiler knows all possible types of, say, `Event`s that your system can handle. This means not only that you no longer need a discard pattern but, crucially, if you add a new type of `Event`, the compiler points out any places in which `Event`s are handled, effectively guiding your development process. (You get compiler errors showing you where you need to handle a new case instead of run-time errors thrown from matching a discard pattern.)

Notice that this data-driven approach where you use data (such as different types of events or commands) in order to perform different logic is completely at odds with the open-closed principle so dear to OO programmers.

13.2.5 *Reconstructing the current state from past events*

Now that you've seen how to represent states and events and how to combine them with state transitions, you're ready to see how an entity's current state can be computed from the history of events that affected that entity in the past. This is represented graphically in figure 13.4.

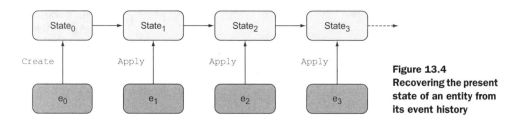

Figure 13.4 Recovering the present state of an entity from its event history

You have a list of events that affected an account, and you want to compute the account's current state. Here are three considerations to keep in mind:

- When you start out with a list and want to end up with a single value, you use `Aggregate`.

- The first event in the list caused the account to be created, whereas subsequent events involve state transitions.
- One final detail: imagine you query the DB for all events concerning account 123, and you get an empty list. This means that the account has no history, so effectively, it doesn't exist, and you should get a None.

The following listing shows how to compute an account's state from its event history.

Listing 13.4 Computing the state of an entity from its event history

```
public static Option<AccountState> From
   (IEnumerable<Event> history)          ◁──┐ Given the history
   => history.Match                            of events
   (
      Empty: () => None,
      Otherwise: (created, otherEvents) => Some          Creates a new account
      (                                                  from the first event, using
         otherEvents.Aggregate                           it as an accumulator
         (
            seed: Account.Create((CreatedAccount)created),   ◁──────┘
            func: (state, evt) => state.Apply(evt)   ◁──┐ Applies each
         )                                                subsequent event
      )
   )
);
```

Let's look at the signature first. We're taking a sequence of events: the entity's history. This is the list of events you get from the DB when you query all the events for a given account ID. I'm assuming that the sequence is sorted; events that happened first should be at the top of the list. You must enforce this when you retrieve events from the database, and this often comes for free: because events are persisted as they occur, they're appended in order, and this ordering is normally preserved when they're retrieved.

We then use the Match method defined in section 12.1.3. This allows you to handle the case of an empty event history, in which case, the account effectively doesn't exist, and the code returns None. This is why the desired return type of AccountState is wrapped in an Option.

If the list is not empty, it's destructured into its head and tail. The head must be a CreatedAccount event, while the tail contains all following events. The code computes the initial state of the account from the CreatedAccount event, and then uses that as an accumulator for Aggregate, which applies all subsequent events to this initial state, thus obtaining the current state.

Notice that if you wanted to see not the current state of the account but its state at any point in the past, this can be done trivially by evaluating the same function but only including events that occurred before the desired date. For this reason, event sourcing is a valuable model when you need an audit trail and need to see how an entity has changed through time.

Now that you've seen how event sourcing offers a viable, append-only model for persistence from which present or past states can be easily computed, let's see what an event-sourced system looks like from a high-level architectural point of view.

13.3   *Architecture of an event-sourced system*

The data flows in an event-sourced system are different from those in a traditional system, where data is backed up by a relational store. As figure 13.5 shows, in CRUD-oriented systems, the program deals in entities or, better, in states. States are saved in the DB; states are retrieved by the server; states are sent to the client. The transformations between the *model* (the data stored in the DB) and the *view model* (the data sent to the client) are often minor.

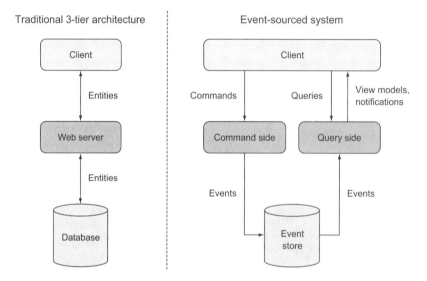

Figure 13.5   High-level comparison of data flows in a traditional vs. event-sourced system

In an event-sourced system, things are quite different. What we persist is events. But users won't want to see an event log, so the data that we surface for the users' consumption must be structured in a meaningful way. For this reason, an event-sourced system can be split neatly into two separate parts—typically, two separate server applications:

- *The command side*—This side has the job of writing data, which consists mainly of handling commands received from clients. Commands are first validated, and valid commands result in events being persisted and published.
- *The query side*—This side has the job of reading data. View models are dictated by what you want to show on the client, and the query side must populate those view models from the stored events. Optionally, the query side can also publish notifications to the client when new events cause the views to change.

This natural split between the command and query sides results in smaller, more focused components. It also gives you flexibility: the command and query sides can be completely separate applications and can, therefore, be scaled and deployed independently. This is advantageous when you think that the load on the query side is likely to be much greater than on the command side. For example, think about how little data you post when you visit a site like Twitter or Facebook compared to the amount of data you retrieve.

Conversely, on the command side, you may need to synchronize writes to prevent concurrent changes. This is much more easily accomplished if there's a single instance of the command side. This separation (which goes by the name of *CQRS* for command/query responsibility segregation), allows you to easily scale the data-intensive query side to satisfy demand, while keeping fewer or perhaps even a single instance of the command side.

The command and query sides don't have to be separate applications. Both can live in the same application. But if you use event sourcing, there's still an internal separation between the two sides. Let's see how you could go about implementing them, starting with the command side.

13.3.1 Handling commands

Commands are, if you like, the earliest source of data. Commands are sent to your application by clients and are handled by the command side, which must do the following:

- Validate the command
- Turn the command into an event
- Persist the event and publish it to interested parties

Let's start by comparing commands and events, which are similar yet distinct:

- *Commands*—Represent requests from a client. It's possible for a command to be disobeyed or disregarded for some reason. Maybe the command fails validation or maybe the system crashes while handling it. Commands should be named in the imperative form, such as `MakeTransfer` or `FreezeAccount`.
- *Events*—Represent things that have already happened. As a result, they can't fail or be disregarded. They should be named in the past tense, such as `DebitedTransfer` or `FrozeAccount`. In the context of ES, the term *event* refers to events that cause state transitions and, therefore, must be persisted (if you have other, more transient events in your system that need not be persisted, make sure you clearly differentiate between them).

Other than that, commands and events generally capture the same information, and creating an event from a command is a matter of copying field by field (sometimes with some variations). The following listing provides an example.

Listing 13.5 Translating a command into an event

```
using Boc.Domain.Events;        ◁─┐ Events are part of the domain definition.

namespace Boc.Commands;              ◁─┐ Commands are part of the
                                         higher-level, client-facing code.
public abstract record Command(DateTime Timestamp);

public record FreezeAccount
(
    DateTime Timestamp,
```

```
    Guid AccountId
)
    : Command(Timestamp)
{
    public FrozeAccount ToEvent() => new
    (
        EntityId: this.AccountId,
        Timestamp: this.Timestamp
    );
}

// more commands here...
```

Translates a command
into an event by copying
values field by field

I've defined similar `ToEvent` methods for each command in the BOC application. Note
that events are defined in your domain (hence, the `Boc.Domain.Events` namespace),
while commands are effectively part of your client-facing code (potentially, events can
be defined in a lower-level assembly on which your command-handling code depends).

An event directly affects a single entity, but events are broadcast within your system
so they may trigger the creation of other events that affect other entities. For example,
a transfer directly affects a bank account but indirectly affects the bank's cash reserve.

Next, let's look at the main workflow on the command side, as figure 13.6 illustrates.

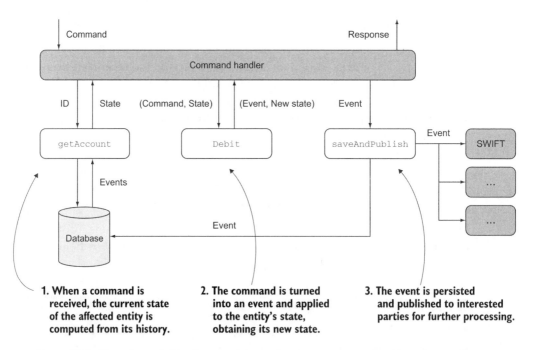

1. **When a command is
   received, the current state
   of the affected entity is
   computed from its history.**

2. **The command is turned
   into an event and applied
   to the entity's state,
   obtaining its new state.**

3. **The event is persisted
   and published to interested
   parties for further processing.**

Figure 13.6 **The command side of an event-sourced system**

To start with, I'll disregard validation and error handling, so that you can concentrate
on the essentials of the data flow. The following listing shows the entry point and main
workflow on the command side.

Listing 13.6 Top-level command-handling workflow

```
public static void ConfigureMakeTransferEndpoint
(
    WebApplication app,
    Func<Guid, AccountState> getAccount,
    Action<Event> saveAndPublish
)
=> app.MapPost("/Transfer/Make", (MakeTransfer cmd) =>
{
    var account = getAccount(cmd.DebitedAccountId);

    var (evt, newState) = account.Debit(cmd);

    saveAndPublish(evt);

    return Ok(new { newState.Balance });
});
```

Handles receiving a command (pointing to `=> app.MapPost("/Transfer/Make", (MakeTransfer cmd) =>`)

Retrieves the account (pointing to `var account = getAccount(cmd.DebitedAccountId);`)

Performs the state transition; returns a tuple with the event and the new state (pointing to `var (evt, newState) = account.Debit(cmd);`)

Persists the event and publishes to interested parties (pointing to `saveAndPublish(evt);`)

Returns information to the client about the new state (pointing to `return Ok(new { newState.Balance });`)

This code depends on two functions:

- getAccount—Retrieves the current state of the affected account (computed from its event history, as you saw in section 13.2.5)
- saveAndPublish—Persists the given event to storage and publishes it to any interested parties

Now for the endpoint itself. It receives a command to make a transfer and uses the getAccount function to retrieve the state of the account to be debited. It then feeds the retrieved account state and the command to the Debit function, which performs the state transition.

Debit returns a tuple containing both the created event and the account's new state. The code then destructures the tuple into its two elements: the created event, which is passed to saveAndPublish, and the account's new state, which is used to populate the response that's sent back to the client. Let's look at the Debit function:

```
public static class Account
{
    public static (Event Event, AccountState NewState) Debit
    (
        this AccountState currentState,
        MakeTransfer transfer
    )
    {
        Event evt = transfer.ToEvent();
        AccountState newState = currentState.Apply(evt);

        return (evt, newState);
    }
}
```

Translates the command into an event (pointing to `Event evt = transfer.ToEvent();`)

Computes the new state (pointing to `AccountState newState = currentState.Apply(evt);`)

Debit converts the command into an event and feeds that event, along with the account's current state, to the Apply function, obtaining the account's new state. Notice that this is the same Apply function that's used when computing the account's current state from its event history.[4] This ensures that state transitions are consistent regardless of whether the event is just occurring now or has occurred in the past and is being replayed.

13.3.2 Handling events

Where do we actually send the money to the recipient? That's done as part of save-AndPublish: the newly created event should be propagated to interested parties. A dedicated service should subscribe to these events and send the money to the receiving bank (via SWIFT or another interbank platform) as appropriate. Several other subscribers may consume the same event for other reasons, such as recomputing the bank's cash reserve, sending a toast notification to the client's phone, and so on.

This may throw some light on why the function is called saveAndPublish: both things should happen atomically. If the process saves the event and then crashes before all subscribers are able to handle the event, the system may be left in an inconsistent state. For example, the account may be debited but the money not sent to SWIFT.

How this atomicity is achieved is somewhat intricate and strictly depends on the infrastructure you're targeting (both for storage and for event propagation). For instance, if you use Event Store, you can take advantage of *durable* subscriptions to event streams, which guarantee that the event is delivered at least once to the subscriber (that's the meaning of *durable* in this context).

By using Event Store, you could simplify the logic in saveAndPublish to only save the event. Event handlers then subscribe to Event Store's event streams, as figure 13.7 shows.

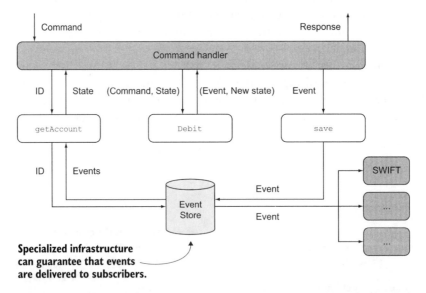

Figure 13.7   Event handlers can subscribe to event streams published by Event Store.

---

[4] Other authors on ES would allow for a command to be translated into several events at this point, but I find this tends to add complexity without any real benefit. Instead, I find that a command should be translated into a single event. When this event is then published, downstream event handlers can create other events, affecting the same but more frequently other entities.

13.3.3 Adding validation

Let's now add validation so that the command is only accepted and turned into an event if the current state of the account allows it. This is shown in the following listing.

Listing 13.7 Ensuring only valid transitions take place

```
public static class Account
{
    public static Validation<(Event Event, AccountState NewState)> Debit
        (this AccountState account, MakeTransfer transfer)
    {
        if (account.Status != AccountStatus.Active)
            return Errors.AccountNotActive;

        if (account.Balance - transfer.Amount < account.AllowedOverdraft)
            return Errors.InsufficientBalance;

        Event evt = transfer.ToEvent();
        AccountState newState = account.Apply(evt);

        return (evt, newState);
    }
}
```

Here `Debit` performs some account-specific validation, so the return type is wrapped in a `Validation`:

- If validation fails, the code returns an `Error` (here I'm demonstrating the approach described in section 8.3.1, where an `Errors` class exposes a property for each error that may occur in your app).
- If all goes well, it returns a tuple with the event and the new state.

In either case, the returned value is implicitly lifted into a `Validation` in the appropriate state. With this in place, let's revisit the main workflow, adding validation as the following listing shows.

Listing 13.8 Command handling with validation

```
public static void ConfigureMakeTransferEndpoint
(
    WebApplication app,
    Func<MakeTransfer, Validation<MakeTransfer>> validate,
    Func<Guid, Option<AccountState>> getAccount,
    Action<Event> saveAndPublish
)
=> app.MapPost("/Transfer/Make", (MakeTransfer transfer)
    => validate(transfer)
        .Bind(t => getAccount(t.DebitedAccountId)
            .ToValidation($"No account found for {t.DebitedAccountId}"))
        .Bind(acc => acc.Debit(transfer))
        .Do(result => saveAndPublish(result.Event))
        .Match(
            Invalid: errs => BadRequest(new { Errors = errs }),
            Valid: result => Ok(new { result.NewState.Balance })));
```

This listing has a new dependency, validate, which should perform some general validation of the command, such as ensuring that the IBAN and BIC codes are in the right format and the like.

I mentioned in section 13.2.5 that retrieving an account should return an Option to reflect the case that no history exists for the requested account. Here we use ToValidation to convert the Option into a Validation, providing an Error value to use if the given Option is None. (This is another example of a natural transformation that we saw in section 6.5.)

The validation of the command, the validation that the entity exists, and the account-specific validation in Debit are all modeled as functions that return a Validation and can therefore be combined with Bind.

The next step of the workflow happens inside a Do function (see the following sidebar). This calls saveAndPublish and passes on the result of Debit, which is therefore available in the subsequent call to Match: the final step in the workflow, where we send an appropriate response to the client, depending on the outcome of the validation.

The Do function

You can use Do to perform side effects in the middle of a workflow. Do is similar to ForEach in that it takes a side-effecting function. Whereas ForEach throws away the inner value, Do passes the value along, making it available for subsequent logic. The implementation of Do is simple:

```
public static Validation<T> Do<T>
   (this Validation<T> val, Action<T> action)
{
   val.ForEach(action);
   return val;
}
```

Alternatively to using Do, you could use Map, giving it a function that performs a side effect and returns its input; however, it is preferable to be explicit, so use Do to highlight the fact that a side effect is being performed, while reserving Map for data transformations that are free of side effects.

Do is also known as Tap or Tee. The name "Tee" is quite descriptive. Think in terms of pipelines: Do is like a T-shaped piece of pipeline (the data comes in at one end and goes out both toward the side-effecting function and toward the following function in the pipeline, as the following figure illustrates).

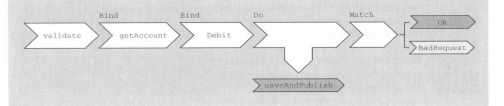

Compared to our initial skeleton in listing 13.6, the code in listing 13.8 adds validation but not exception handling. Because getAccount and saveAndPublish perform I/O, either of them could fail. To express this, we'd have to combine Validation with another effect such as Exceptional. You'll see how this can be achieved in chapter 18.

You should now have a pretty good idea of how the command side of an event-sourced system works. Let's now look at the query side.

13.3.4 Creating views of the data from events

Now that we've seen the functioning of the command side of an event-sourced system, let's look at the query side. We'll again start our exploration from the client. The client displays data in the format that's best suited for the user's needs, and the server is meant to provide data that appears in these views—the view models.

Let's take a bank account statement as a typical view of a bank account. It contains a list of transactions that occurred within a given period (let's assume that periods coincide with calendar months) as well as the balance at the start and at the end of the period. Figure 13.8 shows an example.

Your summary for:		July 2016	
Starting Balance		**550**	
Transactions			
Date	**Description**	**Credited**	**Debited**
2016-07-03	Cash deposit	200	-
2016-07-10	Transfer to Rose Stephens	-	350
2016-07-03	Direct debit payment to Electro	-	65
End Balance		**335**	

Figure 13.8 Example structure of a bank statement

Next, let's define the structure of the view model, containing the data necessary to populate the bank statement. We'll have a parent object, AccountStatement, with a list of Transactions, as the following listing shows.

Listing 13.9 The view model for a bank statement

```
public record AccountStatement
(
    int Month,
    int Year,
```

```
   decimal StartingBalance,
   decimal EndBalance,
   IEnumerable<Transaction> Transactions
);

public record Transaction
(
    DateTime Date,
    string Description,
    decimal DebitedAmount = 0m,
    decimal CreditedAmount = 0m
);
```

Note that `AccountStatement` is related to but completely separate from the `Account-State` you saw in listing 13.2:

- `AccountState` is used on the command side to process commands that may affect an account, so the server logic determines what data should be included.
- `AccountStatement` is part of the query side, so the client determines what data is required.

Both types refer to the same entity, but they may be defined in different namespaces, assemblies, or even applications.

Next, we need to populate this data from the event history of a given account. Notice that we need the *full* history of events. The following listing shows a function that populates an `AccountStatement` for a given period, given that account's event history.

Listing 13.10   Populating the `AccountStatement` view model

```
public static AccountStatement Create
(
    int month,              The period for which we want
    int year,               to populate a statement
    IEnumerable<Event> events        ◁─┐ The account's full
)                                        │ event history
{
    var startOfPeriod = new DateTime(year, month, 1);
    var endOfPeriod = startOfPeriod.AddMonths(1);

    var (eventsBeforePeriod, eventsDuringPeriod) = events
        .TakeWhile(e => endOfPeriod < e.Timestamp)
        .Partition(e => e.Timestamp <= startOfPeriod);

    var startingBalance = eventsBeforePeriod
        .Aggregate(0m, BalanceReducer);
    var endBalance = eventsDuringPeriod
        .Aggregate(startingBalance, BalanceReducer);

    return new
    (
        Month: month,
        Year: year,
        StartingBalance: startingBalance,
```

```
    EndBalance: endBalance,
    Transactions: eventsDuringPeriod.Bind(CreateTransaction)
  );
}
```

Let's go through the code. First, the list of events is split up. We'll need all events that occurred before the start of the statement period in order to calculate the account balance at the start of the period and all events that occurred during the period to calculate the balance at the end.

To calculate the starting balance, we aggregate all prior events using 0 as a seed value and a reducer function (see section 9.6) that increments or decrements the balance, depending on how an event affected the balance. The following listing shows this approach.

Listing 13.11 A reducer modeling how each event affects the account balance

```
static decimal BalanceReducer(decimal bal, Event evt)
  => evt switch
  {
    DepositedCash e => bal + e.Amount,            Events that affect
    DebitedTransfer e => bal - e.DebitedAmount,   the balance
    _ => bal         ◁──┐ Other events don't affect the balance, so this
  };                       default clause returns the running balance.
```

Not all events affect the balance, so the discard pattern of the switch expression returns the running balance.

To calculate the end balance, the same logic can be used, except that we'll use the starting balance as a seed and aggregate the events that occurred within the statement period.

Now for the list of transactions. Some events (like making a transfer) involve a transaction; others (like changes to the account status) don't. I've modeled this in a function, CreateTransaction, that populates a Transaction from an Event:

```
static Option<Transaction> CreateTransaction(Event evt)
  => evt switch
  {
    DepositedCash e => new Transaction
    (
      CreditedAmount: e.Amount,
      Description: $"Deposit at {e.BranchId}",
      Date: e.Timestamp.Date
    ),

    DebitedTransfer e => new Transaction
    (
      DebitedAmount: e.DebitedAmount,
      Description: $"Transfer to {e.Bic}/{e.Iban}; {e.Reference}",
      Date: e.Timestamp.Date
    ),
```

```
        _ => None
    };
```

Events that don't affect the account's balance don't involve a transaction; hence, this function returns an `Option`. You can use this function to compute all the transactions that belong in the statement. But instead of using `Map`, which would yield a `IEnumerable` `<Option<Transaction>>`, you can use `Bind`, which filters out all the `None`s, as we saw in section 6.5.

As you can see, populating a view model from a list of events requires some work and a bit of thinking. The data transformations involved can usually be performed through the usual `Map`, `Bind`, and `Aggregate` functions. View models stay centered on the user experience and are completely decoupled from the underlying representation.

Populating a view model can be computationally intensive if it involves processing a large number of events, so some optimization is often required to avoid recomputing a view model every time it's required. One such optimization is for the query side to cache the current version for every view model and to update it as new events are received. In this case, the query side subscribes to events published by the command side and, upon receiving these, updates the cached version and (optionally) publishes the updated view model to connected clients.

As you can see, if you want an event-sourced model with the performance characteristics of a relational database (or better), some extra work is required to precompute and maintain view models. Some more sophisticated optimizations involve a dedicated DB for the query side, where data is stored in an optimized format for querying. For example, if you need to query views with arbitrary filters, this can be a relational DB. This *query model* is always a by-product of past events so that, in case of discrepancies, the event store always acts as a *source of truth*.

13.4   *Comparing different approaches to immutable storage*

In this chapter, you've had a fairly comprehensive overview of ES—an event-based approach to data storage. You've seen why it's a functional technique at heart and how storing data about state transitions rather than state provides some important benefits.

The other approach I mentioned in the opening of the chapter is the *assertion-based approach*. This is more like the relational model in the sense that you still define entities and attributes, which are essentially like rows and columns in a relational DB. (For example, you could define a `Person` entity with an `Email` attribute.)

You'd modify this DB through *assertions*—things like "starting now, the `Email` attribute of the `Person` with ID 123 has the value jobl@manning.com." In the future, this attribute may become associated with a different value, but the fact that it was associated with the value jobl@manning.com within a particular time range is never forgotten, overwritten, or destroyed. In this model, the DB becomes an ever-growing collection of facts. You can then query the DB in much the same manner that you would a relational DB, but you get to specify whether you want to query the current state or the state at any point in time.

With both the assertion-based and event-based approaches, you get the following:

- An audit trail, making it possible to query the state of an entity at any point in time
- No database contention because no data is ever overwritten

These benefits are inherent in the fact that both approaches embrace immutability. Let's look at some other factors that may influence your choice between these two approaches.

13.4.1 Datomic vs. Event Store

The assertion-based approach really only has one embodiment, Datomic (http://www.datomic.com/), which, apart from the principles discussed here, implements other interesting design decisions that give it good characteristics in terms of performance and scalability. Datomic is a proprietary product with a free version that's limited in terms of scalability. It would be an arduous task to roll out your own assertion-based storage system.

Implementing an event-sourced system, on the other hand, is relatively simple: most of what's required was covered in this chapter. You can write an effective implementation using any DB (either NoSQL or relational) as underlying storage. For a large-scale application, it still pays to use a DB specifically designed for ES, such as Event Store, which is open source.[5] In short, if you want an assertion-based approach, you pretty much have to use Datomic; with ES, you may need or choose to use Event Store.

Because Event Store was developed in .NET, it provides a .NET client for communicating with the store via TCP, and the project has good visibility in the .NET community. Datomic was developed in Clojure, and interoperability with .NET is not good.[6] These aspects have tilted the scales in favor of Event Store and, partly as a result of that, we've seen much wider adoption of ES (whether using Event Store or not) among .NET users.

13.4.2 How event-driven is your domain?

The most important consideration when deciding on any technology is the specific requirements of your domain: some applications are intrinsically event-driven and others aren't.

How can you assess whether ES is a good fit? First, look at what you consider events in your domain. How important are they? Second, see if there's a natural difference between the sort of data being provided and the data being consumed by the parties involved.

---

[5] Although Event Store is particularly attractive for .NET users, it's not the only database designed around event streams. Another stack built on the same principles is Apache Kafka (which manages event streams) and Samza (a framework for maintaining view models computed from these streams).

[6] As of 2021, there is no native .NET client, so it's only possible to connect to Datomic via a RESTful API, which is considered obsolete. For more information, see https://docs.datomic.com/on-prem/reference/languages.html.

Consider, for example, the domain of online auctions. A typical event would be when a client places a bid on an item. This event triggers changes: the client becomes the high bidder, and the value for the next bid is raised. Another important event is when the hammer comes down. The high bidder is bound to purchase the item, which is no longer for sale, and so on. This domain is definitely event-driven.

Furthermore, the data consumed by clients tends to be in a completely different shape from the data they produce: most clients produce single bids, but they may consume data containing the details of an item for sale, the history of bids placed so far on an item, or the list of items they purchased. So there's already a natural decoupling between user actions (commands) and the data they consume (queries). ES is a natural fit for this domain.

By contrast, imagine an application enabling an insurance provider to manage its products. What events can you think of? A new policy can be created, or it can be retired, or some parameter can be modified . . . but, wait, these are essentially the CRUD operations! You still require an audit log because modifying the characteristics of a product may affect thousands of contracts once the modification comes into effect. This is a much better fit for an assertion-based DB.

Immutable data storage is an area to watch for future developments, as both approaches to immutable storage provide important responses to the needs and challenges of modern applications.

Summary

- Thinking functionally about data also encompasses storage. Instead of mutating stored data, consider the database as a big immutable collection: you can append new data but never overwrite existing data.
- There are two main approaches to immutable storage:
  - *Event-based*—The DB is an ever-growing collection of events.
  - *Assertion-based*—The DB is an ever-growing collection of facts.
- Event sourcing means persisting event data as events occur. The state of an entity need not be stored because it can always be computed as the "sum" of all events that affected the entity.
- An event-sourced system naturally separates the concerns of reading and writing data, enabling a CQRS architecture that separates between
  - *The command side*—Commands are received, validated, and turned into events that are persisted and published.
  - *The query side*—Events are combined to create view models, which are served to clients and, optionally, cached for better performance.
- Event-sourced systems include the following components:
  - *Commands*—Simple, immutable data objects encapsulating a request from a client.

- *Events*—Simple, immutable data objects capturing what happened.
- *States*—Data objects representing the state of an entity at a certain point in time.
- *State transitions*—Functions that take a state and an event and produce a new state.
- *View models*—Data objects for populating views. They're computed from events.
- *Event handlers*—These subscribe to events to perform business logic (on the command side) or to update view models (on the query side).

Part 4

Advanced techniques

This part tackles the complex topics of state management, asynchrony, and concurrency.

Chapter 14 discusses the benefits of lazy evaluation and how lazy computations can be composed. This is a general pattern for which you'll see several practical uses.

Chapter 15 shows how you can implement stateful programs without state mutation and how stateful computations can also be composed.

Chapter 16 deals with computations that deliver a single value or a stream of values asynchronously, an important part of modern computing.

Chapter 17 shows how to combine different effects discussed throughout the book—still an open topic of research in FP.

Chapter 18 discusses the Reactive Extensions (Rx), a vast library for working with data streams.

Finally, chapter 19 introduces message-passing concurrency, a style of lock-free concurrency that can be used when writing stateful concurrent programs.

Each chapter in part 4 introduces important techniques that have the potential to completely alter the way you think about writing software. Many of these topics are too vast to be discussed comprehensively, so these chapters aim to provide an introduction and a starting point for further exploration.

Lazy computations, continuations, and the beauty of monadic composition

This chapter covers

- Lazy computations
- Exception handling with `Try`
- Monadically composing functions
- Escaping the pyramid of doom with continuations

In this chapter, you'll first learn why it's sometimes desirable to define *lazy computations*, functions that may or may not be evaluated. You'll then see how these functions can be composed with other functions independently of their evaluation.

Once you've got your feet wet with lazy computations, which are just plain functions, you'll see how the same techniques can be extended to computations that have some useful effect other than laziness. Namely, you'll learn how to use the `Try` delegate to safely run code that may throw an exception and how to compose several `Trys`. You'll then learn how to compose functions that take a callback without ending up in *callback hell*.

What holds all these techniques together is that, in all cases, you're treating functions as *things* that have certain specific characteristics, and you can compose them independently of their execution. This requires a leap in abstraction, but the result is quite powerful.

> **NOTE** The contents of this chapter are challenging, so don't be discouraged if you don't get it all on your first reading.

14.1   *The virtue of laziness*

Laziness in computing means deferring a computation until its result is needed. This is beneficial when the computation is expensive, and its result may not be needed.

To introduce the idea of laziness, consider the following example of a method that randomly picks one of two given elements. You can try it out in the REPL:

```
var rand = new Random();

T Pick<T>(T l, T r) =>
    rand.NextDouble() < 0.5 ? l : r;

Pick(1 + 2, 3 + 4) // => 3, or 7
```

The interesting thing to point out here is that when you invoke `Pick`, both the expressions `1 + 2` and `3 + 4` are evaluated, even though only one of them is needed in the end.[1] So, the program is performing some unnecessary computation. This is suboptimal and should be avoided if the computation is expensive enough. To prevent this, we could rewrite `Pick` to take not two values but two lazy computations instead; that is, functions that can produce the required values:

```
T Pick<T>(Func<T> l, Func<T> r) =>
    (rand.NextDouble() < 0.5 ? l : r)();

Pick(() => 1 + 2, () => 3 + 4) // => 3, or 7
```

`Pick` now first chooses between the two functions and then evaluates one of them. As a result, only one computation is performed.

In summary, if you're not sure whether a value will be required and it may be expensive to compute it, pass the value lazily by wrapping it in a function that computes the value.

> **NOTE** Integer addition is an extremely fast operation, so in this particular example, the cost of allocating the two lambdas outweighs the benefit of making the computations lazy. This technique is only justified in case of operations that are computationally intensive or that perform I/O.

Next, you'll see how such a lazy API can be beneficial when working with `Option`.

---

[1] This is because C# is a language with strict or eager evaluation (expressions are evaluated as soon as they're bound to a variable). Although strict evaluation is more common, there are languages, notably Haskell, that use lazy evaluation so that expressions are evaluated only as needed.

14.1.1 Lazy APIs for working with Option

The Option API provides a couple of examples that nicely illustrate how laziness can be useful. Let's look at those.

PROVIDING A FALLBACK OPTION

Imagine you have an operation that returns an Option, and you want to provide a fallback—another Option-producing operation to use if the first operation returns None. Combining two such Option-returning functions in this way is a common scenario and is achieved through the OrElse function, which is defined as follows:

```
public static Option<T> OrElse<T>
   (this Option<T> left, Option<T> right)
   => left.Match
   (
      () => right,
      (_) => left
   );
```

OrElse simply yields the left Option if it's Some; otherwise, it falls back to the right Option. For example, say you define a repository that looks items up from a cache, failing which, it goes to the DB:

```
interface IRepository<T> { Option<T> Lookup(Guid id); }

class CachingRepository<T> : IRepository<T>
{
   IDictionary<Guid, T> cache;
   IRepository<T> db;

   public Option<T> Lookup(Guid id)
      => cache.Lookup(id).OrElse(db.Lookup(id));
}
```

Can you see the problem in the preceding code? Because OrElse is always called, its argument is always evaluated, meaning that you're hitting the DB even if the item is found in the cache. This defeats the purpose of the cache altogether!

This can be solved by using laziness. For such scenarios, I've defined an overload of OrElse, taking not a fallback Option but a function that will be evaluated, if necessary, to produce the fallback Option:

```
public static Option<T> OrElse<T>
   (this Option<T> opt, Func<Option<T>> fallback)
   => opt.Match
   (
      None: fallback,        ◁──┐  Only evaluates the fallback
      Some: _ => opt            │  function in the None case
   );
```

In this implementation, the fallback function will only be evaluated if opt is None. (Compare this to the previously shown overload, where the fallback option right is always evaluated.) You can accordingly fix the implementation of the caching repository as follows:

```
public Option<T> Lookup(Guid id)
   => cache.Lookup(id).OrElse(() => db.Lookup(id));
```

Now, if the cache lookup returns `Some`, `OrElse` is still called, but not `db.Lookup`, achieving the desired behavior.

As you can see, to make the evaluation of an expression lazy, instead of providing an expression, you provide a function that when called will evaluate that expression. Instead of a `T`, provide a `Func<T>`.

Using the `||` operator as a terse alternative to `OrElse`

Here's an interesting aside that is relevant to this example, although unrelated to the main topic of this chapter. C# allows you to overload logical operators, which I've done in `Option` for `|`:

```
public static Option<T> operator |
(
    Option<T> l,
    Option<T> r
)
=> l.isSome ? l : r;

public static bool operator true(Option<T> opt) => opt.isSome;
public static bool operator false(Option<T> opt) => !opt.isSome;
```

As a result, you can use the short-circuiting `||` operator instead of `OrElse`, and our `Lookup` function can be rewritten as follows:

```
public Option<T> Lookup(Guid id)
   => cache.Lookup(id) || db.Lookup(id));
```

Because `||` is short-circuiting, if the left side (the lookup from the cache) is `Some`, the right side will not be evaluated. The code is terse and efficient and gives us the behavior that we want.

PROVIDING A DEFAULT VALUE

A similar scenario is when you want to extract the inner value from an `Option`, providing a fallback value in case it's `None`. This operation is called `GetOrElse`. For instance, you may need to look up a value from configuration and use a default value instead if no value is specified:

```
string DefaultApiRoot => "localhost:8000";

string GetApiRoot(IConfigurationRoot config)
   => config.Lookup("ApiRoot").GetOrElse(DefaultApiRoot);
```

Assume that `Lookup` returns a duly populated `Option` whose state depends on whether the value was specified in configuration. Notice that the `DefaultApiRoot` property is evaluated regardless of the state of the `Option`.

In this case, that's OK because it simply returns a constant value. But if `Default-ApiRoot` involved an expensive computation, you'd prefer to only perform it if needed by passing the default value lazily. This is why I've also provided two overloads of `GetOrElse`:

```
public static T GetOrElse<T>(this Option<T> opt, T defaultValue)
    => opt.Match
    (
        () => defaultValue,
        (t) => t
    );

public static T GetOrElse<T>(this Option<T> opt, Func<T> fallback)
    => opt.Match
    (
        () => fallback(),
        (t) => t
    );
```

The first overload takes a regular fallback value, `T`, which is evaluated when `GetOrElse` is called. The second overload takes a `Func<T>`, a function that is evaluated only when necessary.

When should an API take values lazily?

As a guideline, when a function might not use some of its arguments, those arguments should be specified as lazy computations.

In some cases, you may choose to provide two overloads: one taking a value as an argument and another taking a lazy computation. Then the client code can decide on the most appropriate overload to call:

- If computing the value is expensive enough, pass the value lazily (more efficient).
- If the cost of computing the value is negligible, pass the value (more readable).

14.1.2 *Composing lazy computations*

In the rest of this chapter, you'll see how lazy computations can be composed and why doing so is a powerful technique. We'll start with the plain-vanilla lazy computation, `Func<T>`, and then move on to lazy computations that include some useful effect, such as handling errors or state.

You saw that `Func<T>` is a lazy computation that can be invoked to obtain a `T`. It turns out that `Func<T>` can be treated as a functor over `T`. Remember, a functor is something that has an inner value over which you can `Map` a function. How is that possible? The functors you've seen so far are all containers of some sort. How can a function possibly be a container, and what's its inner value?

Well, you can think of a function as containing its potential result. If, say, `Option<T>` "maybe-contains" some value of type `T`, you can say that `Func<T>` "potentially-contains" some value of type T or, perhaps more accurately, contains the potential to produce a value of type T. A function's inner value is the value it yields when it's evaluated.

You may know the tale of Aladdin's magic lamp. When rubbed, it would produce a powerful genie. Clearly, such a lamp could have the power to contain anything: put a genie into it, and you can rub it to get the genie back out; put your grandma in it, and you can rub it to get grandma back. And you can think of it as a functor: map a "turn blue" function onto the lamp and, when you rub the lamp, you'll get the contents of the lamp turned blue. Func<T> is such a container, where rubbing is function invocation.

In reality, you know that a functor must expose a Map method with a suitable signature. If you follow the functor pattern (see section 6.1.4), the signature of Map for Func<T> will involve

- An input functor of type () → T, a function that can be called to generate a T. Let's call it f.
- A function to be mapped of type T → R. Let's call it g.
- An expected result of type () → R, a function that can be called to generate an R.

The implementation is quite simple: invoke f to obtain a T, and then pass it to g to obtain an R, as figure 14.1 illustrates. Listing 14.1 shows the corresponding code.

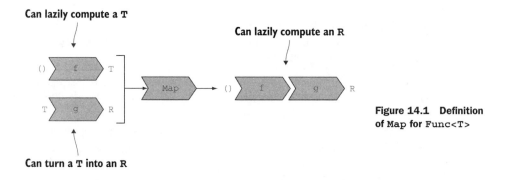

Can lazily compute a T

Can lazily compute an R

Can turn a T into an R

Figure 14.1   Definition of Map for Func<T>

Listing 14.1   Definition of Map for Func<T>

```
public static Func<R> Map<T, R>
   (this Func<T> f, Func<T, R> g)
   => () => g(f());
```

Notice that Map doesn't invoke f. It takes a lazily evaluated T and returns a lazily evaluated R. Also notice that the implementation is just function composition.

To see this in action, open the REPL, import LaYumba.Functional as usual, and type the following:

```
var lazyGrandma = () => "grandma";
var turnBlue = (string s) => $"blue {s}";
var lazyGrandmaBlue = lazyGrandma.Map(turnBlue);

lazyGrandmaBlue() // => "blue grandma"
```

To better understand the laziness of the whole computation, you can bake in some debug statements:

```
var lazyGrandma = () =>
{
   WriteLine("getting grandma...");
   return "grandma";
};

var turnBlue = (string s) =>
{
   WriteLine("turning blue...");
   return $"blue {s}";
};

var lazyGrandmaBlue = lazyGrandma.Map(turnBlue);      ◁──┐ None of the functions
                                                          │ are evaluated yet.
lazyGrandmaBlue()                   ◁──┐ All previously composed
// prints: getting grandma...          │ functions are evaluated now.
//          turning blue...
// => "blue grandma"
```

As you can see, the functions `lazyGrandma` and `turnBlue` aren't invoked until the last line. This shows that you can build up complex logic without executing anything until you decide to fire things off.

Once you've thoroughly understood the preceding examples, experimented in the REPL, and understood the definition of `Map`, it will be easy to understand the definition of `Bind` shown in the following listing.

Listing 14.2 Definition of `Bind` for `Func<T>`

```
public static Func<R> Bind<T, R>
   (this Func<T> f, Func<T, Func<R>> g)
   => () => g(f())();
```

`Bind` returns a function that, when evaluated, will evaluate `f` to get a `T`, apply `g` to it to get a `Func<R>`, and evaluate it to get the resulting `R`.

This is all very interesting, but how useful is it exactly? Because functions are already built into the language, being able to treat `Func` as a monad might not give you a lot. On the other hand, knowing that functions can be composed like any other monad, we can bake some interesting effects into how those functions behave. This is what the rest of this chapter is about.

14.2 Exception handling with Try

In chapter 8, I showed how you could go from an `Exception`-based API to a functional one by catching exceptions and returning them in an `Exceptional`—a structure that can hold either an exception or a successful result. For instance, if you want to safely create a `Uri` from a `string`, you could write a method as follows:

```
Exceptional<Uri> CreateUri(string uri)
{
    try { return new Uri(uri); }
    catch (Exception ex) { return ex; }
}
```

This works, but should you do this for every method that can throw an exception? Surely, after a couple of times, you'll start to feel that all this trying and catching is boilerplate. Can we abstract it away?

14.2.1 *Representing computations that may fail*

Indeed we can, with Try—a delegate representing an operation that may throw an exception. It's defined as follows:

```
public delegate Exceptional<T> Try<T>();
```

Try<T> is simply a delegate you can use to represent a computation that normally returns a T but may throw an exception instead; hence, its return value is wrapped in an Exceptional.

Defining Try as a separate type allows you to define extension methods specific to Try (most importantly, Run), which safely invokes it and returns a suitably populated Exceptional:

```
public static Exceptional<T> Run<T>(this Try<T> f)
{
    try { return f(); }
    catch (Exception ex) { return ex; }
}
```

Run does the try-catch ceremony once and for all, so you never have to write a try-catch statement again. Refactoring the previous CreateUri method to use Try, you can write:

```
Try<Uri> CreateUri(string uri) => () => new Uri(uri);
```

Notice how Try enables you to define CreateUri without any boilerplate code for handling exceptions, and yet, you can still execute CreateUri safely by using Run to invoke it. Test it for yourself by typing the following into the REPL:

```
Try<Uri> CreateUri(string uri) => () => new Uri(uri);

CreateUri("http://github.com").Run()
// => Success(http://github.com/)

CreateUri("rubbish").Run()
// => Exception(Invalid URI: The format of the URI could not be...)
```

Also notice that the body of CreateUri returns a Uri, but Try<Uri> is defined to return an Exceptional<Uri>. This is fine because I've defined implicit conversion from T to Exceptional<T>. Here again, the details of error handling have been abstracted away, so you can concentrate on the code that matters.

As a shorthand notation, if you didn't want to define `CreateUri` as a dedicated function, you could use the `Try` function (defined in F), which simply transforms a `Func<T>` into a `Try<T>`:

```
Try(() => new Uri("http://google.com")).Run()
// => Success(http://google.com/)
```

14.2.2 Safely extracting information from a JSON object

Now comes the interesting part—the reason why it's important that you can compose lazy computations. If you have two (or more) computations that may fail, you can "monadically" compose them into a single computation that may fail by using `Bind`. For example, imagine you have a string representing an object in JSON format with the following structure:

```
{
  "Name": "github",
  "Uri": "http://github.com"
}
```

You want to define a method that creates a `Uri` from the value in the "Uri" field of the JSON object. The following listing shows an *unsafe* way to do this.

Listing 14.3 **Unsafely extracting data from a JSON object**

```
using System.Text.Json;

record Website(string Name, string Uri);

Uri ExtractUri(string json)
{
    var website = JsonSerializer.Deserialize<Website>(json);      ← Deserializes the
                                                                    string into a
    return new Uri(website.Uri);      ← Creates a                   Website
}                                       Uri instance
```

Both `JsonSerializer.Deserialize` and the `Uri` constructor throw an exception if their input isn't well formed.

Let's use `Try` to make the implementation safe. We can start by wrapping the method calls that can throw an exception into a `Try` as follows:

```
Try<Uri> CreateUri(string uri) => () => new Uri(uri);
Try<T> Parse<T>(string s) => () => JsonSerializer.Deserialize<T>(s);
```

As usual, the way to compose several operations that return a `Try` is with `Bind`. We'll look at its definition in a moment. For now, trust that it works, and let's use it to define a method that combines the two preceding operations into another `Try`-returning function:

```
Try<Uri> ExtractUri(string json)
    => Parse<Website>(json)
        .Bind(website => CreateUri(website.Uri));
```

This works, but it's not particularly readable. The `LaYumba.Functional` library includes the implementation of the LINQ query pattern (see the sidebar "A reminder on the LINQ query pattern") for `Try` and all other included monads, so we can improve readability by using a LINQ expression instead, as the following listing demonstrates.

Listing 14.4   Safely extracting data from a JSON object

```
Try<Uri> ExtractUri(string json) =>              Deserializes the string
    from website in Parse<Website>(json)         into a Website
    from uri in CreateUri(website.Uri)      Creates a
    select uri;                             Uri instance
```

Listing 14.4 is the safe counterpart to the unsafe code in listing 14.3. You can see that we could make this refactoring without compromising on readability. Let's feed a few sample values to `ExtractUri` to see that it works as intended:

```
ExtractUri(
    @"{
        ""Name"":""Github"",
        ""Uri"":""http://github.com""
    }")
    .Run()
// => Success(http://github.com/)

ExtractUri("blah!").Run()
// => Exception('b' is an invalid start of a value...)

ExtractUri("{}").Run()
// => Exception(Value cannot be null...)

ExtractUri(
    @"{
        ""Name"":""Github"",
        ""Uri"":""rubbish""
    }")
    .Run()
// => Exception(Invalid URI: The format of the URI...)
```

Remember, everything happens lazily. When you call `ExtractUri`, you just get a `Try` that can eventually perform some computation. Nothing really happens until you call `Run`.

14.2.3 *Composing computations that may fail*

Now that you've seen how to use `Bind` to compose several computations that may fail, let's look under the hood and see how `Bind` is defined for `Try`.

Remember that a `Try<T>` is just like a `Func<T>` for which we now know that invocation may throw an exception. Let's start by quickly looking at `Bind` for `Func` again:

```
public static Func<R> Bind<T, R>
    (this Func<T> f, Func<T, Func<R>> g)
    => () => g(f())();
```

A cavalier way of describing this code is that it first invokes f and then g. Now we need to adapt this to work with Try. First, replacing Func with Try gives us the correct signature. (This is often half of the work because for the core functions, if the implementation type checks, it usually works.) Second, because invoking a Try directly may throw an exception, we need to use Run instead. Finally, we don't want to run the second function if the first function fails. The following listing shows the implementation.

Listing 14.5 Definition of Bind for Try<T>

```
public static Try<R> Bind<T, R>
   (this Try<T> f, Func<T, Try<R>> g)
   => ()
   => f.Run()                                              ◁──┐  Uses Run to
     .Match                                                   │  safely execute
     (                      If the first Try fails, doesn't   │  each Try
        Exception: ex => ex,  ◁──┘ execute the second one     │
        Success: t => g(t).Run()                           ◁──┘
     );
```

Bind takes a Try and a Try-returning function g. It then returns a function that when invoked runs the Try and, if it succeeds, runs g on the result to obtain another Try, which is also run.

If we can define Bind, we can always define Map, which is usually simpler. I suggest you define Map as an exercise.

A reminder on the LINQ query pattern

A fundamental idea of this chapter is that you can use Bind to sequence computations, and for this reason, I'll be showing the implementations of Bind.

In order to use LINQ expressions with monadic types (in this case, Try), you additionally need to implement the LINQ query pattern that I discussed in section 10.4.2. Here's a reminder of how to do this:

- Alias Map as Select.
- Alias Bind as SelectMany.
- Define an additional overload of SelectMany that takes a binary projection function. This additional overload can be defined in terms of Map and Bind, although a more efficient implementation can usually be defined.

I won't clutter up this chapter by showing all these method implementations, which are available in the code samples. By now, you have all the tools to understand them.

14.2.4 Monadic composition: What does it mean?

In this chapter and the next, you'll often read about *monadically composing* computations. That sounds complicated, but it really isn't, so let's take the mystery out of it.

First, let's recap "normal" function composition, which I covered in chapter 7. Suppose you have two functions:

```
f : A → B
g : B → C
```

You can compose them by simply piping the output of f into g, obtaining a function A → C. Now imagine you have the following functions:

```
f' : A → Try<B>
g' : B → Try<C>
```

These functions obviously don't compose because f' returns a Try<B>, whereas g' expects a B, but it's fairly clear that you may want to combine them by extracting the B from the Try<B> and feeding it to g'. This is monadic composition, and it's exactly what Bind for Try does, as you've seen.

In other words, monadic composition is a way to combine functions that's more general than function composition and involves some logic dictating how the functions are composed. This logic is captured in the Bind function.

There are several variations on this pattern. Imagine the following functions:

```
f" : A → (B, K)
g" : B → (C, K)
```

Could we compose these into a new function of type A → (C, K)? Given an A, it's easy to compute a C: run f" on the A, extract the B from the resulting tuple, and feed it to g". In the process, we've computed two K's, so what should we do with them? If there's a way to combine two K's into a single K, then we could return the combined K. For example, if K is a list, we could return all elements from both lists. Functions in the preceding form can be monadically composed if K is of a suitable type.[2]

The functions for which I'll demonstrate monadic composition in this book are listed in table 14.1, but there are many more possible variations.

Table 14.1   Monadically composable computations demonstrated in this book

Delegate	Signature	Section	Scenario
Try<T>	() → T	14.2	Exception handling
Middleware<T>	(T → R) → R	14.3	Adding behavior before or after a given function
Generator<T>	int → (T, int)	15.2	Generating random data
StatefulComputation<S, T>	S → (T, S)	15.3	Keeping state between computations

---

[2] This is referred to as the *writer monad* in the literature, and types for which two instances can always be combined into one are called *monoids*.

14.3 Creating a middleware pipeline for DB access

In this section, I'll start by showing how using HOFs in some cases leads to deeply nested callbacks, affectionately called "callback hell" or "the pyramid of doom." I'll use DB access as the specific scenario to illustrate this problem and show how you can leverage the LINQ query pattern to create flat, monadic workflows instead.

This section contains advanced material that isn't required to understand coming chapters, so if this is your first reading, feel free to skip to chapter 15.

14.3.1 Composing functions that perform setup/teardown

In section 2.3, you learned about functions that perform some setup and teardown and are parameterized with a function to be invoked in between. An example of this was a function that managed a DB connection, parameterized with a function that used the connection to interact with the DB:

```
public static class ConnectionHelper
{
   public static R Connect<R>
      (ConnectionString connString, Func<SqlConnection, R> f)
   {
      using var conn = new SqlConnection(connString);
      conn.Open();
      return f(conn);
   }
}
```

This function can be consumed in client code like so:

```
public void Log(LogMessage message)
   => Connect(connString, c => c.Execute("sp_create_log"
      , message, commandType: CommandType.StoredProcedure));
```

Let's define a similar function that can be used to log a message before and after an operation:

```
public static class Instrumentation
{
   public static T Trace<T>(ILogger log, string op, Func<T> f)
   {
      log.LogTrace($"Entering {op}");
      T t = f();
      log.LogTrace($"Leaving {op}");
      return t;
   }
}
```

If you want to use both functions (opening/closing a connection as well as tracing entering/leaving a block), you'd write something like the following listing shows.

Listing 14.6   Nested callbacks are hard to read

```
public void Log(LogMessage message)
    => Instrumentation.Trace("CreateLog"
        , () => ConnectionHelper.Connect(connString
            , c => c.Execute("sp_create_log"
                , message, commandType: CommandType.StoredProcedure)));
```

This is starting to become hard to read. What if you wanted some other setup of work to be done as well? For every HOF you add, your callbacks are nested one level deeper, making the code harder to understand. That's why it's called "the pyramid of doom."

Instead, what we'd ideally like to have is a clean way to compose a *middleware pipeline*, as figure 14.2 illustrates. We want to add some behavior (like connection management, diagnostics, and so on) to each trip to the DB. Conceptually, this is similar to the middleware pipeline for handling HTTP requests in ASP.NET Core.

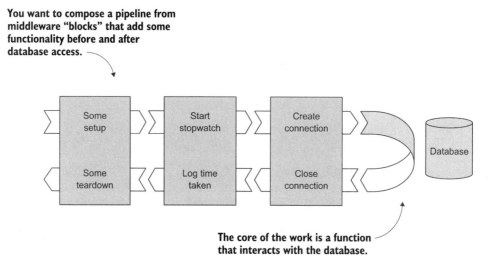

Figure 14.2   A middleware pipeline for accessing the DB

In a normal, *linear* function pipeline, the output of each function is piped into the next function. Each function has no control over what happens downstream. A middleware pipeline, on the other hand, is U-shaped: each function passes some data along, but it also receives some data on the way out, so to speak. As a result, each function is able to perform some operations before *and* after the functions downstream.

I'm going to call each of these functions or blocks a *middleware*. We want to be able to nicely compose such middleware pipelines to add logging, timing, and so on. But, because each middleware must take a callback function as an input argument (otherwise, it can't intervene after the callback has returned), how can we escape the pyramid of doom?

14.3.2 A recipe against the pyramid of doom

It turns out that one way we can look at `Bind` is as a recipe against the pyramid of doom. For instance, you may remember how in chapter 8, we used `Bind` to combine several `Either`-returning functions:

```
WakeUpEarly()
    .Bind(ShopForIngredients)
    .Bind(CookRecipe)
    .Match
    (
        Left: PlanB,
        Right: EnjoyTogether
    );
```

If you expand the calls to `Bind`, the preceding code looks like this:

```
WakeUpEarly().Match
(
    Left: planB,
    Right: u => ShopForIngredients(u).Match
    (
        Left: planB,
        Right: ingr = CookRecipe(ingr).Match
        (
            Left: planB,
            Right: EnjoyTogether
        )
    )
);
```

You can see that `Bind` effectively enables us to escape the pyramid of doom in this case: the same would apply to `Option` and so on. But can we define `Bind` for our middleware functions?

14.3.3 Capturing the essence of a middleware function

To answer this question, let's look at the signatures of our middleware functions and see if there's a pattern that we can identify and capture in an abstract way. These are the functions we've seen so far:

```
Connect : ConnectionString → (SqlConnection → R) → R
Trace : ILogger → string → (() → R) → R
```

Let's imagine a couple more examples where we might like to use middleware. We could use a timing middleware that logs how long an operation has taken and another middleware that begins and commits a DB transaction. The signatures would look like this:

```
Time : ILogger → string → (() → R) → R
Transact : SqlConnection → (SqlTransaction → R) → R
```

`Time` has the same signature as `Trace`: it takes a logger and a string (the name of the operation that's being timed) and the function being timed. `Transact` is similar to

Connect, but it takes a connection that's used to create a transaction and a function that consumes the transaction.

Now that we have four reasonable use cases, let's see if there's a pattern in the signatures:

```
ConnectionString → (SqlConnection → R) → R
ILogger → string → (() → R) → R
SqlConnection → (SqlTransaction → R) → R
```

Each function has some parameters that are specific to the functionality it exposes, but there's definitely a pattern. If we abstract away these specific parameters (which we can provide with partial application) and only concentrate on the arguments shown in bold, all functions have a signature in this form:

```
(T → R) → R
```

They all take a callback function (although, in this context, it's usually called a *continuation*) that produces an R, and they return an R (presumably, the very R returned by the continuation or a modified version of it). The essence of a middleware function is that it takes a continuation of type T → R, supplies a T to it to obtain an R, and returns an R, as figure 14.3 shows.

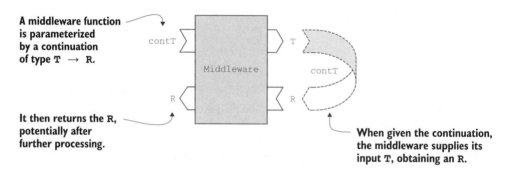

A middleware function is parameterized by a continuation of type T → R.

It then returns the R, potentially after further processing.

When given the continuation, the middleware supplies its input T, obtaining an R.

Figure 14.3   A single middleware function

Let's capture this essence with a delegate:

```
// (T → dynamic) → dynamic
public delegate dynamic Middleware<T>(Func<T, dynamic> cont);
```

But wait. Why is it returning dynamic rather than R?

The problem is that T (the input to the continuation) and R (its output) are not known at the same time. For example, suppose you want to create a Middleware instance from a function such as Connect, which has this signature:

```
public static R Connect<R>(ConnectionString connString
    , Func<SqlConnection, R> func) // ...
```

The continuation accepted by Connect takes a SqlConnection as input, so we can use Connect to define a Middleware<SqlConnection>. That means the T type variable in Middleware<T> resolves to SqlConnection, but we don't yet know what the given continuation will yield, so we can't yet resolve the R type variable in Connect<R>.

Unfortunately, C# doesn't allow us to partially apply type variables, hence, dynamic. So although, conceptually, we're thinking of combining HOFs of this type

```
(T → R) → R
```

we're in fact modeling them as follows:

```
(T → dynamic) → dynamic
```

Later, you'll see that you can still work with Middleware without compromising on type safety.

The interesting—and mind-bending—thing is that Middleware<T> is a monad over T, where (remember) T is the type of the *input* argument taken by the continuation that is given to the middleware function. This seems counterintuitive. A monad over T is usually something that contains a T or some Ts. But this still applies here: if a function has the signature (T → R) → R, then it can provide a T to the given function T → R, so it must contain or somehow be able to produce a T.

14.3.4 *Implementing the query pattern for middleware*

It's time to learn how to combine two middleware blocks with Bind. Essentially, Bind attaches a downstream middleware block to a pipeline, as figure 14.4 shows.

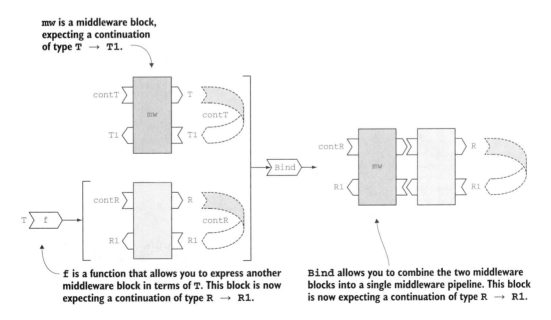

mw is a middleware block, expecting a continuation of type T → T1.

f is a function that allows you to express another middleware block in terms of T. This block is now expecting a continuation of type R → R1.

Bind allows you to combine the two middleware blocks into a single middleware pipeline. This block is now expecting a continuation of type R → R1.

Figure 14.4 Bind adds a middleware block to the pipeline.

The implementation of `Bind` is simple to write but not easy to fully grasp:

```
public static Middleware<R> Bind<T, R>
   (this Middleware<T> mw, Func<T, Middleware<R>> f)
   => cont
   => mw(t => f(t)(cont));
```

We have a `Middleware<T>` expecting a continuation of type (T → dynamic). We then have a function, f, that takes a T and produces a `Middleware<R>`, expecting a continuation of type (R → dynamic). What we get as a result is a `Middleware<R>` that, when supplied a continuation, cont, runs the initial middleware, giving it as continuation a function that runs the binder function f to obtain the second middleware, to which it will pass cont. Don't worry if this doesn't fully make sense at this point.

Let's look at `Map` now:

```
public static Middleware<R> Map<T, R>
   (this Middleware<T> mw, Func<T, R> f)
   => cont
   => mw(t => cont(f(t)));
```

`Map` takes a `Middleware<T>` and a function f from T to R. The middleware knows how to create a T and supply it to a continuation that takes a T. By applying f, it now knows how to create an R and supply it to a continuation that takes an R. You can visualize `Map` as adding a transformation T → R before the continuation or, alternatively, as adding a new setup/teardown block to the pipeline, performing a transformation as the setup and passing the result along as the teardown, as figure 14.5 shows.

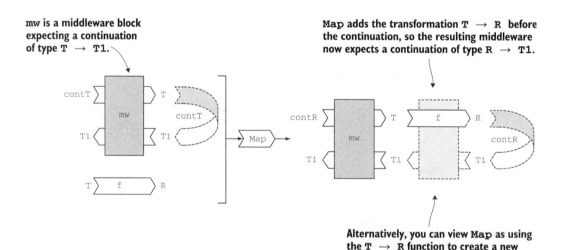

mw is a middleware block expecting a continuation of type T → T1.

Map adds the transformation T → R before the continuation, so the resulting middleware now expects a continuation of type R → T1.

Alternatively, you can view Map as using the T → R function to create a new middleware block that turns a T into an R on the way in and passes the result on the way out.

Figure 14.5 `Map` adds a transformation to the pipeline.

Finally, once we've composed the desired pipeline, we can run the whole pipeline by passing a continuation:

```
Middleware<A> mw;
Func<A, B> cont;

dynamic exp1 = mw(cont);
```

The preceding code shows that if you have a `Middleware<A>` and a continuation function `cont` of type A → B, you can directly supply the continuation to the middleware.

There's still a small crease to iron out. Notice that when we provide the continuation, we get a `dynamic` back, where we really expect a B. To maintain type safety, we can define a `Run` function that runs the pipeline with the identity function as continuation:

```
public static T Run<T>(this Middleware<T> mw)
   => (T)mw(t => t);
```

Because `mw` is a `Middleware<T>` (meaning that `mw` can provide a value of type T to its continuation) and because the continuation in this case is the identity function, we know that the continuation produces a T, so we can confidently cast the result of running the middleware to T.

When we want to run a pipeline, instead of directly providing the continuation, we can use `Map` to map the continuation and then call `Run`:

```
Middleware<A> mw;
Func<A, B> cont;

B exp2 = mw.Map(cont).Run()
```

Here we map our continuation A → B onto our `Middleware<A>`, obtaining a `Middleware<B>`, and then run it (with the identity function) to obtain a B. Notice that exp2 from this snippet is identical to exp1 from the previous one, but we've regained type safety.[3]

Let's put this all to work by refactoring the `DbLogger` from section 2.3 to use `Middleware` rather than HOFs:

```
public class DbLogger
{
   Middleware<SqlConnection> Connect;

   public DbLogger(ConnectionString connString)
   {
      Connect = f => ConnectionHelper.Connect(connString, f);
   }
```

---

[3] This is because when computing exp2, we first compute `mw.Map(cont)`, which composes `cont` with the continuation that will eventually be given. Then, by calling `Run`, we provide the identity function as continuation. The resulting continuation is the composition of `cont` and identity, which is exactly the same as providing `cont` as the continuation.

```
public void Log(LogMessage message) => (
   from conn in Connect
   select conn.Execute("sp_create_log", message
      , commandType: CommandType.StoredProcedure)
).Run();
```

In the constructor, we essentially use partial application to bake the connection string into the Connect function, which now has the right signature to be used as a Middleware<SqlConnection>.

In the Log method, we create a pipeline with a single middleware block, which creates the DB connection. We can then use LINQ syntax to refer to conn (the connection that will be available when the pipeline is run) when calling Execute, the main operation that will interact with the DB.

Of course, we could have written Log more concisely by just passing a callback to Connect. But the whole point here is to avoid callbacks. As we add more blocks to the pipeline, we'll be able to do this by just adding from clauses to our LINQ comprehension. You'll see this next.

14.3.5 *Adding middleware that times the operation*

Suppose we have a DB operation that sometimes takes longer than expected, so we'd like to add another middleware that logs how long the DB access operation took. For this, we could define the following HOF:

```
public static class Instrumentation
{
   public static T Time<T>(ILogger log, string op, Func<T> f)
   {
      var sw = new Stopwatch();
      sw.Start();

      T t = f();

      sw.Stop();
      log.LogDebug($"{op} took {sw.ElapsedMilliseconds}ms");
      return t;
   }
}
```

Time takes three arguments: a logger, to which it will log the diagnostic message; op, the name of the operation being performed, which will be included in the logged message; and a function representing the operation whose duration is being timed.

There's a slight problem because Time takes a Func<T> (a function with *no* input arguments), whereas we defined the continuations accepted by our middleware to be in the form T→dynamic (there should always be an input parameter). We can bridge the gap with Unit, as usual, but this time on the input side. For this, I've defined an adapter function that converts a function taking Unit to a function that takes no arguments:

```
public static Func<T> ToNullary<T>(this Func<Unit, T> f)
   => () => f(Unit());
```

With this in place, we can enrich our pipeline with a block for logging the time taken for DB access as the following listing shows.

Listing 14.7   Combining timing and connection management

```
public class DbLogger
{
   Middleware<SqlConnection> Connect;
   Func<string, Middleware<Unit>> Time;

   public DbLogger(ConnectionString connString, ILogger log)
   {
      Connect = f => ConnectionHelper.Connect(connString, f);
      Time = op => f => Instrumentation.Time(log, op, f.ToNullary());
   }

   public void DeleteOldLogs() => (
      from _    in Time("DeleteOldLogs")
      from conn in Connect
      select conn.Execute
         ( "DELETE [Logs] WHERE [Timestamp] < @upTo"
         , new { upTo = 7.Days().Ago() })
   ).Run();
}
```

Once we've wrapped the call to `Instrumentation.Time` in a `Middleware`, we can use it in the pipeline by adding an additional `from` clause. Notice that the `_` variable will be assigned the `Unit` value returned by `Time`. You can disregard it, but LINQ syntax doesn't allow you to omit it.

14.3.6   *Adding middleware that manages a DB transaction*

As a final example, let's add one more type of middleware that manages a DB transaction. We can abstract simple transaction management into a HOF like this:

```
public static R Transact<R>
   (SqlConnection conn, Func<SqlTransaction, R> f)
{
   using var tran = conn.BeginTransaction();

   R r = f(tran);
   tran.Commit();

   return r;
}
```

`Transact` takes a connection and a function `f` that consumes the transaction. Presumably, `f` involves multiple DB operations that we need to be performed atomically. As an effect of how the `using` declaration is interpreted, the transaction will be rolled back if an exception is thrown by `f`. The following listing provides an example of integrating `Transact` into a pipeline.

Listing 14.8   A pipeline that provides connection and transaction management

```
Middleware<SqlConnection> Connect(ConnectionString connString)     ◁──┐  Adapters to turn
   => f => ConnectionHelper.Connect(connString, f);                    │  existing HOFs into
                                                                       │  Middleware
Middleware<SqlTransaction> Transact(SqlConnection conn)            ◁──┘
   => f => ConnectionHelper.Transact(conn, f);

Func<Guid, int> DeleteOrder(ConnectionString connString)     ◁──┐  The connection
   => (Guid id) =>                                                │  string is injected.
{
   SqlTemplate deleteLinesSql = "DELETE OrderLines WHERE OrderId = @Id";
   SqlTemplate deleteOrderSql = "DELETE Orders WHERE Id = @Id";

   object param = new { Id = id };

   Middleware<int> deleteOrder =
      from conn in Connect(connString)
      from tran in Transact(conn)
      select conn.Execute(deleteLinesSql, param, tran)
           + conn.Execute(deleteOrderSql, param, tran);

   return deleteOrder.Run();
};
```

`Connect` and `Transact` simply wrap existing HOFs into a `Middleware`. `DeleteOrder` is written in curried form so that we can provide the connection string at startup and the ID of the order to delete at run time as explained in section 9.4. Now look at the interesting bit—the middleware pipeline declared as `deleteOrder`:

- `Connect` defines a block that creates (and then disposes) the connection.
- `Transact` defines another block that consumes the connection and creates (and then disposes) a transaction.
- Within the `select` clause, we have two DB actions that use the connection and the transaction and which will, therefore, be executed atomically. Because `Execute` returns an `int` (the number of affected rows), we can use `+` to combine the two operations.

As you already saw in previous chapters, the `Guid` of the order being deleted is used to populate the `Id` field of a `param` object, and as a result, it replaces the `@Id` token of the SQL template strings.

Once the middleware functions are set up, adding or removing a step from the pipeline is a one-line change. If you're logging timing information, do you only want to time the DB actions or also the time taken to acquire the connection? Whatever the case, you can change that by simply changing the order of middleware in the pipeline as the following snippets show:

Acquiring the connection counts toward the time that will be logged.

```
from _ in Time("slowQuery")     ◁──┐
from conn in Connect
select conn.Execute(mySlowQuery)
```

Only the DB action is timed.

```
from conn in Connect
from _ in Time("slowQuery")     ◁──
select conn.Execute(mySlowQuery)
```

The flat layout of LINQ queries makes it easy to see and change the order of the middleware functions. And, of course, this solution avoids the pyramid of doom. Although I've used the idea of middleware and the somewhat specific scenario of DB access to illustrate it, the concept of continuations is wider and applies to any function in this form:[4]

```
(T → R) → R
```

This also means that we could have avoided defining a custom delegate `Middleware`. The definitions of `Map`, `Bind`, and `Run` have nothing specific to this scenario, and we could have used `Func<Func<T, dynamic> dynamic>` instead of `Middleware<T>`. This might even save a few lines of code because it removes the need for creating delegates of the correct type. I opted for `Middleware` as a more explicit, domain-specific abstraction, but that's a personal preference.

In this chapter, you've seen how delegate-based monads like `Try` and `Middleware` provide powerful and expressive constructs. They allow us to elegantly address general problems like exception handling and more specific scenarios like middleware pipelines. We'll explore some more scenarios in chapter 15.

Summary

- Laziness means deferring a computation until its result is needed. It's especially useful when the result may not be required in the end.
- Lazy computations can be composed to create more complex computations that can then be triggered as needed.
- When dealing with an exception-based API, you can use the `Try` delegate type. The `Run` function safely executes the code in the `Try` and returns the result wrapped in an `Exceptional`.
- HOFs in the form (T → R) → R (functions that take a callback or *continuation*) can also be composed monadically, enabling you to use flat LINQ expressions rather than deeply nested callbacks.

---

[4] In the literature, this is known as *the continuation monad*, which again is a misnomer because the monad here isn't the continuation but the computation that takes a continuation as input.

15

Stateful programs and stateful computations

This chapter covers

- What makes a program stateful?
- Writing stateful programs without mutating state
- Generating random structures
- Composing stateful computations

Since chapter 1, I've been preaching against state mutation as a side effect that should be avoided at almost any cost, and you've seen several examples of refactoring programs to avoid state mutation. In this chapter, you'll see how the functional approach works when keeping state is a requirement rather than an implementation detail of your program.

But what's a *stateful* program exactly? It's a program whose behavior differs, depending on past inputs or events.[1] By analogy, if somebody says, "Good morning," you'll probably mindlessly greet them in return. If that person immediately says, "Good morning" again, your reaction will certainly differ: Why in the world

---

[1] This means that a program may be considered stateful/stateless depending on where you draw the program boundary. You may have a stateless server that uses a DB to keep state. If you consider both as one program, it's stateful; if you consider the server in isolation, it's stateless.

would somebody say "Good morning" twice in a row? A stateless program, on the other hand, would keep answering "Good morning" just as mindlessly as before because it has no notion of past inputs. Every time is like the first time.

In this chapter, you'll see how two apparently contradictory ideas—keeping state in memory and avoiding state mutation—can be reconciled in a stateful functional program. You'll then see how functions that handle state can be composed using the techniques you learned in chapter 14.

15.1 Programs that manage state

In this section, you'll see a simple command-line program that enables the user to look up foreign exchange rates (FX rates). A sample interaction with the program would be as follows (bold letters indicate user input):

```
Enter a currency pair like 'EURUSD', or 'q' to quit
usdeur
fetching rate...
0.9162
gbpusd
fetching rate...
1.2248
q
```

If you've downloaded the code samples, you can try it out for yourself:

```
cd Examples
dotnet run CurrencyLookup_Stateless
```

The following listing shows an initial stateless implementation.

Listing 15.1 Stateless implementation of a simple program to look up FX rates

```
WriteLine("Enter a currency pair like 'EURUSD', or 'q' to quit");
for (string input; (input = ReadLine().ToUpper()) != "Q";)
   WriteLine(RatesApi.GetRate(input));
```

```
static class RatesApi
{
    public static decimal GetRate(string ccyPair)
    {
        WriteLine($"fetching rate...");
        // ...                                    Performs a web request to
    }                                             fetch the requested rate
}
```

You can disregard the implementation details of RatesApi.GetRate; all we care about is that it takes a currency pair identifier such as EURUSD (for Euros/US Dollars) and returns the exchange rate.

The program works, but if you repeatedly ask it for the same currency pair, it will perform an HTTP request every time. There are several reasons why you might want to avoid unnecessary remote requests, such as performance, network use, or cost incurred per request. Next, we'll introduce an in-memory cache to avoid looking up rates we've already retrieved.

15.1.1 Caching data in memory

We want to store rates in a cache when they're retrieved and only make HTTP requests for rates we haven't requested before, as figure 15.1 shows. (In practice, you'd want values stored in the cache to expire after some time, but I'll disregard this requirement in order to concentrate on the essential aspects of keeping state.)

Of course, as functional programmers, we want to do this without state mutation. What will be the type of the program's state? A dictionary would be a natural choice, mapping each pair identifier (such as EURUSD) to the corresponding exchange rate. Just to make sure we don't mutate it, let's make it an immutable dictionary: ImmutableDictionary<string, decimal>. And because that's quite an ugly type, we'll alias it as Rates to make the code less verbose.

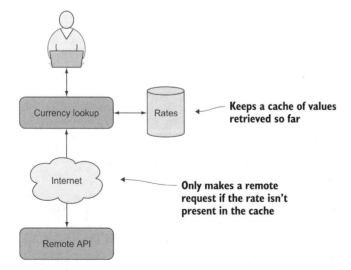

Figure 15.1   Keeping a cache of previously retrieved rates

The following listing provides an implementation that stores already retrieved rates in the cache and only calls the remote API if the rate wasn't previously retrieved. It does this without state mutation.

Listing 15.2 Stateful implementation keeping a cache of rates

```
using Rates = System.Collections.Immutable       A readable name for
    .ImmutableDictionary<string, decimal>;        the program state

public class Program
{
    public static void Main()
    {
        WriteLine("Enter a currency pair like 'EURUSD', or 'q' to quit");
        MainRec(Rates.Empty);        ◁─── Sets up an initial state and
    }                                      passes control to MainRec

    static void MainRec(Rates cache)
    {
        var input = ReadLine().ToUpper();
        if (input == "Q") return;
                                                    Gets a result as well
        var (rate, newState) = GetRate(input, cache);  ◁─── as the new state
        WriteLine(rate);
        MainRec(newState);     ◁─── Recursively calls itself
    }                               with the new state

    static (decimal, Rates) GetRate(string ccyPair, Rates cache)
    {
        if (cache.ContainsKey(ccyPair))     Uses the cached
            return (cache[ccyPair], cache);  rate if available

                                                    Performs a
        var rate = RatesApi.GetRate(ccyPair);  ◁─── web request

        return (rate, cache.Add(ccyPair, rate));   ◁─┐ Returns a tuple with the
    }                                                 │ retrieved rate and the updated
}                                                     │ state of the program
```

Look at the signatures of the two `GetRate` functions:

```
RatesApi.GetRate : string → decimal
Program.GetRate  : string → Rates → (decimal, Rates)
```

The first signature is the stateless version; the second is the stateful version. The latter also takes (along with the requested currency pair) the current state of the program, and it returns (along with the resulting rate) the new state of the program.

> **IMPORTANT** If global variables can't be mutated, you must pass state around via arguments and return values. This is the key to writing stateful applications without mutation.

Let's now move up to `MainRec` (for recursive), which contains the basic control flow of the program. The thing to note here is that it takes as an input parameter the current state of the program, which it passes on to `GetRate` to retrieve the new state (along with the rate, which is printed). It ends by calling itself with the new state.

Finally, `Main` simply calls `MainRec` with the initial state of the program, which is an empty cache. You can view the entire program execution as a loop with `MainRec` recursively calling itself, passing the current version of the state as a parameter.

Note that although there are no global variables in the program, it's still a stateful program. The program keeps some state in memory, which affects how the program operates.

Generally speaking, recursion is a risky business in C#, as it can blow the stack if more than about 10,000 recursive calls are made. If you want to avoid the recursive definition, you can use a loop instead. The following listing shows the `Main` method rewritten to use a loop.

Listing 15.3   Converting a recursive function to a loop

```
public static void Main()
{
    WriteLine("Enter a currency pair like 'EURUSD', or 'q' to quit");
    var state = Rates.Empty;        ◁─┐ The initial state

    for (string input; (input = ReadLine().ToUpper()) != "Q";)
    {
        var (rate, newState) = GetRate(input, state);
        state = newState;    ◁─┐ Reassigns the state variable
        WriteLine(rate);       │ for the next iteration
    }
}
```

Here, instead of the recursive call, we keep a local mutable variable, `state`, which is reassigned to the new state as needed. We're not mutating any global state, so the fundamental idea still holds.

For the remaining examples in this chapter, I'll stick to the recursive version, which I find cleaner. In a real-life application, you'll want to use the iterative version to avoid stack overflow.

15.1.2 Refactoring for testability and error handling

You've seen how you can create a stateful program that doesn't require mutation. Before we move on, I'd like to make some improvements to the program in order to illustrate some of the ideas around testability and error handling, which you saw in previous chapters.

You'll notice that although there are no side effects in terms of state mutation, there are I/O side effects everywhere, so the program isn't at all testable. We can refactor `GetRate` to take the function performing the HTTP request as an input argument, following the pattern explained in chapter 3:

```
static (decimal, Rates) GetRate
    (Func<string, decimal> getRate, string ccyPair, Rates cache)
{
```

```
    if (cache.ContainsKey(ccyPair))
        return (cache[ccyPair], cache);
    var rate = getRate(ccyPair);
    return (rate, cache.Add(ccyPair, rate));
}
```

Now `GetRate` has no side effects other than those that may occur by calling the given delegate `getRate`. As a result, it's easy to unit test this function by providing a delegate with a predictable behavior. `MainRec` could likewise be brought under test by injecting functions to invoke for I/O.

Next, there's no error handling at all: if you enter the name of a currency pair that doesn't exist, the program crashes. Let's put `Try` to good use. First, we'll wrap the stateless `GetRate` method in a `Try`:

```
static class RatesApi
{                                                            The safe function
    public static Try<decimal> TryGetRate(string ccyPair)   returns a Try.
        => () => GetRate(ccyPair);

    static decimal GetRate(string ccyPair) // ...    The unsafe version
}                                                    works just like before.
```

The stateful `Program.GetRate` method must now change its signature to not take a function returning a `decimal` but a `Try<decimal>`. Accordingly, its return type will also be wrapped in a `Try`. Here's the signature before and after:

```
before : (string → decimal) → string → (decimal, Rates)
after  : (string → Try<decimal>) → string → Try<(decimal, Rates)>
```

The following listing shows the refactored implementation.

Listing 15.4 The program refactored to use `Try` for error handling

```
public class Program
{
    public static void Main()
        => MainRec("Enter a currency pair like 'EURUSD', or 'q' to quit"
          , Rates.Empty);

    static void MainRec(string message, Rates cache)
    {
        WriteLine(message);

        var input = ReadLine().ToUpper();
        if (input == "Q") return;

        GetRate(RatesApi.TryGetRate, input, cache).Run().Match
        (
          ex => MainRec($"Error: {ex.Message}", cache),
          result => MainRec(result.Rate.ToString(), result.NewState)
        );
    }
}
```

```
static Try<(decimal Rate, Rates NewState)> GetRate
  (Func<string, Try<decimal>> getRate, string ccyPair, Rates cache)
{
  if (cache.ContainsKey(ccyPair))
    return Try(() => (cache[ccyPair], cache));
  else return from rate in getRate(ccyPair)
    select (rate, cache.Add(ccyPair, rate));
}
}
```

You could try it out for yourself with

```
dotnet run CurrencyLookup_StatefulSafe
```

Here's a sample interaction with the program:

```
Enter a currency pair like 'EURUSD', or 'q' to quit
eurusd
fetching rate...
1.2066
eurusd                        ⎤ Returns the
1.2066            ⟵───────────⎦ cached rate
rubbish
fetching rate...                                              ⎤ Handles errors
Error: The given key 'BISH' was not present in the dictionary.  ⟵──⎦ gracefully
q
```

Notice how we were able to add testability and error handling in a relatively painless way without puffing up the implementation with interfaces, try-catch statements, and so on. Instead, we have more powerful function signatures and more explicit relationships between functions via parameter passing.

15.1.3 *Stateful computations*

As you've seen in this section, if you want to handle state functionally (without state mutation), state must be made available to functions as an input argument, and functions that affect the state must return the updated state as part of their result. The remaining part of this chapter focuses on *stateful computations*, which are functions that interact with some state.

> **NOTE** *Stateful computations* are functions that take a state (as well as, potentially, other arguments) and return a new state (along with, potentially, a return value). They're also called *state transitions*.

Stateful computations may appear both in stateful and stateless programs. You've already seen a few examples. In the previous scenario, GetRate is a stateful computation because it takes some state (the cache) along with a currency pair and returns the updated state along with the requested rate. In chapter 13, the static Account class contained only stateful computations, each taking an AccountState (along with a command) and returning a new AccountState (along with an event to store), although in this case, things were slightly complicated by the result being wrapped in a Validation.

If you want to combine several stateful computations (the process of always passing the state into a function), extracting it from the result and passing it to the next function can become quite tedious. Fortunately, stateful computations can be composed monadically in a way that hides the state-passing, as you'll see next.

The rest of this chapter contains advanced material, which is not required to understand the following chapters, in case you decide to skip to the next chapter.

15.2 A language for generating random data

Random data has many legitimate practical uses, including property-based testing (which I discussed in chapter 10), load testing (where you generate lots of random data and then bombard your system to see how it holds up), and simulation algorithms like Monte Carlo. In this context, I'm mainly interested in presenting random generation as a good introductory example of how stateful computations compose. To get started, type the following into the REPL:

```
var r = new Random(100);
r.Next() // => 2080427802
r.Next() // => 341851734
r.Next() // => 1431988776
```

Because you're explicitly passing the value 100 as a seed for the random generator, you should get *exactly* the same results. As you can see, it's not that random after all. It's next to impossible to get real randomness with our current computers; instead, we use pseudo-random generators, which use a scrambling algorithm to deterministically produce an output that *looks* random. Typically, you don't want to get the same sequence of values every time, so a Random instance is usually initialized without an explicit seed; in this case, the current time is used.

If Random is deterministic, how does it produce a different output every time you call Next? The answer is that Random is stateful: every time you call Next, the state of the Random instance is updated. In other words, Next has side effects.

Next is called with no input arguments and yields an int as its explicit output. But it has an implicit input (the current state of the Random instance) that determines the output, as well as another implicit output, that is, the new state of the Random instance. This will in turn determine the output of the following call to Next.

We're going to create a side-effect-free random generator where all inputs and outputs are explicit. Generating a number is a stateful computation because it requires a seed, and it must also generate a new seed to be used in the following generation. We don't want to only generate integers but values of any type, so the type of a generator function can be captured with the following delegate:

```
public delegate (T Value, int Seed) Generator<T>(int seed);
```

A Generator<T> is a stateful computation that takes an int value as a seed (the state) and returns a tuple consisting of the generated T and a new seed, which can be used to generate a subsequent value. In arrow-notation, the signature for Generator<T> is

```
int → (T, int)
```

To run a generator, we can define the following `Run` methods:

```
public static T Run<T>(this Generator<T> gen, int seed)
   => gen(seed).Value;

public static T Run<T>(this Generator<T> gen)
   => gen(Environment.TickCount).Value;
```

The first overload runs the generator with the given seed and returns the generated value, disregarding the state. The second overload uses the clock to get a different seed value each time it's called (it's therefore impure and not testable, unlike the first overload). Next, let's create some generators.

15.2.1 *Generating random integers*

The basic building block we need is a generator that scrambles the seed value into a new int. The following listing shows one possible implementation.

> **Listing 15.5   A stateful computation returning a pseudorandom number**

```
public static Generator<int> NextInt = (seed) =>
{
    seed ^= seed >> 13;
    seed ^= seed << 18;
    int result = seed & 0x7fffffff;
    return (result, result);
};
```

This is a generator that, when given a seed, scrambles it to obtain another integer that *looks* unrelated.[2] It then returns that value both as a result value and as a seed to be used in the following computation.

Things start to get exciting when you want to generate more complex values. It turns out that if you can generate a random int, you can generate random values for arbitrarily complex types. But let's start with baby steps: Knowing you can generate a random int, how could you write a generator for a simpler type such as a Boolean?

15.2.2 *Generating other primitives*

Remember, a generator takes a seed and returns a new value (in this case, the generated Boolean) along with a new seed. The skeleton of a `Generator<bool>` would be as follows:

```
public static Generator<bool> NextBool = (seed) =>
{
    bool result = // ???
    int newSeed = // ???
    return (result, newSeed);
};
```

---

[2] The specifics of the algorithm are irrelevant for the purposes of this discussion. There are many algorithms for generating pseudorandom numbers.

How can we go about implementing it? We already have a generator for an int, so we can generate an int and return true/false depending on whether it's even/odd. We also need to return a new seed, and for this, we can take advantage of the new seed computed when generating the int. Essentially, we're using NextInt, transforming the resulting int into a bool and reusing the seed. Figure 15.2 illustrates this.

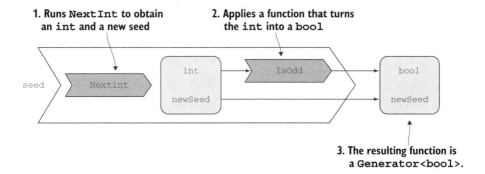

Figure 15.2   Using the NextInt generator to generate a Boolean

The implementation is as follows:

```
public static Generator<bool> NextBool = (seed) =>
{
    var (i, newSeed) = NextInt(seed);
    return (i % 2 == 0, newSeed);
};
```

Now, let's think of this differently. What we're doing here is effectively mapping a function that turns an int into a bool while reusing the new seed returned by the existing NextInt generator. We can generalize this pattern to define Map: if you have a Generator<T> and a function f : T → R, you can obtain a Generator<R> as follows: run the generator to obtain a T and a new seed; apply f to obtain an R; return the resulting R along with the new seed. The following listing shows the implementation of Map.

Listing 15.6   Definition of Map for Generator<T>

```
public static Generator<R> Map<T, R>
(
    this Generator<T> gen,
    Func<T, R> f
)
=> seed =>                          Map returns a generator
{                                   that, when given a seed...
    var (t, newSeed) = gen(seed);   ... runs the given generator gen
    return (f(t), newSeed);         to obtain a T and a new seed...
};                                  ... then uses f to turn the T into an R,
                                    which is returned along with the new seed.
```

We can now define generators for types that carry less information than an `int` (such as `bool` or `char`) much more concisely, as in the following listing.

Listing 15.7   Building upon `NextInt` to generate other types

```
public static Generator<bool> NextBool =>          Generates an int...
    from i in NextInt
    select i % 2 == 0;          ...returns whether it's even

public static Generator<char> NextChar =>
    from i in NextInt
    select (char)(i % (char.MaxValue + 1));
```

That's much more readable because we don't have to explicitly worry about the seed, and we can read the code in terms of "generate an int, and return whether it's even."

15.2.3 *Generating complex structures*

Now let's move on and see how we can generate more complex values. Let's try to generate a pair of integers. We'd have to write something like this:

```
public static Generator<(int, int)> PairOfInts = (seed0) =>
{
    var (a, seed1) = NextInt(seed0);
    var (b, seed2) = NextInt(seed1);
    return ((a, b), seed2);
};
```

Here you see that for each stateful computation (or for each time we generate a random value), we need to extract the state (the newly created seed) and pass it on to the next computation. This is rather noisy. Fortunately, we can do away with the explicit state-passing by composing the generators with a LINQ expression as the following listing shows.

Listing 15.8   Defining a function that generates a pair of random integers

```
public static Generator<(int, int)> PairOfInts =>        Generates an int
    from a in NextInt                                     and calls it a
    from b in NextInt                   Generates another
    select (a, b);      Returns the pair   int and calls it b
                        of a and b
```

This is much more readable, but under the covers, it's the same as before. This works because I've defined an implementation of `Bind/SelectMany` that takes care of "threading the state," passing it from one computation to the next. Graphically, figure 15.3 shows how `Bind` works. Listing 15.9 shows the corresponding code.

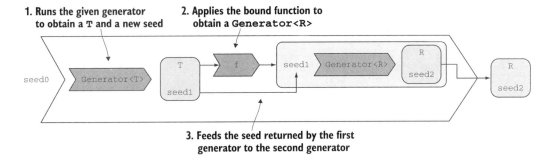

1. Runs the given generator to obtain a T and a new seed

2. Applies the bound function to obtain a `Generator<R>`

3. Feeds the seed returned by the first generator to the second generator

Figure 15.3 Definition of `Bind` for `Generator<T>`

Listing 15.9 Definition of `Bind` for `Generator<T>`

```
public static Generator<R> Bind<T, R>
(
    this Generator<T> gen,
    Func<T, Generator<R>> f
)
=> seed0 =>
{
    var (t, seed1) = gen(seed0);
    return f(t)(seed1);
};
```

Now we have all the building blocks to generate arbitrarily complex types. Say we want to create an `Option<int>`. That's easy—generate a Boolean for the state of the `Option` and an `int` for the value:

```
public static Generator<Option<int>> OptionInt =>
    from some in NextBool
    from i in NextInt
    select some ? Some(i) : None;
```

This should look familiar. You saw some similar code in section 10.1.3 when we were using FsCheck to define property tests and we needed to provide a method for generating random `Options`. Indeed, FsCheck's random generator is defined along the same lines as this one.

The following listing shows a slightly more complex example, that of generating a sequence of ints.

Listing 15.10 Generating a list of random numbers

```
public static Generator<IEnumerable<int>> IntList
    => from empty in NextBool
        from list in empty ? Empty : NonEmpty
        select list;
```

```
static Generator<IEnumerable<int>> Empty
   => Generator.Return(Enumerable.Empty<int>());

static Generator<IEnumerable<int>> NonEmpty
   => from head in NextInt
      from tail in IntList
      select List(head).Concat(tail);

public static Generator<T> Return<T>(T value)
   => seed => (value, seed);
```

Let's start with the top-level `IntList`. We generate a random Boolean to tell us if the sequence should be empty.[3] If so, we use `Empty`, which is a generator that always returns an empty sequence; otherwise, we return a non-empty sequence by calling `NonEmpty`. This generates an `int` as the first element and a random sequence to follow it. Note that `Empty` uses the `Return` function for `Generator`, which lifts a value into a generator that always returns that value and doesn't affect the state it's given.

What about generating a string? A string is essentially a sequence of characters, so we can generate a list of `int`s, convert each `int` to a `char`, and build a string from the resulting sequence of characters. As you can see, we follow this approach to generate a language for combining generators of various types into generators for arbitrarily complex types.

15.3 A general pattern for stateful computations

There are many other scenarios in which we may want to compose several stateful computations, other than generating random values. For this, we can use a more general delegate, `StatefulComputation`:

```
delegate (T Value, S State) StatefulComputation<S, T>(S state);
```

A `StatefulComputation<T>` is a function in this form:

```
S → (T, S)
```

`T` is the function's result value, and `S` is the state.[4] You can compare this to the signature of `Generator<T>` to see how similar they are:

```
StatefulComputation<T> : S   → (T, S)
Generator<T>           : int → (T, int)
```

With `Generator`, the state that gets passed in and out is always an `int`. With the more general `StatefulComputation`, the state could be of an arbitrary type `S`. Thus, we can define `Map` and `Bind` in the same way (the only difference being an additional type

---

[3] This means that, statistically, half the generated lists will be empty, a quarter of the lists will have one element, and so on, so this generator is unlikely to produce a long list. You can follow a different approach and generate a random length first, presumably within a given range, and then populate the values. As this shows, once you start to generate random data, it's important to define parameters that govern the random generation.

[4] In FP lingo, this is called *the state monad*. This is a truly terrible name to describe a function that takes some state as an argument. This unfortunate name is probably the greatest hurdle to understanding it.

parameter) and let them take care of threading the state between one computation and the next.

In chapter 11, we discussed trees, and you saw how you could define a `Map` function that creates a new tree, where each element is the result of applying a function to each value in the original tree. Imagine that you now want to assign a number to each element, as figure 15.4 shows.

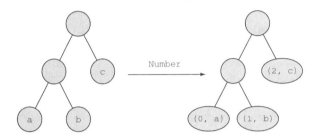

Figure 15.4 Numbering each element in a tree

This operation is similar to `Map` in the sense that you must traverse the tree and apply a function to each element. But, additionally, you must keep some state (a counter value) that needs to be incremented as you visit each element and used to label each leaf.

Let's start by defining a `Numbered<T>` type that wraps a `T` and a number:

```
public record Numbered<T>(T Value, int Number);
```

This means the operation we're trying to model can be expressed as a function from `Tree<T>` to `Tree<Numbered<T>>`.

The following listing shows an initial implementation that traverses the tree, explicitly passing the state (a counter value) around.

Listing 15.11 Numbering the leaves of a tree by explicitly passing state

```
using LaYumba.Functional.Data.BinaryTree;

public Tree<Numbered<T>> Number<T>(Tree<T> tree)        Calls the stateful overload,
   => Number(tree, 0).Tree;                             passing 0 as the initial state

(Tree<Numbered<T>> Tree, int Count) Number<T>
(
   Tree<T> tree,
   int count
)
=> tree.Match
(
   Leaf: t =>
      (
                                                        Labels this leaf with
         Tree.Leaf(new Numbered<T>(t, count)),          the current count
         count + 1        Returns the incremented
      ),                  count as the new state
```

```
    Branch: (l, r) =>
    {
        var (left, count1) = Number(l, count);          Recursively calls Number on
        var (right, count2) = Number(r, count1);        the left and right subtrees
        return (Tree.Branch(left, right), count2);      ◁──── Returns the new tree
    }                                                          with the updated count
);
```

We start the computation with a count of 0. The numbering function simply matches on the type of tree. If it's a leaf, then it contains a T, so Number returns a pair, containing as the result a Numbered<T> (wrapping the T and the current count) and as the new state the incremented counter. If it's a branch, then we recursively call Number on the left and right subtrees. Because each of these operations returns an updated state, we must thread the state along and return it in the result value.

Although I find the preceding solution satisfactory, it's true that manually passing state along introduces some noise. We can get rid of that by refactoring the code to use the StatefulComputation delegate instead.

We'll start by defining a simple stateful computation that takes an int (the state, which in this case is the counter) and returns the counter as the value and the incremented state as the new state:

```
static StatefulComputation<int, int> GetAndIncrement
    = count => (count, count + 1);

GetAndIncrement(0) // => (0, 1)
GetAndIncrement(6) // => (6, 7)
```

Remember, a stateful computation returns both a *value* and a *new state*. GetAndIncrement returns the current counter value as the returned value and the incremented counter as the new state.

The interesting thing about GetAndIncrement is that it allows you to peek into the state: because the current counter value becomes the inner value of the computation, you can refer to it in a LINQ expression. You can see this in the following code, where we assign the current count value to the count variable.

The following listing shows how we can rewrite our tree numbering function using LINQ to take care of passing the state.

Listing 15.12   Numbering the leaves of a tree using LINQ

```
StatefulComputation<int, Tree<Numbered<T>>> Number<T>
(
    Tree<T> tree
)
=> tree.Match                    Assigns the current count to the
(                                count variable, while assigning the       The result is a new leaf
    Leaf: t =>                   incremented count to the state            containing the original
        from count in GetAndIncrement           ◁──┐                       leaf value, numbered
        select Tree.Leaf(new Numbered<T>(t, count)),  ◁──┘                  with the current count.
```

```
    Branch: (left, right) =>
        from newLeft in Number(left)
        from newRight in Number(right)
        select Tree.Branch(newLeft, newRight)
);
```

As you can see, when you're composing a sequence of several stateful computations as in the Branch case, LINQ can really improve readability. Otherwise, I find that passing the state around explicitly is clearer. Note that the preceding function returns a computation, which does nothing until it's given an input state:

```
Number(tree).Run(0)
```

Although stateful computations are ubiquitous, the need to chain several computations isn't as frequent. It does crop up often in certain areas, though, such as simulations or parsers. A functional parser, for example, is usually modeled as a function that takes a string (the state), consumes part of the string, and produces a result consisting of a structured representation of what's been parsed and the remainder of the string that's left to parse (the new state).

Summary

- When writing stateful programs, you can avoid changing state as a side effect by always passing the state explicitly as part of your functions' input and output.
- Stateful computations are functions in the form $S \to (T, S)$. They take some state and return a value as well as an updated state.
- Stateful computations can be composed monadically to reduce the syntactic burden of passing the state from one computation to the next.

16
Working with asynchronous computations

This chapter covers
- Using `Task` to represent asynchronous computations
- Composing asynchronous operations sequentially and in parallel
- Working with asynchronous sequences

In today's world of distributed applications, many operations are performed asynchronously. A program can begin some operation that takes a relatively long time, such as requesting data from another application, but it doesn't sit idle, waiting for that operation to complete. Instead, it goes on to do other work and resumes the operation once the data has been received.

Asynchrony certainly is the bread and butter of today's programmer. I waited until this late in the book to deal with it because it adds a level of complexity that I wanted to postpone in order to make the ideas presented so far more approachable.

Asynchronous operations are represented in C# using `Task`, and in this chapter, you'll see that `Task<T>` is not so different from other containers such as `Option<T>`,

Try<T>, and so on. While Task<T> represents a single value that is delivered asynchronously, IAsyncEnumerable<T> is a recent addition to the language that is used to represent a sequence of values delivered asynchronously. I'll discuss this in the second part of this chapter.

16.1 *Asynchronous computations*

In this section, I'll start by introducing the need for asynchrony and how we can use Task to model the asynchronous delivery of a value. You'll then see that Task<T> is just another container for a T and, therefore, supports operations like Map and Bind. We'll then address some frequently recurring concerns when working with Tasks: combining several asynchronous operations, handling failure, performing multiple retries, and running tasks in parallel.

> ### Task **and** ValueTask
>
> The BCL also includes ValueTask, which is a value type and is otherwise similar to Task in terms of usage. It is recommended that an asynchronous method return ValueTask rather than Task when
>
> - It's called on a hot path, so performance is critical.
> - It can involve asynchrony, but often completes synchronously; for example, methods that read from a file or a remote API and cache the retrieved data.
>
> In such cases, using ValueTask is more efficient because you're not allocating a Task on the heap. For the purposes of this chapter, when you find a mention of Task, the idea also holds for ValueTask. To learn more about ValueTask and how it differs from Task, head to https://youtu.be/fj-LVS8hqlE to hear about it from its creator Stephen Toub.

16.1.1 *The need for asynchrony*

Some operations take longer than others—massively longer! Whereas the time required to perform a typical computer instruction is in the order of nanoseconds, I/O operations such as reading from the filesystem or making a network request are in the order of milliseconds or even seconds.

To get a better grasp of how big the difference is, let's scale things up to something more human: if an in-memory instruction such as adding two numbers were to take about a second, then a typical I/O operation would take months or years. And, as in real life, you can wait a few seconds at the water cooler while your cup is filled, but you wouldn't wait around at the bank for weeks while your mortgage application is processed. Instead, you'd file your application, go back to your daily life, and expect to be notified of the result at some point in the future.

Figure 16.1   When an operation can be performed quickly, we're happy to wait for the operation to complete, ceasing other work. This is the way synchronous code works.

Figure 16.2   When we initiate an operation that takes a long time to complete, we then go on to do other work, expecting to be notified when the operation is complete. This is how asynchronous code works.

This is the idea behind asynchronous computations: kick off an operation that takes a long time, move on to doing other work, and then come back once the operation completes.

16.1.2 *Representing asynchronous operations with Task*

The main tool for working with asynchronous computations since C# 4 is the *Task-based Asynchronous Pattern*. I assume you're already familiar with it to some extent; if not, you'll find ample documentation online. In a nutshell, here's what it consists of:

- Use `Task` and `Task<T>` to represent asynchronous operations.
- Use the `await` keyword to await the `Task`, which frees the current thread to do other work while the asynchronous operation completes.

For instance, in section 15.1, we discussed a program that fetches FX rates from the web. The following listing shows the code that actually performs the web request, which I previously omitted.

Listing 16.1 Blocking the current thread while a network call completes

```
public static decimal GetRate(string ccyPair)
{
    Task<string> request = new HttpClient()
        .GetStringAsync(UriFor(ccyPair));

    string body = request.Result;          ⟵┐ Calling Result blocks the thread
                                             │ until the operation completes.
    var response = JsonSerializer.Deserialize<Response>(body, opts);
    return response.ConversionRate;
}

record Response(decimal ConversionRate);

const string ApiKey = "1a2419e081f5940872d5700f";

static string UriFor(string ccyPair)
{
    var (baseCcy, quoteCcy) = ccyPair.SplitAt(3);
    return $"https://v6.exchangerate-api.com/v6/{ApiKey}"
        + $"/pair/{baseCcy}/{quoteCcy}";
}

static readonly JsonSerializerOptions opts = new()
    { PropertyNamingPolicy = new SnakeCaseNamingPolicy() };
```

Let's go through the code in GetRate, which performs the remote API call. We call UriFor to compute the URI needed to retrieve the desired FX rate and then use an HttpClient to perform the API query.

When calling Result on the resulting Task, the current thread pauses and waits for the response to be received from the remote API. It then deserializes the response body into the appropriate type and extracts the requested rate.

Blocking until the response is received is OK for a simple console application, but it would be unacceptable for most real-world applications, whether client or server. There's no need to block a thread while waiting for a network call to complete.

You can refactor GetRate to perform the request asynchronously, as the following listing shows.

Listing 16.2 Using Task to represent an asynchronous operation

```
                                       ┌ The method has the async
public static async Task<decimal>  ⟵──┘ modifier and returns a Task.
    GetRateAsync(string ccyPair)        ⟵┐ By convention, the method
{                                        │ name has the Async suffix.
    Task<string> request = new HttpClient()
        .GetStringAsync(UriFor(ccyPair));
                                         ┌ await frees the current thread
    string body = await request;    ⟵──┘ until the operation completes.

    var response = JsonSerializer.Deserialize<Response>(body, opts);
    return response.ConversionRate;
}
```

Notice the changes:

- The method now returns not a decimal but a Task<decimal>.
- await suspends the current context (freeing the thread to do other work), which is resumed when the asynchronous operation has completed and its result is available.
- You have to mark a method async when you use await in its body.[1]
- By convention, Task-returning methods are named with the Async suffix.[2]

So far, no surprises. Now let's look at Task<T> from a more functional point of view.

16.1.3 *Task as a container for a future value*

Given the perspective we've been building in this book, it's natural to look at Task<T> as just another container of T. If Option<T> can be seen as a box that *may* contain a T and Func<T> as a container that can be run to get a T, then Task<T> can be seen as a container within which a T will materialize at some point in the future. So Task<T> is a construct that adds the effect of asynchrony.

> **NOTE**   Again, there's a vexing dichotomy between the non-generic Task and the generic Task<T>, respectively representing asynchronous operations that yield void and a T.
>
> In this chapter, I'll always use a return value (at least Unit), so even if I write Task for brevity, you should take it to mean Task<T>.

To put this idea of Task as a container into code, I've defined its Return, Map, and Bind functions. These functions effectively make Task<T> a monad over T, and their implementation is shown in the following listing.

Listing 16.3   Map and Bind can be defined trivially in terms of await

```
public static Task<T> Async<T>(T t)
   => Task.FromResult(t);

public static async Task<R> Map<T, R>
   (this Task<T> task, Func<T, R> f)
   => f(await task);
```

---

[1]   This is a bit of a shame as async adds noise, especially when used in lambdas. Strictly speaking, it's not needed: it's possible to design the language syntax without async; however, it was added to enable backward compatibility back when await was first added to the language.

[2]   I have strong feelings *against* this naming convention. It was proposed by Microsoft in the early days of async. For one thing, you don't name methods that return a string with a special -Str suffix, do you? So why would you with Task? The idea behind the convention was, I believe, to facilitate disambiguation in APIs that expose both synchronous and asynchronous variants of the same operation. But this leads to bad design: if there's a reason for a method to be asynchronous, then using the synchronous variant is suboptimal. An API should encourage doing the right thing by only exposing the asynchronous version. If both versions are exposed, then, if anything, the synchronous version should be labeled with the -Sync suffix, which would stick out like an eyesore. Good design makes it easy to do the right thing, so forcing longer, noisier names for the asynchronous version is bad design. Unfortunately, this convention has become widespread enough to be considered the standard.

```
public static async Task<R> Bind<T, R>
    (this Task<T> task, Func<T, Task<R>> f)
    => await f(await task);
```

I'll use `Async` as the `Return` function for `Task`, which lifts a `T` into a `Task<T>`. It's just a shorthand for .NET's `Task.FromResult` method.

Notice how easy it is to define `Map` and `Bind` with the `await` keyword. Why is it so easy? Remember, `Map` *extracts* the inner value(s) from a container, applies the given function, and wraps the result back up into a container. But this unwrapping and wrapping is exactly what the `await` language feature does: it extracts the `Task`'s inner value (the value the operation returns when it completes), and when a method contains an `await`, its result is automatically wrapped in a `Task`.[3] All that's left for `Map` to do is to apply the given function to the awaited value.

`Bind` is similar. It awaits the given `Task<T>`, and when this completes, the resulting `T` can be supplied to the bound function. This in turn returns a `Task<R>`, which must also be awaited before the desired result of type `R` is obtained.

I've implemented the LINQ query pattern for `Task` along the same lines, so you can rewrite the `GetRateAsync` function using a LINQ comprehension as the next listing shows.

Listing 16.4 Using LINQ comprehensions with `Tasks`

```
public static Task<decimal> GetRateAsync(string ccyPair) =>
    from body in new HttpClient().GetStringAsync(UriFor(ccyPair))
    let response = JsonSerializer.Deserialize<Response>(body, opts)
    select response.ConversionRate;
```

In the LINQ comprehension in listing 16.4, the `from` clause takes the inner value of the `Task` and binds it to the variable `body` (more generally, when you see a clause like `from s in m`, you can read it as, "extract the inner value of m and call it s, then   "); this is exactly what `await` does. The difference is that `await` is specific to `Task`, whereas LINQ comprehensions can be used with any monad.

Compare this with listing 16.2, and you'll see that it performs the same operations. Also, notice that the `async` modifier is gone because the method body does not include the `await` operator.

Of course, once you've implemented `Bind`/`SelectMany`, you can use it to combine several asynchronous operations. The following listing demonstrates this; for best performance, instead of `GetStringAsync`, it uses `GetStreamAsync`, which yields a stream that can be consumed asynchronously by the deserializer.

---

[3] `await` works not only with `Task` but any *awaitable* (any value for which a `GetAwaiter` [instance or extension] method returning an `INotifyCompletion` is defined).

Listing 16.5   Using LINQ comprehensions to chain asynchronous operations

```
public static Task<decimal> GetRateAsync(string ccyPair) =>
   from str in new HttpClient()
      .GetStreamAsync(UriFor(ccyPair))
   from response in JsonSerializer
      .DeserializeAsync<Response>(str, opts)
   select response.ConversionRate;
```

This is the version that leverages asynchrony the most and avoids storing the response in memory (which would be inefficient when handling large payloads). Note that two `from` clauses are required, given that we now have two asynchronous operations (corresponding to two occurrences of the `await` operator if we weren't using a LINQ comprehension).

Lazy vs. asynchronous computations

Lazy and asynchronous computations both allow you to write code that "runs in the future." That is, at a certain point, your program defines what to do with a value `T` returned by a lazy computation `Func<T>` or an asynchronous computation `Task<T>`, but those instructions are then executed at a later point.

There are also important differences between the two. From the point of view of the code that defines the computation

- Creating a lazy computation (like a `Func`, `Try`, `StatefulComputation`, and so on) doesn't start the computation. In fact, it does nothing (no side effects).
- Creating a `Task` kicks off an asynchronous computation.

From the point of view of the code consuming the computed result

- The code consuming a lazy value "decides" when to run the computation, obtaining the computed value.
- The code consuming an asynchronous value has no control over when it will receive the computed value.

16.1.4   *Handling failure*

I mentioned that you can think of `Task<T>` as a construct that adds the effect of asynchrony. In fact, it also captures error handling. Because asynchronous operations are, most frequently, I/O operations, there's a high chance of something going wrong. Fortunately, `Task<T>` also has error handling via the `Status` and `Exception` properties.

This is important. Imagine that you have a synchronous computation and are using `Exceptional<T>` to model a computation that may fail. If you now want to make the computation asynchronous, you don't need a `Task<Exceptional<T>>` but only a `Task<T>`.

To see some examples of how various asynchronous computations can be composed, let's look at some slightly more complex variations on the scenario of retrieving exchange rates.

Imagine that your company has purchased a subscription to CurrencyLayer, a company providing good quality exchange rate data (that is, data with a short delay compared to the market) via an API. If, for some reason, a call to CurrencyLayer's API fails, you want to fall back to RatesAPI, which is what we've been using so far. First, assume you define two classes encapsulating access to the APIs:

```
public static class CurrencyLayer
{
    public static Task<decimal> GetRateAsync(string ccyPair) => //...
}
public static class RatesApi
{
    public static Task<decimal> GetRateAsync(string ccyPair) => //...
}
```

CurrencyLayer is implemented along the same lines as RatesApi, but it's adapted to CurrencyLayer's API, which returns data with a different structure. The interesting part is combining the two calls to GetRateAsync. For this kind of task, you can use the OrElse function, which takes a task and a fallback to use in case the task fails (the idea is similar to the OrElse function defined for Option in chapter 14):

```
public static Task<T> OrElse<T>
    (this Task<T> task, Func<Task<T>> fallback)
    => task.ContinueWith(t =>
        t.Status == TaskStatus.Faulted
            ? fallback()
            : Async(t.Result)
    )
    .Unwrap();
```

> **Flattens a Task<Task<T>> into a Task<T>**

Notice that OrElse assumes that a Task either fails or succeeds. In reality, C# Tasks also support cancellation, but this feature is rarely used and complicates the API, so I won't deal with cancellation here. You can use OrElse as follows:

```
CurrencyLayer.GetRateAsync(ccyPair)
    .OrElse(() => RatesApi.GetRateAsync(ccyPair))
```

The result is a new Task that produces the value returned by CurrencyLayer if the operation is successful and, otherwise, the value returned by RatesAPI.

There is, of course, always the possibility that both calls fail—if, say, the network is down. So we also need a function to specify what to do when a task fails. I'll call it Recover:

```
public static Task<T> Recover<T>
(
    this Task<T> task,
    Func<Exception, T> fallback
)
=> task.ContinueWith(t =>
    t.Status == TaskStatus.Faulted
        ? fallback(t.Exception)
        : t.Result);
```

You can use `Recover` as follows:

```
RatesApi
   .GetRateAsync("USDEUR")
   .Map(rate => $"The rate is {rate}")
   .Recover(ex => $"Error fetching rate: {ex.Message}")
```

`Recover` is something you'd typically use at the end of a workflow to specify what to do if an error occurs somewhere along the way. You can use `Recover` in the same way you'd use `Match` for things like `Option` or `Either`. But `Match` works synchronously; a `Task` doesn't have anything to match on because its status isn't available until some point in the future, so technically, `Recover` is more like `Map` for the faulted case (you can confirm this by looking at its signature).

It's also reasonable to define an overload of `Map` that takes a handler for both the success and failure cases:

```
public static Task<R> Map<T, R>
(
    this Task<T> task,
    Func<Exception, R> Faulted,
    Func<T, R> Completed
)
=> task.ContinueWith(t =>
    t.Status == TaskStatus.Faulted
        ? Faulted(t.Exception)
        : Completed(t.Result));
```

This could then be used as follows:

```
RatesApi.GetRateAsync("USDEUR").Map(
    Faulted: ex => $"Error fetching rate: {ex.Message}",
    Completed: rate => $"The rate is {rate}")
```

16.1.5 *An HTTP API for currency conversion*

Let's put it all together by writing an API endpoint that allows clients to convert an amount from one currency to another. A sample interaction with this API is as follows:

```
$ curl http://localhost:5000/convert/1000/USD/to/EUR -s
896.9000

$ curl http://localhost:5000/convert/1000/USD/to/JPY -s
103089.0000

$ curl http://localhost:5000/convert/1000/XXX/to/XXX -s
{"message":"An unexpected error has occurred"}
```

You can call the API on a route such as "convert/1000/USD/to/EUR" to find out how many Euros are equivalent to 1,000 US Dollars. Here's the implementation:

```
Task<IResult> Convert
(
    decimal amount,
    string baseCcy,
```

```
    string quoteCcy
)                                                              Fall back to a
=> RatesApi.GetRateAsync(baseCcy + quoteCcy)                   secondary API.
    .OrElse(() => CurrencyLayer.GetRateAsync(baseCcy + quoteCcy))   ◁────
    .Map(rate => amount * rate)      ◁──┐ Performs the
    .Map                                │ rate conversion.
    (
        Faulted: ex => StatusCode(500),   ◁──┐ Specify what to do
        Completed: result => Ok(result)       │ in case of failure
    );
```

```
app.MapGet("convert/{amount}/{baseCcy}/to/{quoteCcy}", Convert);
```

When the application gets a request, it calls the CurrencyLayer API to get the relevant rate. If this fails, it calls RatesAPI. Once it has a rate, it uses it to calculate the equivalent amount in the target currency. Finally, it maps a successful result to a 200 and failure to a 500.

You may remember from chapter 8 that once you're in the elevated world, you should stay in it for as long as possible. This is all the more true of Task: being in the world of Task means writing code that runs in the future, so leaving the elevated world in this case means blocking the thread and waiting for the future to catch up. We hardly ever want to do that.

Note that the method handling the request returns a Task<IResult>: ASP.NET sends the response to the client when the Task has run to completion, and you don't need to worry about when this will take place. You *never* need to leave the elevated world of Task in this case.

16.1.6 If it fails, try a few more times

When remote operations (such as a call to an HTTP API) fail, the reasons for failure are often transient: maybe there's a glitch in connectivity, or the remote server is being restarted. In other words, an operation that fails once may succeed if you retry a few seconds or minutes later.

The need to retry when an operation fails is a common requirement when dealing with third-party APIs over whose health you have no control. The following listing shows one simple and elegant solution that performs an asynchronous operation, retrying for a specified number of times if it fails.

Listing 16.6 Retrying with exponential backoff

```
public static Task<T> Retry<T>
    (int retries, int delayMillis, Func<Task<T>> start)
    => retries <= 0
        ? start()                    ◁──┤ Last attempt        If the attempt fails,
        : start().OrElse(() =>                                wait for a while
            from _ in Task.Delay(delayMillis)                 and then retry.
            from t in Retry(retries - 1, delayMillis * 2, start)
            select t);
```

To use it, simply wrap the function performing the remote operation in an invocation to the `Retry` function:

```
Retry(10, 1000, () => RatesApi.GetRateAsync("GBPUSD"))
```

This specifies that the operation should be retried at most 10 times, with an initial delay of one second between attempts. The last argument is the operation to perform, specified lazily because invoking the function kicks off the task.

Notice that `Retry` is recursive: if the operation fails, it waits for the specified interval and then retries the same operation, decreasing the number of retries left and doubling the interval to wait the next time around (a retry strategy known as *exponential backoff*).

16.1.7 *Running asynchronous operations in parallel*

Because `Task` is used to represent operations that take time, it's only natural that you may want to execute them in parallel when possible.

Imagine you want to check prices offered by different airlines. Assume you have several classes encapsulating access to the airlines' APIs, each implementing the `Airline` interface:

```
interface Airline
{
    Task<Flight> BestFare(string origin, string dest, DateTime departure);
}
```

`BestFare` gets you the cheapest flight available on a given route and date. The flight details are queried via a remote API, so naturally the results are wrapped in a `Task`.

Now imagine for a second that we're back in the 90s, and you're interested in touring Europe on a shoestring. You'd need to look at the only two low-cost airlines on the market: EasyJet and Ryanair. You could then find the best price offered between two airports on a given date like so:

```
Airline ryanair;
Airline easyjet;

Task<Flight> BestFareM(string origin, string dest, DateTime departure)
    => from r in ryanair.BestFare(origin, dest, departure)
       from e in easyjet.BestFare(origin, dest, departure)
       select r.Price < e.Price ? r : e;
```

This works, but it's not optimal. Because LINQ queries are monadic, `easyjet.BestFare` will only be called after `ryanair.BestFare` has completed (you'll see why in a moment). But why wait? After all, the two calls are completely independent, so there's no reason we can't make the two calls in parallel.

You may remember from chapter 10 that when you have independent computations, you can use applicatives. The following listing shows `Apply` defined for `Task`, which again is implemented rather trivially in terms of `await`.

Listing 16.7 Implementation of `Apply` for `Task`

```
public static async Task<R> Apply<T, R>
   (this Task<Func<T, R>> f, Task<T> arg)
   => (await f)(await arg);

public static Task<Func<T2, R>> Apply<T1, T2, R>
   (this Task<Func<T1, T2, R>> f, Task<T1> arg)
   => Apply(f.Map(F.Curry), arg);
```

As with other containers, the important overload is the first one (where a unary function is wrapped in a container), and overloads for greater arities can be defined by just currying that function. As with `Map` and `Bind`, the implementation simply uses the `await` keyword to reference the `Task`'s inner value. `Apply` awaits the wrapped function, awaits the wrapped argument, and applies the function to the argument. The result is wrapped in a task automatically as a result of using `await`.

The following listing shows how you can use `Apply` to find the cheaper fare more efficiently.

Listing 16.8 Performing two `Task`s in parallel with `Apply`

```
Task<Flight> BestFareA(string origin, string dest, DateTime departure)
{
   var pickCheaper = (Flight l, Flight r)
      => l.Price < r.Price ? l : r;

   return Async(pickCheaper)
      .Apply(ryanair.BestFare(origin, dest, departure))
      .Apply(easyjet.BestFare(origin, dest, departure));
}
```

In this version, the two calls to `BestFare` are kicked off independently, so they run in parallel. The total time needed for `BestFareA` to complete is determined by the time required for the longer of the API calls to complete—not their sum.

To get a better understanding of why `Apply` runs the task in parallel, while `Bind` does so sequentially, have a look at the following listing, which shows `Bind` and `Apply` side by side.

Listing 16.9 `Bind` runs tasks sequentially, `Apply` in parallel

```
public static async Task<R> Bind<T, R>
   (this Task<T> task, Func<T, Task<R>> f)
   => await f(await task);

public static async Task<R> Apply<T, R>
   (this Task<Func<T, R>> f, Task<T> arg)
   => (await f)(await arg);
```

`Bind` first awaits the given `Task<T>` and only then evaluates the function starting the second task. It runs the tasks sequentially and can't do otherwise because a value for `T` is required in order to create the second task.

Apply, on the other hand, takes two `Tasks`, meaning that both tasks have been started. With this in mind, let's revisit this code:

```
Async(PickCheaper)
    .Apply(ryanair.BestFare(origin, dest, departure))
    .Apply(easyjet.BestFare(origin, dest, departure));
```

When you call `Apply` the first time (with the Ryanair task), it *immediately* returns a new `Task` without waiting for the Ryanair task to complete (that's the behavior of the `await` inside `Apply`). Then the program immediately goes on to create the EasyJet task. As a result, both tasks run in parallel. In other words, the difference in behavior between `Bind` and `Apply` is dictated by their signatures:

- With `Bind`, the first `Task` must be awaited in order to create the second task, so it should be used when the creation of a `Task` depends on the return value of another.
- With `Apply`, both tasks are provided by the caller, so you should use it when the tasks can be started independently.

What if you have not two, but a long list of low-cost airlines to compare, as is the case today? To tackle this more complex scenario, we'll need a new tool: `Traverse`, which we'll see in section 17.1. But first, we'll conclude this chapter by looking at sequences of asynchronous values.

16.2   Async streams

`Task<T>` is good for modeling operations that take some time to deliver a single `T`, allowing you to write asynchronous code without excessive complexity. However, we often have operations that return not a single `T`, but several `T`'s, which can be delivered individually or in batches with a relatively long time between items or batches. Here are some examples:

- *Retrieving several pages from a paginated API.* Each page is retrieved with a single asynchronous operation and includes a certain number of resources, but you need to retrieve several pages in order to retrieve all the resources you require.
- *Reading a file.* Instead of reading the whole content of a file into memory, you can read it line by line asynchronously; this allows you to start processing the lines read so far while the rest of the file is still being read.
- *Retrieving data from a cloud-hosted DB.*

As with any long-running operation, we don't want to wait while the requested values are delivered. Instead, we want the calling thread to be freed as soon as the async request is kicked off, as figure 16.3 shows.

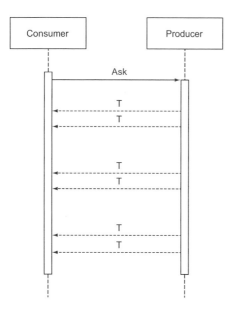

Figure 16.3 An asynchronous sequence. The consumer of information asks for some data, which is returned asynchronously by the producer of information with a non-negligible delay between the produced values.

We can model such scenarios as *async streams*—streams of values that are delivered asynchronously. These are represented with the IAsyncEnumerable<T> interface, and C# 8 introduced dedicated syntax to create and consume IAsyncEnumerables.

IAsyncEnumerable is like Task (in that it provides asynchrony) and like IEnumerable (in that it provides aggregation). It combines both effects, if you like. Table 16.1 shows the relationship between these different abstractions.

Table 16.1 How IAsyncEnumerable compares with other abstractions

	Synchronous	**Asynchronous**
Single value	T	Task<T>
Multiple values	IEnumerable<T>	IAsyncEnumerable<T>

So, you may ask, "How is IAsyncEnumerable<T> different from Task<IEnumerable<T>>?" Crucially, with Task<IEnumerable<T>>, you have to wait for the enclosing Task to complete before you can consume the resulting T's. With IAsyncEnumerable<T>, on the other hand, you can start consuming the incoming T's as soon as they are received without waiting for the end of the stream. Let's explore some concrete scenarios.

16.2.1 Reading from a file as an async stream

Imagine you're working in e-commerce and have to keep track of how many items are available in the warehouse for each product. The logistics side of the business uses an obsolete protocol: stock deliveries to the warehouse are recorded as comma-separated values in a CSV file, which is uploaded at the end of each day. You have to write a process that reads from the CSV file (each line represents delivery of stock of a particular product) and updates the e-commerce DB accordingly.

Because reading from a file is relatively slow, it's natural to model this as an asynchronous operation; furthermore, you can read the contents of the file line by line. This is more efficient than storing the entire contents of a large file into memory. Hence, you can use an IAsyncEnumerable as the following listing demonstrates.

Listing 16.10   Reading the contents of a file as an async stream of strings

```
using System.Collections.Generic;
using System.IO;

static async IAsyncEnumerable<string> ReadLines(string path)
{
   using StreamReader reader = File.OpenText(path);
   while (!reader.EndOfStream)
      yield return await reader.ReadLineAsync();
}
```

Notice that to generate an IAsyncEnumerable, you use yield return (like you do with IEnumerable) in combination with await. In fact, every time you have an asynchronous operation (a method that returns a Task<T> as is the case with ReadLineAsync here) that needs to be called repeatedly, you can consider using an IAsyncEnumerable<T>. Now that we have an async stream of strings, we can use each line to populate a data object (I'll call this Delivery), and use it to update the DB:

```
record Delivery(long ArticleID, int Quantity);          ←── Models a
                                                             delivery
static Delivery Parse(string s)     ←──┐ Populates a Delivery
{                                      │ from a line from the file
   string[] ss = s.Split(',');
   return new(long.Parse(ss[0]), int.Parse(ss[1]));
}                                                    ┌ Updates the DB with
static void UpdateDb(Delivery r) => // ...    ←──────┘ information from the delivery
```

With these building blocks in place, we can write the program that updates the DB with the values from the CSV file:

```
public static async Task Main()                               ┌ Consumes the
{                                                             │ stream of lines
   await foreach (var line in ReadLines("warehouse.csv"))  ←──┘ from the CSV file
   {
      Delivery d = Parse(line);         ←──┐ Parses each line
      UpdateDb(d);    ←──┐ Saves the Delivery │ into a Delivery
   }                    │ to the DB
}
```

Notice that here we consume the values in the IAsyncEnumerable with await foreach. This is similar to how you consume the elements of an IEnumerable with foreach.

16.2.2 Consuming async streams functionally

I hope that you're now thinking, "But we never want to use `foreach` to explicitly loop over the elements in a collection; instead, we want to use `Map` or a LINQ comprehension to transform each line into a `Delivery` and `ForEach` to update the DB!"

And, of course, you would be right to think that because that's the approach I've been following throughout the book. The only catch is that the relevant extension methods on `IAsyncEnumerable` must be imported by referencing the `System .Interactive.Async` package. Once you have this reference in place, you can rewrite the program as the following listing shows.

Listing 16.11 Leveraging the extension methods in `System.Interactive.Async`

```
using System.Linq;                              ◁──┐ Extensions on IAsyncEnumerable
                                                   │ are in this namespace.
public static async Task Main()
   => await ReadDeliveries("warehouse.csv")     ┌─ Performs a side effect for
      .ForEachAsync(UpdateDb);                  ◁─┘ each element in the stream

static IAsyncEnumerable<Delivery> ReadDeliveries(string path)
   => from line in ReadLines(path)              │ Applies a function to each
      select Parse(line);                       │ element in the stream
```

Here we use a LINQ comprehension to transform each asynchronously delivered string into a `Delivery` and `ForEachAsync` to update the DB. Why is it called `ForEach-Async` instead of just `ForEach`? Because it completes only when all values in the stream have been processed, it returns a `Task`, and the convention is to use the `Async` suffix for `Task`-returning operations.

Notice that I've defined `UpdateDb` to be synchronous. In practice, you would probably make this operation asynchronous as well; in which case, it would return a `Task` rather than `void`. You would then need to modify the program as follows, using `ForEachAwaitAsync` rather than `ForEachAsync`:

```
public static async Task Main()
   => await ReadDeliveries("warehouse.csv")
      .ForEachAwaitAsync(UpdateDbAsync);

static Task UpdateDbAsync(Delivery r) => // ...
```

16.2.3 Consuming data from several streams

So far, you've seen how to define an async stream and how to consume its values using `Select` for data transformations (whether directly or through a LINQ comprehension with a single `from` clause) and `ForEachAsync` or `ForEachAwaitAsync` to perform side effects. Next, we'll look at using a LINQ comprehension with multiple `from` clauses. As you know from section 10.4, this resolves to `SelectMany`, which is essentially `Bind`.

Imagine your client has not one but several warehouses. They all upload their respective CSV files into a directory at the end of the day, so your program needs to change to process multiple files. The change is quite simple. Instead of taking a path to a file, ReadDeliveries can take the directory path and process all files present in that directory:

```
static IAsyncEnumerable<Delivery> ReadDeliveries(string dir)
   => from path in Directory.EnumerateFiles(dir).ToAsyncEnumerable()
      from line in ReadLines(path)
      select Parse(line);
```

That's it! A one-line change. EnumerateFiles yields an IEnumerable<string>. This needs to be promoted to an IAsyncEnumerable<string> so that it can be used in a LINQ comprehension with the streams generated by processing each file. Note that the files will be processed sequentially; therefore, the resulting stream will have all the deliveries from the first file before moving on to the second file, and so on.

16.2.4 *Aggregation and sorting with async streams*

Async streams are powerful in that they enable you to start consuming the values in the stream before the stream has ended. In our example, this means that you can start updating the DB while the CSV file is still being read. In some scenarios, this can give you huge gains in efficiency.

Now imagine that the warehouse receives several deliveries throughout the day, potentially including several deliveries of the same product, so the CSV file may include several entries for the same product ID. If this is the case, you want to perform a single DB update for that product. Your code would then need to change as follows:

```
public static async Task Main()
   => await ReadDeliveries("warehouse.csv")
      .GroupBy(r => r.ProductID)
      .SelectAwait(async grp => new Delivery(grp.Key
        , await grp.SumAsync(r => r.Quantity)))
      .ForEachAwaitAsync(UpdateDbAsync);
```

The gist here is that you are grouping the elements in the stream by their product IDs; this is done with GroupBy, just as you would do with IEnumerable. Within each grouping, you then take the sum of all quantities to create a single Delivery for each product. But notice that you cannot use Sum like you would on IEnumerable; instead, you have to use SumAsync, which returns a Task (because you have to wait until you receive all items before you can compute their sum).

As a result, although the code is correct, you'll notice that we've effectively lost some of the gains of asynchrony. We need to wait until all elements are received to compute their sum or any other aggregate operation. Therefore, in this case, IAsyncEnumerable ends up being no better than Task<IEnumerable>. This is also the case if you want the values to be sorted.

Summary

- Task<T> represents a computation that asynchronously delivers a T.
- Tasks should be used when the underlying operation may have significant latency, such as most I/O operations.

- Task-returning functions can be composed with `Map`, `Bind`, and several other combinators to specify error handling or multiple retries.
- If `Task`s are independent, they can be run in parallel. You can use `Task` as an applicative, and composing several `Task`s with `Apply` runs them in parallel.
- `IAsyncEnumerable<T>` represents a sequence of `T`'s that are delivered asynchronously.
- Use the extension methods in `System.Interactive.Async` to work with `IAsyncEnumerable`; this also includes the implementation of the LINQ query pattern.
- Keep in mind that some operations on async streams, such as sorting and aggregation, require all elements in the stream, therefore losing some of the efficiency gained by using an async stream.

Traversable and stacked monads

17

This chapter covers

- Traversables: handling lists of elevated types
- Combining the effects of different monads

So far in the book you've seen a number of different containers that add some effect to the underlying value(s)—Option for optionality, IEnumerable for aggregation, Task for asynchrony, and so on. As our list of containers keeps growing, we'll inevitably hit the problem of combining different containers:

- If you have a list of Tasks that you want to execute, how can you combine them into a single Task that will complete when all the operations have completed?
- If you have a value of type Task<Validation<T>>, how do you compose it with a function of type T → Task<R> with the least amount of noise?

This chapter will give you the tools to combine the effects of different containers and show how to avoid an excess of nested containers.

17.1 Traversables: Working with lists of elevated values

Traverse is one of the slightly more esoteric core functions in FP, and it allows you to work with lists of elevated values. It's probably easiest to approach through an example.

Imagine a simple command-line application that reads a comma-separated list of numbers entered by the user and returns the sum of all the given numbers. We could start along these lines:

```
using Double = LaYumba.Functional.Double;          ← Exposes an Option-returning
using String = LaYumba.Functional.String;              function for parsing a double
                                                   ← Exposes a static
var input = Console.ReadLine();                        Trim function

var nums = input.Split(',')    // Array<string>
   .Map(String.Trim)           // IEnumerable<string>
   .Map(Double.Parse);         // IEnumerable<Option<double>>
```

We split the input string to get an array of strings and remove any whitespace with `Trim`. We can then map onto this list the parsing function `Double.Parse`, which has the signature `string → Option<double>`. As a result, we get an `IEnumerable<Option<double>>`.

Instead, what we really want is an `Option<IEnumerable<double>>`, which should be `None` if *any* of the numbers failed to parse. In this case, we can warn the user to correct their input.[1] We saw that `Map` yields a type where the effects are stacked up in the opposite order than the one we need.

This is a common enough scenario that there's a specific function called `Traverse` to address it, and a type for which `Traverse` is defined is called a *traversable*. Figure 17.1 shows the relationship between `Map` and `Traverse`.

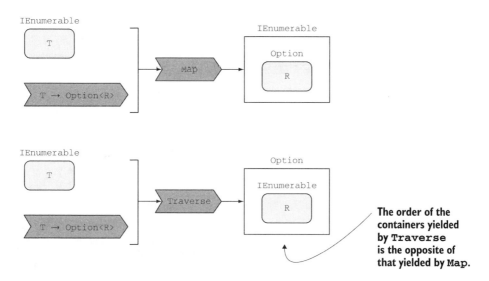

Figure 17.1 Comparing `Map` and `Traverse`

---

[1] You may remember from chapter 6 that we could use `Bind` instead of `Map` to filter out all the `None` values and only add up the numbers that were successfully parsed. That's not desirable for this scenario: we'd be silently removing values that the user probably mistyped in error, effectively giving an incorrect result.

Let's generalize the idea of a traversable:

- We have a traversable structure of T's, so let's indicate this with Tr<T>. In this example, it's IEnumerable<string>.
- We have a world-crossing function, f : T → A<R>, where A must be at least an applicative. In this example, it's Double.Parse, which has type string → Option<double>.
- We want to obtain an A<Tr<R>>.

The general signature for Traverse is in this form

```
Tr<T> → (T → A<R>) → A<Tr<R>>
```

Particularized for this example, it's

```
IEnumerable<T> → (T → Option<R>) → Option<IEnumerable<R>>
```

17.1.1 *Validating a list of values with monadic Traverse*

Let's see how we can go about implementing Traverse with the preceding signature. If you look at the top-level types in the signature, you'll see that we start with a list and end up with a single value. Remember, we reduce lists to a single value using Aggregate, which was covered in section 9.6.

Aggregate takes an accumulator and a reducer function, which combines each element in the list with the accumulator. The accumulator is returned as the result if the list is empty. This is easy; we just create an empty IEnumerable and lift it into an Option using Some, as the following listing shows.

> **Listing 17.1 Monadic `Traverse` with an `Option`-returning function**

```
public static Option<IEnumerable<R>> Traverse<T, R>
(
    this IEnumerable<T> ts,
    Func<T, Option<R>> f
)
=> ts.Aggregate
(
    seed: Some(Enumerable.Empty<R>()),      ◁  If the traversable is empty,
                                               lifts an empty instance
    func: (optRs, t) =>                     ◁  Extracts the accumulated list
        from rs in optRs                       of R's from the Option
        from r in f(t)                      ◁  Applies the function to
        select rs.Append(r)      ◁             the current element, and
);                                Appends the value to the    extracts the value from
                                  list, and lifts the resulting  the resulting Option
                                  list into an Option
```

Now, let's look at the reducer function—that's the interesting bit. Its type is

```
Option<IEnumerable<R>> → T → Option<IEnumerable<R>>
```

When we apply the function f to the value t, we get an Option<R>. After that, we must satisfy the signature:

```
Option<IEnumerable<R>> → Option<R> → Option<IEnumerable<R>>
```

Let's simplify this for a moment by removing the `Option` from each element:

```
IEnumerable<R> → R → IEnumerable<R>
```

Now it becomes clear that the problem is that of appending a single `R` to an `IEnumerable<R>`, yielding an `IEnumerable<R>` with all the elements traversed so far. The appending should happen within the elevated world of `Option` because all the values are wrapped in an `Option`. As you learned in chapter 10, we can apply functions in the elevated world in the applicative or the monadic way. Here we use the monadic flow.

Now that you've seen the definition of `Traverse`, let's go back to the scenario of parsing a comma-separated list of numbers typed by the user. The following listing shows how we can achieve this with `Traverse`.

Listing 17.2 Safely parses and sums a comma-separated list of numbers

```
using Double = LaYumba.Functional.Double;
using String = LaYumba.Functional.String;

var input = Console.ReadLine();
var result = Process(input);
Console.WriteLine(result);

static string Process(string input)
   => input.Split(',')          // Array<string>
      .Map(String.Trim)         // IEnumerable<string>
      .Traverse(Double.Parse)   // Option<IEnumerable<double>>
      .Map(Enumerable.Sum)      // Option<double>
      .Match
      (
         () => "Some of your inputs could not be parsed",
         (sum) => $"The sum is {sum}"
      );
```

In the preceding listing, the top-level statements perform I/O, while all the logic is in the `Process` function. Let's test it to see the behavior:

```
Process("1, 2, 3")
// => "The sum is 6"

Process("one, two, 3")
// => "Some of your inputs could not be parsed"
```

17.1.2 *Harvesting validation errors with applicative Traverse*

Let's improve error handling so we can tell the user which values are wrong. For that, we need `Validation`, which can contain a list of errors. This means we'll need an implementation of `Traverse` that takes a list of values and a `Validation`-returning function. This is shown in the following listing.

Listing 17.3 Monadic `Traverse` with a `Validation`-returning function

```
public static Validation<IEnumerable<R>> TraverseM<T, R>
(
   this IEnumerable<T> ts,
```

```
    Func<T, Validation<R>> f
)
=> ts.Aggregate
(
    seed: Valid(Enumerable.Empty<R>()),
    func: (valRs, t) => from rs in valRs
                        from r in f(t)
                        select rs.Append(r)
);
```

This implementation is similar to the implementation that takes an Option-returning function (listing 17.1) except for the signature and the fact that the Return function being used is Valid instead of Some. This duplication is due to the lack of an abstraction common to both Option and Validation.[2]

Notice that I've called the function TraverseM (for monadic) because the implementation is monadic. If one item fails validation, the validation function won't be called for any of the subsequent items.

If, instead, we want errors to accumulate, we should use the applicative flow (if you need a refresher on why this is the case, refer back to section 10.5). We can, therefore, define TraverseA (for applicative) with the same signature but using the applicative flow, as the following listing shows.

> **Listing 17.4   Applicative Traverse with a Validation-returning function**

```
static Func<IEnumerable<T>, T, IEnumerable<T>> Append<T>()
    => (ts, t) => ts.Append(t);

public static Validation<IEnumerable<R>> TraverseA<T, R>
(
    this IEnumerable<T> ts,
    Func<T, Validation<R>> f
)
=> ts.Aggregate
(
    seed: Valid(Enumerable.Empty<R>()),          ◁─── If the traversable is empty,
    func: (valRs, t) =>                                lifts an empty instance
        Valid(Append<R>())       ◁─── Lifts the Append function,
            .Apply(valRs)             particularized for R      Applies it to the
            .Apply(f(t))              ◁───                      accumulator ◁───
);                             ◁─── Applies f to the current element; the R wrapped in the
                                    resulting Validation is the second argument to Append.

public static Validation<IEnumerable<R>> Traverse<T, R>         For Validation, Traverse
    (this IEnumerable<T> list, Func<T, Validation<R>> f)        should default to the
    => TraverseA(list, f);         ◁───                         applicative implementation.
```

The implementation of TraverseA is similar to TraverseM, except that in the reducer function, the appending is done with the applicative rather than the monadic flow. As a result, the validation function f is called for *each* T in ts, and all validation errors will accumulate in the resulting Validation.

---

[2] The reasons for this were discussed in chapter 6, in the "Why is functor not an interface?" sidebar.

Because this is the behavior we usually want with `Validation`, I've defined `Traverse` to point to the applicative implementation `TraverseA`, but there's still scope for having `TraverseM` if you want a short-circuiting behavior.

The following listing shows the program, refactored to use `Validation`.

Listing 17.5 Safely parsing and summing a comma-separated list of numbers

```
static Validation<double> Validate(string s)
   => Double.Parse(s).Match
   (
      () => Error($"'{s}' is not a valid number"),
      (d) => Valid(d)
   );

static string Process(string input)
   => input.Split(',')          // Array<string>
      .Map(String.Trim)         // IEnumerable<string>
      .Traverse(Validate)       // Validation<IEnumerable<double>>
      .Map(Enumerable.Sum)      // Validation<double>
      .Match
      (
         errs => string.Join(", ", errs),
         sum => $"The sum is {sum}"
      );
```

The listing only shows the updated implementation of `Process` (the top-level statements are the same as previously). If we test this enhanced implementation, we now get this:

```
Process("1, 2, 3")
// => "The sum is 6"

Process("one, two, 3")
// => "'one' is not a valid number, 'two' is not a valid number"
```

As you can see, in the second example, the validation errors have accumulated as we have traversed the list of inputs. If we used the monadic implementation, `TraverseM`, we'd only get the first error.

17.1.3 *Applying multiple validators to a single value*

The preceding example demonstrates how to apply a single validation function to a list of values you want to validate. What about the case in which you have a single value to validate and many validation functions?

We tackled such a scenario in section 9.6.3, where we had a request object to validate and a list of validators, each checking that certain conditions for validity are met. As a reminder, we defined a `Validator` delegate to capture a function performing validation:

```
// T => Validation<T>
public delegate Validation<T> Validator<T>(T t);
```

The challenge was to write a single `Validator` function combining the validation of a list of `Validator`'s, harvesting all errors. We had to jump through a few hoops to define a `HarvestErrors` function with this behavior (listing 9.22).

Now that you know about using `Traverse` with a `Validation`-returning function, we can rewrite `HarvestErrors` much more concisely, as the following listing shows.

```
public static Validator<T> HarvestErrors<T>
   (params Validator<T>[] validators)
   => t
   => validators
      .Traverse(validate => validate(t))
      .Map(_ => t);
```

Here, `Traverse` returns a `Validation<IEnumerable<T>>`, collecting all the errors. If there are no errors, the inner value of type `IEnumerable<T>` will contain as many instances of the input value `t` as there are validators. The subsequent call to `Map` disregards this `IEnumerable` and replaces it with the original object being validated. Here's an example of using `HarvestErrors` in practice:

```
Validator<string> ShouldBeLowerCase
   = s => (s == s.ToLower())
      ? Valid(s)
      : Error($"{s} should be lower case");

Validator<string> ShouldBeOfLength(int n)
   => s => (s.Length == n)
      ? Valid(s)
      : Error($"{s} should be of length {n}");

Validator<string> ValidateCountryCode
   = HarvestErrors(ShouldBeLowerCase, ShouldBeOfLength(2));

ValidateCountryCode("us")
// => Valid(us)

ValidateCountryCode("US")
// => Invalid([US should be lower case])

ValidateCountryCode("USA")
// => Invalid([USA should be lower case, USA should be of length 2])
```

17.1.4 *Using Traverse with Task to await multiple results*

`Traverse` works with `Task` much as it does with `Validation`. We can define `TraverseA`, which uses the applicative flow and runs all tasks in parallel, `TraverseM`, which uses the monadic flow and runs the tasks sequentially, and `Traverse`, which defaults to `TraverseA` because running independent asynchronous operations in parallel is usually preferable. Given a list of long-running operations, we can use `Traverse` to obtain a single `Task` that we can use to await all the results.

In section 16.1.7, we looked at comparing flight fares from two airlines. With `Traverse`, we're equipped to deal with a list of airlines. Imagine that each airline's flights can be queried with a method that returns a `Task<IEnumerable<Flight>>`, and we want to get all flights available on a given date and route, sorted by price:

```
interface Airline
{
    Task<IEnumerable<Flight>> Flights
        (string origin, string destination, DateTime departure);
}
```

How do we get all flights from all the airlines? Notice what happens if we use `Map`:

```
IEnumerable<Airline> airlines;

IEnumerable<Task<IEnumerable<Flight>>> flights =
    airlines.Map(a => a.Flights(from, to, on));
```

We end up with an `IEnumerable<Task<IEnumerable<Flight>>>`. This isn't at all what we want!

With `Traverse`, instead, we'll end up with a `Task<IEnumerable<IEnumerable <Flight>>>`, a single task that completes when *all* airlines have been queried (and fails if any query fails). The task's inner value is a list of lists (one list for each airline), which can then be flattened and sorted to get our list of results sorted by price:

```
async Task<IEnumerable<Flight>> Search(IEnumerable<Airline> airlines
    , string origin, string dest, DateTime departure)
{
    var flights = await airlines
        .Traverse(a => a.Flights(origin, dest, departure));
    return flights.Flatten().OrderBy(f => f.Price);
}
```

`Flatten` is simply a convenience function that calls `Bind` with the identity function, hence flattening the nested `IEnumerable` into a single list including flights from all airlines. This list is then sorted by price.

Most of the time, you'll want the parallel behavior, so I've defined `Traverse` to be the same as `TraverseA`. On the other hand, if you have 100 tasks and the second task fails, then monadic traverse will save you from running 98 tasks that would still be kicked off when using applicative traverse. So the implementation you choose depends on the use case, and this is the reason for including both.

Let's look at one final variation on this example. In real life, you probably don't want your search to fail if one of perhaps dozens of queries to a third-party API fails. Imagine you want to display the best results available, like on many price comparison websites. If a provider's API is down, results from that provider won't be available, but we still want to see results from all the others.

The change is easy! We can use the `Recover` function shown in section 16.1.4 so that *each* query returns an empty list of flights if the remote query fails:

```
async Task<IEnumerable<Flight>> Search(IEnumerable<Airline> airlines
    , string origin, string dest, DateTime departure)
{
    var flights = await airlines
        .Traverse(a => a.Flights(origin, dest, departure)
                        .Recover(ex => Enumerable.Empty<Flight>()));

    return flights.Flatten().OrderBy(f => f.Price);
}
```

Here we have a function that queries several APIs in parallel, disregards any failures, and aggregates all the successful results into a single list sorted by price. I find this a great example of how composing core functions like `Traverse`, `Bind`, and others allows you to specify rich behavior with little code and effort.

17.1.5 *Defining Traverse for single-value structures*

So far you've seen how to use `Traverse` with an `IEnumerable` and a function that returns an `Option`, `Validation`, `Task`, or any other applicative. It turns out that `Traverse` is even more general. `IEnumerable` isn't the only traversable structure out there; you can define `Traverse` for many of the constructs you've seen in the book. If we take a nuts and bolts approach, we can see `Traverse` as a utility that stacks effects up the opposite way as when performing `Map`:

```
Map      : Tr<T> → (T → A<R>) → Tr<A<R>>
Traverse : Tr<T> → (T → A<R>) → A<Tr<R>>
```

If we have a function that returns an applicative `A`, `Map` returns a type with the `A` on the inside, whereas `Traverse` returns a type with the `A` on the outside.

For example, in chapter 8, we had a scenario in which we used `Map` to combine a `Validation`-returning function with an `Exceptional`-returning function. The code went along these lines:

```
Func<MakeTransfer, Validation<MakeTransfer>> validate;
Func<MakeTransfer, Exceptional<Unit>> save;

public Validation<Exceptional<Unit>> Handle(MakeTransfer request)
   => validate(request).Map(save);
```

What if, for some reason, we wanted to return an `Exceptional<Validation<Unit>>` instead? Well, now you know the trick: just replace `Map` with `Traverse`!

```
public Exceptional<Validation<Unit>> Handle(MakeTransfer request)
   => validate(request).Traverse(save);
```

But can we make `Validation` traversable? The answer is yes. Remember that we can view `Option` as a list with at most one element. The same goes for `Either`, `Validation`, and `Exceptional`: the success case can be treated as a traversable with a single element; the failure case as empty.

In this scenario, we need a definition of `Traverse` taking a `Validation` and an `Exceptional`-returning function. The following listing shows the implementation.

Listing 17.7 Making `Validation` traversable

```
public static Exceptional<Validation<R>> Traverse<T, R>
(
   this Validation<T> valT,
   Func<T, Exceptional<R>> f
)
=> valT.Match
```

```
(
    Invalid: errs => Exceptional(Invalid<R>(errs)),
    Valid: t => f(t).Map(Valid)
);
```

The base case is if the Validation is Invalid; that's analogous to the empty list case. Here we create a value of the required output type, *preserving* the validation errors. If the Validation is Valid, that means we should "traverse" the single element it contains, named t. We apply the Exception-returning function f to it to get an Exceptional<R> and then we Map the Valid function on it, which lifts the inner value r into a Validation<R>, giving us the required output type, Exceptional<Validation<R>>.

You can follow this pattern to define Traverse for the other one-or-no-value structures. Notice that once you've defined Traverse, then when you have, say, a Validation<Exceptional<T>> and want to reverse the order of the effects, you could just use Traverse with the identity function.

In summary, Traverse is useful not just to handle lists of elevated values but, more generally, whenever you have stacked effects. As you encode your application's requirements through Option, Validation, and others, Traverse is one of the tools you can use to ensure that the types don't get the better of you.

17.2 Combining asynchrony and validation (or any other two monadic effects)

Most enterprise applications are distributed and depend on a number of external systems, so much if not most of your code runs asynchronously. If you want to use constructs like Option or Validation, soon enough you'll deal with Task<Option<T>>, Task<Validation<T>>, Validation<Task<T>>, and so on.

17.2.1 The problem of stacked monads

These nested types can be difficult to work with. When you work within one monad, such as Option, everything is fine because you can use Bind to compose several Option-returning computations. But what if you have a function that returns an Option<Task<T>> and another function of type T → Option<R>? How can you combine them? And how would you use an Option<Task<T>> with a function of type T → Task<Option<R>>?

We can refer to this more generally as the problem of *stacked monads*. In order to illustrate this problem and how it can be addressed, let's revisit one of the examples from chapter 13. The following listing shows a skeletal version of the endpoint that handles API requests to make a transfer.

> **Listing 17.8 Skeleton of the `MakeTransfer` command handler**

```
public static void ConfigureMakeTransferEndpoint
(
    WebApplication app,
    Func<Guid, AccountState> getAccount,
    Action<Event> saveAndPublish
)
```

```
=> app.MapPost("/Transfer/Make", (MakeTransfer cmd) =>     <——|  Handles receiving
{                                                               a command

   var account = getAccount(cmd.DebitedAccountId);   <——|  Retrieves the account

   var (evt, newState) = account.Debit(cmd);              <—  Performs the state
                                                              transition; returns a
   saveAndPublish(evt);        <——|  Persists the event and publishes    tuple with the event
                                     it to interested parties            and the new state

   return Ok(new { newState.Balance });   <——|  Returns information to the
});                                              client about the new state
```

The preceding code serves as an outline. Next, you'll see how to add asynchrony, error handling, and validation.

First, we'll inject a new dependency to perform validation on the MakeTransfer command. Its type will be Validator<MakeTransfer>, which is a delegate with this signature:

```
MakeTransfer → Validation<MakeTransfer>
```

Next, we need to revise the signatures of the existing dependencies. When we call getAccount to retrieve the current state of an account, that operation will hit the database. We want to make it asynchronous, so the result type should be wrapped in a Task. Furthermore, errors can occur when connecting to the DB. Fortunately, Task already captures this. Finally, there's the possibility that the account doesn't exist (no events were ever recorded for the given ID), so the result should also be wrapped in an Option. The full signature will be

```
getAccount : Guid → Task<Option<AccountState>>
```

Saving and publishing an event should also be asynchronous so that the signature should be

```
saveAndPublish : Event → Task
```

Finally, remember that Account.Debit also returns its result wrapped in a Validation:

```
Account.Debit :
   AccountState → MakeTransfer → Validation<(Event, AccountState)>
```

Now let's write a skeleton of the command handler with all these effects in place:

```
public static void ConfigureMakeTransferEndpoint
(
   WebApplication app,
   Validator<MakeTransfer> validate,
   Func<Guid, Task<Option<AccountState>>> getAccount,
   Func<Event, Task> saveAndPublish
)
=> app.MapPost("/Transfer/Make", (MakeTransfer transfer) =>
{
   Task<Validation<AccountState>> outcome = // ...

   return outcome.Map
   (
```

```
Faulted: ex => StatusCode(StatusCodes.Status500InternalServerError),
Completed: val => val.Match
(
    Invalid: errs => BadRequest(new { Errors = errs }),
    Valid: newState => Ok(new { Balance = newState.Balance })
)
    );
});
```

So far, we've listed the dependencies with the new signatures, established that the main workflow will return a `Task<Validation<AccountState>>` (because there will be some asynchronous operations, and there will be some validation), and mapped its possible states to appropriately populated HTTP responses. Now comes the real work: How do we put together the functions we need to consume?

17.2.2 *Reducing the number of effects*

First, we'll need a couple of adapters. Notice that `getAccount` returns an `Option` (wrapped in a `Task`), meaning we should cater for the case in which no account is found. What does it mean if there's no account? It means the command is incorrectly populated, so we can map `None` to a `Validation` with an appropriate error.

`LaYumba.Functional` defines `ToValidation`, a natural transformation that "promotes" an `Option` to a `Validation`. It maps `Some` to `Valid`, using the `Option`'s inner value, and `None` to `Invalid`, using the provided `Error`:

```
public static Validation<T> ToValidation<T>
    (this Option<T> opt, Error error)
    => opt.Match
    (
        () => Invalid(error),
        (t) => Valid(t)
    );
```

In the case of `getAccount`, the returned `Option` is wrapped in a `Task` so that we don't apply `ToValidation` directly, but use `Map` instead:

```
Func<Guid, Task<Option<AccountState>>> getAccount;

Func<Guid, Task<Validation<AccountState>>> getAccountVal
    = id => getAccount(id)
        .Map(opt => opt.ToValidation(Errors.UnknownAccountId(id)));
```

At least now we're only dealing with two monads: `Task` and `Validation`.

Second, `saveAndPublish` returns a `Task`, which doesn't have an inner value, so it won't compose well. Let's write an adapter that returns a `Task<Unit>` instead:

```
Func<Event, Task> saveAndPublish;

Func<Event, Task<Unit>> saveAndPublishF
    = async e =>
    {
        await saveAndPublish(e);
        return Unit();
    };
```

Let's look again at the functions we must compose in order to compute the workflow's outcome:

```
validate        : MakeTransfer → Validation<MakeTransfer>
getAccountVal   : Guid → Task<Validation<AccountState>>
Account.Debit   : AccountState → MakeTransfer
                  → Validation<(Event, AccountState)>
saveAndPublishF : Event → Task<Unit>
```

If we used `Map` the whole way through, we'd get a result type of `Validation<Task<Validation<Validation<Task<Unit>>>>>`. We could try using a sophisticated combination of calls to `Traverse` to change the order of monads and `Bind` to flatten them. Honestly, I tried. It took me about half an hour to figure it out, and the result was cryptic and not something you'd be keen to ever refactor!

We have to look for a better way. Ideally, we'd like to write something like this:

```
from tr in validate(transfer)
from acc in GetAccount(tr.DebitedAccountId)
from result in Account.Debit(acc, tr)
from _ in SaveAndPublish(result.Event)
select result.NewState
```

We'd then have some underlying implementations of `Select` and `SelectMany` that figure out how to combine the types together. Unfortunately, this can't be achieved in a general enough way: add too many overloads of `SelectMany` and this will cause overload resolution to fail. The good news is that we can have a close approximation. You'll see this next.

17.2.3 *LINQ expressions with a monad stack*

We can implement `Bind` and the LINQ query pattern for a specific monad stack; in this case, `Task<Validation<T>>`.[3] This allows us to compose several functions that return a `Task<Validation<>>` within a LINQ expression. With this in mind, we can adapt our existing functions to this type by following these rules:

- If we have a `Task<Validation<T>>` (or a function that returns such a type), then there's nothing to do. That's the monad we're working in.
- If we have a `Validation<T>`, we can use the `Async` function to lift it into a `Task`, obtaining a `Task<Validation<T>>`.
- If we have a `Task<T>`, we can map the `Valid` function onto it to again obtain `Task<Validation<T>>`.
- If we have a `Validation<Task<T>>`, we can call `Traverse` with the identity function to swap the containers around.

---

[3] I won't show the implementation, which is included in the code samples. This really is library code, not code that a library user should worry about. You may also ask whether an implementation is required for every stack of monads, and indeed, this is the case, given the pattern-based approach we've been following in the book.

So our previous query needs to be modified as follows:

```
from tr in Async(validate(transfer))
from acc in GetAccount(tr.DebitedAccountId)
from result in Async(Account.Debit(acc, tr))
from _ in SaveAndPublish(result.Event).Map(Valid)
select result.NewState;
```

**Uses `Async` to lift the `Validation`
into a `Task<Validation<>>`**

**Uses `Map(Valid)` to
turn a `Task` into a
`Task<Validation<>>`**

`GetAccount` **returns a `Task<Validation<>>`,
which is the monad stack we're working with.**

This will work as long as the appropriate implementations of `Select` and `SelectMany` for `Task<Validation<T>>` are defined. As you can see, the resulting code is still reasonably clean and easy to understand and refactor. We just had to add a few calls to `Async` and `Map(Valid)` to make the types line up. The following listing shows the complete implementation of the command handler, refactored to include asynchrony and validation.

Listing 17.9 The command handler, including asynchrony and validation

```
public static void ConfigureMakeTransferEndpoint
(
    WebApplication app,
    Validator<MakeTransfer> validate,
    Func<Guid, Task<Option<AccountState>>> getAccount,
    Func<Event, Task> saveAndPublish
)
{
    var getAccountVal = (Guid id) => getAccount(id)
        .Map(opt => opt.ToValidation(Errors.UnknownAccountId(id)));

    var saveAndPublishF = async (Event e)
        => { await saveAndPublish(e); return Unit(); };

    app.MapPost("/Transfer/Make", (MakeTransfer transfer) =>
    {
        Task<Validation<AccountState>> outcome =
            from tr in Async(validate(transfer))
            from acc in getAccountVal(tr.DebitedAccountId)
            from result in Async(Account.Debit(acc, tr))
            from _ in saveAndPublishF(result.Event).Map(Valid)
            select result.NewState;

        return outcome.Map
        (
            Faulted: ex => StatusCode(StatusCodes.Status500InternalServerError),
            Completed: val => val.Match
            (
                Invalid: errs => BadRequest(new { Errors = errs }),
                Valid: newState => Ok(new { Balance = newState.Balance })
            )
        );
    });
}
```

Let's look at the code. First, the operations that need to be completed as part of the workflow are injected as dependencies. Next, we have a couple of adapter functions to go from `Option` to `Validation` and from `Task` to `Task<Unit>`. We then configure the endpoint that handles transfer requests. Here, we use a LINQ comprehension to combine the different operations in the workflow. Finally, we translate the resulting outcome into an object representing the HTTP response we'd like to return.

As you saw in this chapter, although monads are nice and pleasant to work with in the context of a single monadic type, things get more complicated when you need to combine several monadic effects. Note that this isn't just the case in C# but even in functional languages. Even in Haskell, where monads are used everywhere, stacked monads are usually dealt with via the rather clunky *monad transformers*. A more promising approach is called *composable effects*, and it has first-class support in a rather niche functional language called Idris. It's possible that the programming languages of the future will not only have syntax optimized for monads, such as LINQ, but also syntax optimized for monad stacks.

As a practical guideline, remember that combining several monads adds complexity, and limit the nesting of different monads to what you really need. For instance, once we simplified things in the previous example by transforming `Option` to `Validation`, we only had to deal with two stacked monads rather than three. Similarly, if you have a `Task<Try<T>>`, you can probably reduce it to a `Task<T>` because `Task` can capture any exceptions raised when running the `Try`. Finally, if you find yourself always using a stack of two monads, you can write a new type that encapsulates both effects into that single type. For example, `Task` encapsulates both asynchrony and error handling.

Summary

- If you have two monads, A and B, you might like to stack them up in values like A<B<T>> to combine the effects of both monads.
- You can use `Traverse` to invert the order of monads in the stack.
- Implementing the LINQ query pattern for such a stack allows you to combine A's, B's, and A<B<>>'s with relative ease.
- Still, stacked monads tend to be cumbersome, so use them sparingly.

18

Data streams and
the Reactive Extensions

This chapter covers

- Using `IObservable` to represent data streams
- Creating, transforming, and combining
  `IObservables`
- Knowing when you should use `IObservable`

If you've ever been to a financial hub like Wall Street or Canary Wharf, you've probably seen a *ticker board*, a luminous board displaying the latest price at which the most widely traded stocks are being traded. This is a good representation of a *data stream*: a stream of related values that are delivered through time.

Traders (both human and algorithms) keep an eye on the prices so that they can *react* to price changes: if a stock's price rises or falls to a given level, they may decide to buy or sell, according to their investment strategy. This is, in essence, how *reactive programming* works: you define and consume data streams, potentially transforming the data in the streams in interesting ways, and define how your program should react to the data it consumes.

For example, if you have an Internet of Things in your home, you may have sensors that broadcast certain parameters (like room brightness or temperatures) and devices that react to changes in those parameters (regulating the window shutters or the air conditioning).

Or, in an event-sourced system like I described in chapter 13, you can publish the events as a stream and define downstream processing of those events in order to, say, recompute an account's balance with every transaction and send the account holder a notification if the balance turns negative.

In this chapter, you'll learn to model data streams with the `IObservable` interface and to use the Reactive Extensions (Rx) to create, transform, and combine `IObservables`. We'll also discuss what sort of scenarios benefit from using `IObservable`.

Rx is a set of libraries for working with `IObservables`, much like LINQ provides utilities for working with `IEnumerables`. Rx is a rich framework, so thorough coverage is beyond the scope of this chapter. Instead, we'll just look at some basic features and applications of `IObservable` and how it relates to other abstractions we've covered so far.

18.1 *Representing data streams with IObservable*

If you think of an array as a sequence of values in space (space in memory, that is), then you can think of `IObservable` as a sequence of values in time:

- With an `IEnumerable`, you can enumerate its values at your leisure.
- With an `IObservable`, you can observe the values as they come.

As with `IAsyncEnumerable`, which we discussed in chapter 16, `IObservable` is like an `IEnumerable` in that it contains several values, and it's like a `Task` in that values are delivered asynchronously. Table 18.1 shows how `IObservable` relates to other abstractions.

Table 18.1 How `IObservable` compares with other abstractions

	Synchronous	Asynchronous
Single value	T	Task<T>
Multiple values	IEnumerable<T>	IAsyncEnumerable<T> IObservable<T>

`IObservable` is, therefore, more general than both `IEnumerable` and `Task`. You can view `IEnumerable` as a special case of `IObservable` that produces all its values right away, and you can think of `Task` as a special case of `IObservable` that only produces a single value. What's the difference between `IObservable` and `IAsyncEnumerable`, and why do we need both?

- `IAsyncEnumerable` is consumer-centric: the component that consumes the data asks the producer for some data and receives an async stream of values in return—the data is "pulled" by the consumer. The consumer *interacts* with the producer, hence the libraries developed to work with `IAsyncEnumerable` are called the *Interactive Extensions* (Ix). These packages are named System .Interactive.*. (IAsyncEnumerable itself is included in the BCL in the System.Collections.Generic namespace.)

- IObservable is producer-centric: the consumer subscribes to the data, which is "pushed" out by the producer. The consumer merely *reacts* to the values it receives; hence the libraries developed to work with IObservable are called the *Reactive Extensions* (Rx). These packages are named System.Reactive.*. (IObservable itself is included in the BCL in the System namespace.)

> **NOTE** Both Rx and Ix are maintained by the .NET Foundation; they are open source and hosted at https://github.com/dotnet/reactive.

Rx has been around for many years (there are implementations of Rx not only in .NET but in many other languages), so there are more resources and know-how at your disposal. By comparison, async streams and Ix are a recent addition; and yet, because of native language support since C# 8 via the yield return and await keywords (which we saw in chapter 16), it feels easier to create and consume them.

18.1.1 A sequence of values in time

The easiest way to develop an intuition about IObservable is through *marble diagrams*. Figure 18.1 shows a few examples. Each IObservable is represented with an arrow, representing time, and marbles, representing values produced by the IObservable.

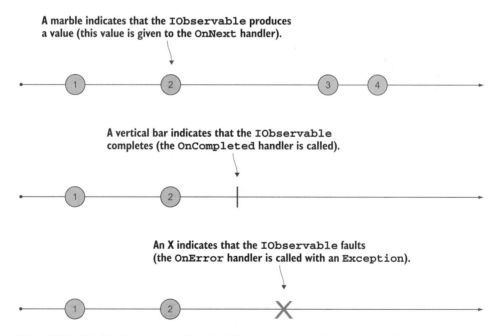

Figure 18.1 Marble diagrams provide an intuitive way to understand IObservables.

The image illustrates that an `IObservable` can produce three different kinds of messages:

- `OnNext` signals a new value, so if your `IObservable` represents a stream of events, `OnNext` will be fired when an event is ready to be consumed. This is an `IObservable`'s most important message, and often the only one you'll be interested in.
- `OnCompleted` signals that the `IObservable` is done and will signal no more values.
- `OnError` signals that an error has occurred and provides the relevant `Exception`.

The `IObservable` contract

The `IObservable` contract specifies that an `IObservable` should produce messages according to the following grammar:

```
OnNext* (OnCompleted|OnError)?
```

That is, an `IObservable` can produce an arbitrary number of `T`'s (`OnNext`), possibly followed by a single value indicating either successful completion (`OnCompleted`) or an error (`OnError`). This means that there are three possibilities in terms of completion. An `IObservable` can

- Never complete
- Complete normally with a completion message
- Complete abnormally; in which case, it produces an `Exception`

An `IObservable` *never* produces any values after it's completed regardless of whether it completes normally or with an error.

18.1.2 *Subscribing to an IObservable*

Observ-*ables* work in tandem with observ-*ers*. Simply put,

- Observers produce values
- Observers consume them

If you want to consume the messages produced by an `IObservable`, you can create an observer and associate it with an `IObservable` via the `Subscribe` method. The simplest way to do this is by providing a callback that handles the values produced by the `IObservable` like so:

```
using System;
using System.Reactive.Linq;

IObservable<int> nums = //...

nums.Subscribe(Console.WriteLine);
```

Exposes the `IObservable` interface

Exposes the `Subscribe` extension method used below

When I say that `nums` "produces" an `int` value, all I really mean is that it calls the given function (in this case, `Console.WriteLine`) with the value. The result of the preceding code is that when `nums` produces an `int`, it's printed out.

I find the naming a bit confusing; you'd expect an `IObservable` to have an `Observe` method, but instead, it's called `Subscribe`. Basically, you can think of the two as synonyms: an observer is a subscriber, and in order to observe an `IObservable` you subscribe to it.

What about the other types of messages an `IObservable` can produce? You can provide handlers for those as well. For instance, the following listing shows a convenience method, `Trace`, that attaches an observer to an `IObservable`; this observer simply prints a diagnostic messages whenever the `IObservable` signals. We'll use this method later for debugging.

Listing 18.1 Subscribing to the messages produced by an `IObservable`

```
using static System.Console;

public static IDisposable Trace<T>
    (this IObservable<T> source, string name)
    => source.Subscribe
    (
        onNext: t => WriteLine($"{name} -> {t}"),
        onError: ex => WriteLine($"{name} ERROR: {ex.Message}"),
        onCompleted: () => WriteLine($"{name} END")
    );
```

`Subscribe` actually takes three handlers (all are optional arguments) to handle the different messages that an `IObservable<T>` can produce. It should be clear why the handlers are optional: if you don't expect an `IObservable` to ever complete, there's no point in providing an `onComplete` handler.

A more OO option for subscribing is to call `Subscribe` with an `IObserver`, an interface that, unsurprisingly, exposes `OnNext`, `OnError`, and `OnCompleted` methods.[1]

Also notice that `Subscribe` returns an `IDisposable` (the subscription). By disposing it, you unsubscribe.

In this section, you've seen some of the basic concepts and terminology around `IObservable`. It's a lot to absorb, but don't worry, things will become clearer as you see some examples. These are the basic ideas to keep in mind:

- Observables produce values; observers consume them.
- You associate an observer with an observable by using `Subscribe`.
- An observable produces a value by calling the observers' `OnNext` handler.

18.2 Creating IObservables

You now know how to consume the data in a stream by subscribing to an `IObservable`. But how do you get an `IObservable` in the first place? The `IObservable` and `IObserver` interfaces are included in .NET Standard, but if you want to create or perform many

---

[1] `IObserver` is the method declared in the `IObservable` interface. The overload that takes the callbacks is an extension method.

other operations on `IObservables`, you'll typically use the Reactive Extensions (Rx) by installing the `System.Reactive` package.[2]

The recommended way to create `IObservables` is by using one of several dedicated methods included in the static `Observable` class; we'll look at some next. I recommend you follow along in the REPL whenever possible.

18.2.1 Creating a timer

A timer can be modeled with an `IObservable` that signals at regular intervals. We can represent it with a marble diagram as follows:

This is a good way to start experimenting with `IObservables` because it's simple but does include the element of time. The code in the following listing uses `Observable.Interval` to create a timer.

> **Listing 18.2 Creating an `IObservable` that signals every second**

```
using System.Reactive.Linq;

var oneSec = TimeSpan.FromSeconds(1);
IObservable<long> ticks = Observable.Interval(oneSec);
```

Here we define `ticks` as an `IObservable` that will begin signaling after one second, producing a `long` counter value that increments every second, starting at 0. Notice I said "will begin" signaling? The resulting `IObservable` is lazy, so unless there's a subscriber, nothing will actually happen. Why talk, if nobody's listening?

If we want to see some tangible results, we need to subscribe to the `IObservable`. We can do this with the `Trace` method defined earlier:

```
ticks.Trace("ticks");
```

At this point, you'll start to see the following messages appear in the console, one second apart:

```
ticks -> 0
ticks -> 1
ticks -> 2
ticks -> 3
ticks -> 4
...
```

---

[2] Rx includes several libraries. The main library, `System.Reactive`, bundles the packages you'll most commonly need: `System.Reactive.Interfaces`, `System.Reactive.Core`, `System.Reactive.Linq`, and `System.Reactive.PlatformServices`. There are several other packages that are useful in more specialized scenarios, such as if you're using Windows forms.

Because this IObservable never completes, you'll have to reset the REPL to stop the noise—sorry!

18.2.2 Using Subject to tell an IObservable when it should signal

Another way to create an IObservable is by instantiating a Subject. A Subject is an IObservable you can imperatively tell to produce a value, which it will, in turn, push out to its observers. For example, the following listing shows a program that turns inputs from the console into values signaled by a Subject.

Listing 18.3 Modeling user inputs as a stream

```
using System.Reactive.Subjects;
using static System.Console;

var inputs = new Subject<string>();          ◁── Creates
                                                  a Subject
using (inputs.Trace("inputs"))      ◁──  Subscribes to
{                                        the Subject
    for (string input; (input = ReadLine()) != "q";)      Tells the Subject to
        inputs.OnNext(input);                      ◁──    produce a value, which it
                                                          pushes to its observers
    inputs.OnCompleted();           ◁──  Tells the Subject
}       ◁──  Leaving the using block       to signal completion
             disposes the subscription.
```

Every time the user types in some input, the code pushes that value to the Subject by calling its OnNext method. When the user types "q," the code exits the for loop and calls the Subject's OnCompleted method, signaling that the stream has ended. Here we've subscribed to the stream of inputs using the Trace method defined in listing 18.1, so we'll get a diagnostic message printed for each user input.

An interaction with the program looks like this (user inputs in bold):

```
hello
inputs -> hello
world
inputs -> world
q
inputs END
```

> **Avoid using** Subject
>
> Subject is useful for demonstrative purposes, but it works *imperatively* (you tell the Subject when to fire) and this goes somewhat counter to the *reactive* philosophy of Rx (you specify how to react to certain things when they happen).
>
> For this reason, it's recommended that you avoid Subjects whenever possible and instead use other methods such as Observable.Create, which you'll see next.
>
> As an exercise, try to rewrite the code in listing 18.3 using Observable.Create to create an IObservable of user inputs.

18.2.3 *Creating IObservables from callback-based subscriptions*

If your system subscribes to an external data source, such as a message queue, event broker, or publisher/subscriber, you can model that data source as an IObservable.

For example, Redis can be used as a publisher/subscriber. Redis's API exposes a Subscribe method allowing you to register a callback that receives messages published on Redis on a given channel (a Redis channel is just a string; it allows subscribers to specify what messages they're interested in). The following listing shows how you can use Observable.Create to create an IObservable that will signal whenever messages are received from Redis.

Listing 18.4 Creating an `IObservable` from messages published to Redis

```
using StackExchange.Redis;
using System.Reactive.Linq;

ConnectionMultiplexer redis
    = ConnectionMultiplexer.Connect("localhost");

IObservable<RedisValue> RedisNotifications          Create takes an observer, so the
(                                                    given function is only called
    RedisChannel channel                             when a subscription is made.
)
=> Observable.Create<RedisValue>(observer =>    ◁    Converts from the callback-
{                                                    based implementation of
    var sub = redis.GetSubscriber();                 Subscribe to values
    sub.Subscribe(channel, (_, val) => observer.OnNext(val));   produced by the IObservable
    return () => sub.Unsubscribe(channel);    ◁    Returns a function that will be called
});                                                 when the subscription is disposed
```

The preceding method returns an IObservable that produces the values received from Redis on the given channel. You could use this as follows:

```
RedisChannel weather = "weather";               Gets an IObservable that
                                                signals when messages are
var weatherUpdates = RedisNotifications(weather);  ◁  published on the weather channel
weatherUpdates.Subscribe(
    onNext: val => WriteLine($"It's {val} out there"));  ◁  Subscribes to the
                                                            IObservable
redis.GetDatabase(0).Publish(weather, "stormy");
// prints: It's stormy out there                Publishing a value causes
                                                weatherUpdates to
                                                signal; the onNext handler
                                                is called as a result.
```

You may ask, "What have we gained exactly?" After all, we could have registered a callback using Redis's Subscribe method to handle messages; instead, we now have an IObservable and need to Subscribe to *it* to handle messages. The point is, with an IObservable, we can leverage the many operators included in Rx (which we'll discuss in section 18.3) as well as the schedulers (which are used to optimize performance and are beyond the scope of this chapter).

18.2.4 *Creating IObservables from simpler structures*

I said that IObservable<T> is more general than a value T, a Task<T>, or an IEnumerable <T>, so let's see how each of these can be promoted to an IObservable. This becomes useful if you want to combine one of these less powerful structures with an IObservable.

Return allows you to lift a single value into an IObservable that looks like this:

That is, it immediately produces the value and then completes. Here's an example:

```
IObservable<string> justHello = Observable.Return("hello");
justHello.Trace("justHello");

// prints: justHello -> hello
//         justHello END
```

Return takes a value, T, and lifts it into an IObservable<T>. This is the first container where the Return function is actually called Return!

Let's see about creating an IObservable from a single asynchronous value—a Task. Here, we have an IObservable that looks like this:

After some time, we'll get a single value, immediately followed by the signal for completion. In code, it looks like this:

```
Observable.FromAsync(() => RatesApi.GetRateAsync("USDEUR"))
    .Trace("singleUsdEur");

// prints: singleUsdEur -> 0.92
//         singleUsdEur END
```

Finally, an IObservable created from an IEnumerable looks like this:

That is, it immediately produces all the values in the IEnumerable and completes:

```
IEnumerable<char> e = new[] { 'a', 'b', 'c' };
IObservable<char> chars = e.ToObservable();
chars.Trace("chars");

// prints: chars -> a
//         chars -> b
//         chars -> c
//         chars END
```

You've now seen many, but not all, methods for creating `IObservable`s. You may end up creating `IObservable`s in other ways; for example, in GUI applications, you can turn events such as mouse clicks into event streams by using `Observable.FromEvent` and `FromEventPattern`.

Now that you know about creating and subscribing to `IObservable`, let's move on to the most fascinating area: transforming and combining different streams.

18.3 *Transforming and combining data streams*

The power of using streams comes from the many ways in which you can combine them and define new streams based on existing ones. Rather than dealing with individual values in a stream (like in most event-driven designs), you deal with the stream as a whole.

Rx offers a lot of functions (often called *operators*) to transform and combine `IObservable`s in a variety of ways. I'll discuss the most commonly used ones and add a few operators of my own. You'll recognize the typical traits of a functional API: purity and composability.

18.3.1 *Stream transformations*

You can create new observables by transforming an existing observable in some way. One of the simplest operations is mapping. This is achieved with the `Select` method, which works (as with any other container) by applying the given function to each element in the stream, as figure 18.2 shows.

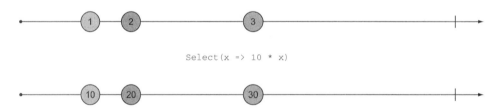

Figure 18.2 `Select` **maps a function onto a stream.**

Here's some code that creates a timer and then maps a simple function on it:

```
var oneSec = TimeSpan.FromSeconds(1);
var ticks = Observable.Interval(oneSec);

ticks.Select(n => n * 10)
   .Trace("ticksX10");
```

We're attaching an observer on the last line with the `Trace` method, so the preceding code will cause the following messages to be printed every second:

```
ticksX10 -> 0
ticksX10 -> 10
ticksX10 -> 20
```

```
ticksX10 -> 30
ticksX10 -> 40
...
```

Because `Select` follows the LINQ query pattern, we can write the same thing using LINQ:

```
from n in ticks select n * 10
```

Using `Select`, we can rewrite our simple program that checks exchange rates (first introduced in listing 15.1) in terms of observables:

```
public static void Main()
{
    var inputs = new Subject<string>();        The stream of values
                                               entered by the user

    var rates =
        from pair in inputs                    Maps user inputs to the
        select RatesApi.GetRateAsync(pair).Result;    corresponding retrieved values

    using (inputs.Trace("inputs"))      Subscribes to both streams
    using (rates.Trace("rates"))        to produce debug messages
        for (string input; (input = ReadLine().ToUpper()) != "Q";)
            inputs.OnNext(input);
}
```

Here, `inputs` represents the stream of currency pairs entered by the user, and in `rates`, we map those pairs to the corresponding values retrieved from the web. We're subscribing to both observables with the usual `Trace` method, so an interaction with this program could be as follows:

```
eurusd
inputs -> EURUSD
rates -> 1.0852
chfusd
inputs -> CHFUSD
rates -> 1.0114
```

Notice, however, that in the code, we have a blocking call to `Result`. In a real application, we wouldn't want to block a thread, so how could we avoid that?

We saw that a `Task` can easily be promoted to an `IObservable`. If we promote the `Task` of retrieving each rate from the remote API to an `IObservable` rather than waiting for its result, then we get an `IObservable` of `IObservables`. Sound familiar? `Bind`! We can use `SelectMany` instead of `Select`, which flattens the result into a single `IObservable`. We can, therefore, rewrite the definition of the `rates` stream as follows:

```
var rates = inputs.SelectMany
    (pair => Observable.FromAsync(() => RatesApi.GetRateAsync(pair)));
```

`Observable.FromAsync` promotes the `Task` returned by `GetRateAsync` to an `IObservable`, and `SelectMany` flattens all these `IObservables` into a single `IObservable`.

Because it's always possible to promote a `Task` to an `IObservable`, an overload of `SelectMany` exists that does just that (this is similar to how we overloaded `Bind` to work with an `IEnumerable` and an `Option`-returning function in section 6.5). This means we can avoid explicitly calling `FromAsync` and return a `Task` instead. Furthermore, we can use a LINQ query:

```
var rates =
    from pair in inputs
    from rate in RatesApi.GetRateAsync(pair)
    select rate;
```

The program thus modified works the same way as before but without the blocking call to `Result`.

IObservable also supports many of the other operations that are supported by IEnumerable, such as filtering with `Where`, `Take` (takes the first *n* values), `Skip`, `First`, and so on.

18.3.2   *Combining and partitioning streams*

There are also many operators that allow you to combine two streams into a single one. For example, `Concat` produces all the values of one `IObservable`, followed by all the values in another, as figure 18.3 shows.

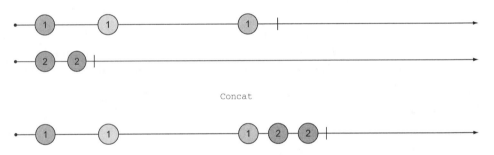

Figure 18.3   Concat waits for an IObservable to complete and then produces elements from the other IObservable.

For instance, in our exchange rate lookup, we have an observable called `rates` with the retrieved rates. If we want an observable of all the messages the program should output to the console, this must include the retrieved rates but also an initial message prompting the user for some input. We can lift this single message into an `IObservable` with `Return` and then use `Concat` to combine it with the other messages:

```
IObservable<decimal> rates = //...

IObservable<string> outputs = Observable
    .Return("Enter a currency pair like 'EURUSD', or 'q' to quit")
    .Concat(rates.Select(Decimal.ToString));
```

In fact, the need to provide a starting value for an `IObservable` is so common that there's a dedicated function for it—`StartWith`. The preceding code is equivalent to this:

```
var outputs = rates.Select(Decimal.ToString)
    .StartWith("Enter a currency pair like 'EURUSD', or 'q' to quit");
```

Whereas Concat waits for the left IObservable to complete before producing values from the right observable, Merge combines values from two IObservables without delay, as figure 18.4 shows.

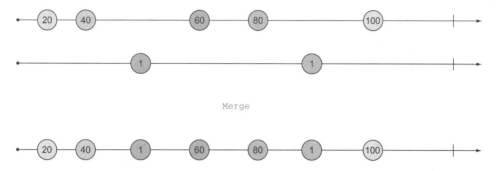

Figure 18.4 **Merge merges two IObservables into one.**

For example, if you have a stream of valid values and one of error messages, you could combine them with Merge as follows:

```
IObservable<decimal> rates = //...
IObservable<string> errors = //...

var outputs = rates.Select(Decimal.ToString)
   .Merge(errors);
```

Just as you might want to merge values from different streams, the opposite operation—partitioning a stream according to some criterion—is also often useful. Figure 18.5 illustrates this.

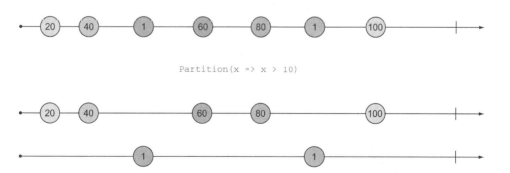

Figure 18.5 **Partitioning an IObservable according to a predicate**

Partition returns a pair of IObservables, so you can destructure it like this:

```
var (evens, odds) = ticks.Partition(x => x % 2 == 0);
```

Partitioning an `IObservable` of values is roughly equivalent to an `if` when dealing with a single value, so it's useful when you have a stream of values that you want to process differently, depending on some condition. For example, if you have a stream of messages and some criterion for validation, you can partition the stream into two streams of valid and invalid messages and process them accordingly.

18.3.3 *Error handling with IObservable*

Error handling when working with `IObservable` works differently from what you might expect. In most programs, an uncaught exception either causes the whole application to crash or causes the processing of a single message/request to fail, while subsequent requests work fine. To illustrate how things work differently in Rx, consider this version of our program for looking up exchange rates:

```
var inputs = new Subject<string>();

var rates =
    from pair in inputs
    from rate in RatesApi.GetRateAsync(pair)
    select rate;

var outputs = from r in rates select r.ToString();

using (inputs.Trace("inputs"))
using (rates.Trace("rates"))
using (outputs.Trace("outputs"))
    for (string input; (input = ReadLine().ToUpper()) != "Q";)
        inputs.OnNext(input);
```

The program captures three streams, each dependent on another (`outputs` is defined in terms of `rates`, and `rates` is defined in terms of `inputs`, as figure 18.6 shows), and we're printing diagnostic messages for all of them with `Trace`.

Figure 18.6 Simple dataflow between three `IObservable`s

Now look what happens if you break the program by passing an invalid currency pair:

```
eurusd
inputs -> EURUSD
rates -> 1.0852
outputs -> 1.0852
chfusd
inputs -> CHFUSD
rates -> 1.0114
outputs -> 1.0114
xxx
inputs -> XXX
rates ERROR: Input string was not in a correct format.
outputs ERROR: Input string was not in a correct format.
chfusd
inputs -> CHFUSD
eurusd
inputs -> EURUSD
```

What this shows is that once `rates` errors, it never signals again. This behavior is as specified in the `IObservable` contract (see the sidebar on "The **IObservable** contract"). As a result, everything downstream is also "dead." But `IObservables` upstream of the failed one are fine: `inputs` is still signaling, as would any other `IObservables` defined in terms of `inputs`.

To prevent your system from going into such a state, where a branch of the dataflow dies while the remaining graph keeps functioning, you can use the techniques you learned for functional error handling.

The following listing shows the implementation of `Safely`, a helper function included in `LaYumba.Functional` that allows you to safely apply a `Task`-returning function to each element in a stream. The result is a pair of streams: a stream of successfully computed values and a stream of exceptions.

Listing 18.5 Safely performing a `Task` and returning two streams

```
public static (IObservable<R> Completed, IObservable<Exception> Faulted)
   Safely<T, R>(this IObservable<T> ts, Func<T, Task<R>> f)
   => ts
      .SelectMany(t => f(t).Map(              Converts each Task<R> to a
         Faulted: ex => ex,                   Task<Exceptional<R>> to
         Completed: r => Exceptional(r)))     get a stream of Exceptionals
      .Partition();

static (IObservable<T> Successes, IObservable<Exception> Exceptions)
   Partition<T>(this IObservable<Exceptional<T>> excTs)
{
   bool IsSuccess(Exceptional<T> ex)                  Partitions a stream of
      => ex.Match(_ => false, _ => true);            Exceptionals into
                                                     successfully computed
   T ExtractValue(Exceptional<T> ex)                 values and exceptions
      => ex.Match(_ => default, t => t);

   Exception ExtractException(Exceptional<T> ex)
      => ex.Match(exc => exc, _ => default);

   var (ts, errs) = excTs.Partition(IsSuccess);
   return
   (
      Successes: ts.Select(ExtractValue),
      Exceptions: errs.Select(ExtractException)
   );
}
```

For each `T` in the given stream, we apply the `Task`-returning function `f`. We then use the binary overload of `Map` defined in section 16.1.4 to convert each resulting `Task<R>` to a `Task<Exceptional<R>>`. This is where we gain safety: instead of an inner value `R` that throws an exception when it's accessed, we have an `Exceptional<R>` in the appropriate state. `SelectMany` flattens away the `Tasks` in the stream and returns a stream of `Exceptionals`. We can then partition this in successes and exceptions.

With this in place, we can refactor our program to handle errors more gracefully:

```
var (rates, errors) = inputs.Safely(RatesApi.GetRateAsync);
```

18.3.4 Putting it all together

The following listing showcases the various techniques you've learned in this section. It shows the exchange rates lookup program, refactored to safely handle errors, and without the debug information.

Listing 18.6   The program refactored to safely handle errors

```
public static void Main()
{
    var inputs = new Subject<string>();

    var (rates, errors) = inputs.Safely(RatesApi.GetRateAsync);

    var outputs = rates
        .Select(Decimal.ToString)
        .Merge(errors.Select(ex => ex.Message))
        .StartWith("Enter a currency pair like 'EURUSD', or 'q' to quit");

    using (outputs.Subscribe(WriteLine))
        for (string input; (input = ReadLine().ToUpper()) != "Q";)
            inputs.OnNext(input);
}
```

The dataflow diagram in figure 18.7 shows the various IObservables involved and how they depend on one another.

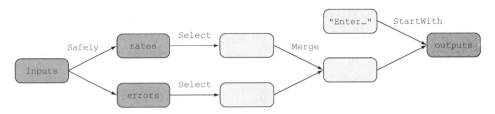

Figure 18.7   Dataflow with a separate branch for handling errors

Notice how Safely allows us to create two branches, each of which can be processed independently until a uniform representation for both cases is obtained, and they can be merged.

This program nicely illustrates the three parts that typically compose a program that uses IObservables:

- *Set up the data sources*—In our case, this is captured by inputs.
- *Process the data*—This is where you use functions like Select, Merge, and so on.
- *Consume the results*—Observers consume the most downstream IObservables (in this case, outputs) to perform side effects.

18.4   Implementing logic that spans multiple events

So far I've mostly aimed at familiarizing you with IObservables and the many operators that can be used with them. For this, I've used familiar examples like the exchange rates lookup. After all, given that you can promote any value T, Task<T>, or IEnumerable<T> to an IObservable<T>, you could pretty much write all of your code in terms of IObservables! But should you?

The answer, of course, is probably not. The area in which IObservable and Rx really shine is when you can use them to write stateful programs without any explicit state manipulation. By *stateful programs*, I mean programs in which events aren't treated independently; past events influence how new events are treated. In this section, you'll see a few such examples.

18.4.1 Detecting sequences of pressed keys

At some point, you've probably written an event handler that listens to a user's keypresses and performs some actions based on what key and key modifiers were pressed. A callback-based approach is satisfactory for many cases, but what if you want to listen to a specific sequence of keypresses? For example, say you want to implement some behavior when the user presses the combination Alt-K-B.

In this case, pressing Alt-B should lead to different behavior, based on whether it was shortly preceded by the leading Alt-K, so keypresses can't be treated independently. If you have a callback-based mechanism that deals with single keypressed events, you effectively need to set in motion a state machine when the user presses Alt-K, and then wait for the possible Alt-B that will follow, reverting to the previous state if no Alt-B is received in time. It's actually pretty complicated!

With IObservable, this can be solved much more elegantly. Let's assume that we have a stream of keypress events, keys. We're looking for two events—Alt-K and Alt-B—that happen on that same stream in quick succession. In order to do this, we need to explore how to combine a stream with itself. Consider the following diagram:

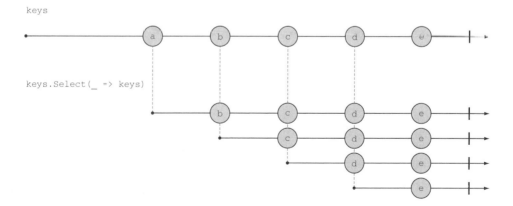

It's important to understand this diagram. The expression keys.Select(_ => keys) yields a new IObservable that maps each value produced by keys to keys itself. Therefore, when keys produces its first value, "a," this new IObservable produces an

IObservable that has all following values in keys. When keys produces its second value, "b," the new IObservable produces another IObservable that has all the values that follow "b," and so on.[3]

Looking at the types can also help clarify this:

```
keys                      : IObservable<KeyInfo>
_ => keys                 : KeyInfo → IObservable<KeyInfo>
keys.Select(_ => keys)  : IObservable<IObservable<KeyInfo>>
```

If we use SelectMany instead, all these values are flattened into a single stream:

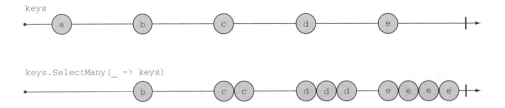

Of course, if we're looking for two consecutive keypresses, we don't need *all* values that follow an item but just the next one. Instead of mapping each value to the whole IObservable, let's reduce it to the first item with Take:

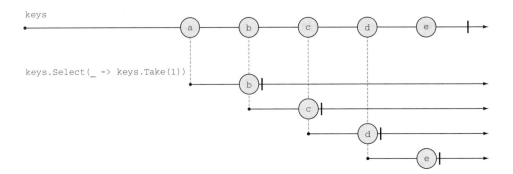

We're getting close. Now, let's make the following changes:

- Instead of ignoring the current value, pair it with the following value.
- Use SelectMany to obtain a flat IObservable.
- Use LINQ syntax.

---

[3] Imagine what keys.Select(_ => keys) would look like if keys were an IEnumerable: for each value, you'd be taking the whole IEnumerable. In the end, you'd have an IEnumerable containing *n* replicas of keys (*n* being the length of keys). With IObservable, the behavior is different because of the element of time, so when you say, "Give me keys," what you really get is all values keys will produce in the future.

The resulting expression pairs each value in an `IObservable` with the previously emitted value:

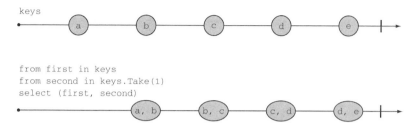

This is a pretty useful function in its own right, and I'll call it `PairWithPrevious`. We'll use it later.

But for this particular scenario, we only want pairs to be created if they're sufficiently close in time. This can be achieved easily by using an overload of `Take` that takes a `Timespan` as the following listing shows.

Listing 18.7   Detecting when the user presses the Alt-K-B key sequence

```
IObservable<ConsoleKeyInfo> keys = //...
var halfSec = TimeSpan.FromMilliseconds(500);

var keysAlt = keys
    .Where(key => key.Modifiers.HasFlag(ConsoleModifiers.Alt));

var twoKeyCombis =
    from first in keysAlt
    from second in keysAlt.Take(halfSec).Take(1)
    select (First: first, Second: second);

var altKB =
    from pair in twoKeyCombis
    where pair.First.Key == ConsoleKey.K
       && pair.Second.Key == ConsoleKey.B
    select Unit();
```

> For any keypress, pairs it with the next keypress that occurs within a half-second

As you can see, the solution is simple and elegant. You can apply this approach to recognize more complex patterns within sequences of events—all without explicitly keeping track of state and introducing side effects!

You've probably also realized that coming up with such a solution isn't necessarily easy. It takes a while to get familiar with `IObservable` and its many operators, and to develop an understanding of how to use them.

18.4.2 *Reacting to multiple event sources*

Imagine we have a bank account denominated in Euros, and we'd like to keep track of its value in US Dollars. Both changes in balance and changes in the exchange rate cause the dollar balance to change. To react to changes from different streams, we could use `CombineLatest`, which takes the latest values from two observables when one of them signals, as figure 18.8 shows.

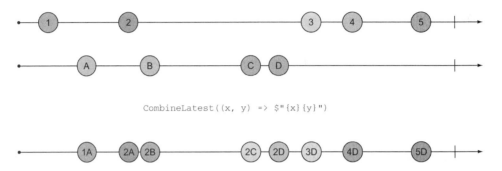

CombineLatest((x, y) => $"{x}{y}")

Figure 18.8   `CombineLatest` **signals whenever one of two** `IObservables` **signals.**

Its usage would be as follows:

```
IObservable<decimal> balance = //...
IObservable<decimal> eurUsdRate = //...

var balanceInUsd = balance.CombineLatest(eurUsdRate
    , (bal, rate) => bal * rate);
```

This works, but it doesn't take into account the fact that the exchange rate is much more volatile than the account balance. In fact, if exchange rates come from the FX market, there may well be dozens or hundreds of tiny movements every second! Surely this level of detail isn't required for a private client who wants to keep an eye on their finances. Reacting to each change in exchange rate would flood the client with unwanted notifications.

This is an example of an `IObservable` producing too much data (see the sidebar on "Backpressure"). For this, we can use `Sample`, an operator that takes an `IObservable` that acts as a data source, and another `IObservable` that signals *when* values should be produced. `Sample` is illustrated in figure 18.9.

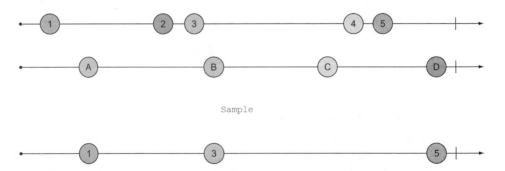

Sample

Figure 18.9   `Sample` **produces the values from a source stream when a sampler stream signals.**

In this scenario, we can create an `IObservable` that signals at 10-minute intervals and use it to sample the stream of exchange rates, as the following listing shows.

Listing 18.8 Sampling a value from an `IObservable` every 10 minutes

```
IObservable<decimal> balance = //...
IObservable<decimal> eurUsdRate = //...

var tenMins = TimeSpan.FromMinutes(10);
var sampler = Observable.Interval(tenMins);
var eurUsdSampled = eurUsdRate.Sample(sampler);

var balanceInUsd = balance.CombineLatest(eurUsdSampled
   , (bal, rate) => bal * rate);
```

This is another scenario in which our logic spans multiple events, and using Rx operators `CombineLatest` and `Sample` allows us to encode this logic without explicitly keeping any state.

Backpressure: When an `IObservable` produces data too quickly

When you iterate over the items in an `IEnumerable` or an `IAsyncEnumerable`, you're "pulling" or requesting items, so you can process them at your own pace. With `IObservable`, items are "pushed" to you (the consuming code). If an `IObservable` produces values more rapidly than they can be consumed by the subscribed observers, this can cause excessive *backpressure*, causing strain on your system.

To ease backpressure, Rx provides several operators:

- `Throttle`
- `Sample`
- `Buffer`
- `Window`
- `Debounce`

Each has different behavior and several overloads, so we won't discuss them in detail. The point is that with these operators, you can easily and declaratively implement logic like, "I want to consume items in batches of 10 at a time," or "If a cluster of values come in quick succession, I only want to consume the last one." Implementing such logic in a callback-based solution, where each value is received independently, would require you to manually keep some state.

18.4.3 Notifying when an account becomes overdrawn

For a final, more business-oriented example, imagine that in the context of the BOC application, we consume a stream of all transactions that affect bank accounts, and we want to send clients a notification if their account's balance becomes negative.

An account's balance is the sum of all the transactions that have affected it, so at any point, given a list of past `Transactions` for an account, you could compute its current balance using `Aggregate`.

There is an `Aggregate` function for `IObservable`; it waits for an `IObservable` to complete and aggregates all the values it produces into a single value. But this isn't what we need: we don't want to wait for the stream to complete, but to recompute the balance every time we receive a new `Transaction`. For this, we can use `Scan` (see figure 18.10), which is similar to `Aggregate` but aggregates all previous values with every new value that is produced.

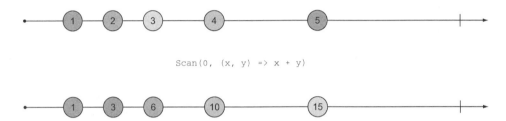

Figure 18.10 `Scan` **aggregates all values produced so far.**

As a result, we can effectively use `Scan` to keep state. Given an `IObservable` of `Trans-actions` affecting a bank account, we can use `Scan` to add up the amounts of all past transactions as they happen, obtaining an `IObservable` that signals with the new balance when the account balance changes:

```
IObservable<Transaction> transactions = //...
decimal initialBalance = 0;

IObservable<decimal> balance = transactions.Scan(initialBalance
    , (bal, trans) => bal + trans.Amount);
```

Now that we have a stream of values representing an account's current balance, we need to single out what changes in balance cause the account to "dip into the red," going from positive to negative.

For this, we need to look at changes in the balance, and we can do this with `Pair-WithPrevious`, which signals the current value together with the previously emitted value. You saw the implementation of `PairWithPrevious` in section 18.4.1, but here it is again for reference:

```
// ----1-------2---------3--------4------>
//
//              PairWithPrevious
//
// -----------(1,2)-----(2,3)----(3,4)-->
//
public static IObservable<(T Previous, T Current)>
    PairWithPrevious<T>(this IObservable<T> source)
    => from first in source
       from second in source.Take(1)
       select (Previous: first, Current: second);
```

This is one of many examples of custom operations that can be defined in terms of existing operations. The preceding snippet also shows how you can use ASCII marble diagrams to document your code.

We can use `PairWithPrevious` to signal when an account dips into the red as follows:

```
IObservable<Unit> dipsIntoTheRed =
    from bal in balance.PairWithPrevious()
    where bal.Previous >= 0
        && bal.Current < 0
    select Unit();
```

Now let's make things a bit closer to the real world. If your system receives a stream of transactions, this will probably include transactions for all accounts. Therefore, we must group them by account ID in order to correctly compute the balance. `GroupBy` works for `IObservable` similarly to how it does for `IEnumerable`, but it returns a stream of streams.

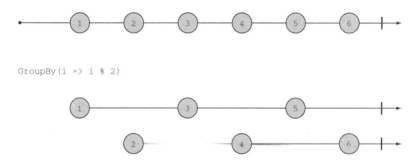

The following listing shows how to adapt the logic, assuming an initial stream of transactions for all accounts.

Listing 18.9 Signalling whenever an account becomes overdrawn

```
IObservable<Transaction> transactions = //...          ◁⎯ Includes transactions
                                                          from all accounts
IObservable<Guid> dipsIntoRed = transactions
    .GroupBy(t => t.AccountId)                          ◁⎯ Groups by account ID
    .Select(DipsIntoTheRed)                             ◁⎯ Signals dips into the red
    .MergeAll();                                              for any particular account
                                   ◁⎯ Flattens the result
static IObservable<Guid> DipsIntoTheRed    into a single observable
    (IGroupedObservable<Guid, Transaction> transactions)
{
    Guid accountId = transactions.Key;
    decimal initialBalance = 0;

    var balance = transactions.Scan(initialBalance
        , (bal, trans) => bal + trans.Amount);
```

```
    return from bal in balance.PairWithPrevious()
           where bal.Previous >= 0
              && bal.Current < 0
           select accountId;        ⟵┐  Signals the ID of the
}                                    │  offending account

public static IObservable<T> MergeAll<T>
   (this IObservable<IObservable<T>> source)
   => source.SelectMany(x => x);
```

Now we're starting with a stream of Transactions for all accounts, and we end up with a stream of Guids that will signal whenever an account dips into the red, including the Guid identifying the offending account. Notice how this program is effectively keeping track of the balances of all accounts without the need for us to do any explicit state manipulation.

18.5   *When should you use IObservable?*

In this chapter, you've seen how you can use IObservable to represent data streams and Rx to create and manipulate IObservables. There are many details and features of Rx that we haven't discussed at all, but we've still covered enough ground for you to start using IObservables and to further explore the features of Rx as needed.[4]

As you've seen, having an abstraction that captures a data stream enables you to detect patterns and specify logic that spans across multiple events within the same stream or across different streams. This is where I'd recommend using IObservable. The corollary is that, if your events can be handled independently, then you probably shouldn't use IObservables because using them will probably reduce the readability of your code.

An important thing to keep in mind is that because OnNext has no return value, an IObservable can only push data downstream and never receives any data back. Hence, IObservables are best combined into *one-directional dataflows*. For instance, if you read events from a queue and write some data into a DB as a result, IObservable can be a good fit; likewise if you have a server that communicates with web clients via WebSockets, where messages are exchanged between client and server in a fire-and-forget fashion.

On the other hand, IObservables are not well-suited to a request-response model such as HTTP. You could model the received requests as a stream and compute a stream of responses, but you'd then have no easy way to tie these responses back to the original requests.

Finally, if you have complex synchronization patterns that can't be captured with the operators in Rx, and you need more fine-grained control over how messages are sequenced and processed, you may find the building blocks in the System.DataFlow namespace (based on in-memory queues) more appropriate.

---

[4] To give you an idea of what was not covered, there are many more operators along with important implementation details of Rx: schedulers (which determine how calls to observers are dispatched), *hot* versus *cold* observables (not all observables are lazy), and Subjects with different behaviors, for example.

Summary

- `IObservable<T>` represents a *stream* of Ts, a sequence of values in time.
- An `IObservable` produces messages according to the grammar

  `OnNext* (OnCompleted|OnError)?.`

- Writing a program with `IObservable`s involves three steps:
  - Create `IObservable`s using the methods in `System.Reactive.Linq` `.Observable`.
  - Transform and combine `IObservable`s using the operators in Rx or other operators you may define.
  - Subscribe to and consume the values produced by the `IObservable`.
- Associate an observer to an `IObservable` with `Subscribe`.
- Remove an observer by disposing of the subscription returned by `Subscribe`.
- Separate side effects (in observers) from logic (in stream transformations).
- When deciding on whether to use `IObservable`, consider the following:
  - `IObservable` allows you to specify logic that spans multiple events.
  - `IObservable` is good for modeling unidirectional dataflows.

19

An introduction to message-passing concurrency

This chapter covers

- Why shared mutable state is sometimes required
- Understanding message-passing concurrency
- Programming with agents in C#
- Hiding agent-based implementations behind conventional APIs

Every seasoned developer has some first-hand experience of how difficult it can be to deal with problems such as deadlocks and race conditions. These are the hard problems that can arise in concurrent programs that involve shared mutable state ("shared," that is, between processes that execute concurrently).

This is why, throughout this book, you've seen many examples of how to solve problems *without* making recourse to shared mutable state. Indeed, my recommendation is to avoid shared mutable state *whenever possible*, and FP provides an excellent paradigm for doing so.

In this chapter, you'll see why it's not always possible to avoid shared mutable state, and what strategies there are to synchronize access to shared mutable state. We'll then concentrate on one of these strategies: *agent-based concurrency*, a style of concurrent programming that relies on message-passing between agents that "own" some state that they access in a single-threaded way. Programming with agents is popular with F# programmers, but you'll see that it's perfectly doable in C#.

19.1 The need for shared mutable state

It's generally possible to avoid shared mutable state when designing parallel algorithms. For instance, if you have a computationally intensive problem that you'd like to parallelize, you can usually break the data set or the tasks down in such a way that several threads compute an intermediate result *independently*. Hence, these threads can do their work without the need to share any state. Another thread may compute the final result by combining all the intermediate results.

The problem, however, is that avoiding shared mutable state isn't always possible. Although it can generally be achieved in the case of parallel computations, it's much more difficult if the source of concurrency is multithreading. For example, imagine a multithreaded application, such as a server handling requests on multiple threads, that needs to do the following:

- Keep an application-wide counter so that unique, *sequential* account numbers can be generated.
- Cache some resources in memory to improve efficiency.
- Represent real-world entities like items for sale, trades, contracts, and so on, ensuring that you don't sell the same (unique, real-world) item twice if two concurrent requests to buy it are received.

In such scenarios, it's essentially a requirement to share mutable state between the many threads that the server application uses to more efficiently handle requests. To prevent concurrent access from leading to data inconsistencies, you need to ensure the state can't be accessed (or, at least, updated) concurrently by different threads. That is, you need to *synchronize* access to shared mutable state.

In mainstream programming, this synchronization is usually achieved using locks. *Locks* define critical sections of the code that can only be entered by one thread at a time. When one thread enters a critical section, it blocks other threads from entering it. Functional programmers tend to avoid using locks and resort, instead, to alternative techniques:

- *Compare-and-swap (CAS)*—CAS allows you to atomically read and update a single value, which can be done in C# using the `Interlocked.CompareExchange` methods.
- *Software transactional memory (STM)*—STM allows you to update mutable state within transactions, which offers some interesting guarantees about how these updates take place:
  - *Each thread performs a transaction in isolation.* It sees a view of the program state that is unaffected by transactions that occur concurrently on other threads.

- *Transactions are then committed atomically.* Either all changes in the transaction are saved or none.[1]
- *Conflicting transactions don't necessarily fail.* If a transaction fails because of conflicting changes made in another, concurrent transaction, it can be retried with a fresh view of the data.

- *Message-passing concurrency*—The idea of this approach is that you set up lightweight processes that have exclusive ownership of some mutable state. Communication between processes is via message-passing, and processes handle messages sequentially, hence preventing concurrent access to their state. There are two main embodiments of this approach:

  - *The actor model*—This was most famously implemented at Ericsson in conjunction with the Erlang language, but implementations for other languages, including C#, abound. In this model, processes are called *actors*, and they can be distributed across different processes and machines.
  - *Agent-based concurrency*—This is inspired by the actor model, but it's much simpler because processes, called *agents*, only exist within one application.

CAS only allows you to deal with a single value, so it provides an effective solution for a very limited number of scenarios.

STM is an important paradigm for in-process concurrency, and it's particularly popular among Clojure and Haskell developers because these languages come with a compelling and battle-tested implementation of STM. If you want to explore this paradigm in C#, language-ext contains an implementation of `Atom` and `Ref`, the primitives allowing you to atomically update data shared between threads.[2]

In the rest of this chapter, I'll concentrate on message-passing concurrency, especially agent-based concurrency. You'll later see how agents and actors differ in more detail. Let's begin by looking at message-passing concurrency as a programming model.

19.2   *Understanding message-passing concurrency*

You can think of an agent (or actor; the fundamental idea is the same) as a process that has exclusive ownership of some mutable state. Communication between actors is via message passing so that the state can never be accessed from outside of the actor. Furthermore, incoming messages are processed sequentially so that concurrent state updates can never take place.

---

[1] In fact, there are several different strategies for implementing STM with different characteristics. Some implementations also enforce *consistency*, meaning that it's possible to enforce invariants that a transaction can't violate. Do the properties atomicity, consistency, and isolation sound familiar? That's because they are three of the ACID properties guaranteed by many databases—the last one being *durability*, which, of course, does not apply to STM as it specifically pertains to in-memory data.

[2] I already mentioned language-ext, a functional library for C#, in the front matter. The code is available at https://github.com/louthy/language-ext, and for some basic code samples showing how to use the STM features, see https://github.com/louthy/language-ext/wiki/Concurrency.

Figure 19.1 illustrates an agent: a process that runs in a loop. It has an inbox in which messages are queued, and it has some state. When a message is dequeued and processed, the agent typically does some of the following:

- Performs side effects
- Sends messages to other agents
- Creates other agents
- Computes its new state

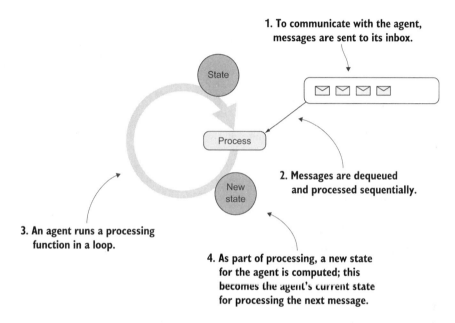

1. To communicate with the agent, messages are sent to its inbox.

2. Messages are dequeued and processed sequentially.

3. An agent runs a processing function in a loop.

4. As part of processing, a new state for the agent is computed; this becomes the agent's current state for processing the next message.

Figure 19.1 An agent consists of a message inbox and a processing loop.

The new state will be used as the current state at the next iteration, when the following message is processed.

Let's begin with an idealized, almost pseudocode implementation of an agent as I just described. Look at the code in the following listing in detail and see how each part corresponds to what's depicted in figure 19.1.

Listing 19.1 Idealized implementation of an agent

```
public sealed class Agent<State, Msg>
{                                                    Uses a concurrent queue
    BlockingCollection<Msg> inbox          ◁────     as a message inbox
        = new BlockingCollection<Msg>(new ConcurrentQueue<Msg>());

    public void Tell(Msg message)          Telling a message to the agent
        => inbox.Add(message);             simply enqueues the message.
```

```
public Agent                              Creates an agent by providing an
(                                         initial state and a processing function
   State initialState,
   Func<State, Msg, State> process
)
{
   void Loop(State state)
   {                                      Dequeues a message as
      Msg message = inbox.Take();         soon as it's available
      State newState = process(state, message);      Processes the message,
      Loop(newState);     Loops with the             determining the new
   }                      new state                  state of the agent

   Task.Run(() => Loop(initialState));         The actor runs in
}                                              its own process.
}
```

There are several interesting things to point out here. First, notice that there are only two public members, so only two interactions with an agent are allowed:

- You can create (or *start*) an agent.
- You can *tell* it a message, which simply enqueues the message in the agent's inbox.

You can define more complex interactions from these primitive operations.

Let's now look at the processing loop, encoded in the Loop function. This dequeues the first message from the inbox (or waits until a message becomes available) and processes it using the agent's processing function and its current state. This yields the agent's new state, which is used in the next execution of the loop.

Notice that the implementation is side-effect free, apart from any side effects that may occur when calling the given processing function. The way changes in state are captured is by always passing the state as an argument to the Loop function (a technique you already saw in chapter 15).

Notice also that this implementation assumes that State must be an immutable type; otherwise, it could be shared by the process function and updated arbitrarily outside of the scope of the agent's processing loop. As a result, the state only "appears" to be mutable because a new version of the state is used with each invocation of Loop.

Finally, take a moment to look at the signature for the constructor. Does it remind you of anything? Compare it with Enumerable.Aggregate. Can you see that it's essentially the same? The current state of an agent is the result of reducing all the messages it's received so far, using the initial state as an accumulator value and the processing function as a reducer. It's a fold in time over the stream of messages received by the agent.

This implementation is elegant, and it would work well in a language with tail-call elimination. This is not featured in C#, so we'll need to make some changes for a stack-safe implementation. Furthermore, we can also dispense with many of the low-level details by using existing functionality in .NET. We'll look at this next.

19.2.1 *Implementing agents in C#*

.NET includes an implementation of agents called `MailboxProcessor`, but it was designed for use from F# and is awkward to use from C#. And, although the preceding implementation is useful for understanding the idea, it's not optimal. Instead, in the coming examples, I'll use a more practical implementation of an agent, which is included in LaYumba.Functional and shown in the following listing.

> **Listing 19.2 Implementation of an agent that builds on `Dataflow.ActionBlock`**

```
using System.Threading.Tasks.Dataflow;

public interface Agent<Msg>
{
   void Tell(Msg message);
}

class StatefulAgent<State, Msg> : Agent<Msg>
{
   private State state;
   private readonly ActionBlock<Msg> actionBlock;

   public StatefulAgent
   (
      State initialState,
      Func<State, Msg, State> process
   )
   {
      state = initialState;

      actionBlock = new ActionBlock<Msg>(msg =>
      {
         var newState = process(state, msg);
         state = newState;
      });
   }

   public void Tell(Msg message)
      => actionBlock.Post(message);
}
```

Processes the message with the current state

Assigns the result to the stored state

Queueing and processing messages is managed by the `ActionBlock`.

Here I've replaced the recursive call (which could lead to stack overflow) with a single mutable variable `state` that keeps track of the agent's state and is reassigned as each message is processed. Although this is a side effect, messages are processed sequentially, therefore preventing concurrent writes.

I've also dispensed with the details of managing the queue and process by using `ActionBlock`, one of the building blocks in .NET's `Dataflow` library. An `ActionBlock` contains a buffer (by default, unbounded in size) that acts as the agent's inbox and that only allows a fixed number of threads to enter the block (by default, a single thread), ensuring messages are processed sequentially.

`State` should still be an immutable type (otherwise, as previously pointed out, it could be shared by the `process` function and mutated outside the scope of the `ActionBlock`). If this is observed, the code is thread-safe.

From the point of view of the client code, nothing has changed: we still only have two public members with the same signatures as before. The reason for the `Agent<Msg>` interface is twofold:

- From the point of view of the client code consuming an agent, you can only tell it messages, so by using the interface, we avoid exposing the type parameter for the state. After all, the type of the state is an implementation detail of the agent.
- You can envisage other implementations such as stateless agents or agents that persist their state.

Finally, here are some convenience methods for easily creating agents:

```
public static class Agent
{
   public static Agent<Msg> Start<State, Msg>
      ( State initialState
      , Func<State, Msg, State> process)
      => new StatefulAgent<State, Msg>(initialState, process);

   public static Agent<Msg> Start<Msg>(Action<Msg> action)
      => new StatelessAgent<Msg>(action);
}
```

The first overload simply creates an agent with the given arguments. The second takes an action and is used to create a *stateless agent*: an agent that processes messages sequentially but doesn't keep any state. (The implementation is trivial, as it just creates an `ActionBlock` with the given `Action`). We can also define agents with an asynchronous processing function/action; I've omitted the overloads for brevity, but the full implementation is in the code samples. Next, we'll get started using agents.

19.2.2   Getting started with agents

Let's look at some simple examples of using agents. We'll build a couple of simple agents that interact as figure 19.2 shows.

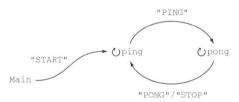

Figure 19.2   Simple interaction between agents by exchanging messages

We'll start with a really simple, stateless agent that takes a message of type `string` and just prints it out. You can follow along in the REPL:

```
Agent<string> logger = Agent.Start((string msg) => WriteLine(msg));

logger.Tell("Agent X");
// prints: Agent X
```

Next, let's define the ping and pong agents that interact with the logger and with each other:

```
Agent<string> ping, pong = null;

ping = Agent.Start((string msg) =>
{
   if (msg == "STOP") return;

   logger.Tell($"Received '{msg}'; Sending 'PING'");
   Task.Delay(500).Wait();
   pong.Tell("PING");
});

pong = Agent.Start(0, (int count, string msg) =>
{
   int newCount = count + 1;
   string nextMsg = (newCount < 5) ? "PONG" : "STOP";

   logger.Tell($"Received '{msg}' #{newCount}; Sending '{nextMsg}'");
   Task.Delay(500).Wait();
   ping.Tell(nextMsg);

   return newCount;
});

ping.Tell("START");
```

Here, we define two additional agents. ping is stateless; it sends a message to the logger agent and a PING message to the pong agent, unless the message it's told is STOP, in which case, it does nothing. It's quite common for an agent to have different behavior depending on the message, that is, to interpret the message as a command.

Now let's see a stateful agent: pong. The implementation is quite similar to ping. It sends PONG to ping, but it also keeps a counter as state. The counter is incremented with every message, and after five messages, the agent sends a STOP message instead.

The whole ping-pong is set in motion when we send the initial START message to ping on the last line. Running the program causes the following to be printed:

```
Received 'START'; Sending 'PING'
Received 'PING' #1; Sending 'PONG'
Received 'PONG'; Sending 'PING'
Received 'PING' #2; Sending 'PONG'
Received 'PONG'; Sending 'PING'
Received 'PING' #3; Sending 'PONG'
Received 'PONG'; Sending 'PING'
Received 'PING' #4; Sending 'PONG'
Received 'PONG'; Sending 'PING'
Received 'PING' #5; Sending 'STOP'
```

Now that you've seen some simple agents interact, it's time to move on to something closer to real-world requirements.

19.2.3 *Using agents to handle concurrent requests*

Let's revisit the scenario of a service that provides exchange rates. The service should retrieve rates from the Rates API and cache them. We saw a simple implementation in section 15.1, but there the interaction was via the command line so that requests necessarily came in one by one.

Let's change that. Let's imagine that the service is part of a larger system and that other components may request rates via a message broker, as figure 19.3 illustrates.

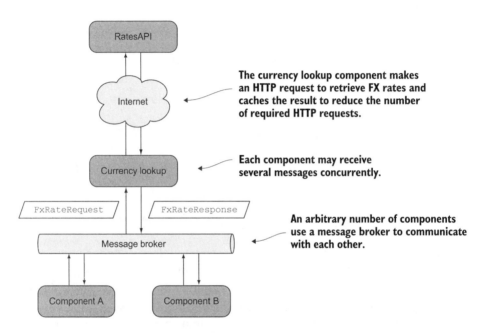

Figure 19.3   A system in which several requests may be received concurrently

Components communicate with each other by sending messages via the message broker. To communicate with the currency lookup service, the following messages are defined:

```
record FxRateRequest
(
    string CcyPair,
    string Sender
);

record FxRateResponse
(
    string CcyPair,
    decimal Rate,
    string Recipient
);
```

The currency pair whose rate is being requested

The sender and recipient fields allow the message broker to correctly route messages.

We'll assume that the message broker is multithreaded, so that our service may receive multiple requests on different threads at exactly the same time.

In this case, sharing state between threads is a requirement: if we had a different cache for every thread, that would be suboptimal. So we need some synchronization to ensure that we don't perform unnecessary remote lookups and that cache updates don't cause race conditions.

Next, we'll see how we can use agents to achieve this. First, we'll need a bit of setup code, defining the interaction with the message broker. This is shown in listing 19.3. Note that the code isn't specific to any particular message broker; we just need to be able to subscribe to it to receive requests and to use it to send responses. (The code samples include an implementation of `MessageBroker` that uses Redis as its underlying transport.)

Listing 19.3 Setting up the interaction with the message broker

```
public static void SetUp(MessageBroker broker)
{                                                          An agent that
    Agent<FxRateResponse> sendResponse = Agent.Start(     sends the responses
        (FxRateResponse res) => broker.Send(res.Recipient, res));    <───

                                        An agent that processes the
    Agent<FxRateRequest> processRequest     requests and uses the previously
        = StartReqProcessor(sendResponse);  <──┘ defined agent to send the response

    broker.Subscribe<FxRateRequest>("FxRates", processRequest.Tell);   <────
}
                                                            When a request
                                                        is received, passes it to
                                                          the processing agent
```

Starting at the bottom, we subscribe to receive requests broadcast on the "FxRates" channel, providing a callback to handle the request. This callback (which will be called on multiple threads) simply passes the request to the processing agent, defined on the previous line. Hence, although requests are received on multiple threads, they'll be immediately queued up in the processing agent's inbox and processed sequentially.

Does this mean that processing is now single-threaded, and we lose any benefit of multithreading? Not necessarily! If the processing agent did *all* the processing, that would indeed be the case. Instead, let's take a more granular approach: we can have an agent for each currency pair in charge of fetching and storing the rate for its particular pair. The request-processing agent will just be in charge of managing these per-currency-pair agents and delegating the work to them, as figure 19.4 shows.

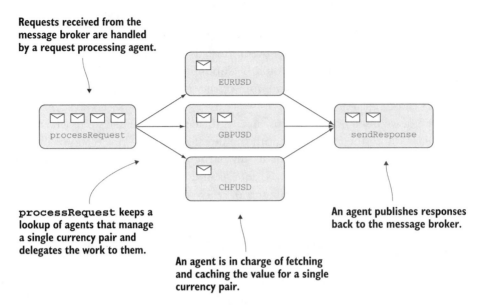

Requests received from the message broker are handled by a request processing agent.

processRequest keeps a lookup of agents that manage a single currency pair and delegates the work to them.

An agent is in charge of fetching and caching the value for a single currency pair.

An agent publishes responses back to the message broker.

Figure 19.4   Breaking up the work between agents that can run concurrently

Let's now look at the definitions of the agents. The following listing shows the higher-level agent, which handles incoming requests and starts the lower-level per-currency-pair agents, delegating work to them.

Listing 19.4   A coordinating agent routes requests to a per-currency-pair agent

```
using CcyAgents = System.Collections.Immutable
    .ImmutableDictionary<string, Agent<string>>;

static Agent<FxRateRequest> StartReqProcessor
    (Agent<FxRateResponse> sendResponse)

    => Agent.Start(CcyAgents.Empty
        , (CcyAgents state, FxRateRequest request) =>
    {
        string ccyPair = request.CcyPair;

        Agent<string> agent = state
            .Lookup(ccyPair)
            .GetOrElse(() => StartAgentFor(ccyPair, sendResponse));

        agent.Tell(request.Sender);
        return state.Add(ccyPair, agent);
    });
```

If required, starts a new agent for the requested currency pair

Passes the request to the agent in charge of the pair

As you can see, the request-processing agent holds not a cache of values, but of agents—one for each currency pair. It starts those agents as needed and forwards the requests to them.

The benefit of this solution is that requests for one currency, say GBPUSD, won't impact requests for another, say EURUSD. On the other hand, if you get several requests for GBPUSD at the same time, only one remote request is made to fetch that rate while other requests are queued.

Finally, the following listing provides the definition of the agent that manages the rate for a single currency pair.

Listing 19.5 An agent managing the FX rate for a single currency pair

```
static Agent<string> StartAgentFor
(
    string ccyPair,
    Agent<FxRateResponse> sendResponse
)
=> Agent.Start<Option<decimal>, string>
(
    initialState: None,
    process: async (optRate, recipient) =>
    {
        decimal rate = await optRate.Map(Async)
            .GetOrElse(() => RatesApi.GetRateAsync(ccyPair));

        sendResponse.Tell(new FxRateResponse
        (
            CcyPair: ccyPair,
            Rate: rate,
            Recipient: recipient
        ));

        return Some(rate);
    }
);
```

If necessary, fetches the rate from the remote API ←

Sends the response ←

The agent's new state ←

This agent's state is the rate for a single pair; it's wrapped in an Option because, when the agent is first created, it has no rate available yet. Upon receiving a request, the agent decides whether a remote lookup is required (you could easily improve this to fetch the rate if the cached value is expired).

To keep the example simple, I've avoided the question of expiry as well as error handling. I'm also assuming that sending the request to the message broker is a fire-and-forget operation with minimal latency so that it's OK to have a single agent performing it.

The main point of the example is that using agents with their sequential processing of messages can be quite efficient. It does, however, require a mental shift, both from the functional approach we've been pursuing in this book and from the traditional approach of using locks.

19.2.4 Agents vs. actors

Agents and actors are closely related. In both cases, a single thread processes messages sequentially and communicates with other actors/agents by sending them messages. There are also important differences:

- *Agents run within a single process, whereas actors are designed for distributed systems.* In the examples we've looked at so far, a reference to an agent refers to a specific instance in the current process. References to actors, on the other hand, are location-transparent; when you have a reference to an actor, that actor may be running in the same process or in another process, possibly on a remote machine. A reference to an agent is a pointer, whereas a reference to an actor is an ID that the actor model implementation uses to route messages across processes as appropriate.

- *Actor model implementations are designed to be fault-tolerant.* For example, Erlang includes *supervisors*: actors that monitor supervised actors and take action when they fail. Regular actors handle the happy path, whereas supervisors take care of recovery, ultimately improving the robustness of the system. There's no counterpart to this with agents.

- *The state of an agent (or an actor) should be immutable and never shared outside the scope of the agent.* In our agent implementation, however, there's nothing stopping an inexperienced developer from creating an agent whose state is mutable and from passing that mutable state to other components, thus allowing that state to be changed from outside the scope of the agent. With actors, messages are serialized, so this should never occur.

As you can see, although the fundamental idea behind agents and actors is the same, the actor model is richer and more complex. You should only consider using the actor model if you require coordination of concurrent operations across different applications or machines; otherwise, the operational and setup cost would be unjustified, and you should rely on agents instead.

Although I was able to implement an actor with just a few lines of code, implementing the actor model is much more complex. So if you want to use actors, you'll probably use one of several implementations of the actor model for .NET:

- *Orleans* (https://github.com/dotnet/orleans) is Microsoft's take on the actor model. It has a distinctly object-oriented feel. The underlying philosophy is that less experienced developers can interact with actors (called *grains*) as though they were local objects, without being exposed to any additional complexities specific to the actor model. Orleans takes care of managing the grains' lifecycle, meaning that their state is kept in memory or persisted to storage automatically. Persistence can be to a variety of media including SQL Server and cloud storage on Azure.

- *Akka.NET* (http://getakka.net/) is a community-driven port of the Akka framework popular with Scala developers. It predates Orleans and is much more explicit about its message-driven nature, so the barrier to entry is higher. A variety of options are available for message transport and persistence of the actors' state.

- *echo* (https://github.com/louthy/echo-process) is the .NET implementation closest to Erlang, and was developed by Paul Louth. It's the most lightweight option, both in terms of syntax and configuration: you can create an actor (called a *process*) with a function like we did with agents, or you can use an interface-based approach (which reads more naturally if you need to handle different kinds of messages). Out of the box, echo only supports messaging across application domains and persistence via Redis, but you can implement adapters to target different infrastructure.

All these actor model implementations differ both in terminology and in important technical details, so it's difficult to offer a description of *the* actor model without being somewhat specific to one implementation. This is one of the reasons why I've opted to illustrate the fundamental ideas of message-passing concurrency with a simple implementation of agents instead. You can carry these principles over to actor-based programming, but you'll need to learn other principles such as error handling with supervisors and the guarantees for message delivery offered by the specific implementation you're using.

19.3 Functional APIs, agent-based implementations

Is agent-based programming even functional? Although agents and actors were developed in the context of functional languages (remember, in our idealized implementation an agent was side-effect free), agent-based programming differs starkly from the functional techniques you've seen throughout this book:

- You tell an agent a message, and this is usually interpreted as a command, so the semantics are rather imperative.
- An agent often performs a side effect or tells a message to another agent, which will, in turn, perform a side effect.
- Most importantly, telling an agent a message returns no data, so you can't compose tell operations into pipelines the way you can with functions.
- FP separates logic from data; agents contain data and at least some logic in the processing function.

As a result, agent-based programming "feels" different from FP as you've seen it so far, so it's debatable whether or not agent-based concurrency is actually a functional technique. If you think it's not (as I'm inclined to), then you must conclude that FP is not good at certain types of concurrency (where shared mutable state can't be avoided), and it needs to be complemented with a different paradigm such as agent-based programming or the actor model.

With agents, it's easy to program *unidirectional data flows*: the data always flows forward (to the next agent), and no data is ever returned. In the face of this, we have two choices:

- *Embrace the idea of unidirectional data flow, and write your applications in this style.* In this approach, if you had clients connecting to a server, you wouldn't use a request-response model like HTTP but rather a message-based protocol such as WebSockets or a message broker. This is a viable approach, especially if your domain is event-driven enough that you already have a messaging infrastructure in place.

- *Hide the agent-specific details behind a more conventional API.* This implies that agents should be able to return a response to a message sender. In this approach, agents are used as concurrency primitives that are implementation details (just as locks are) and that should not dictate the program's design. We'll explore this approach next.

19.3.1 *Agents as implementation details*

The first thing we need is a way to get a reply from an agent, a "return value" of sorts. Imagine that a sender creates a message that includes a handle that it can wait on. It then tells the message to an agent, which signals a result on that handle, making it available to the sender. With this, we can effectively have two-way communication on top of the fire-and-forget `Tell` protocol.

`TaskCompletionSource` provides a suitable handle for this purpose: the sender can create a `TaskCompletionSource`, add it to the message payload, and await its `Task`. The agent will do its work and set the result on the `TaskCompletionSource` when ready. Doing this manually for every message for which you want a response would be tedious, so instead, I've included in my `LaYumba.Functional` library a beefed-up agent that takes care of all this wiring. I won't include the implementation details here, but the interface definition is as follows:

```
public interface Agent<Msg, Reply>
{
    Task<Reply> Tell(Msg message);
}
```

Notice that this is a completely new interface with not one but two generic arguments: the type of messages that the agent accepts and the type that it replies with. Telling a message of type `Msg` to this agent returns a `Task<Reply>`. To start an agent of this type, we'll use a processing function of type

```
State → Msg → (State, Reply)
```

or its asynchronous version

```
State → Msg → Task<(State, Reply)>
```

which is a function that, given the agent's current state and the received message, computes not only the agent's new state, but also a reply to be returned to the sender.

Let's look at a simple example—an agent that keeps a counter and can be told to increment the counter, and also returns the counter's new value:

```
var counter = Agent.Start(0
    , (int state, int msg) =>
    {
        var newState = state + msg;        ┐  Returns the new state to be
        return (newState, newState);    ◄──┘  stored and the reply to the sender
    });
```

You can now consume this agent like this:

```
var newCount = await counter.Tell(1);
newCount // => 1
newCount = await counter.Tell(1);
newCount // => 2
```

Notice that `Tell` returns a `Task<int>`, so the caller can just await the reply, as with any asynchronous function. Essentially, you can use this agent as a thread-safe, stateful, asynchronous version of a function of type `Msg → Reply`:

- *Thread safe* because it internally uses an `ActionBlock` that processes one message at a time
- *Stateful* because the state kept by the agent can change as a result of processing a message
- *Asynchronous* because your message may have to wait while the agent processes other messages in its queue

This means that, compared to using locks, you're not only gaining in safety (no deadlocks) but also in performance (locks block the current thread, whereas `await` frees the thread to do other work).

19.3.2 *Hiding agents behind a conventional API*

Now that we have a mechanism for two-way communication in place, we can improve the API by hiding the specifics of agent-based programming. For example, in the case of a counter, we could define a `Counter` class as the following listing shows.

Listing 19.6 Hiding an agent-based implementation behind a public API

```
public sealed class Counter
{
    readonly Agent<int, int> counter =          ◁── The agent is an
        Agent.Start(0, (int state, int msg) =>       implementation detail.
        {
            var newState = state + msg;
            return (newState, newState);
        });
                                                ◁── Public interface
    public Task<int> IncrementBy(int amount)         of the Counter
        => counter.Tell(amount);
}
```

Now a consumer of `Counter` can be blissfully unaware of its agent-based implementation. A typical interaction would look like this:

```
var counter = new Counter();
var newCount = counter.IncrementBy(10);
await newCount // => 10
```

19.4   *Message-passing concurrency in LOB applications*

In LOB applications, the need to synchronize access to some shared state usually arises from the fact that entities in the application represent real-world entities, and we need to ensure that concurrent access doesn't leave them in an invalid state or otherwise break business rules. For example, two concurrent requests to purchase a particular item shouldn't result in that item being sold twice. Similarly, concurrent moves in a multiplayer game shouldn't lead to an invalid state of the game.

Let's see how this would play out in our banking scenario. We need to ensure that when different transactions (debits, credits, transfers) happen concurrently, they don't leave the account in an invalid state. Does this mean we need to synchronize access to the account data? Not necessarily! Let's see what happens if we don't take any special measures with respect to concurrency.

Imagine an account with a balance of 1,000. An automated direct debit payment occurs causing 800 to be debited from the account. Concurrently, a transfer of 200 is requested so that the amount of 200 is also debited. If we use the event-sourced approach shown so far in this book, we get the following result:

- The direct debit request causes the creation of an event, capturing a debit of 800, and the caller will receive an updated state with a balance of 200.
- The transfer request likewise causes the creation of an event, capturing a debit of 200, and the caller will receive an updated state with a balance of 800.
- When the account is loaded next, its state is computed from all past events so that its state will correctly have a balance of 0.
- As new events are published, any clients that subscribe to updates can reflect those changes in state. (For example, the client device on which the transfer request was made can be notified when the direct debit has taken place so that the account balance shown to the user is always up to date.)

In short, if you use immutable objects and event sourcing, you don't get inconsistent data as a result of concurrent updates; this is an important benefit of event sourcing.

Let's now enrich this scenario with a new business requirement. Each account is assigned a maximum allowed overdraft, meaning that an account's balance can never go below a certain amount. Now imagine that we have the following:

- An account with a balance of 1,000 and a maximum overdraft of 500
- A direct debit payment of 800
- Concurrently, a transfer request also for 800

If you don't synchronize access to the account data, both requests will succeed, leading to the account having an overdraft of 600, which violates our business requirement that the overdraft should never exceed 500. To enforce the maximum allowed overdraft, we need to synchronize the execution of actions that modify the account balance, as a result of which one of the concurrent requests in this scenario should fail. Next, you'll see how to achieve this using actors.

19.4.1 *Using an agent to synchronize access to account data*

To ensure that the account data can't be affected concurrently by different requests, we can associate an agent with each account. Notice that agents are lightweight enough that it's OK to have thousands or even millions of them. Also notice that I'm assuming there's a single server process through which accounts can be affected. If this weren't the case, you'd need to use an implementation of the actor model instead, but the gist of the following implementation would still be valid.

To associate an agent with an account, we'll define an `AccountProcess` class with an agent-based implementation. This means we're now using three classes to represent accounts:

- `AccountState`—A record that represents the state of an account at a given moment in time
- `Account`—A static class that only contains pure functions used to calculate state transitions
- `AccountProcess`—An agent-based implementation that tracks the current state of an account and handles any commands that affect the account's state

You saw implementations of `Account` and `AccountState` in chapter 13, and those don't need to change. The following listing shows the implementation of `AccountProcess`.

> **Listing 19.7 Sequential processing of commands that affect an account**

```
using Result = Validation<(Event Event, AccountState NewState)>;

public class AccountProcess
{
   Agent<Command, Result> agent;

   public AccountProcess
   (
      AccountState initialState,
      Func<Event, Task<Unit>> saveAndPublish
   )
   => this.agent = Agent.Start(initialState
      , async (AccountState state, Command cmd) =>
      {
         Result result = cmd switch
         {
            MakeTransfer transfer => state.Debit(transfer),      ⟵ Uses pure functions
            FreezeAccount freeze => state.Freeze(freeze),           to calculate the result
         };                                                         of the command

         await result.Traverse(tpl => saveAndPublish(tpl.Event));   ⟵─┐
         var newState = result
            .Map(tpl => tpl.NewState)          Persists the event within the block so
            .GetOrElse(state);                that the agent doesn't process new
                                              messages in a nonpersisted state
         return (newState, result);
      });
```

```
public Task<Result> Handle(Command cmd)        All commands are queued
   => agent.Tell(cmd);                         and processed sequentially.
}
```

Each instance of `AccountProcess` internally holds an agent, so that all commands affecting an account can be processed sequentially. Let's look at the body of the agent: first, we calculate the result of the command, given the command and the current state. This is done using pure, static functions only.

The result, remember, is a `Validation` with an inner value including the resulting `Event` and the new account state. If the result is `Valid`, we proceed to save and publish the created event (the check is done as part of `Traverse`).

It's important to note that persistence happens *within* the processing function. That is, the agent shouldn't update its state and start processing new messages before it has successfully persisted the event representing its current state transition. (Otherwise, persisting the event could fail, leading to a mismatch between the agent's state and the state captured by the persisted events.)

Finally, we return the account's updated state (which is used when processing subsequent commands) and the result of the command. This result includes both the new state and the created event, wrapped in a `Validation`. This makes it easy to send back to the client the details of the success and result of this request.

Notice how agents (and actors) complect state, behavior, and persistence (as such, they have been labeled "more object-oriented than objects"). In this implementation, I'm injecting a function for persisting the events, whereas most implementations of the actor model include some configurable mechanism for persisting an actor's state.

19.4.2 Keeping a registry of accounts

We now have an `AccountProcess` that can process commands applicable to a specific account in a thread-safe manner. But how does the code in an API endpoint get the instance of `AccountProcess` for the relevant account? And how do we ensure that we never accidentally create two `AccountProcesses` for the same account?

What we need is a single, application-wide registry that holds all live `Account-Processes`. It needs to manage their creation and serve them by ID so that the code handling client requests can get an `AccountProcess` simply by providing the account ID included in the request.

Actor model implementations have such a registry built in, allowing you to register any particular actor against an arbitrary ID. In our case, we'll build our own simple registry. The following listing shows a first attempt at doing this.

> **Listing 19.8 Storing and managing the creation of `AccountProcesses`**

```
using AccountsCache = ImmutableDictionary<Guid, AccountProcess>;

public class AccountRegistry
{
   Agent<Guid, Option<AccountProcess>> agent;
```

```
public AccountRegistry
(
    Func<Guid, Task<Option<AccountState>>> loadState,
    Func<Event, Task<Unit>> saveAndPublish
)
=> this.agent = Agent.Start
(
    initialState: AccountsCache.Empty,
    process: async (AccountsCache cache, Guid id) =>
    {
        if (cache.TryGetValue(id, out AccountProcess account))
            return (cache, Some(account));

        var optAccount = await loadState(id);

        return optAccount.Map(accState =>
        {
            AccountProcess account = new(accState, saveAndPublish);
            return (cache.Add(id, account), Some(account));
        })
        .GetOrElse(() => (cache, None));
    }
);

public Task<Option<AccountProcess>> Lookup(Guid id)
    => agent.Tell(id);
}
```

> If the requested `AccountProcess` is not in the cache, loads the current state from the DB

> Creates an `AccountProcess` with the retrieved state

In this implementation, we have a single agent that manages a cache where all live instances of AccountProcess are kept. If no AccountProcess is found for the given ID, the account's current state is retrieved from the DB and used to create a new AccountProcess, which is added to the cache. Notice that, as usual, the loadState function returns a Task<Option<AccountState>> to acknowledge that the operation is asynchronous and that it's possible that no data is found for a given ID.

Before you read on, go through the implementation again. Can you see any problems with this approach? Let's see: loading the account state from the DB is done *within* the agent body; is that warranted? This means that reading the state for account *x* will block another thread that's interested in account *y*. That's certainly suboptimal!

19.4.3 *An agent is not an object*

This is the kind of schoolboy error that's common when you're getting used to programming with agents or actors. Although agents and actors are similar to objects, you can't think of them as such. The error in listing 19.8 is that we're conceptually giving the agent the responsibility of providing the caller with the requested AgentProcess, and this gives us a suboptimal solution.

Instead, agents should only have the responsibility of managing some state. The agent in question manages a dictionary, so we can call it to look up an item, or to add a new item, but going to the DB to retrieve data is a relatively slow operation that's not directly pertinent to managing the cache of AgentProcesses.

With this in mind, let's think of an alternative solution. A thread that wants to get hold of an `AgentProcess` for an account ID should do the following:

1 Ask the agent to look up the ID.

2 If no `AgentProcess` is stored, retrieve the state of the account from the DB (this time-consuming operation will be done in the calling thread, therefore without affecting the agent).

3 Ask the agent to create and register a new `AgentProcess` with the given state and ID.

This means that we may need to go to the agent twice, so we need two different message types to specify what we want the agent to do. The following listing shows that different types of messages can be defined to convey the caller's intention.

Listing 19.9 Different message types convey the caller's intention

```
public class AccountRegistry
{
   abstract record Msg(Guid Id);
   record LookupMsg(Guid Id) : Msg(Id);
   record RegisterMsg(Guid Id, AccountState AccountState) : Msg(Id);
}
```

I've defined these message types as inner classes because they're only used within the `AccountRegistry` class to communicate with its agent.

We can now define the `Lookup` method, which constitutes the `AccountRegistry`'s public API (and is, therefore, executed on the caller's thread), as follows:

```
public class AccountRegistry
{
   Agent<Msg, Option<Account>> agent;
   Func<Guid, Task<Option<AccountState>>> loadState;

   public Task<Option<Account>> Lookup(Guid id)          Tells the agent to
      => agent                                           look up the given ID
         .Tell(new LookupMsg(id))          ◁
         .OrElse(() =>                                   If the lookup fails, the state
            from state in loadState(id)    ◁             is loaded in the calling thread.
            from account in agent.Tell(new RegisterMsg(id, state))    ◁
            select account);
}
                                                         Tells the agent to register
                                                         a new process with the
                                                         given state and ID
```

It first asks the agent to look up the ID; if the lookup fails, then the state is retrieved from the DB. Note that this is done on the calling thread, leaving the agent free to handle other messages. Finally, a second message is sent to the agent asking it to create and register an `AccountProcess` with the given account state and ID.

Notice that everything happens within the `Task<Option<>>` stack because this is the type returned both by `loadState` and by `Tell`. Even `OrElse` here resolves to an overload I've defined on `Task<Option<T>>`, which executes the given fallback function if the `Task` has faulted or if the inner `Option` is `None`.

All that's left to show is the revised definition of the agent, which is started in the `AccountRegistry`'s constructor. The following listing shows this.

Listing 19.10 An agent storing a registry of `AccountProcesses`

```
using AccountsCache
   = ImmutableDictionary<Guid, Agents.Account>;

public class AccountRegistry
{
   Agent<Msg, Option<Account>> agent;
   Func<Guid, Task<Option<AccountState>>> loadState;

   public AccountRegistry
   (
      Func<Guid, Task<Option<AccountState>>> loadState,
      Func<Event, Task<Unit>> saveAndPublish
   )
   {
      this.loadState = loadState;

      this.agent = Agent.Start
      (
         initialState: AccountsCache.Empty,
         process: (AccountsCache cache, Msg msg)
            => msg switch                            ⟵——  The agent uses pattern matching
         {                                                 to perform different actions
                                                           depending on the message it's sent.
            LookupMsg m => (cache, cache.Lookup(m.Id)),

            RegisterMsg m => cache.Lookup(m.Id).Match      An edge case in which two
            (                                              concurrent requests have both
               Some: acc => (cache, Some(acc)),     ⟵——    loaded the account state
               None: () =>
               {
                  AccountProcess acc                       Creates and
                     = new(m.AccountState, saveAndPublish);  registers a new
                  return (cache.Add(m.Id, acc), Some(acc));  AccountProcess
               }
            )
         }
      );
   }

   public Task<Option<Account>> Lookup(Guid id) => // as above...
}
```

This implementation is slightly more complex but more efficient, and this example has given us the chance to see a common pitfall when programming with agents: namely, performing an expensive operation in the body of an agent that doesn't strictly require synchronized access to the agent's state.

On the other hand, in both proposed implementations, once an `AccountProcess` is created, it's never terminated; it will persist events to the DB to keep the stored version in sync with the in-memory state, but we read from the DB at most once. Is this a good thing or bad? It depends on how much data you'll eventually have in memory and how much memory you have available. It's potentially a huge optimization because access to in-memory data is orders of magnitude faster than access to the DB. The ability to keep all your data in memory is one of the big draws of the actor model: because actors can be distributed across machines, there's no effective limit on the amount of memory you can use, and accessing memory (even over the network) is much faster than accessing even a local DB.

19.4.4 *Putting it all together*

With the previous building blocks in place, let's see how our implementation for the API endpoint changes:

```
public static void ConfigureMakeTransferEndpoint
(
   WebApplication app,
   Validator<MakeTransfer> validate,        Required to get an
   AccountRegistry accounts             ◁── AccountProcess by account ID
)
{                                            Changes from Task<Option<>>
   var getAccountVal = (Guid id)     ◁──── to Task<Validation<>>
      => accounts
         .Lookup(id)
         .Map(opt => opt.ToValidation(Errors.UnknownAccountId(id)));


   app.MapPost("/Transfer/Make", (MakeTransfer transfer) =>
   {
      Task<Validation<AccountState>> outcome =
         from cmd in Async(validate(transfer))
         from acc in getAccountVal(cmd.DebitedAccountId)
         from result in acc.Handle(cmd)    ◁──┐ The AccountProcess handles the
         select result.NewState;              │ command, updating the account state and
                                              │ persisting/publishing the corresponding event.
      return outcome.Map(
         Faulted: ex => StatusCode(500),
         Completed: val => val.Match(
            Invalid: errs => BadRequest(new { Errors = errs }),
            Valid: newState => Ok(new { Balance = newState.Balance })));
   });
}
```

The endpoint implementation depends on a `Validator` for validating the command and on the `AccountRegistry` for retrieving an `AccountProcess` for the relevant account.

The main change, compared to the version in chapter 13, is that the `result` tuple is only returned for feedback, whereas persisting and publishing the event happens in the `AccountProcess`'s `Handle` method. This, as you've seen, is required to prevent concurrent modifications to the account's state, which could violate business rules such as limiting the account's maximal overdraft.

I'm not including the implementation for the functions that read and write events to storage because they're so technology-specific and don't entail any particularly interesting logic.

You've now seen all the main components of an end-to-end solution for handling a money transfer with the added constraints of synchronized access to the account state.

Summary

- Shared mutable state that's accessed concurrently can cause difficult problems.
- For this reason, you should avoid shared mutable state entirely whenever possible. This is often the case in parallel processing scenarios.
- In other types of concurrency, notably in multithreaded applications that need to model real-world entities, shared mutable state is often required.
- Access to shared mutable state must be serialized to avoid inconsistent changes to the data. This can be achieved using locks but also using lock-free techniques.
- Message-passing concurrency is a technique that avoids locks by restricting state mutation to processes (actors/agents) that have exclusive ownership of some state, which they can access single-threadedly in reaction to messages they're sent.
- An actor/agent is a lightweight process featuring
  - An inbox in which messages sent to it are queued up
  - Some state of which it has exclusive ownership
  - A processing loop in which it processes messages sequentially, taking actions such as creating and communicating with other agents, changing its state, and performing side effects
- Agents and actors are fundamentally similar, but there are important differences:
  - Actors are distributed, whereas agents are local to a single process.
  - Unlike with agents, the actor model includes error handling provisions such as *supervisors*, which take action if the supervised actor fails.
- Message-passing concurrency feels quite different from other FP techniques, mainly because FP works by composing functions, whereas actors/agents tend to work in a fire-and-forget fashion.
- It's possible to write high-level functional APIs with underlying agent-based or actor-based implementations.

appendix
Working with previous version of C#

This second edition of the book was written for C# 10 and takes advantage of the language's latest features, given that they're relevant to FP. If you're working on legacy projects that use previous versions of C#, you can still apply all of the ideas discussed in this book. This appendix shows you how.

A.1 *Immutable data objects before C# 9*

In the book, I've used records and structs for all data objects. Records are immutable by default, and structs are copied by value when passed between functions so that they too are perceived as being immutable. If you want to work with immutable data objects but need to use a version prior to C# 9, you have to rely on one of the following options:

- Treat objects as immutable by convention.
- Manually define immutable objects.
- Use F# for your domain objects.

To illustrate each of these strategies, I'll go back to the task of writing an `Account-State` class to represent the state of a bank account in the BOC application. We saw this in section 11.3.

A.1.1 *Immutability by convention*

Before the introduction of records, C# developers usually defined data objects with an empty constructor and property getters and setters. The following listing shows how you could model the state of a bank account using this approach.

401

> **Listing A.1   A simple model for the state of a bank account**

```
public enum AccountStatus
{ Requested, Active, Frozen, Dormant, Closed }

public class AccountState
{
   public AccountStatus Status { get; set; }
   public CurrencyCode Currency { get; set; }
   public decimal AllowedOverdraft { get; set; }
   public List<Transaction> TransactionHistory { get; set; }

   public AccountState()
      => TransactionHistory = new List<Transaction>();
}
```

This allows us to create new instances elegantly with the object initializer syntax as in the following listing.

> **Listing A.2   Using the convenient object initializer syntax**

```
var account = new AccountState
{
   Currency = "EUR"
};
```

This creates a new account with the `Currency` property set explicitly; other properties are initialized to their default values. Note that the object initializer syntax calls the parameterless constructor and the public setters defined in `AccountState`.

A.1.2   *Defining copy methods*

If we want to represent a change in state, such as if the account is frozen, we'll create a new `AccountState` with the new `Status`. We can do this by adding a convenience method on `AccountState` as the following listing shows.

> **Listing A.3   Defining a copy method**

```
public class AccountState
{
   public AccountState WithStatus(AccountStatus newStatus)
      => new AccountState
      {
         Status = newStatus,              ⟵⎯ The updated field
         Currency = this.Currency,
         AllowedOverdraft = this.AllowedOverdraft,      All other fields are copied
         TransactionHistory = this.TransactionHistory   from the current state.
      };
}
```

`WithStatus` is a method that returns a copy of the instance, identical to the original in everything except the `Status`, which is as given. This is similar to the behavior you get with AddDays and similar methods defined on DateTime: they all return a new instance (see section 11.2.1).

Methods like WithStatus are called *copy methods* or *with-ers* because the convention is to name them With[Property]. The following listing shows an example of calling a copy method to represent a change in the state of the account.

Listing A.4 Obtaining a modified version of the object

```
var newState = account.WithStatus(AccountStatus.Frozen);
```

Copy methods are similar to with expressions in records, in that they return a copy of the original object, where one property has been updated.

> **NOTE** The cost of representing changes through copy methods is not as high as you might think, as already discussed in section 11.3 (specifically in the sidebar on "Performance impact of using immutable objects"). This is because a copy method like WithStatus creates a *shallow copy* of the original: an operation that is fast and sufficient to guarantee safety (assuming that all the object's children are immutable as well).

A.1.3 Enforcing immutability

The implementation shown so far uses property setters to initially populate an object (section A.1.1) and copy methods to obtain updated versions (section A.1.2). This approach is called *immutability by convention*: you use convention and discipline to avoid mutation. The setters are exposed, but they should never be called after the object has been initialized. But this doesn't prevent a mischievous colleague who's not sold on immutability from setting the fields directly:

```
account.Status = AccountStatus.Frozen;
```

If you want to prevent such destructive updates, you'll have to make your object immutable by removing property setters altogether. New instances must then be populated by passing all values as arguments to the constructor as the following listing shows.

Listing A.5 Refactoring towards immutability: removing all setters

```
public class AccountState
{
    public AccountStatus Status { get; }
    public CurrencyCode Currency { get; }
    public decimal AllowedOverdraft { get; }
    public List<Transaction> Transactions { get; }

    public AccountState
    (
        CurrencyCode Currency,
        AccountStatus Status = AccountStatus.Requested,
        decimal AllowedOverdraft = 0,
```

```
            List<Transaction> Transactions = null
    )
    {
        this.Status = Status;
        this.Currency = Currency;
        this.AllowedOverdraft = AllowedOverdraft;
        this.Transactions = Transactions ?? new List<Transaction>();
    }

    public AccountState WithStatus(AccountStatus newStatus)
        => new AccountState
        (
            Status: newStatus,
            Currency: this.Currency,
            AllowedOverdraft: this.AllowedOverdraft,
            Transactions: this.TransactionHistory
        );
}
```

In the constructor, I've used named parameters and default values in such a way that I can create a new instance with a syntax that is similar to the object initializer syntax we were using before. We can now create a new account with sensible values like this:

```
var account = new AccountState
(
    Currency: "EUR",
    Status: AccountStatus.Active
);
```

The `WithStatus` copy method works just like before. Notice that we've now enforced that a value must be provided for `Currency`, which isn't possible when you use the object initializer syntax. So we've kept readability while making the implementation more robust.

> **TIP** Forcing the clients of your code to use a constructor or a factory function to instantiate an object improves the robustness of your code because you can enforce business rules at this point, making it impossible to create an object in an invalid state, such as an account with no currency.

A.1.4   *Immutable all the way down*

We're still not done because for an object to be immutable, all its constituents must be immutable too. Here we're using a mutable `List`, so your mischievous colleague could still effectively mutate the account state by writing this:

```
account.Transactions.Clear();
```

The most effective way to prevent this is to create a copy of the list given to the constructor and store its contents in an immutable list. The following listing shows how to do this using the `ImmutableList` type in the `System.Collections.Immutable` library.[1]

---

[1] The `System.Collections.Immutable` library was developed by Microsoft to complement the mutable collections in the BCL, so its feel should be familiar. You must get it from NuGet.

Listing A.6 Preventing mutation by using immutable collection

```
using System.Collections.Immutable;          Marks the class as sealed to
                                             prevent mutable subclasses
public sealed class AccountState      ◄──┘
{
    public IEnumerable<Transaction> TransactionHistory { get; }

    public AccountState(CurrencyCode Currency
        , AccountStatus Status = AccountStatus.Requested
        , decimal AllowedOverdraft = 0
        , IEnumerable<Transaction> Transactions = null)
    {                                             Creates and stores
        // ...                                    a defensive copy
        TransactionHistory = ImmutableList.CreateRange   of the given list
            (Transactions ?? Enumerable.Empty<Transaction>());
    }
}
```

When a new `AccountState` is created, the given list of transactions is copied and stored in an `ImmutableList`. This is called a *defensive copy*. Now the list of transactions of an `AccountState` can't be altered by any consumers, and it remains unaffected even if the list given in the constructor is altered at a later point. Fortunately, `Create-Range` is smart enough that if it's given an `ImmutableList`, it just returns it so that copy methods won't incur any additional overhead.

Furthermore, `Transaction` and `Currency` must also be immutable types. I've also marked `AccountState` as `sealed` to prevent the creation of mutable subclasses. Now `AccountState` is truly immutable, at least in theory. In practice, one could still mutate an instance using reflection so that your mischievous colleague can still have the upper hand.[2] But at least now there's no room for mutating the object by mistake.

How can you add a new transaction to the list? You don't. You create a new list that has the new transaction as well as all existing ones and that will be part of a new `AccountState`, as the following listing demonstrates.

Listing A.7 Adding an element to a list requires a new parent object

```
using LaYumba.Functional;        ◄──┐  Includes Prepend as an extension
                                     │  method on IEnumerable
public sealed class AccountState
{
    public AccountState Add(Transaction t)
        => new AccountState             A new IEnumerable
        (                               including existing values
            Transactions: TransactionHistory.Prepend(t),  ◄──┘ and the one being added
            Currency: this.Currency,
            Status: this.Status,        All other fields are
            AllowedOverdraft: this.AllowedOverdraft   copied as usual.
        );
}
```

----

[2] The utilities in `System.Reflection` allow you to view and modify the value of any field at run time, including `private` and `readonly` fields and the backing fields of autoproperties.

Notice that in this particular case, we're *prepending* the transaction to the list. This is domain-specific; in most cases, you're interested in the latest transactions, so it's most efficient to keep the latest ones at the front of the list.

A.1.5 *Copy methods without boilerplate?*

Now that we've managed to properly implement `AccountState` as an immutable type, let's face one of the pain points: *writing copy methods is no fun!* Imagine an object with 10 properties, all of which need copy methods. If there are any collections, you'll need to copy them into immutable collections and add copy methods that add or remove items from those collections. That's a lot of boilerplate!

The following listing shows how to mitigate this by including a single `With` method with named optional arguments, much like how we used them in the `AccountState` constructor in listing A.5.

Listing A.8 A single `With` method that can set any property

```
public AccountState With
(
    AccountStatus? Status = null,        │ null indicates that
    decimal? AllowedOverdraft = null     │ the field isn't specified.
 )                                                   If no value is specified,
=> new AccountState                                    uses the current
(                                                      instance's value
    Status: Status ?? this.Status,
    AllowedOverdraft: AllowedOverdraft ?? this.AllowedOverdraft,
    Currency: this.Currency,                │ You can prevent
    Transactions: this.TransactionHistory   │ arbitrary changes.
);
```

The default value of `null` indicates that the value hasn't been specified; in which case, the current instance's value is used to populate the copy. For value-type fields, you can use the corresponding nullable type for the argument type to allow a default of `null`. Because the default value `null` indicates that the field hasn't been specified, and hence the current value will be used, it's not possible to use this method to set a field to `null`. Given the discussion on `null` versus `Option` in section 5.5.1, you can probably see that this isn't a good idea anyway.

Notice that in listing A.8, we're only allowing changes to two fields because we're assuming that we can never change the currency of a bank account or make arbitrary changes to the transaction history. This approach allows us to reduce boilerplate while still retaining fine-grained control over what operations we want to allow. The usage is as follows:

```
public static AccountState Freeze(this AccountState account)
    => account.With(Status: AccountStatus.Frozen);

public static AccountState RedFlag(this AccountState account)
    => account.With
    (
```

```
      Status: AccountStatus.Frozen,
      AllowedOverdraft: 0m
    );
```

This not only reads clearly but gives us better performance compared to using the classic With[Property] methods: if we need to update multiple fields, a single new instance is created. I definitely recommend using this single With method over defining a copy method for every field.

Another approach is to define a generic helper that does the copying and updating without the need for any boilerplate. I've implemented such a general-purpose With method in the LaYumba.Functional.Immutable class, and it can be used as the following listing shows.

> **Listing A.9 Using a general-purpose copy method**

```
using LaYumba.Functional;

var oldState = new AccountState("EUR", AccountStatus.Active);
var newState = oldState.With(a => a.Status, AccountStatus.Frozen);

oldState.Status    // => AccountStatus.Active
newState.Status    // => AccountStatus.Frozen
newState.Currency  // => "EUR"
```

Here, With is an extension method on object that takes an Expression identifying the property to be updated and the new value. Using reflection, it then creates a bitwise copy of the original object, identifies the backing field of the specified property, and sets it to the given value.

In short, it does what we want—for any field and any type. On the upside, this saves us from having to write tedious copy methods. On the downside, reflection is relatively slow, and we lose the fine-grained control available when we explicitly choose what fields can be updated in With.

A.1.6 Comparing strategies for immutability

In summary, before the introduction of records in C# 9, enforcing immutability was a thorny business, and one of the biggest hurdles when programming functionally.

Here are the pros and cons of the two approaches I've discussed:

- *Immutability by convention*—In this approach, you don't do any extra work to *prevent* mutation; you just *avoid* it like you probably avoid the use of goto, unsafe pointer access, and bitwise operations (just to mention a few things that the language allows but that have proven problematic). This can be a viable choice if you're working independently or with a team that's sold on this approach from day one. The downside is, of course, that mutation can creep in.
- *Define immutable objects in C#*—This approach gives you a more robust model that communicates to other developers that the object shouldn't be mutated. It

is preferable if you're working on a project where immutability isn't used across the board. Compared to immutability by convention, it requires at least some extra work in defining constructors.

To make things even more complicated, third-party libraries may have limitations that dictate your choices. Traditionally, deserializers and ORMs for .NET have used the empty constructor and settable properties to create and populate objects. If you're relying on libraries with such requirements, immutability by convention may be your only option.

A.2   *Pattern matching before C# 8*

Pattern matching is a language feature that allows you to execute different code depending on the *shape* of some data—most importantly, its type. It's a staple of statically typed functional languages, and we've used it extensively in the book, whether through `switch` expressions or through the definition of a `Match` method.

In this section, I'll describe how support for pattern matching has evolved through successive versions in C# and show you a solution to use pattern matching even if you're working on an older version of C#.

A.2.1   *C#'s incremental support for pattern matching*

For a long time, C# had poor support for pattern matching. Until C# 7, the `switch` statement only supported a very limited form of pattern matching, allowing you to match on the exact value of an expression. What about matching on the *type* of an expression? For example, suppose you have the following simple domain:

```
enum Ripeness { Green, Yellow, Brown }

abstract class Reward { }

class Peanut : Reward { }
class Banana : Reward { public Ripeness Ripeness; }
```

Up to C# 6, computing a description of a given `Reward` had to be done as the following listing shows.

Listing A.10   Matching on the type of an expression in C# 6

```
string Describe(Reward reward)
{
    Peanut peanut = reward as Peanut;
    if (peanut != null)
        return "It's a peanut";

    Banana banana = reward as Banana;
    if (banana != null)
        return $"It's a {banana.Ripeness} banana";

    return "It's a reward I don't know or care about";
}
```

For such a simple operation, this is incredibly tedious and noisy. C# 7 introduced some limited support for pattern matching so that the preceding code could be abridged as the next listing shows.

Listing A.11 Matching on type in C# 7 with `is`

```
string Describe(Reward reward)
{
   if (reward is Peanut _)
      return "It's a peanut";

   if (reward is Banana banana)
      return $"It's a {banana.Ripeness} banana";

   return "It's a reward I don't know or care about";
}
```

Or, alternatively, using the `switch` statement as the following listing shows.

Listing A.12 Matching on type in C# 7 with `switch`

```
string Describe(Reward reward)
{
   switch (reward)
   {
      case Peanut _:
         return "It's a peanut";
      case Banana banana:
         return $"It's a {banana.Ripeness} banana";
      default:
         return "It's a reward I don't know or care about";
   }
}
```

This is still fairly awkward, especially because in FP, we'd like to use expressions, whereas both `if` and `switch` expect statements in each branch.

Finally, C# 8 introduced `switch` expressions (you saw several examples in the book), allowing us to write the preceding code as the following listing shows.

Listing A.13 A `switch`-expression in C# 8

```
string Describe(Reward reward)
   => reward switch
   {
      Banana banana => $"It's a {banana.Ripeness} banana",
      Peanut _ => "It's a peanut",
      _ => "It's a reward I don't know or care about"
   };
```

A.2.2 *A custom solution for pattern matching expressions*

If you're working on a codebase that uses a version prior to C# 8, you can still pattern match on type using the `Pattern` class I've included in `LaYumba.Functional`. It can be used as in the following listing.

Listing A.14 A custom `Pattern` class for expression-based pattern matching

```
string Describe(Reward reward)
    => new Pattern<string>
    {
        (Peanut _) => "It's a peanut",
        (Banana b) => $"It's a {b.Ripeness} banana"
    }
    .Default("It's a reward I don't know or care about")
    .Match(reward);
```

The generic parameter specifies the type that's returned when calling `Match`.

A list of functions; the first one with a matching type is evaluated.

Optionally adds a default value or handler

Supplies the value on which to match

This isn't as performant as first-class language support nor does it have all the bells and whistles like deconstruction, but it's still a good solution if you're just interested in matching on type.

You first set up the functions that handle each case (internally, `Pattern` is essentially a list of functions, so I'm using list initializer syntax). You can optionally call `Default` to provide a default value or a function to use if no matching function is found. Finally, you use `Match` to supply the value to match on; this will evaluate the first function whose input type matches the type of the given value.

There's also a non-generic version of `Pattern` in which `Match` returns `dynamic`. You could use this in the preceding example by simply omitting `<string>`, making the syntax a bit cleaner still.

> **TIP** In this book, you saw implementations of a `Match` method for `Option`, `Either`, `List`, `Tree`, and so on. These effectively perform pattern matching. Defining such methods makes sense when you know from the start all the cases you'll need to handle (for instance, `Option` can only be `Some` or `None`). By contrast, the `Pattern` class is useful for types that are open for inheritance, like `Event` or `Reward`, where you can envisage adding new subclasses as the system evolves.

A.3 *Revisiting the event sourcing example*

To illustrate the techniques described previously, let's revisit our event sourcing scenario from section 13.2 and suppose we can only use C# 6. We don't have records, so to represent the state of an account, we'll define `AccountState` as an immutable class. All properties will be read-only and will be populated in the constructor. The following listing shows the implementation.

Listing A.15 An immutable class representing the state of an account

```
public sealed class AccountState
{
   public AccountStatus Status { get; }
   public CurrencyCode Currency { get; }      All properties
   public decimal Balance { get; }            are read-only.
   public decimal AllowedOverdraft { get; }

   public AccountState
   (
      CurrencyCode Currency,
      AccountStatus Status = AccountStatus.Requested,
      decimal Balance = 0m,
      decimal AllowedOverdraft = 0m
   )
   {
      this.Currency = Currency;
      this.Status = Status;                   Initializes properties
      this.Balance = Balance;                 in the constructor
      this.AllowedOverdraft = AllowedOverdraft;
   }

   public AccountState WithStatus(AccountStatus newStatus)  ◄─┐
      => new AccountState
      (
         Status: newStatus,
         Balance: this.Balance,
         Currency: this.Currency,              Exposes copy
         AllowedOverdraft: this.AllowedOverdraft    methods for
      );                                        creating
                                                modified copies
   public AccountState Debit(decimal amount)   ◄─┤
      => Credit(-amount);

   public AccountState Credit(decimal amount)  ◄─┘
      => new AccountState
      (
         Balance: this.Balance + amount,
         Currency: this.Currency,
         Status: this.Status,
         AllowedOverdraft: this.AllowedOverdraft
      );
}
```

Other than properties and the constructor, AccountState has a WithStatus copy method that creates a new AccountState with an updated status. Debit and Credit are also copy methods that create a copy with an updated balance. (This pretty long class definition replaces the record definition in listing 13.2, which was only seven lines.)

Now, about state transitions. Remember that we use the first event in the account's history to create an AccountState and then use each event to compute the account's new state after the event. The signature for a state transition is

```
AccountState → Event → AccountState
```

In order to implement the state transition, we pattern match on the type of event and update the `AccountState` accordingly:

Listing A.16   Modeling state transitions with pattern matching

```
public static class Account
{
    public static AccountState Create(CreatedAccount evt)        ◁──┐  CreatedAccount
        => new AccountState                                         │  is a special case
            (                                                       │  because there
                Currency: evt.Currency,                            │  is no prior state.
                Status: AccountStatus.Active
            );

    public static AccountState Apply
        (this AccountState account, Event evt)      │  Calls the relevant transition,
        => new Pattern                          ◁──┘  depending on the type of the event
        {
            (DepositedCash e) => account.Credit(e.Amount),
            (DebitedTransfer e) => account.Debit(e.DebitedAmount),
            (FrozeAccount _) => account.WithStatus(AccountStatus.Frozen),
        }
        .Match(evt);
}
```

Without being able to rely on language support for pattern matching, this code uses the pattern matching solution shown in section A.2.2 to great effect.

A.4   *In conclusion*

As you saw, all the techniques discussed in this book can be used on legacy projects that use older versions of C#. Of course, if you can, do upgrade to the latest version of C# to take advantage of new language features, especially records and pattern matching.

epilogue
What next?

Congratulations on taking up the challenge of learning FP and making it to the end of the book! You're now familiar with all the fundamental concepts of FP as well as several advanced techniques. I hope that you've enjoyed the book, and I encourage you to share your impressions through a review, social media, or just by talking with colleagues. By way of goodbye, I want to give you some suggestions on where to look next if you'd like to take your exploration of FP further.

Firstly, I invite you to watch my talk on *Logic vs. side effects*, given at NDC Sydney 2017. In it, I outline a summary on how to tame side effects using different techniques, including *free monads*, the most radical approach to separating logic from side effects. It's available here: https://youtu.be/wJq86IXkFdQ.

Your next step would probably be to learn a functional language (or a few). C# is a multiparadigm language, so you can mix and match as you like. A functional language, on the other hand, forces you to use the functional approach throughout, for example, by not allowing any state mutation at all. You'll also find that functional languages have better syntactic support for the techniques presented in this book. An additional benefit of learning a functional language is that it allows you to take advantage of other learning resources: books, blogs, talks, and so on.

Most learning material on FP available today has code samples in Haskell or Scala. The natural choice would be to learn Haskell, which is the functional language of reference and a lingua franca among functional programmers. For this, I recommend you read *Learn You a Haskell for Great Good* by Miran Lipovaca (No Starch Press, 2011).[1] Another good way to learn Haskell is to do so while following Erik Meijer's online course on FP.[2]

---

[1] You can read the full contents online for free at http://learnyouahaskell.com/ but do consider buying a copy to reward the author's hard work.

[2] Erik Meijer is, among other things, one of the main contributors to LINQ and Rx. His online course on FP is available on edX (https://www.edx.org/), and you can follow along in Haskell or one of several other languages.

Scala is a multiparadigm language with an emphasis on FP that runs on the Java virtual machine. The Scala community is active in addressing the question of how the ideas of FP, which tend to originate in academia, can best be put to work in industry. If you want to learn Scala, I recommend you do so by following Martin Odersky's online courses.[3]

Two younger functional languages I'm fond of are Elm and Elixir, both of which are supported by an enthusiastic user community and are gaining popularity, especially among startups. I hope to see these two languages gain wider adoption and recognition in the next few years.

Elm (http://elm-lang.org/) is a strongly typed, purely functional client-side language that compiles to JavaScript. The syntax is terse, similar to Haskell or F#, but the language and tooling are much more user-friendly. It includes a framework that takes care of managing state and performing side effects. As a result, the programmer only writes pure functions. Simply put, Elm puts any existing JavaScript framework to shame. If you're a full-stack web developer, consider using Elm for the frontend.

Elixir (http://elixir-lang.org/) is a dynamically typed language that runs on the Erlang virtual machine, which is based on the actor model discussed in chapter 15, and as such, it's particularly well suited if your interest is in systems with a high degree of concurrency. You'll want to further explore message-passing concurrency.

Finally, I recommend you take a look at Edwin Brady's *Type-Driven Development with Idris* (Manning, 2017). Even if you only read a few chapters and never plan to write a program in Idris, seeing how type driven development works in a language that it optimized for it can stimulate you to bring some of those techniques into your coding practice.

There are many more functional and multiparadigm languages out there (sorry if I forgot to include your favorite!), each with its own appeal. But the ideas of FP that you've learned in this book are language-independent and will enable you to acquire a basic working knowledge of any functional language within a couple of days or weeks at most.

Goodbye.

---

[3] Martin Odersky is the creator of Scala, and his online courses are available on Coursera (https://www.coursera .org/).

index